D1480912

This Book
has been presented to the
CHURCH LIBRARY
of _OUR REDEEMER LUTHERAN_

_1967_

IN MEMORY OF
Mrs. John Schoenberger

by
Mr. Jaegers
Bible Class.

IRON CURTAIN CHRISTIANS

IRON CURTAIN CHRISTIANS

CHRISTIANS

The Church in Communist
Countries Today

BY KURT HUTTEN

Translated by
WALTER G. TILLMANNS

Augsburg Publishing House
Minneapolis, Minnesota

IRON CURTAIN CHRISTIANS
Copyright © 1967 Augsburg Publishing House
All rights reserved
Library of Congress Catalog Card No. 67-11727

This book is a translation of *Christen hinter dem Eisernen Vorhang*
by Kurt Hutten published in 1962 by Quell-Verlag,
Stuttgart, Germany

Preface

The establishment of Communist rule in a number of countries which have a Christian tradition and the clash between the churches and militant atheism, which has been raised to the status of an official confession in those countries, represent one of the most decisive chapters in the history of the church. The contest has developed into a life-or-death struggle. Large and small church bodies of all denominations are involved in it. As far as past experiences have shown, there have been victories and defeats, retreats and flights into the catacombs, compromises, breathing spells, and times of apparent peace. The battle is not yet over, not for a long time, and the final results are hidden from the eyes of all people. The developments in the various countries show a certain similarity in the strategy of the political leaders although their strategy is often strongly influenced by the extent of the resistance offered by the church. The most important element of this resistance is not the action of the church leaders, but the quiet strength with which the Christian congregations continue to exist in a totalitarian dictatorship, even where the organization of the church has been shattered and where individual Christians are constantly being exposed to the pounding of atheistic propaganda, where they are threatened by officials of the state, and yet dare to live their faith.

Press and radio in the West have reported concerning these events behind the Iron Curtain. We are here using these reports. But for him who cannot follow these reports continuously and who cannot fit them into the total picture, for him who cannot fully understand them, I have tried to summarize the happenings of the past years in a comprehensive survey.

The type of materials which are at my disposal forces me to make a few remarks about their limitations. The sources are, to be sure, extremely rich: press releases from the West and the East; official pronouncements by the leaders of the churches, by governments, and by organizations of the Communist Party; reports by travelers and refugees; and various laws, agreements, decrees, and the like. But these materials are not always reliable. The news is incomplete since the Iron Curtain acts as a filter. The press releases are often contradictory and colored according to the political and philosophical viewpoint of the writer. In the case of the official documents published by the churches, we must ask to what extent these documents reflect the true voice of the churches or are subject to certain forms prescribed by the state. As far as the official agencies of the state and of the party are concerned, we must take into account that the contents of their pronouncements are determined by political and propaganda motives. Reports of travelers, newspapermen, and refugees are naturally fragmentary. The most important source material is deposited in the archives of the states and the churches and probably in numerous hiding places in the various countries. Only after these documents have been made fully available, will it be possible to write an exact account of the history of the churches in the Communist countries.

As long as these documents are not at hand, we must be satisfied with preliminary accounts. Therefore I have purposely limited my account. It is more a chronicle than a history. In its center are the known facts. In order to gain a fairly complete picture I have critically evaluated a large body of information and have eliminated some of it. But it is quite clear that complete accuracy cannot be attained under present conditions. I had to forego an investigation of the underlying causes, motives, and developments, for I wanted to spare the reader mere assumptions and hypotheses. Only where authentic and creditable material was available did I make an exception. I have also been careful not to judge hastily the decisions and actions of the leading churchmen, and I would recommend the same caution to my readers. For who can see into their hearts and put himself into their places, realizing the conditions and the responsibilities which they are facing? In a word, who has the right to be a judge?

Finally, I have also avoided discussing the basic questions which challenge us in view of the existence of the church in the Communist world, as for example: What is the historical guilt of the Christian church? To what extent is she responsible for the rise of Communism? What are the theological implications of Communist atheism? What is the problem of coexistence in a totalitarian and anti-theistic state, and what is the character of the proclamation of the Christian message in this world? To what extent is the church permitted to make compromises? What are the reasons why the various churches react so differently to their Communist rulers? Of course, the reader will again and again meet these problems head-on. But we would want to alert him to recognize them when they occur in the course of this account. The same variety is also found in the answers and solutions which the individual churches have tried to find to these questions.

The following pages want to inform. They want to serve as orientation. But they also want to call the reader to clear thinking and meditation. It is not our doing that we are permitted to live in a free world. Furthermore, this freedom is not guaranteed to us for all future times. But we know one thing: As of now it is possible for us to make our decisions as free citizens and to live as Christians in complete liberty. This opportunity is a gift that must be protected. All around us we are threatened by internal and external disasters. The fate of the Christians behind the Iron Curtain should be a warning to us: We should treasure and preserve the things that have been taken away from them and that have been preserved for us; we should hear the voice of God behind the happenings of our times, a voice that calls us to examine ourselves, to re-evaluate our values, and to remap our route. We should learn from the terrible experiences of the oppressed churches so that we may be well prepared if the hour of trial should ever strike for us.

KURT HUTTEN

Contents

CHAPTER ONE

THE SOVIET UNION

A. THE RUSSIAN ORTHODOX CHURCH

1. Attack

" 'Religion is the opiate of the people'—these words of Marx are the cornerstone of the whole ideology of Marxism in matters of religion. Marxism looks upon all present-day forms of religion and upon all churches, upon each and every religious organization as organs of bourgeois reaction." Or: "Is the fiction of God perhaps not the worst way of spitting into your own face? Every human being that occupies himself with the creation of the fiction of God or even permits such fiction to exist is thereby spitting into his own face in the worst way possible."

These sentences were written by Lenin. The irreconcilable enmity against any kind of religion is one of the fundamental tenets of Communist ideology and of the Communist program. The deliverance of the enslaved and exploited masses and the attainment of happiness in fraternal collectivism demand the liberation of the masses from all types of religious "superstition," for this superstition is merely a means of deflecting man's longing for happiness from this world to the next. Moreover, the Christian church has always been allied with the exploiters of the human race and permitted herself to be abused by them in their endeavor to paralyze the proletariat in its struggle. Therefore she must be liquidated as a spiritual and organizational power by the use of the most radical means.

Paragraph 13 of the Russian Communist Party program proclaimed: "The Communist Party of the Soviet Union is convinced that only a conscious and determined planning of the total social and economic activities of the masses will bring about the end of

1

religious superstition. The Party is fighting for the complete abolition of all connections between the exploiting classes and the organizations of religious propaganda and wants to facilitate the liberation of the working masses from religious superstition and wants to organize the most effective possibility for scientific educational and anti-religious propaganda. At the same time it will carefully strive to avoid all offense to the religious feelings of the believers, because such offense may lead to an intensifying of religious fanaticism."

2. The Noose of the Law

In the October Revolution of 1917 Communism gained control of an immense empire. At the same time the Russian Orthodox Church came under its power. The church has always been identified most intimately with the government of the Czars and with the feudalism that had passed from the stage of history only recently. Therefore the main thrust of the revolutionaries was directed against the church. Socialist-revolutionary class-hatred was added to the basic ideological enmity against the church. This was the cause of the bloody persecution which the church had to suffer.

At the time of the Revolution the Orthodox Church numbered 70 dioceses, 130 bishops, 50,960 priests, 94,629 monks and nuns and over 100 million faithful. Immediately after the Revolution she was deprived of her external privileged position by means of various legal and administrative actions. On December 4, 1917, all ecclesiastical property was confiscated. On December 11 the separation of church and school was ordered, on December 18 civil marriage was introduced, and on January 1, 1918, all subsidies by the state were stopped. A decree by the Council of People's Commissars of January 23, 1918, guaranteed the free exercise of religious "cultic activities" (paragraph 5) as long as they did not interfere with the maintenance of public order. But paragraph 9 of the same decree forbade religious instruction in schools and permitted it only under private auspices. Paragraph 10 decreed that all churches would henceforth be associations of public law. Paragraph 12 deprived the churches of their corporate character and forbade them to own property. Finally, paragraph 13 declared all cultic objects belonging to the churches to be the property of the people, but permitted congregations to use buildings and equipment without payment of fees. By another decree issued by the People's Commissar for Justice on August 27, 1920, the "liquidation of all relics" was ordered; they had to be surrendered to the state museums. In 1921 it was further ordered that "all treasures of the church must be removed" from her control.

On April 8, 1929, all previous anti-religious laws were summarized in the *Law Concerning Religion* which up to the present time has been basic for the relationship between the Soviet state and the religious organizations or "associations" operating within the territory of the USSR. The following stipulations of this law are of importance:

PARAGRAPH 3: "A religious association is a local society of citizens belonging to one and the same cult, confession, tendency, or direction, who have completed the eighteenth year of their life. This society must have no less than twenty members who meet to satisfy their religious needs. Believers who for lack of numbers are not allowed to form a religious society have the right to form a 'group of believers.' Religious associations, societies, and groups do not possess the rights of legal persons."

PARAGRAPH 4: "Religious societies and groups of believers can be active only after they have registered their societies or groups with the Commission for Religious Affairs of the City Soviet or with the Rayon Executive Committee."

PARAGRAPH 8: "The membership lists of a religious society or group of believers must be reported together with the names of ministers . . . at stated times to the office where they have been registered."

PARAGRAPH 13: "Religious societies by open ballot shall elect from their members assembled in a general meeting an executive committee which shall be responsible for the immediate exercise of all functions related to the administration and the use of religious objects and shall represent the religious society to the outside; religious societies shall elect three persons; groups of believers shall elect one representative."

PARAGRAPH 14: "The offices which are entrusted with the registration of such societies and groups reserve the right to exclude individuals from the executive committees of religious societies and groups of believers."

PARAGRAPH 17: "Religious societies are forbidden:

"(a) To collect funds for mutual assistance, to form consumers' organizations and production associations, and to use the property which is at their disposal for any purposes other than the satisfaction of their religious needs;

"(b) To grant material assistance to their members;

"(c) To organize prayer meetings and the like for children, youth, or women; also meetings, groups, circles, sections devoted to the study of the Bible; circles devoted to literature, the crafts, handwork, religious instruction, and similar purposes; to establish children's playgrounds, libraries, or reading rooms; to organize sanatoriums and hospitals. In prayer rooms and buildings only such books may be kept as are necessary for the carrying on of the exercises of the religious cult in question."

PARAGRAPH 19: "The field of activity of the ministers of religion, preachers, teachers, etc., is limited to the place of residence of the members of the religious society whom they are serving, and the place of their respective prayer houses."

PARAGRAPH 25: "The property which is needed for the religious exercises, whether it belonged to the believers by treaty or was purchased by them or was given to them in recent times for the satisfaction of their religious needs, is herewith nationalized. It shall be registered with the Commission of Religious Affairs of the City Soviet or Rayon Executive Committee in question and shall be put at the disposal of the believers for their use."

PARAGRAPH 29: "In the agreement which the believers make with the City Soviet or the Rayon Executive Committee it shall be stipulated that the persons who are using a religious building or religious objects agree:

"(a) To keep and preserve them as state property which is entrusted to their care;

"(b) To carry out repairs of religious buildings and to bear the costs that are connected with the possession and use of such property, as, for example, heating, insurance, protection, taxes, local fees, etc.;

"(c) To use such property exclusively for the satisfaction of religious needs;

"(d) To compensate the state if the property is damaged or destroyed."

PARAGRAPH 54: "Members of groups of believers and religious societies have the right to take up collections of voluntary offerings both inside and outside of the building but only among the members of their respective religious societies and only for purposes connected with the maintenance of prayer houses, religious objects, ministers of religion, and religious executive committees. Any obligatory assessment of fees for the maintenance of religious societies will be punished according to the penal code of the Russian Federated Socialist Soviet Republic."

PARAGRAPH 58: "The exercise of religious rites and ceremonies and the keeping of religious objects are not permitted in institutions and buildings of the state, and in any public, cooperative, or private place. This prohibition does not include the exercise of rites connected with a religious cult done in rooms that have been especially set aside at the request of a dying or seriously ill patient confined to a hospital and penal institution, and to the observation of religious rites in cemeteries and crematories."

The stipulation of the law that a minister can be active only at his place of residence (see paragraph 19) led to a complete isolation of the bishops from their dioceses. By a decree of December 27, 1932, concerning the requirement to carry passports, all "nonworkers," including clergymen, were deprived of the right to reside in the larger urban centers and their suburbs. The contact between the various congregations or between congregations and their church leaders became all but impossible.

The new *Constitution of 1936* declared in its paragraph 124: "In order to assure to its citizens freedom of conscience the church in the USSR is separated from the state, and the school is separated from the church. Freedom in the exercise of a religious cult and of the freedom for anti-religious propaganda is guaranteed to all citizens."

The stipulations concerning the separation of church and school were interpreted to mean that religious instruction of young people under eighteen years of age was forbidden. Private instruction was permitted, if not more than three persons assembled. Thus, "freedom in the exercise of a religious cult" meant clearly that the church was merely permitted to hold services. Any proclamation of the Word outside of the church building, such as mission work, evangelism, and cultural contributions to the community, was forbidden.

3. The League of Militant Atheists

The Communist Party began energetically to establish atheism in the souls of the Russian people in place of religious faith. This task was assigned to the League of Militant Atheists. Its beginning was the publishing house *Atheist*, established in 1922, which provided the working masses with anti-religious propaganda. They published two magazines, *Atheists at the Workbench*, and *Beshboshnik* ("The Godless"). At first the readers of these two magazines banded together in the larger cities under the title of *Society of the Friends of Beshboshnik*. In their desire to organize themselves and others interested in these magazines they called a meeting, in April 1925, which a few months later led to the organization of the *League of Atheists*. During the Second All-Russian Congress of June 1929 the name of the society was changed to *League of Militant Atheists* in order to indicate that the goal of the league was "an active, militant fight against all religion."

According to its constitution the League was set up as a "voluntary proletarian organization . . . which has the following task: To unite the working masses of the USSR to engage in an active and systematic fight against religion in all its forms and appearances which hinder the establishment of the socialist state and the cultural revolution." Children between the ages of eight and fourteen were united in "Groups of Godless Youth." The Thirteenth Congress of the Communist Party of the USSR passed a resolution which made it obligatory for every member of the Communist Party to join the League. Its membership increased rapidly. In the first year of its existence (1926) it numbered 87,000 members. By 1929 it had increased to 465,000 members and by 1930 to three million. The subscriptions to the magazine *Beshboshnik* increased from 62,500 in 1927 to 500,000 in 1932. In 1935 the League consisted of 50,000 "cells" or chapters with about five million active members and two million members of the Godless Youth organization. Its leader, Emilian Jaroslavsky, left no doubt about its aims. He stated: "It is our aim to cast all the churches on earth into a giant sea of flames. Our godless movement has become a tremendous force which will exterminate all religious feeling. The movement is one of the most important branches of the anti-religious class war. We must constantly increase our anti-religious work which undermines the foundations of the old world. The ministers of all religions must learn to know that no God, no saint, no prayer can save the world of capitalism from perdition."

In connection with the Second Five-Year Plan of 1933-1937, an anti-religious five-year plan was propagated. It contained a detailed time schedule for the closing of all houses of worship during the first year of its operation. The second year's goal called for the liquidation of all "religious cells" in the family, the removal of all believers from offices and factories, and the suppression of all religious publications. During the third year "cells of the godless" were to be established, and at least 150 anti-religious films were to be produced. All ministers of religion who refused to give up their religious calling were to be banished. During the fourth year all former churches were to be converted into movie houses and clubs. And during the fifth year the "idea of God" was to be liquidated from the hearts and minds of people.

The League called on all atheistic organizations to mobilize their strength according to plan. They were asked to train "specialists in godlessness" and to organize squadrons of atheists which would be active in the mines and factories. Every godless worker was assigned a special task that he had to carry out under constant supervision. In every factory, office, school, and collective farm "cells of atheists" were to be organized so that the whole thinking of all workers and peasants could be permeated with atheism. Every activity in the front-line of socialist reconstruction was to be saturated with anti-religious content. Special courses were organized for women and a special type of women's literature was published. Finally, anti-religious spying was strongly urged upon all members. The League of Militant Atheists was put in charge of supervising even the inner life of the religious associations and, if necessary, to interfere so that clergy and other religious propagandists would not exploit the religious emotions of women.

In preparation for the elections which took place at the end of 1937 about 15,000 agitators were trained, who, during one month alone, delivered 300,000 speeches against the influence of the church. The League planned the observance of a "Godless Month" during which 250,000 young people were to be enrolled in its anti-religious work. Clergymen who voluntarily forsook their congregations during this "Godless Month" were enrolled as former ministers of religion in the anti-religious groups and their propaganda war. Prizes in the amounts of 25,000, 15,000 and 10,000 rubles were offered to the writers of the best "godless hymns." Similarly, a contest for the publication of a "Bible for the Godless" was organized. A special textbook for atheists was published which was to be used in the schools. Various publishing houses throughout the Soviet Union inundated the country with blasphemous pamphlets, such as *The Plague of God, The Drunken Christ*. Biographies of 120 famous blasphemers were published and several godless songbooks. Envelopes bore godless markings, such as: "Attack and Socialist Zeal Is the Best Weapon in the Fight Against All Religions" and "The Fight Against Religion Is a Fight for Socialism." The issuance of a special Godless Stamp was used to finance the work of the League of Militant Atheists. The League was also entrusted with the reeducation of the inmates of penal institutions and of concentration camps. Machine shops and tractor combines were singled out to lead the fight against religious remnants throughout the country. The political cells of these groups were entrusted with organizing what were called "Anti-Religious Caravans" whose task it was to promote atheistic expositions and meetings in the villages.

Science, too, was enlisted in the anti-religious propaganda war.

The Central Committee of the League decided to found an Academy of Atheism. The Soviet government issued a decree for the establishment of a chair of "Professor of Atheism" whose first occupant became Jaroslavsky. Later chairs of atheism were established at various universities and other institutions of learning.

Numerous anti-religious museums were opened. Favorite homes for such museums were, of course, former churches. An inscription on the anti-religious museum of Kiev read: "After the take-over of power by the workers and by the Executive Committee of the USSR, the chief monastery in Kiev was converted on September 29, 1926, from a place of religious opium into a city of proletarian culture bearing the proud name: All-Ukrainian Museum City." In the anti-religious museum housed in the former Isaac's Cathedral of Leningrad the origin of mankind according to Genesis was ridiculed and corrected on the basis of the monistic philosophy of Ernst Häckel. Two glass coffins were placed in the center of the nave. "This is supposed to be a saint," the guide said as he pointed at a dried-up mummy. "This saint is supposed to be 240 years old. And now, comrades, here are two other corpses, also 240 years old. Although they were not saints, but counterfeiters, the corpses of these men were preserved just as well as the corpse of the saint." A special exhibit, entitled: "The Church as an Organization for the Exploitation of the People" showed that baptisms, funerals, religious processions, and even the ringing of bells were used to fill the coffers of the church. On a red flag which was hanging on a wall were inscribed these words: "Against God, Liquor, and Illiteracy." Besides photos and statistics which depicted the destruction of the orthodox religion the Central Anti-Religious Museum in the former Monastery of the Passion in Moscow showed the dissolute life of monks, the raping of minors by clergymen, and a large canvas called "The Burning of the Ikons" with laughing citizens of the Soviet Union standing in front of a burning heap of ikons. The state publishing house of the Soviet Union published a special illustrated edition of the "Exposition of the Gods" so that those who could not personally come to the museums of atheism in Moscow and Leningrad would be able to get a clearer understanding of the development of faith in God. The title page of the publication showed a typical atheist who confronted the Russian people with the slogan "Without God" and proclaimed to all people and animals listening to him: "There is no God." At the end the book stated: "All priests and leaders of the various cults which are still existing today in other nations hate Russia on account of her godless government, on account of her attitude against the gods and their protectors, the capitalists and the priests. But in Russia priests become fewer and fewer from day to day. Even in the most remote corners and villages people begin to understand that there are no gods and that exploiters have invented them."

The Communist Party also saw to it that the large mass organizations, the labor unions and the *Komsomol* (the League of Communist Youth) took part in the anti-religious struggle. The Sixteenth Congress of the Communist Party in 1930 instructed the labor unions to intensify their anti-religious activities. Anti-religious missionaries were trained in special seminaries of the godless, large sums of money were spent, and radio and press were enlisted to the hilt in the cause. Theoretically every worker was made into a fighter against religion by virtue of his being a member of the labor unions. The Komsomol took a stand against religion and for atheism. Its constitution stipulated that every Soviet youth "must be truthful and honest, must keep comrades from committing evil deeds, must observe the rules of socialist cooperation, and must fight against drunkenness, rowdyism, the remnants of religious prejudices, and uncomradely attitudes toward women."

4. Deportations, Executions, and the Closing of Churches

Starting with the thesis that "all present-day religions and churches are organs of bourgeois reaction which serve the purpose of exploitation and which benumb the senses of the working class," as *Antireligiosnik* (1937, No. 8) stated, logical deductions led to the accusation that the church was allied with the forces of the counter-revolution. Thus the Communists looked upon priests and believers as their enemies who, as *Beshboshnik* (1937, No. 7) expressed it, "have put on the mask of religion. . . . Espionage by clerics and sectarians is one of the most potent proofs that religious organizations are the enemies of working people everywhere. The espionage conducted by the churches and sects is the poisoned weapon of the Fascists who are preparing to attack the USSR. Therefore all Bolsheviks must constantly strive to unmask as early as possible the spy activities of the servants of religion and to liquidate them."

With these statements the stage was set for the mobilization of police power and of the courts to fight against the church, or, as had been done during the early years of the revolution, for giving a free hand to the lynch justice of the masses. Numerous churchmen were condemned to death, heavy prison terms, or deportation on the basis of these political charges against them. Bishop B. in the Ural region was accused of having established a terror organization which had planned to dynamite ammunition dumps and carry on espionage against the Red Army. According to *Isvestija* another spy in bishop's cassock was accused of having plotted the assassination of leading members of the Soviet hierarchy. Still another bishop near Voronesh was accused of having tried to infiltrate the Supreme Soviet. Terrorists confessed that they had removed safety devices from mines and industrial plants. The Archbishop of Leningrad, Benedict Plotnikov, was accused of having organized an espionage network and was shot. In Orjol, the press reported, "a band of counter-revolutionary churchmen" had appealed to their people "to resist the measures of the Communist Party and the power of the Soviets." They were tried before a court. Twenty-two of the thirty-two accused were condemned and shot.

The number of bishops, priests, and laymen who were liquidated cannot be statistically ascertained. Up to 1923 about 28 bishops and well over 1,200 priests had been murdered; many others had been deported, forced from their parishes or driven underground. Toward the end of 1927 a total of 117 bishops were listed as imprisoned or banished. In the years from 1929 to 1931 the attacks against the clergy gained new momentum during the troubles attending the collectivization of peasants. In 1934 four bishops were shot. According to Roman Catholic estimates a total of about 42,000 priests and bishops had been eliminated by the beginning of 1936.

This figure included all those who had been executed, imprisoned, or put into concentration camps.

Many priests changed their occupations, but the Communist press complained again and again that they were only leaving their regular congregations while not renouncing their priestly calling. Thus *Beshboshnik* (1935, No. 12) wrote: "In the past year the Priest Korolev came to the Third Fish Smoking Plant of Leningrad where he offered to work as an electrician. He did not wear his priestly garb, nor did he have long hair. His external appearance was accepted as sufficient proof by the directorate of the factory to accept him as a member of the workers' association. No one seemed to think to ask the stranger for his workers' documents. Soon this priest was issued ration cards . . . and for a whole year he was considered one of the workers. When he saw that he had not been unmasked, he began to propagate his religious views to the less progressive among the workers. Some of them were persuaded to take his place at the workbench during those days when he went to church in order to celebrate the main service and the vespers. We ask, Where was the watchfulness of the working class of the Third Fish Smoking Plant?"

In the year 1941, when Hitler attacked Russia, there were still 28 active bishops and 5,665 parish priests. Numerous congregations had been orphaned. They were without a house of worship. Churches could be closed at any time, without even an excuse, since all religious buildings were the property of the state. This included all cultic objects necessary for the worship of the believers. The law of April 8, 1929, had given to the state the authority to take back the property which belonged to it.

The following were considered sufficient reason for confiscation: financial inability on the part of the believers to pay the high taxes or to make needed repairs on buildings; statements or activities at meetings, interpreted as not serving the satisfaction of religious requirements; serious emergencies in state and society, such as a lack of housing, clubs, rooms, hospitals; demands on the part of the militant atheists to close the churches because of their threat to the atheistic education of the youth; mere suspicion that the church was used as a gathering place for counter-revolutionary elements.

There was never a lack of reasons, and often subterfuges were used with great ingenuity. Before the Revolution, Russia, according to Soviet sources, had had 54,174 churches, 23,593 chapels, and 1,025 monasteries. Twenty years later there were only about 1,500 churches left. In the year 1935 alone, 14,000 churches and chapels had been closed. Of the 1,624 churches existing in Moscow in 1917 only about twenty were left in 1936. Almost all the church bells had been carted off and melted down. Ikons were often expropriated, collected and publicly burned, as were the church records. The bones of saints were dug up, uncovered, and profaned, in order to show the people that all talk about the miraculous preservation of these bones was false. Churches were destroyed or converted into clubs, schools, houses of social culture, children's castles of culture, anti-religious museums, and other types of museums, village social centers, dance halls, warehouses, movies, and the like.

5. The Decision of the Patriarch

The congregations which had been paralyzed, intimidated by propaganda, belabored with so-called "scientific enlightenment," and deprived of their priests and their houses of worship suffered great losses. The indifferent, the undecided, and the timid forsook them. The next generation was taken over by the ideology of the state. Many congregations had disappeared without a trace. But the faith of the believers did not die, and the church outlasted the storms of destruction. How did it happen?

The All-Russian Synod or Council that had been called by the Kerensky government on October 15, 1917—i.e. before the Bolshevist October revolution—in December of that same year reintroduced the patriarchate of the Orthodox Church which had been vacant since 1721 when the Czars had taken over its functions. The Council entrusted the leadership of the Orthodox Church to the Patriarch Tikhon who, in January 1919, pronounced his anathema against all those "who had abused their high positions to persecute the church and the Christian people." In September 1919 Tikhon decreed that the clergy should be completely neutral in politics. He said that for him there were neither Whites nor Reds, but only the children of the one Holy Mother Church who had been driven into blindness, fratricide, and perdition. In the year 1922 the government put Tikhon in prison.

In order to forestall the accusation that the Russian Orthodox Church was allied with political reaction at home and abroad, the Patriarch published, on June 16, 1923, a "self-criticism" which he forwarded to the Supreme Court of the Soviets. In it he said: "Raised in a monarchical society and until my imprisonment exposed to the influence of anti-Soviet circles, I have indeed succumbed to a negative attitude toward Soviet power. My negative attitude has caused me to change from passive to active resistance against the Soviets." Tikhon then mentioned a few examples of such "active resistance," stated that he regretted his past mistakes, and asked to be released from prison. He concluded: "I declare furthermore in the presence of this Supreme Court that from now on I am no longer an enemy of Soviet power. I disavow definitely and clearly any connection with the counter-revolution abroad and the machinations of the monarchists and White Guardists in this country."

What had caused the patriarch to make this declaration? He was concerned about his release from prison not for personal reasons, but for the sake of the church. The church needed him, she was threatened most severely during these months by a schism which had been caused by the founding of the so-called "Living Church." When Tikhon was released from prison, a large crowd of the faithful waited for him and strewed flowers in his path. He remained loyal to the direction on which he started out in his self-criticism. In the first document published after his release he declared: "All monarchists and White Guardists inside and outside of Russia should know that I am not an enemy of the state." In a second declaration he stated that the Orthodox Church in Russia was non-political, that in the future she wanted to be neither White nor Red, that she was a mediating and apostolic church, and that all attempts, no matter from which side they might be undertaken, to pull the church into the political struggle would be rejected and condemned. A third declaration, issued on April 7, 1925, the day of his death, contained a positive confession to Soviet power. In it Tikhon called upon the faithful: "To permit no activity directed against the government, to nourish no hopes for the return of the monarchy, and to be convinced that the Soviet government actually is the power of the workers and the peasants and that for this reason it is unshaken."

It was the merit of Patriarch Tikhon that in the years of the most difficult disturbances he preserved the inner independence of the church. He confessed his full political loyalty to the Soviet state, but he did not give to the state a religious anointing and he did not sell his birthright to the Communist revolutionary ideology. Every one of Tikhon's successors has followed this tradition established by the first patriarch. His decision to recognize the Communist government, even though it was militantly atheistic, as a government given by God was the primary reason for the fact that the church was now permitted to lead a legally recognized life even though it was a very miserable life. Not only in foreign countries, but also in the eyes of many of the believers in the Soviet Union, Tikhon and his successors were looked upon as twilight figures or even as traitors who had made their peace with Antichrist. They accepted this odium silently. Whenever they spoke on political themes, it appeared as if their language was not natural or was strained. But who could know their mind? Who could say whether an inner decision, naked force, or an overwhelming sense of responsibility formulated their words? Perhaps history will render to these men the verdict that they were truly great because they did not choose the easier way of imprisonment, banishment, or death. They were willing to drink the bitter cup of scorn to the last draught so that the church might live.

Since the Kremlin did not permit the election of a new patriarch, the church had to be satisfied to appoint a patriarch-vicar in the person of Metropolitan Peter of Krutitzy. He continued the course that had been charted by Tikhon and issued a loyalty declaration toward the Soviet state. But because he refused to come to terms with the so-called "Living Church," Peter was imprisoned and died in exile in 1936. At the end of 1925 Metropolitan Sergius took over the church's government for the imprisoned patriarch-vicar. In order to establish at least to some degree the administration of the church he asked the government officially, in June 1926, to grant the church administration the permission to convoke a synod. This request was promptly denied and Sergius was arrested in December 1926. After four months he was released from prison and was recognized by the government, in May 1927, as "Administrator of the Church of Moscow." The promise which he had been forced to give in order to obtain this favor from the government was carried out in a pastoral letter issued by the administrator on July 29, 1927. In it Sergius indicated that the activities of the bishops who had emigrated to foreign countries were the reason for the government's distrust of the church. He asked all Orthodox priests in foreign countries to resign from the Russian Church if they could not give their complete loyalty to the Russian government. At the same time he indicated: "We want to remain Orthodox believers and also want to recognize the Soviet Union as our earthly fatherland whose joys and successes will also be our joys and successes, and whose misfortunes will also be our misfortunes. Every blow against the Soviet Union, through war, boycott, natural catastrophe, or assassination on the streets—as recently at Warsaw—we shall consider a blow against ourselves."

Sergius was strongly opposed by the bishops who were interned on the island of Slolovka. In the years 1923-1926 a total of eighty bishops had been interned here. These bishops disapproved the policy of Sergius. But the administrator refused to change his mind. In the beginning of 1929 he was recognized by the overwhelming majority of the church. In his former position as Metropolitan of Gorki he had cultivated good relations with a number of congregations in which workers predominated. In Moscow he became so popular that congregations had to ask him weeks ahead to preach in their crowded services. When the imprisoned Metropolitan Peter died in 1936, Sergius became Patriarch-Vicar in his stead, or, as he was called, "Guardian of the Patriarchal Throne."

6. Schisms

Surrounding the patriarch were the many dangers and temptations of the revolutionary years. Several schisms to the right and to the left took place. In 1920 a supreme church administration was formed, which at first operated from southern Russia with the approval of Tikhon, but was later forced to go into exile where it held its first synod at Karlovac and constituted itself, in November 1921, as "The Russian Orthodox Church in Exile." The former Metropolitan Antony of Kiev became the leader of this church. This group was intent on restoring both the church and the monarchy and began to work for the "spiritual rebirth of Russia." It took the line that this rebirth cannot take place without the restoration of the monarchy under the Romanovs. In March 1922 Tikhon withdrew ecclesiastical recognition from this group. On its part the group (whose headquarters was later located in Munich) accused the Moscow patriarch of becoming a captive of the spirit of evil and trying to please man more than God by attempting to get along with Stalin. In addition, the Orthodox congregations in the West whose membership had increased by over two million Russian emigrants were torn and divided by the question of how they should deal with the Moscow patriarchate to which they had belonged administratively in the past. For a while they formed an autonomous church under the Metropolitan Eulogius of Paris, but later, in 1928, they placed themselves again under the Moscow patriarchate. Finally, in 1930, they acknowledged the Ecumenical Patriarch of Contantinople. In West Germany at present about 15,000 Orthodox belong to this church. The Russian Orthodox Church in the USA remained officially under the patriarch until 1933. At that time the majority of the American Orthodox of Russian extraction dissolved this bond, and since then there have been quite a number of schisms. While the Russian Orthodox Church in Exile, whose leadership moved to New York in 1950, numbers 55,000 members and the Russian Orthodox Greek Catholic Church of America, which is in communion with Constantinople, has 755,000 members, the Exarchate of North and South America, which is affiliated with Moscow, has only an insignificant number of congregations.

More important and more dangerous than these schisms abroad was an inner-Russian schism which had the support of the atheistic state. Under the leadership of some Communist priests, a "Living Church" had been formed, also called the *Obnolenski Movement,* which used the motto: "The causes of Lenin and of Christ are identical." This church opposed the Patriarch Tikhon, usurped the central administrative offices of the church in 1922, and began, with the help of the state, to liquidate its enemies. The patriarch was denounced and deposed from his office. The government recognized the "Living Church" on August 10, 1922, as the only legally established Orthodox Church. In March 1923 its synod decided to abolish the patriarchate altogether and to establish a "Supreme Soviet of the Church," which became its highest lawgiving body. The group permitted the marriage of bishops and also second marriage for priests.

Upon his release from prison, on June 26, 1923, Patriarch Tikhon immediately took steps to outlaw the "Living Church." On July 15 he declared the "Living Church" to be schismatic, and many of its followers thereafter left it. The "Living Church" now took the name "Synodical Church" which was recognized in 1924 by the Ecumenical Patriarch of Constantinople. Both successors of Tikhon, the Patriarch-Vicar Peter and his administrator Sergius, continued to condemn the "Living Church." Its remaining members again changed the title of the church, calling themselves "The Union of Congregations of the Apostolic Church," gave themselves a democratic synodal constitution, but no longer played an important part in the ecclesiastic development of the Soviet Union. In 1945 the remnant submitted humbly to the Moscow patriarchate.

Much more serious was another split, which was not caused by political opportunists but by faithful Christians. Metropolitan Joseph of Leningrad was opposed to the loyalty declaration which the administrator of the patriarchate, Sergius, had issued in 1927. He found numerous followers who gathered around him in the Leningrad Church of the Resurrection. This opposition movement began to feel the wrath of the state to the fullest extent. Its houses of worship were closed, and its most respected leaders were shot. Metropolitan Joseph, together with many clergymen and lay people, was sent to a concentration camp. The persecuted congregations were forced to go underground. In 1928 there were secret services in many private homes in Leningrad. After 1930 the number of the faithful increased considerably, in spite of harsh persecutions by the state. Also in other parts of Russia, especially in

Siberia, congregations met secretly. There was no administrative center nor were there any regular leaders. The faithful considered Metropolitan Joseph as their head. In the years 1929-30 in the concentration camp of Solovski, where a number of Josephine bishops were being held, secret ordinations of priests took place. There were also some secret bishops. In Leningrad services continued to be held in many places, including homes, schools, hospitals, and even in some factories. The persecution of this group became especially violent during the Great Purge of 1937-38. Not much is known of the fate of this church in the catacombs. Perhaps it has disappeared; perhaps it still continues to exist in greatest secrecy. But it has disappeared from the public view. The observer can see, from the fate which befell this church of the faithful, the road of martyrdom which the whole Russian Orthodox Church would have traveled if the patriarch and his successors had not decided to face up to political realities.

7. Church Underground

When, after the Revocation of the Edict of Nantes, the Huguenot church of France was forbidden (1685), the faithful went "into the desert." They gathered on the mountains and in the forests to hold their divine services. Something similar happened in the Soviet Union. Jaroslavski called out angrily at a meeting of the Moscow unions on April 10, 1939: "When a priest is deprived of his congregation, that does not mean that he stops being a priest. He changes into an itinerant priest. He travels around with his primitive tools in the villages, performs religious rites, reads prayers, baptizes children. Such wandering priests at times are more dangerous than those who carry on their ministry at a designated place of residence."

Many priests who were expelled from their congregations made the whole immense extent of Russia their field of pastoral activity. A secret appeal was made: "Take your staff in hand and go out to the highway. If they ask you where you come from, answer: 'I am seeking the faithful of the diaspora on the desecrated face of the earth.'" One report about these wandering priests stated: "When the last church building has been closed in a town, then they take their staff and go from place to place. They teach everywhere, in the villages, in the houses, and in the stables, in the forests and under the open sky in the field. They look pale and miserable, and often their clothing is torn. A few crumbs of bread are their only nourishment. In their little sack they carry a Bible, their most precious belonging. They are warmly received by the people, but woe unto them if they fall into the hands of the stool pigeons of the police."

Also the group of *Starzoi* was reorganized, and the number of pilgrims that traversed the giant realm increased constantly. Formerly the *Starzoi* had busied themselves fighting against the secularization of the Orthodox Church. Now, after the victory of the atheistic powers, their chief concern was the preservation of the faith. A German pastor wrote at that time: "These men are carrying out the work of Christian missionaries by going through the countryside on foot, looking like simple farmers with their fur-caps on their heads, the Gospel and the cross in their knapsacks. They are preachers, seers, prophets, and pastors all in one. They are trying to lead the Russian people back to the original simplicity of the Orthodox Christian faith. Therefore they are beloved and honored by the population and they are hated and persecuted by the Soviet government. These *Starzoi* carry out their high calling in this terrible moment of the history of the Eastern Orthodox Church. They do not permit the fire of the faith to be extinguished and the worm of the conscience to die."

There arose among the people many strange legends and miracle stories which originated as a reaction of the scandalized Christians to the desecration of their sacred places. Such legends spread, beginning in 1923, through the whole Ukraine, and great numbers of pilgrims came to the places where these miracles were said to have occurred. These stories told about the renewal of sacred pictures, crosses, and church steeples which had been destroyed and the miraculous apparitions of sacred objects in the churches. These were some of the examples: Three Bolsheviks were riding on a highway. When they came to a cross, one of them began to shoot at it. He shot several times. After he had hit the cross eight times, blood flowed from the cross. Or the following: At a crossing of the roads a Bolshevik shot at a cross. The bullet richocheted and killed him. But it also wounded the picture of Christ on the left side, and from the picture blood was flowing. There were also eschatological visions. Talismans against the Antichrist were manufactured. Banquets were prepared for pilgrims during which apocalyptic questions were discussed and religious songs were sung. The story is told of a Communist who had been brought by a miracle to baptize his children. Or there was the story of a picture of Christ that had been removed, but could still be seen by children and believing people.

As hard as the closing of the churches was for the congregations, their spiritual life did not starve to death. Faith had a way of avoiding and overcoming obstacles. If there was no way to worship in the house of God one fled to the ikons in the homes. A writer by the name of Oletshchuk wrote disappointedly in the magazine *Antireligiosnik* (1936) that the closing of churches and other prohibitions did not better the conditions but, on the contrary, made them worse. Churches and houses of prayer were established in the dwellings of faithful collective farmers, where pictures were transferred from the prayer corners in the rooms and placed into chests. The part of the priest was taken over by the oldest collective farmer and services were conducted illegally. The oppressed religious remnants were driven underground but not destroyed. Stalin even declared: "The churches of the Soviet Union can easily be closed. All you have to do is to give a command to the OGPU and they are closed. But then the peasant and the peasant woman become a church underground and build the church in their souls. Such churches cannot be controlled by the secret police. Therefore the atheistic movement must use more effective methods. Perhaps we should only in exceptional cases be rough with them and attack them and use repression only as a last resort."

The results of twenty years of persecutions carried on with all means at the disposal of the state were disappointing. According to the Anti-Religious Five-Year Plan the idea of God was supposed to have been eliminated from the hearts of the people by 1937, on the twentieth anniversary of the October Revolution. But it was not eliminated. As a matter of fact, the year 1937 was not at all a year of triumph for the League of Militant Atheists. In that year the power of the League began to decline. In March 1937 *Iswestija* reported that the League had experienced a painful drop in membership. By 1938 its membership had decreased from its peak of 5,000,000 members to 2,000,000. Its activities had slackened off. The old atheists had become tired. At the beginning of 1939 the persecutions of Christians suddenly stopped. The government decreed that all forceful repression of religion must be discontinued. In the meantime world-moving events were taking place on the stage of history. The Second World War started, and in the summer of 1941 the Germans attacked the Soviet Union. German divisions penetrated deep into the heart of Russia. In September 1941 *Beshboshnik* suspended publication on account of paper shortage, and at the same time the League of Militant Atheists was dissolved, because it had lost its meaning.

8. Turning Point During the Second World War

In the situation of great national crisis Stalin decided to adopt a new religious policy. He was forced to mobilize all the resources of Russia for the great patriotic war. His readiness to forget for the time being about old Communist ideas and to come to an understanding with the Orthodox Church was not the result of any change of heart but a political maneuver. It was also proof of the fact that the number of believers still represented a large portion of the people, a fact that was important enough for Stalin to make certain concessions in order to win the church for the support of the patriotic war.

On May 2, 1942, the administrator of the patriarchate, Sergius, was permitted to take the title Metropolitan of Moscow. On September 3, 1943, he was personally received by Stalin. This meant a *de facto* recognition of the patriarchate by the state. On September 8, Sergius was elected to the patriarchal throne by seventeen bishops assembled at a synod. But he died soon afterward, on April 15, 1944.

In January and February 1945, while the Germans were being driven back across their borders by the victorious Red Army, a council was convened in Moscow which decided to adopt a new and strongly centralized church constitution which transferred the essential power of the Holy Synod, which had been the ecclesiastical right arm of the czars from 1721 to 1917, to the patriarch. He was given the right to nominate the bishops, and the bishops received the right to appoint priests. There were no longer any elections in the church. The Russian Orthodox Church inside and outside of Russia was divided into 89 eparchies. Metropolitan Alexei of Leningrad was elected as the new patriarch. The government facilitated the meeting of the council in every possible way. The patriarchate, which until that time had resided in a miserable hut on the outskirts of Moscow, was installed in a palatial building which had once been the German embassy.

The church received numerous favors after 1943. The much-touted freedom of religion which had been officially guaranteed in the constitution of 1936, but had been suppressed *de facto,* became now a reality, at least to some extent. A large number of houses of worship were returned to the church. In Moscow the number of open churches increased from 15 in 1939 to over 50 in 1943. The Orthodox Georgian Church was completely restored and returned to the patriarch. The famous St. Michael's Church of the old Trinity Monastery, which had been secularized after the Revolution, was newly consecrated. The relics of St. Alexis were returned from the Kremlin museum to the cathedral of the patriarch. Also new buildings were erected for which the state made building materials available at a discount. The state helped restore and refurbish priestly vestments, covers, and even bed-linen for the seminarians and put at the disposal of the church automobiles, gasoline, communion wine, wax, printing paper, and the like.

The number of churches in actual operation in the Russia of 1945 was estimated at about 20,000. In June 1946 there were about 25,000 parishes and 30,000 priests. Also monasticism saw a modest rebirth. Important monasteries like the famous Cave Monastery of Kiev and Trinity Monastery of Moscow, which contained the tomb of St. Sergius, were returned to the church. The renowned Alexander Nevski Lavra once more served its original purpose as a monastery. The convent of Novotie Vichi, which was numbered among Russia's oldest and most revered shrines and which, since 1922, had served as a museum, was opened again. In 1946 there were 99 monasteries and convents throughout the USSR. The church was also given the right to educate her future priests. On October 1, 1946, the Orthodox Theological Academy in Moscow began its work. Another academy was opened at Leningrad. In addition to these two academies there were a number of ecclesiastical secondary schools.

On October 12, 1943, the Soviet government established a Council for the Affairs of the Orthodox Church whose chairman was G. Karpov. Another agency of the state for the affairs of non-Orthodox religious bodies was established under the chairmanship of N. Polianski. By decree of August 22, 1945, the government recognized the Orthodox Church as a body of public law. She was allowed to buy property for religious purposes, to build churches and to organize shops for the manufacture of religious objects. The maintenance of church cemeteries and the assessment of church taxes or membership contributions, however, remained forbidden.

Concerning the division of authority between the church administration and the council of the state, Patriarch Alexei said: "The Council helps the church in all matters which need the permission of the civil authorities, for example, the purchase of real estate for the building of churches, monasteries, and church schools, and making such real estate available to the church for church purposes. But everything that concerns the inner life of the church, such as administrative matters, the appointment of bishops and priests, and the transfer of clergymen, is within the power of the patriarch and the Holy Synod." On the other hand, the council of the state exercised a tight control over the church which went to the smallest details. Meetings of the synod and bishops' conferences could take place only with the permission of the government. When a bishop was elected, a representative of the state had to be present to give the decisive vote. As was the patriarch, so every bishop was "assisted" by a Soviet commissar. If a parish was to be organized or property to be purchased or sold, the permission of the state had to be obtained. In every district of the Soviet Union the council of state had a deputy.

When Patriarch-elect Alexei was enthroned on February 2, 1945, Karpov expressed to the church the gratitude and high recognition of the Soviet government for the loyalty and the sacrifices which had been evidenced during the war on the part of the church. Alexei in turn thanked the Soviet government for the support that it had given and blessed the great leader Marshal Stalin. In fact, the church had richly rewarded the government for its leniency and had put at its disposal her whole moral authority, both materially and spiritually. She had collected 300,000,000 rubles and armed an armored division, *Dimitri Donskoi,* which was presented in March 1944 to the Red Army. Metropolitan Nikolai bestowed upon this division the blessings of the church and gave it the following charge: "Go forward, faithful fighters, in the name of the final liberation of our fatherland from the fascists, in the name of a peaceful life and happiness of the people. Begin your holy work. In God's name, forward!" Many priests served on the battlefields in the ranks of the Red Army. Others became partisans behind the lines of the Germans. Many received high Soviet decorations. The church prayed constantly: "Arise, O Lord, help us and give to thy fighters the victory, in thy name we pray." The council of Moscow issued a call to all nations of the world to help in the fight against fascism. High dignitaries of the church were active in the propaganda war against the Germans, and their sentiments were not always Christian. Their utterances could perhaps be excused or at least be explained as strange language forced upon them by their rulers. Thus Archbishop Lucas of Tambov wrote in the magazine of the patriarchate (February 1944): "If we speak of the terrible Germans, can we still think of the sacred command of Christ: Love your enemies? No! Never! Under no circumstances can this be true. One cannot carry out this command, because such love is completely and absolutely impossible, not only for man, but also for the angels and for the God of love himself, because God himself hates evil and liquidates the evildoer. Those terrible Germans are not only our enemies, but also the enemies of God. Who would dare to speak of loving the enemies of God?" In a book, *Patriarch Sergius and His Legacy,* which was published by the patriarchate, the following remarks of the patriarch were printed: "In the fight between good and evil the spiritual front is clearly drawn. The Christians are gathered in the bosom of Orthodoxy, and the anti-Christians are found in the fascist hordes." The late patriarch had considered it the task of the church to fight "side by side with the angels of God who untiringly fight against the evil in the world" until fascism, which he considered the creation of Protestant "subjectivism," had been crushed.

The sufferings of the war led to a religious revival among the people of the USSR. According to an estimate by Jaroslavski, more than half of the soldiers of the Red Army were believers. Church services were crowded once more. The church did not have to worry about recruiting men for the priesthood. She followed faithfully the agreement which she had made with the state and underwrote the policies of the state even after the war. She complied with all the demands made upon her by the state. When Stalin died in 1953, Patriarch Alexei sent the Council of Ministers of the USSR a letter of condolences in which he stated that the church was deeply grieved over the death of "the great creator of the happiness of our people. His passing," he wrote, "is a great misfortune for our fatherland and for all its people. Stalin's death fills the entire Russian Orthodox Church with deep sorrow. She will never forget his benevolence toward us."

Expressions of this kind should not be taken too seriously. But the Orthodox Church clearly showed her political loyalty and her close identification with the people in whose midst she was working. This should not be understood as a religious anointing of Communism by the Gospel. The Orthodox Church never assigned to the Communist state or to any dictatorship a partnership in the way of salvation. She never changed her liturgy and her doctrine in favor of Communist ideology. In the publications of the patriarchate there was no proof that Marxist ideology had ever taken root in the church. In the historical articles published by the church no mention was made that looked like a dialectical-materialistic interpretation of church history. The Communist Party was never mentioned in her writings. The Communist Party did not exist officially as far as the Orthodox Church was concerned. She recognized the Soviet state as a government ordained by God. Bishop Michael of

Smolensk defined the position of the church to the state in his book *The Turning Point in the History of Mankind* as follows: "According to her destiny the church cannot be a state within the state, as is Roman Catholicism. She cannot be an organization which is parallel to the state, as was the old Orthodox Church of Byzantium. She cannot be an executive organ of the state, as was the Russian Orthodox Church before the Revolution. All these forms of relationship to the state are foreign to the Orthodox Church. According to her destiny she must unite those who are living here on earth with those who are living in heaven. She represents thus the family of the heavenly Father. This self-interpretation of the church, which means that her foundation is not built on rights and privileges, but on mutual love of all her members, should never arouse the suspicion of the state. She should never fear the limitation of her spiritual ministry by the state."

Another important aspect was brought out in an article which the famous Russian philosopher of religion Nicholas Berdyaev, who died on March 23, 1948, wrote in the French magazine *The Third Hour*. He stated: "The church can do nothing else but condemn materialism. But that does not mean that she must in the same breath condemn political and social orders which have been established by it. The Russian Church has been accused of being in league with a non-Christian government. But where in the world is there a Christian government which is founded on spiritual foundations? All churches are forced to live in a non-Christian world which is at enmity with Christ. Let us not forget that during the Constantinian period of world history (400-1900) the relationship between church and state was always abnormal. The Soviet state is neither Christian nor Orthodox. Orthodox czarism considered itself sacrosanct, and the church was perverted by Caesaro-Papism. The Soviet state with its materialistic ideology cannot interfere in the inner life of the church, neither can it interest itself in it. All it can do is to regulate the relationship between church and state."

9. Fruits of Collaboration

The new relationship between state and church benefited both of them. The church was able to begin the task of trying to win back the lost exarchates. The Exarchate of Western Europe in Paris remained outside her sphere of influence. The Russian Church in Exile also remained unreconciled. The Russian Orthodox Church in the USA, in spite of all efforts by the patriarch, could not be won back. But Alexei succeeded in taking root in central and western Europe without, however, being able to break the influence of his rival in Constantinople. Furthermore, the patriarchate was able to resume its predominant position among the autocephalous Orthodox churches which its numerical and spiritual importance demanded. In 1945 Patriarch Alexei traveled to Syria, Palestine, and Egypt. Further trips by Russian church leaders followed. There was no lack of exchange visits and there was a great deal of correspondence. The Kremlin too gained from this activity. The Russian Orthodox Church became an important factor in the Pan-Slavic movement and in Communist world propaganda. The small Orthodox churches of Estonia, Latvia, Czechoslovakia, and Hungary, which formerly had been under the Ecumenical Patriarchate of Constantinople, were incorporated into the Russian Church. The dioceses of China were won back in 1945. The Orthodox Churches of Paland, Romania, and Bulgaria formed close alliances with Moscow. But between the Patriarchs of Moscow and Constantinople the old rivalry continued. At the council of Moscow in 1945 the representative of the Ecumenical Patriarch Maximus V emphasized that his church was the mother which had given birth to Russia in Christ. The invitation to a Pan-Orthodox Council which Alexei had issued on April 4, 1945, was rejected by the Ecumenical Patriarch because he alone had the right to call such a council. Alexei denied this and complained that the Ecumenical Patriarch was supporting the Orthodox clergy in Poland, Finland, and Western Europe, who had separated from Moscow, and that in America he had organized whole dioceses and had appointed an exarch for central and western Europe.

The Pan-Orthodox Council met in Moscow July 8-17, 1948. A number of important Orthodox churches from abroad participated in it, for example, the churches of Yugoslavia, Romania, Bulgaria, and the patriarchate of Antioch. At the same time the five-hundredth anniversary of the independence of the patriarchate of Moscow from Contantinople was commemorated. The Council sent an astonishingly frank message to the churches of the world in which it stated: "We, the churches of the Orthodox communion, receive a bad impression because the instigators of a new war are the members of the Roman Catholic and Protestant churches. We are deeply grieved that instead of listening to the voice of peace and of Christian mercy we hear from the bulwark of Roman Catholicism, the Vatican, and from the nest of Protestantism, the United States of America, that a new war is being prepared and hymns of praise are being sung to the atom bomb and similar instruments of destruction of human life. It is our sincere prayer and our warm hope that the pride and power-hunger of the Vatican and of all those who support it, and also the arrogance of Protestant rationalism, will make room for Christian love of peace so that they may all say with the Apostle Paul: 'But by the grace of God I am what I am' (1 Cor. 15:10)! "The statement further complained that the Roman Catholic Church had perverted the truth and had destroyed the purity of doctrine. "Therefore," it continued, "it is not we but the voices of the Church Fathers who proclaim the condemnation of Roman papacy. The Roman bishops have always been on the side of the powerful and against the weak and exploited. The Vatican is the center of international intrigue against the interests of the people, especially the Slavic people. It is the center of international fascism, one of the incendiaries of imperialistic wars, and it is engaged at the present time in the most active way in the preparation for another war. The whole Christian world and all the faithful must realize to what depths of an abyss the papacy has descended. Christians cannot avoid attacking this policy of the Vatican as anti-Christian, anti-democratic, and anti-national."

In a declaration on the unity of the church the Roman idea of unity was rejected as erroneous and the ecumenical movement was criticized because it tried to establish a mere external union. It interfered with international politics and was a body of organized charities, they stated, "which tries to buy human souls through the giving of alms." The Orthodox council declared that there was only one way for the restoration of the true unity of the church, namely the return to the doctrine of the old undivided church. The declaration of the council continued: "The Orthodox Church believes without wavering that it is its most noble and most sacred duty to preserve the testimony of the ancient and undivided church of Jesus Christ."

With this message the newly found self-confidence of the patriarchate of Moscow became evident to the whole Christian world. At the World Council of Churches meeting in Amsterdam in 1948 there were Orthodox representatives, but the patriarch of Moscow declined the invitation to participate in the ecumenical movement in its present form. It was not until 1954 that he changed his position. In 1961 the church of the patriarch joined the World Council of Churches at New Delhi.

The state helped the patriarchate to win a doubtful victory by forcing the Catholic Church of the Byzantine Rite in Ruthenia to transfer her allegiance from Rome to the Russian Orthodox Church. At the beginning of the Second World War this church numbered 3,040 parishes, 4,300,000 faithful, 2,950 priests, 520 monks, 1,100 nuns, and 540 students of theology. It had 9,900 elementary schools, 308 secondary schools, 38 print shops and 35 book stores. When in 1945 the larger part of the territory which formerly belonged to Poland was incorporated into the Soviet Union, the bishops were ordered to break with Rome and to join the Orthodox Church. They refused. The Archbishop of Lemberg, Slipyi, and all his fellow bishops, eight in number, were arrested, imprisoned, and sent to work camps. After the church had been rendered leaderless in such a way, the state convoked a church convention, which on March 8, 1945, met at Lemberg, revoked its union with Rome, and proclaimed the return of the church to the Russian Orthodox communion. Priests and laymen who remained faithful to Rome were bloodily persecuted. Over 50% of the priests were arrested, 10% were able to escape, 10% went underground, and only the 30% remaining priests bowed before the power of the state and joined the Orthodox Church. All seminaries for priests and the monasteries of the church were closed. The faithful were deported in great numbers. The last resistance was broken by drastic punitive action. After 1948 the churches were converted into warehouses, clubs, and movies. All pilgrimage and monastery churches were completely leveled to the ground. At the beginning of 1948 the Russian TASS news agency announced the complete liquidation of the Catholic Church of the Byzantine Rite. But in 1961 there were still complaints in the press that nuns who had gone underground were supported by the faithful; that secret letters were sent by the churches; that perhaps there was even a hierarchical organization, although the regular bishops had been imprisoned or had died; that meetings were held and children were being instructed in the Roman Catholic faith.

The last result of the close connection between church and state was the active participation of the patriarchate and all other churches of the Soviet Union in the Communist Peace Movement. Of course, this activity which was supposed to serve the peace of the world could be bolstered with good biblical reasons, but there was no doubt that the cooperation of the patriarchate was also in the interest of Soviet world politics and that the patriarch was used as a spokesman for Soviet propaganda, as became clear in the spring of 1952. At that time the Communist press leveled severe accusations against the USA because that country had allegedly begun bacteriological warfare in Korea. The news, of course, was false. But the patriarch published a declaration of the Holy Synod in which he protested in the name of the churches and all the faithful against what he called "a crime that cries to highest heaven and which is being committed against the people of China and Korea." He said that the cup of suffering of the Korean people was running over, that there was a suffering hitherto unseen and that there were unheard-of vexations. The weapon of bacteriological warfare had been used by the enemy of all peace-loving people, the American imperialists. Insects exposed to the plague had been dropped by American airplanes on villages not only in Korea, but also in China. He continued: "How deep must the morals of those who have become beasts and wild animals have fallen! They have become calculating mass murderers." From May 9 to 12, 1952, a World Peace Conference of the Church was held in Moscow, which was also attended by some representatives from foreign countries. Before the beginning of the meeting, Ilya Ehrenburg declared in *Pravda:* "As long as our Peace Movement was mainly promoted by

Communist intellectuals and leaders of the working masses the American leaders worried very little about it. But the next World Peace Congress at the end of this year will be attended also by factory owners and merchants, pastors and Quakers, people whom the Americans until now have considered their confederates." These words made clear what high hopes the Kremlin placed in the participation of the churches in the Peace Movement.

10. Atheism with Kid Gloves

Stalin in his role as chief of the government recognized the patriarchate, but the Communist Party was still working behind the facade erected by the state. While the state proclaimed the idea of freedom of belief and of tolerance, the Communist Party continued to demand in its pronouncements that all forms of religion should be completely liquidated. The decrees "Concerning the Elimination of the Remnants of Capitalism on the Consciousness and the Behavior of Man," which were passed during the Twenty-Second Congress of the Communist Party in 1961, stated: "The Party considers the fight against all manifestations of bourgeois ideology and morality, against the psychology of private ownership, and against superstition and religious prejudices an integral part of Communist education." It furthermore stated: "For the education of man in the spirit of scientific materialism and for the purpose of overcoming religious prejudices that Party will use all means at her disposal to influence our people ideologically without permitting the violation of the feelings of the faithful. It is absolutely necessary to show patiently the uselessness of religious attitudes which have arisen in history because of man's fears of the elemental powers of nature and because of the social servitude caused by lack of knowledge of the true causes of the phenomena of nature and society. In this connection it will be necessary to bolster our ideas with the findings of modern science which reveal to us the concept of the world more and more clearly, increase the power of man over nature, and leave no room for religious phantasies concerning supernatural powers."

The elimination of the religious remnants was attempted in a very different way from the methods used immediately after 1917. There were no wild attacks or denials of the legal rights of believers. Patience or, as it was called, "scientific enlightenment," was being used. Communist atheism remained militant, there was no doubt about it, but it had put on kid gloves. From time to time it became apparent that inside these kid gloves there were still the fists of boxers.

In the year 1947 an All-Union Society for the Dissemination of Political and Scientific Knowledge had been organized under the direction of Professor Vavilov, president of the Academy of Sciences of the USSR. He was later succeeded by the highly esteemed scholar I. Oparin. Since the latter's death in 1956 Professor Mark Borisovitch Mitin has headed the movement. In the year 1959 the All-Union Society had 800,000 members. From the very beginnings it had set itself high goals. For the work of enlightenment plans were made in the summer of 1950 to send over 500,000 propagandists with pictures and expositions into all the corners of the Soviet Union and to distribute more than 20,000,000 anti-religious brochures. The Society stated: "The fight against the Gospel and the legend of Christ must be carried on relentlessly with all the means at the disposal of the Communist movement." Two large film studios were commissioned to produce eight anti-religious films which dealt with themes like the following: "The Fairy Tale of the Divine Origin of Life," "Religion as a Tool of Capitalist Oppression," "Princes of the Church as Warmongers," "The Church and the Battle for the Liberation of the Working Class." In the year 1954 the Society conducted 120,000 meetings on atheistic themes, but in 1956 the number had decreased to 84,000. However, propaganda carried on by various publications increased considerably. Bibliographies of the years 1952-1954 show that 979 titles were published against religion and for the promotion of atheism. In 1955 only 157 atheistic books and brochures made their appearance. In 1956 this number further decreased to 145 and in 1957 to 102. Since 1958, however, the production of anti-religious books has increased again. At the request of the party, books like: *Russian Writers on Religion,* and the great reference work, *Vademecum for the Atheist,* a collection, *Why We Have Broken With Religion,* and Jaroslavski's old *Bible for Believers and Unbelievers*—he had died in 1943—were published by the Society. Other books, that bore titles like *Scientific Predictions and Religious Prejudices, How Man Created God, The Miracles of Religion and the Power of Science, The Myth of the Soul*, were also published. The theme of scientific atheistic propaganda concentrated its attacks against religious interpretations of nature and of the human race, because such interpretations seemed to hinder progress and science and injected the superfluous idea of the personal creator into the world picture. Such an injection of the metaphysical dimension into the physical understanding of the world interfered with Communist understanding of the origin of life and of man himself, and the hypotheses concerning the origin of religion in general which the Communists held as their cardinal beliefs. These problems had to be solved from the point of view of materialistic dialectic materialism. This was done in a number of books on astronomy, geology, biology, anthropology, archeology, ethnography, and history.

At a meeting in June 1959 there was a great deal of self-criticism on the part of the Society, and it was decided to publish a new magazine, *Nauka y Religia* (Science and Religion) beginning in September 1959. It was issued in 70,000 copies, later increased to 110,000, and interpreted itself in one of its first editorials as "The Battle Organ of Militant Atheism." It was noteworthy that in this magazine also a Western atheist, the English philosopher Bertrand Russell, wrote an article. He discussed the question, "Does Religion Contribute Anything Valuable to Civilization?" and summarized his answers in the following sentence: "No, except that it has contributed to creating a calendar." He arrived at the conclusion: "It is possible that mankind is already on the threshold of the Golden Age. If this is the case, we must first of all kill the dragon which guards its gates, and this dragon is religion."

In order to advance the training of "propagandist squadrons" it was decided that besides a strong emphasis on the scientific, atheistic theme in all the curricula there should be lecture courses in the schools of higher learning. Already in 1955 the Academy of Sciences had organized a Commission for the Coordination of the Academy of Sciences of the USSR of Questions Dealing With

Scientific Propaganda. Several highly qualified scientists worked in a number of institutes, among them the Museum for the History of Religion and of Atheism in Leningrad which had been founded in 1932 and the sector for the History of Religion and Atheism in the Historical Institute of the Academy of Sciences. Publications issued by these institutes were no mere propaganda, but claimed scientific status. They were very detailed and showed an interest in the history of Russian Orthodoxy which had been hitherto unknown in the Soviet Union.

In 1958 the Ukrainian Soviet Republic introduced in its schools of higher learning compulsory lectures on the foundations of atheism. The courses included in the humanistic and medical academies numbered 24 hours, in the technical, agricultural, and pharmaceutical institutes 14 hours. They were offered in the fourth year of studies. Their purpose was: "To prove to the students the scientifically untenable positions of religion, to criticize sharply the class-conditioned and empirical roots of those religions and sects which are most widely represented in the world, to expose them to sharp criticism, and to show how modern natural and social sciences have gradually eliminated all religious dogmas." The students were to get a clear scientific and atheistic world-view. The course was subdivided into nine themes: Contrast between nature and religion; Origins of religion: Origins and social causes of Christianity; Reactionary essence of Catholicism; Critique of the theology of the Orthodox Church; Religious sects in their reactionary role; Judaism, Buddhism, Islam; The relationship of the Communist Party and the Soviet government to the religions and the churches; Forms and methods of scientific atheist propaganda. As early as 1957 a House of Atheists was established in Odessa for the purpose of utilizing the scientific results in popular form for the struggle against religion. A section, "Demythologized Miracles," carried out experiments which unmasked the so-called religious miracles, and for this cause the chairs of physics and chemistry at the Odessa Institute were enlisted. A section, "People and Superstitions," worked for the propagation of new social customs in place of the old, e.g., Komsomol weddings and festivals connected with the birth of a child. Another section, "Atheistic Discussions," carried on a dialogue, and a literary artistic section was made responsible for the sending of atheistic mobile libraries into housing developments and clubs and to perform anti-religious dramas.

In the Soviet Republic of Turkmenistan a University for Atheism was opened at Ashkhabad in 1958. Each semester there were sixty lectures. The participants were asked to continue the anti-religious attacks in an increasing measure. At the beginning of 1959 a Moscow Club of Young Atheists was founded, formed by students, young academicans, and lectures from all the faculties and from several institutions of learning. According to the statutes of the society, members had the task "of developing their own atheistic ideology and at the same time training young people so that they can participate actively in the education of workers." For discussions members of the churches and of the sects were to be invited. The members of the club were to be active with individual anti-religious propaganda among the believers, especially among the young people.

Besides the press, radio, film, theater, with which the whole public domain was influenced in the spirit of atheism, the schools in particular were assigned the task of educating the youth in a purely atheistic spirit and of making them immune to religious influences. The textbook of the Pedagogical Institute, *Pedagogy*, by Jessipov Gonsharov, gave the following instructions: "In the elementary schools a very effective means of anti-religious influence is the reading of articles on art which show the harm and the deception of religion. The teacher must be perceptive and must use stories and fairy tales, excerpts from the writings of great writers, and good materials culled from newspapers and magazines which are adapted to the understanding of the child. In the Russian language classes pictures should be used to illustrate the fact that religion is being used as a means for the oppression of the masses and for keeping them in ignorance and the servants of the interests of the rich. In history classes the teacher should tell the children that man was not created by the gods, but that the gods were made by man. Children must learn to see how the capitalists are using religion for the enslavement of the masses, how churches and clergymen are serving the interests of exploitation and are enriching themselves at

the expense of the working man, how religion is supporting superstitions and ignorance among the masses, by influencing the latter
against science and culture, and how religion is giving assistance to
the enemies of the revolution. In geography the children should
be instructed in the scientific explanation of natural phenomena
which have been explained in a nonsensical way by religion. Besides this, the children should be taught how the church fought
against science and should be impressed by the accounts of the
martyrs of science like Giordano Bruno, Copernicus, Galileo, and
others. Examples of man's victory over nature and his conquest of
her riches should impress upon the children the senselessness of
religious doctrines and the harm done by them, beginning with a
fatalistic dependence of man on supernatural powers. Instruction in
the natural sciences should make clear to the children the irreconcilability of religion with science. It should show the harm which
religion has done to agriculture and health. Stories from the history
of science will arouse in the child indignation against all kinds of
obscurantism and a desire to fight actively against religion. Besides
this influence of the schools, such as the reading of publications
dealing with scientific and anti-religious themes, going on excursions to the Museum of the Revolution to view the materials concerning the reactionary role of the church, the showing of anti-
religious films and slides, and the discussion of anti-religious works
with parents, should be used outside of regular class instruction."

11. Guidelines for Atheistic Propaganda

The results of all these efforts of scientific atheistic propaganda
were discouraging. Apparently many of the people who were entrusted with this work did not only do it negligently, but against
their better judgment. The Central Committee of the Communist
Party decided, during one of its plenary sessions, that too little
attention was being paid to anti-religious propaganda and demanded, in a decree of July 7, 1954, that the passive attitude toward
religion should speedily be brought to an end. It said: "For the
strengthening of scientific atheistic propaganda all the means and
forms of ideological and political influence, such as lectures or dis-

cussions in the press, radio, movies, and theater, must be used to educate the working man in his own language. For the scientific atheistic propaganda, the best propagandists of the Party and of the Komsomol, the intelligentsia and the scientific forces available to us must be mobilized." Publishing houses were told to edit atheistic propaganda in documentary form for mass distribution, and the press was asked to influence its readers systematically and intensively with atheistic themes. The schools were to increase their educational work in the spirit of militant materialism and to permeate instruction in every field with atheistic contents. The Komsomol was to improve its propaganda among the young people and turn especially to that part of the young people who were still under the influence of the church, while the labor unions were to take care of the spreading of the materialistic ideology among the workers ("especially the women") through lectures and popular scientific films.

In an editorial July 24, 1956, *Pravda* complained that some party organizations were not convinced of the vital necessity of a determined fight against the remnants of capitalism and had shown tolerance toward the spreading of various types of prejudice and superstition. The Ministry of Education and the Ministry of Universities had not devoted as much energy to the education in the spirit of the materialistic ideology as was necessary. The organs of popular education had not considered it their most noble duty to fight against the religious prejudices of the population. The clubs, the Houses and Palaces of Culture, the reading rooms, which were charged with fighting daily and without wavering against religious prejudice and for the spread of scientific knowledge, often had been only insufficiently prepared to do this work. The Ministry of Culture and the Society for the Dissemination of Political and Scientific Knowledge had organized their scientific atheistic propaganda in a very unsatisfactory way. The labor unions and the Komsomol organizations had withdrawn completely from the propaganda. The press had fallen down on its job. Said the editorial, "The Party, whose duty it is to propagate the work of Communist education among the working masses, cannot be satisfied with this neglect of scientific atheistic propaganda. It is the duty of the Party organizations to eliminate in the shortest possible time all the shortcomings in this field and to reactivate scientific atheistic propaganda."

Articles of this type appeared also in other newspapers. Antireligious propaganda was increased. But it took a turn which was not at all desired by the regime. Therefore, on November 10, 1954, the Central Committee of the Communist Party passed the following resolution which was signed by the then Secretary General of the Central Committee, Nikita Khrushchev. This resolution became important for future developments. It said in part: "In accordance with its program the Communist Party carries on a scientific work of enlightenment in the sense of a materialistic ideology which is directed toward the steady development of the consciousness of the working masses and toward their gradual liberation from religious prejudices. But in this work the party deems it advisable to avoid any violation of the feelings of the faithful. The Central Committee has received information which shows that lately serious offenses have been committed in many places while the scientific atheistic propaganda was carried on among the population. Instead of carrying on systematic individual work for the propagation of scientific knowledge and waging an ideological battle against religion, many articles in the central and local newspapers, as well as many speeches by lecturers and other people, have employed insulting attacks against the clergy and those who participate in religious ceremonies. There have been cases in the columns of the press and in oral statements by the propagandists where some members of the clergy and the faithful have without reason been represented as people who do not deserve to be trusted politically. In a number of districts local organizations and individuals have interfered administratively in the activities of religious organizations and groups, and have committed offensive acts against the clergy. Such mistakes in anti-religious propaganda are against the program and the policy of the Communist Party in its fight against religion. They run counter to the repeated instructions of the Party that insults to the feelings of the faithful are not permitted."

The Central Committee also complained that in many cases there had been no careful selection of propaganda speakers and stated: "Not infrequently, scientifically untrained men or people insufficiently trained in atheistic propaganda, as well as occasional bunglers, who for the most part know only anecdotes and fairy tales about the clergy, have been permitted to speak." The area and district committees of the Communist Party and all other party organizations were told "to eliminate the mistakes in atheistic propaganda decisively and in no case to permit any violation of the feelings of the faithful and the clergy or any interference in the administration of the church." Such procedures the Central Committee considered to be contrary to the current party line and the constitution of the USSR. As a result of the incisive changes in the social and economic conditions and of the victory of socialism, it stated: "The majority of the population has freed itself long ago from the religious remnants. There are, however, citizens who are doing their patriotic duty as citizens honestly and sincerely, but who still are under religious influence. The Party has always had a sensitive and attentive attitude toward those of the faithful, and it will demand such an attitude also in the future. Therefore it is stupid and injurious to mistrust politically certain Soviet citizens on account of their religious convictions. Moreover, administrative measures and insults against religion will lead only to a deepening and even a strengthening of religious prejudices among these people."

The Central Committee continued: "It must be taken into account that the position of the church in the Soviet Union cannot be equated with the position of the church in the countries of exploitation. If the church in those countries is a pillar of the ruling classes and if she served in the Russia of the Czars for the strengthening of czarism and if she was to a large extent an enemy of Soviet power after the October Revolution, the social roots of religion have now been undermined and the basis upon which the church has been standing has been eliminated. The majority of the clergy are now just as loyal to the Soviet power as are other citizens. This has been proved by the facts of history. Therefore the battle against religious prejudices is now an ideological battle of a scientific materialistic ideology against an unscientific religious ideology."

"But," said the Central Committee, "the elimination of the mistakes of anti-religious propaganda should not lead to a wavering and weakening in our propaganda. The Communist Party cannot look on without interest and as a neutral observer as long as religion continues to exist. But it deems it necessary to wage an incisive and systematic propaganda war against it. The carrying out of this propaganda requires the greatest attention and care in the selection of official lecturers, other speakers, and authors. Therefore only scientifically qualified persons can be used for this work. Furthermore, an important improvement in the activities of the Palaces of Culture, clubs, libraries, reading rooms, lecture halls, parks set aside for culture and recreation, and other cultural and educational facilities is necessary."

12. Tough Religious Remnants

The complaints about the toughness of religious remnants and the lack of anti-religious propaganda continued. In the *Komsomolskaja Prawda* of February 19, 1957, W. Borisenkov told about a visit to Stalino. He saw many people in St. Hilary's Church, including young people, and he conversed with them. A young worker told him: "A short time ago I brought my child to baptism." To the question whether he believed in these things he answered: "Formerly, perhaps, I did not believe, but now I believe. Where one person drowns, another swims. What is good for the life of one leads another one to perdition." Some old women asked Borisenkov and his companions whether they had been to church. He said: "We denied it, and they persuaded us to go in to see how young people were being married. The women vied with each other in talking about the beauty of the church and the beauty of religious ceremonials. They praised the church, certainly not for the first time."

On the market place newly made ikons and other devotional helps were being sold. Borisenkov related: "These examples can be multiplied to show that the clergy and the preachers of religious sects do not renounce their influence upon the younger generation. On the contrary, they have adjusted the forms of their work to the present conditions and have increased their battle for the winning of the hearts and minds of the young men and women. Just think of the religious holidays. The preparation for and the celebration of these holidays are used to bring young people back into the church. The Baptists follow the following procedure: Each member of the sect is assigned the task of bringing at least one person of their sect to faith. The clergy leave no important occurrence in the life of man unobserved. Marriage, the birth of a child, the death of a near relative, material needs and other matters—everything they use to ingratiate themselves into the minds of men and to spread their influence upon the youth." The Komsomol Committee of Stalino tried to counteract this influence of the church upon the youth, but used inferior means. Thus on Easter Sunday 15 Komsomol members gathered, carried a phonograph into the church, and played records and danced during the service until a policeman ejected them. Said the reporter: "Instead of showing reasons which lead to the spreading of religious influence among young people and of finding more fitting forms of atheist propaganda, the Komsomol members, after their first attempts had misfired, threw their guns away and gave up and withdrew."

Borisenkov thought that it was time to understand that wherever ideological work is neglected the influence of religious ideology becomes stronger. The Central Committee of the Communist Party this time called upon all youth organizations to increase the scientific atheistic propaganda. In April 1957 the Central Committee of the Komsomol published a decree entitled "The Fight Against Dangerous Ideas Among Young People," in which the functionaries were accused of having been fully ineffective in their fight against reactionary ideas among the young people. The Komsomol ordered a propagandistic counteroffensive against the religious feelings among the young. They stated that young people were attracted in increasing numbers to religions and cults. This poisoning influence of religion in their thinking called for a counteroffensive. Another decree called "The Improvement of Scientific Atheistic Propaganda Among the Youth" gave guidelines for the improvement of the inferior working methods of the atheists. But how could one do anything if the atheists whose duty it was to attack religion—and that included all Communist functionaries, scientists, teachers, and so forth—were themselves not immune to the religious poison? On October 14, 1954, *Literaturnaja Gaseta* published the alarming news that among the intellectuals of Leningrad there were secret Christians. Among them was a very well known physiologist who was teaching at a medical institute, had belonged to the Communist Party since 1942, and had given lectures on the irreconcilability of science with religion. Several months before *Pravda* reported that in the North Russian town of Omutinsk in the middle of the night the secretary of the local Komsomol Rayon committee and two Communist Party secretaries had appeared with their children in church and had had them secretly baptized. In 1955 the All-Union Society published a brochure, *On the Atheistic Education of Children.* This brochure told of cases "in which not a single member of a family believed in God, in which the parents gave their children careful atheistic education, and in which these succumbed to religious influences despite their education."

These were puzzling occurrences which contradicted all expectations and needed more careful investigation. During a meeting of the atheists in Moscow in May 1957 the philosopher M. I. Gubanov spoke on the "Reasons for the Existence of Religious Remnants in the Soviet Union." He declared that the number of believers was not increasing, but the intensity of religious propaganda was. But why was there still religion in the Soviet Union after all its social presuppositions had been eliminated? As a reason for the continued existence of religion Gubanov gave the fact that religion was the most conservative form of community consciousness and that it was more independent, relatively speaking, in relation to economic bases than all other ideologies. The majority of the people, to be sure, had broken with religion, and the number of fanatics and activists practicing religion was now unimportant. But the number of people who were wavering was still important. These people sometimes went to church, and under certain conditions became quite pious. He stated that the deprivations and the sufferings of the war also contributed to the preservation of religious feelings. Another reason for the existence of religious remnants, according to Gubanov, was to be found in the elementary forces of nature: drought, early frost, mortality among animals, and other things. Although the feeling of dependence upon natural forces had become less, religion increased when there was a failure of harvest or great mortality among animals. In times of drought the faithful liked to have their processions and their religious observances. A further reason for the survival of religion was the inequality of women who had to face not only the pressures of work but also the ever-present domestic work. Not less than seventy percent of the believers were women. Finally Gubanov expressed his anxiety about the many activities of the church and his disappointment over atheistic propaganda. Church people and sectarian preachers were able to use the freedom of conscience which had been guaranteed to them in the constitution. The church also put architecture, paintings, music, oratory, and singing into the services of religious propaganda. The clergy used insufficient scientific knowledge among the people and falsifications under the guise of science. As an example of such deception Gubanov cited a clergyman who dared to explain the days of the creation story in the sense of long periods of time, notwithstanding the findings of linguistics. The battle against religion, Gubanov felt, had become difficult because of the fact that the religious ideology of the clergy was opposed to the political loyalty of the majority of the believers who had to be taken into consideration. After the classes had been abolished and after the Five-Year Plan had dug up the roots of religion the battle of ideas was still being carried on in depth and it must continue, patiently and with proper preparation.

The question why religious remnants did not disappear was the theme that puzzled everybody and that was being discussed in public everywhere. The catalog of reasons which were adduced to explain this phenomenon was repeated again and again. In the spring issue of 1957 the Moscow magazine *Partinaya Shishny* (Life of the Party) mentioned among the difficulties and contradictions of life which nourish the religious remnants that there were also the international tensions and the influence of the capitalistic world. Besides these objective reasons Gubanov further mentioned: "Lack of work in our social organizations and, at times, lack of activity in our institutions for cultural enlightenment as well as weaknesses of atheistic propaganda" as playing an important part. Only thus could it be explained that a part of the youth was represented among those who were still following religious customs and attending church. Atheistic clubs were cold and uncomfortable and besides dances and sporadic movie presentations nothing was offered. Therefore the young people out of boredom went to church. Here everything was bright, clean, and solemn, and there were sermons on various religious themes. He went on to say: "Especially important is the individual approach in freeing people from these religious remnants. But the organizations do not always support a person whose consciousness has made a radical breach and who experiences a restlessness and wavering concerning questions of ideology. Thus it happens at times that such a person comes under the influence of religious preachers and begins to explain things in life which are not clear to him as the work of God. For him lectures are no longer sufficient. In that case an open, person-to-person discussion is required, but one very often encounters difficulties. It occurs that the mere attempt to discuss a religious theme with a person causes resistance and estrangement among people. However, we should not be discouraged by our first lack of success, but we should state our atheistic point of view with great emphasis and repeatedly. Then success in the final analysis cannot be taken away from us."

As a further reason for the persistence of religious remnants *Voprosi Filosofi* of Moscow mentioned that the first stage of Communism still had certain aspects of capitalism which were unavoidable. It said: "To those belong the difficulties and contradictions of our life which are caused by errors in our agricultural polity. These errors were not at all necessary for the development of our society, and yet for many years they have had a negative influence on the consciousness of many people. Facts like bureaucracy, which should be foreign to Soviet democracy, influence the consciousness of the Soviet people in a negative way . . . Stalin's violation of the Leninist doctrine of leadership was very harmful to the cause of freeing the working man from the remnants of old ideas. As is known, this led to many serious errors in many branches of the party and of the state and to a brutal violation of socialist legality."

The organ of the Central Committee of the Communist Party of the USSR, *Kommunist,* agreed that formerly many atheists had been mistaken when they assumed that religion could be liquidated relatively easily. To be sure, *Kommunist* continued, "it will be liquidated and disappear completely once Communist rule is established. But today we are in the first stage of such a society and the power of tradition through which religion continues to thrive is, as Lenin said, a tremendous power. Added to this must be the active propaganda of ecclesiastical organizations. It is less powerful today than it was at the time of the czars. But," said *Kommunist,* "the clergy and the sectarians use this activity as long as it is at their disposal. They are partly responsible for the fact that the number of the faithful at times is on the increase. Facts show that the young people and the little children are exposed to religious propaganda. Furthermore, the state does not know how to organize the leisure time of its citizens. The work of the clubs and the like is less than adequate. This lack of efficiency is utilized by the church. It is a well-known fact that sectarians work successfully at substitutes for the clubs by organizing musical and dramatic circles, courses in sewing and collections for the support of the needy. As a consequence of the many negative phenomena of Communist life, religious preaching finds a fertile soil. Among these phenomena may be numbered the violation of the rules of socialist ethics, moral corruption, lack of sobriety, rough treatment of women, inconsiderate behavior toward children, uncomradely deportment, theft, and the like. All these things, which are remnants of capitalism in our socialist life, are interpreted by the clergy and the sectarians as the consequences of the spread of atheism. They declare that the reliable basis for all morality has disappeared and that that foundation for the ethical behavior of man has been destroyed. Such arguments make an impression upon some people. Thus a number of girls are married in church because they have been convinced that a church wedding is more enduring than a civil marriage. Parents encourage their children to observe religious customs because, according to their opinions, these customs fortify their moral foundations. In addition, there have been marked changes in the contents of religious ideology. Clergymen have put everything into the background which may discredit religion politically and scientifically."

According to *Kommunist*, "clergymen now condemn themselves for superstitions which they formerly accepted, they throw overboard certain antiquated ideas and dogmas and re-interpret many religious practices in such a way that they do not openly contradict science, and in general they are trying to reconcile religion with science. The defenders of religion even support Communism by calling Christ the first Communist who worked for the poor and for peace. The number of churches and of clergymen has indeed decreased considerably, and the great wealth and power of the church of former days are lacking. But the church has become loyal to the state. Therefore any attempt to unmask the counter-revolutionary activities of the church against the Soviet state is a thing of the past. We can no longer use this argument in our scientific atheistic propaganda. Rather the unscientific basis of religious ideology must be exposed, and it must be shown that the church with the propagandizing of this ideology is still a reactionary force. But we should not use harsh words, anecdotes, and tough language, for the believers demand a quiet analysis, a factual discussion, convincing arguments, and irrefutable logic. Mere trite expressions and mechanical attacks must be avoided. Atheistic propaganda must be a type of ongoing dialogue with the faithful, since only in this way can we penetrate into the depths of their consciousness. Religious discussions with clergymen, mass meetings, and godless carnivals are outmoded and useless. It is better to have lectures, discussion evenings, anti-religious exhibits and publications of anti-religious themes. Especially effective is the method of individual discussions, since the faithful will avoid attendance at scientific materialistic lectures and similar events."

There was a definite lack of anti-religious speakers and propagandists. The All-Union Society had been unable to develop a systematic propaganda effort. The anti-religious specialists, of whom there were not too many and whose intellectual level was not always high, were still the chief protagonists on the atheistic front. It became more and more important to enlarge the circle of anti-religious propagandists and to increase their quality.

In a decree of ideological control the Central Committee of the Communist Party, *Partishnaya Shishny* (No. 18, 1959) stated that the All-Union Society had neglected to carry out her work during the past few years. Many important scientists, writers, composers, and artists had withdrawn from it. Often the functionaries of the society and their propaganda had been compromised by the fact that all kinds of bunglers and other inferior people had been granted the right to speak. They had lacked principle. The possibility of radio and television had been poorly utilized. Not more than 50-60 percent of the members of the All-Union Society were giving public lectures. Therefore large numbers of the population were not influenced by the propaganda of the Society.

Also in the activity of the leading organs of the Society serious deficiencies were noticed. The leadership had very little contact with subordinate organizations and sections, with the Academy of Sciences, the unions, and other associations. Many functionaries did their work without having their heart in it. They used a bureaucratic style. The publishing activities of the Society also showed great deficiencies. The level of some brochures was very low, and they were written in a dry style. As far as popular books and visual materials for the lecturers went, there was very little of them. Therefore the subordinate committees of the Communist Party were asked by the Central Committee to take measures to improve the work of the All-Union Society and to replenish it with experienced help.

In *Iswestija* (October 4, 1959) the Communist Party demanded the establishment of Palaces of Marriage in order to counteract the pull of church ceremonies. The interior of these palaces was to be furnished with an electrical organ or a tape recorder and was to be artistically decorated. It was to have a festival character. The Communists substituted their own anti-Christian celebrations for the days appointed for high Christian festivals. Thus, at Christmas 1958 the Moscow broadcasting station proclaimed that the Sputniks had seen no trace of the paradise of the czar-gods in the heavens. Religious concepts of paradise were called fairy tales. At

Christmas 1959 Moscow radio and all provincial broadcasting stations were alerted to send anti-religious broadcasts, day after day, and especially during the evening hours. On this occasion too, Sputnik was used to discredit religion. There were articles in the newspapers which stated that from now on no one could claim that man does not have power over the kingdom of the heavens. The union paper *Trud* published a caricature in which an Orthodox priest, who looked like a decorative dwarf used in old-fashioned gardens, looked up to a tall, beaming workman. The text read: "The Gospel says that the will of God has created the world. As an answer to this nonsense we have increased the number of planets." At Easter 1959 an Atheistic Week was held. During those days there were meetings of workers and scientists in the factories, the collective farms, clubs, and cultural centers, in the course of which propaganda was made for atheistic publications. But the attendance at divine Easter services was nevertheless much greater than the attendance at the anti-religious meetings. Again at Easter 1960 an atheistic offensive was launched. Moscow radio declared that faith in immortality represented an unspeakable prejudice for the working masses. To be sure, this faith meant a strengthening of the faithful, but it also sapped their energy and prevented them from trying to improve with all their strength their earthly lot. In the overcrowded St. Vladimir's Cathedral in Kiev young atheists caused noisy disturbances which lasted for about an hour. A young fellow holding two consecrated candles in his hands imitated the Metropolitan. It was very embarrassing that these scenes took place in the presence of a number of foreign diplomats. Similar occurrences took place at other Easter services. In 1961 Moscow radio announced that Easter would be declared an anti-religious holiday. Four new anti-religious films were released and the workers of the textile factory Treshgorki in Moscow were invited to a great atheists' ball.

When the first space travel in a manned space craft had succeeded, the atheistic propaganda was increased. In *Iswestija* G. Volkov jubilantly declared: "The cosmonaut flights of man strike at the heart of religion and at the idea of God itself. Now man has freed himself from servitude under a fictitious God and exercises the functions which were considered exclusively the work of God. Man now creates the world anew. All biblical miracles pale before the wonderful actions of human hands. With the beginning of the era of space travel it has become clear that man is almighty and all-powerful."

The primitive tone of these arguments showed how antiquated atheistic propaganda had become. Added to this was the fact of the very noisy and self-confident appeal to science, which alone permitted the interpretation of dialectic materialism as a possible explanation for the origin of the world. This method came under attack from the people who were least expected to oppose it, namely the scientists themselves. The world-renowned physicist, P. R. Kapitza, spoke in 1962 about tensions between the natural sciences and the ideology of the Communist Party and claimed that the Communist ideologists had committed one mistake after another and had severely harmed the development of the natural sciences. For example, they had declared the theory of relativity of Einstein to be reactionary and had stated that cybernetics was the result of the thinking of decadent imperialists. He stated that if the scientists had followed Communist ideologists, the Soviet Union would not possess atomic weapons, space ships, and rockets today. Kapitza demanded that not only physics but also biology and the other branches of the natural sciences should be freed from the unbearable ideological supervision by the Communist Party.

The scientific foundations of atheism were not so solid that they could be protected against all these objections. What an individual was able to do in this respect became clear from a report printed in *Literaturnaja Gaseta* of November 21, 1959. In the village of Voltshanka on the other side of the Volga a young priest, Father John, had appeared. His excellent education and his wide knowledge prompted the believers to show him great respect so that the work of the Communist youth club was almost completely neglected. Atheistic speakers were avoided like poison. Father John felt himself more and more secure. "Brethren," he said, "even if they should send atheistic speakers against us we would put such questions to them with the help of God that they would not be able to give an answer." At this challenge the All-Union Society was swamped with cries for help that an experienced atheistic orator should be sent as quickly as possible. But it was all in vain. Atheistic speakers avoided being confronted by this priest, who was an excellent speaker. Against the background of such occurrences the caricature which the Moscow humorous weekly *Krokodil* published on its title page at the beginning of 1960 could be understood. Three young people, two men and a woman, were kneeling before an ikon and were praying to the enemy that the least one anti-religious speaker would be sent to their district.

But there were also other examples: In *Komsomolskaja Prawda* A. Kuliakin, a young forester, reported how he met religious prejudices in the village of Shockshe in the district of Archangelsk and how he tried in vain to win over the young people for discussions concerning religion. Afterward he gave talks on questions related to forestry and some other related subjects which had good results. But when he attempted to tell his hearers that religion was the opiate for the people, his listeners always reacted in silence. On the next day the women started a conversation on their own and told him about the punishment which the Lord would mete out to all sinners. This conversation led eventually to a revival of atheism in the village. The forester formed a small chorus which he accompanied with the accordion. Their concert was a big success, and new members were won for the chorus. They even practiced during the Lenten season and there developed a group of activists who resented all religious prohibitions. The young people showed themselves more and more willing to learn. The club increased, and when it gained the first prize in the Rayon contest more young people were irresistibly attracted while those who went to church on Sundays became fewer and fewer.

After a village had been won over to atheism the church was usually closed. The village of Berezovki in the Ural Mountains was an example for such a progressive village. In a petition submitted to *Iswestija* the inhabitants declared that the priest, the choir director, and the sexton had until now lived as parasites feasting on the money of the faithful. They declared that the priest's stories about the heavenly paradise and about hell, about God and saints, were ridiculous in the face of present-day knowledge. They said that they realized there was no room for God in the heavens. They stated: "We work our land in such a way that we have harvests without the need for God." Agitators were sent to the village and speeches were made to enlighten the inhabitants. The agitators explained to them the meaning of Sputnik and of the scientific accomplishments and showed them that until now they had been led astray by religion. Finally an apostate priest was introduced to them who appealed to the inhabitants to forsake their religion. The village became unchurched.

When a church was closed a group of soldiers usually appeared who removed ikons and other objects of the cult from the deserted church and took them to a museum. Within an hour another crew would appear which would demolish the church and level it to the ground. In Berezovki the Soviet kindergarten was given possession of all the assets of the closed church. In this way, in 1960 alone about 500 churches were closed and 500 villages became unchurched.

How prevalent was religion among the population, and especially among the young people? There were no statistics, but one piece of research was conducted in 1959 by a research group of the Moscow Academy of Sciences. The research was carried on among collective farmers in the provinces of Kalinin, Ostroka, Gorki, and Jaroslavl, all near the upper course of the Volga River. Its task was to find out certain facts about the way of life and the religious customs of the rural populations in this central region of the Soviet Union. It stated: "The right means for a quick victory over the religious remnants can be found only when it is known in which form and in which milieu they still keep alive and which are the reasons for their vitality." Concerning the results of this research the magazine *Kommunist* (No. 8, 1960) reported: "Measured by the picture which Communist propaganda has drawn of the progressive attitude of workers and collective farmers, the researchers had to admit that this group of people had gone backwards. There was mention that in some villages there were no traces of religious faith, especially on the collective farms. There was also some progress seen in the fact that a considerable part of the farm population had given up regular religious practices and that those who still practiced religion had, with the exception of the very old people, only a very vague idea of their faith. They believed in God and a hereafter, and they believed in the effectiveness of prayer. Still there was a very large number of religious remnants, and the group of researchers was alarmed."

The magazine stated that the group discovered ikons in many farm houses: "These were certainly not harmless anachronisms. Even in the house of an unbelieving collective farmer or of a village activist an ikon could be used for religious propaganda. But when an ikon is found in the house of a believer it is especially dangerous because it can be used for religious instruction and the preservation of the church. Therefore," the magazine concluded, "propaganda has to make it clear to the people that ikons are as harmful as they are unnecessary. To be sure, the whole matter has to be handled with tact, since demands made at the wrong time for the removal of ikons usually have no results."

The research group also found that baptism was still quite generally practiced among the farmers. It stated that it might be more correct to say that baptism had been revived. It had not merely survived. In the 1920's and 1930's baptism had been slowly disappearing, but during the Great War and in the post-war years the trend had been reversed. This observation was especially important since most of the researched areas had not been occupied by the Germans during the war. It seemed that the majority of the children who were baptized received their baptism during or after the war. But baptized members of families belonging to the intelligentsia and to the group of "progressive farmers" were rather the exception.

As a result of the war also church weddings had become more frequent than before. In one area of the province of Kalinin the collective farmers stated frankly that church weddings had become fashionable. Many young people were married in churches because the civil wedding ceremonies conducted by the state were so dull. The Komsomol had established a rite of marriages, but the public seemed to be very little interested in Komsomol weddings.

The report furthermore complained that while many people did not believe in the hereafter, they habitually returned to the comfort which the church offered whenever there was a funeral. It criticized the civil funeral ceremonies for their lack of solemnity.

The great festivals of Christmas, Epiphany, Easter, Pentecost, continued to attract a great number of people to the churches. The report tried to minimize this tendency as remnants of tradition. "However, one should have serious misgivings," it stated, "when one watches the local saints' days which are celebrated in connection with secular village festivals. They are being celebrated differently from village to village, but they remain the great festivals of the country population, and they all have in common that they have absolutely no relevance to the agricultural planning of the state. These people work the whole year and spend their savings in two days of celebrating saints' days." At various times the celebration of saints' days had been forbidden, but always new festivals that had been introduced to take their place, as, for example, the harvest festival, had taken on a religious character. Meetings of collective farmers might pass resolutions to abolish all religious festivals. But when the time came they were celebrated nevertheless.

The report also tried to analyze the religious customs among individual age groups. As far as the sixty-year-olds were concerned, the majority had remained true to their faith. For them faith was associated with their childhood and youth. Should they now be left to themselves since they were dying out anyway? The report warned against neglecting atheistic work among any age group. Nothing would be more wrong than to assume that the old people did not exercise a great influence upon the young people. They were the people who handed down religious beliefs within the families. They demanded of their children and other close relatives that they should live good religious lives. Some of the older people who were asked declared: "Our children belong to us. They should do what we tell them to do." Therefore the elimination of the religious influence of the old people upon the young should be given priority. It had become mandatory to cut the religious ties which bound one generation to the next. The "believing grandmother" was singled out by the report as especially dangerous. She would often refuse to take care of grandchildren unless they had been properly baptized. She taught them how to pray and placed crosses around their necks and even took them along to church and instructed them in the legends of religious superstition.

The majority of the people between forty and sixty years of age took part in the work of socialist reconstruction. Most of them had not been married in church, and their children had not been baptized. They had removed the ikons from their homes. But even in this age group the researchers found many believers, especially among the women. As a reason for the prevalence of women among the believers the report mentioned the quiet life which women led in their homes and the fact that they did not become involved sufficiently in the social and collective life of the Sovchoses (collective farms).

The young people between the ages of twenty and thirty-five had been educated in Soviet schools. For them unbelief was the normal state of affairs. It was not the result of an inner conflict. But even this "native" atheism had its weak points. Most of the young people did not realize how widespread the evil of religion was. Among the young people there were many whose atheism the report called "primitive atheism," i.e. atheism without militant activity against a religion whose essence was largely hidden from their eyes. These people thought of religion as a harmless anachronism. A result of this inactive attitude was that quite a number of the young people were not immune against the religious influences of the family. "Consequently," the report stated, "it is not enough to inculcate in our young people an atheistic ideology, because only in a few cases do they believe in God, but one must teach them to become intolerant of any religious ideology."

The persecution of God and religion which had been going on for almost half a century had not been successful. The Russian people refused to get rid of the infection of religious poison. Therefore it was no wonder that the militant atheists showed impatience and disappointment from time to time. Their attitude expressed itself in excessive attacks against believers. There were repeated disturbances of divine services like the ones that took place outside the Moscow cathedral on Easter morning 1965. Pressure was brought against members of the monastic orders. There were constant interferences with pilgrimages. In January 1961 *Pravda* demanded that anti-religious propaganda should be carried on more tactfully and designations like gangsters and wasp nests applied to religious meetings should not be used. The paper condemned one-sided atheistic propaganda reports that had been published in the Soviet press in recent years and that magnified certain defects among the religious people, as, for example, alleged immorality of the priests. Khrushchev himself declared at that time: "To be an atheist does not include the right to insult the religious feelings of church-goers." *Pravda* regretted that the publications of the atheists had not followed this advice of the Premier. For the advancement of atheism only educational methods should be permitted. At the same time, however, the paper admitted that it was necessary to super-vise carefully the activities of the priests so that they would at all times follow the laws of the state.

13. Orthodoxy After Half a Century of Atheistic Rule

The careful supervision of the clergy did not have to be stressed by *Pravda*. The Party since 1917 had seen to it that nothing was left undone to supervise all activities of the church. Lives and activities of the priests were determined and circumscribed by numerous prohibitions. They were free merely to conduct their religious rites within the four walls of their churches. They were living from the offerings of the faithful or from the sale of blessed candles. That the gifts which they received for taking care of the churches which were still open were generous was reported again and again. Thus in most reports any indications that priests were hungry and ill clad were missing. In the official Communist society they were, nevertheless, considered pariahs. They were not allowed to join labor unions. The union paper *Trud* declared: "Both athe-ists and believers can become members of our unions, but our unions are not open to those loafers who receive their income through religious fraud. The money of the state and the funds of the unions are not designated to support these people and to give them social security."

For almost five decades the Russian Christians had been exposed to an intensive atheistic propaganda. The whole atmosphere in which they were living was atheistic. Religion was defamed as superstition and was placed on a level with the evils of whisky as an enemy of the people. Young people were forced to pass through an intensive atheistic training period. They had to accept this influence —at least outwardly—in order to stay in Komsomol, the powerful youth organization, and in school. It was surprising that in spite of this influence not all children who left school were hard-core atheists. There were many who continued to believe because their church and their home had been stronger than school and Komsomol. There were others who, in spite of the fact that they had been trained in dialectic materialism, did not become convinced fighters for the Communist ideology. Many of them became nihilists. Others coveted the treasures which secularized Western culture offered to the world. In the summer of 1960 *Iswestija* complained that university students at Novo Sherkast were following the "philosophy of despair," somewhat akin to a type of Western existentialism. At another time a reader wrote to the editor of the paper: "It seems that our sons, our young people, have been infected by a dangerous bacillus, for they seem not to believe in the things that we teach them since they do not see the realization of the ideas which we have promised them. They have lost their illusions and are living now only for their own desires." An investigating committee of Komsomol found that "some young people succumb to the pernicious influences of spiritual and moral opinions which are diametrically opposed to our ideas." *Komsomolskaja Prawda* warned: "The wind from foreign countries has penetrated through the cracks in the Russian windows. We are in the midst of an ideological battle; one can even call it a purification process within our own nation. . . . There are many nihilists and there are even those who believe in God."

The church had no opportunity to refute publicly the attacks of atheistic propaganda. The only church paper permitted in the Soviet Union was the official paper of the Moscow Patriarchate, and it was sent only to priests and other church functionaries. The church had no access to radio and television. She had been silenced completely in public life. In this emergency the primitive method of distributing typewritten texts was often used to better prepare the believers for the arguments of the scientists and atheists. On September 20, 1959, *Komsomolskaja Prawda* tried to counteract such an illegal document entitled "Science and Religion: A Thesis for Religious People." Wrote the paper: "As much as we can gather, an anonymous theologian is trying to devaluate the materialistic ideas which have resulted from the development of atomic physics. According to him, many kinds of energy have been found which can be called half-material essences. The idea of half-material essences is a recognition that non-material energies exist. He claims that religious truths can be ascertained outside of matter where we find a purely spiritual principle. In further arguments the author comes to the conclusion that scientific discoveries advance the recognition of the wisdom of the Creator and that there is not at all an insoluble contradiction between science and religion. He says: 'Science has not proved that there is no God. Science does not know whether we continue to live after the destruction of our body or not. A scientific ideology, a scientific philosophy as such, does not exist.'" The paper tried to disprove the conclusions of the "anonymous theologian."

The number of people who could be reached by these and similar mimeographed materials was always small. What was the church able to do against the giant apparatus of public mass media which atheistic propaganda had at its disposal day after day? Could it be considered an act of despair when, as the union paper *Trud* reported, seminarians of the Monastery of St. Sergius near Moscow bought out the entire stock of anti-religious materials that were being sold in the kiosks on the streets of Moscow and in the bookstores of the city?

Yet the fact remained that the discussion about the existence and the power of God had not been silenced, not even among those who had long since broken away from the church. An English student reported in *The Tablet* about her conversations with Russians on the streets of Moscow. The question: "Do you believe in God?" always called, with unfailing certainty, for a lengthy discussion. A young worker told the English girl: "There is a theme which every Russian, no matter which ideology he follows, likes to discuss gladly at any time. It is the theme: 'Is there a God?'" In her first preliminary discussions with passersby this student was asked about many things in the life of the English. Then without a warning a young man asked the question: "Do you believe in God?" She answered simply: "Yes." But her counter-question was answered in the negative by the Russians. She told them: "Your attitude seems to me to be the attitude of the nineteenth century." To this remark quite a number of her listeners agreed. "Quite right, sister," she heard someone say. One of her questioners wanted to know whether many young English people were Christians. When she reported that the Christian movement was increasing among the students and workers of England she heard a murmur in the back rows: "That is good." She asked: "And how is it with you? How many people among you are Christians?" A woman in the crowd replied: "All of us." Another said: "About forty percent." A third woman said: "Nobody knows, but presumably there are quite a number of them."

This report was an interesting sidelight on the Russian situation. However, it would be dangerous to generalize. In Tuapse, a well-known resort on the Black Sea, the local party paper printed in daily installments a fictitious report of a certain author named I. Kris. This report dealt with a cosmic catastrophe. Soviet scientists had suddenly discovered a burning ball mixed with the sun. It was described as a titanic mass of frightening immensity that was approaching the earth with a velocity of 257,400 km. per day. Especially the non-Communist world was struck with horror. People left everything and went into boats in order to save at least their lives, and bourgeois scientists took advantage of the confusion in order to launch an attack against the Soviet Union. They moved through the universe on an earth satellite and wanted to drop a counter-mass against the Soviet Union so that finally all Communists would be destroyed. When the installments of the story by the writer Kris had gotten to this point the readers of the paper began to feel the cold hand of horror. Their nerves began to crack. People were seen in the streets, whispering to each other that the decline of the world was close at hand. According to the fictitious reports only forty days were allotted to them. They reminded themselves of biblical parallels. Some of the more simple-minded people sold their homes and their cows for a song. Many citizens of Tuapse brought out their old ikons from their hiding places and prayed fervently to the God whose non-existence had been proved to them in numerous training courses. They fell on their knees before the cross in the church, and they forgot in a few hours what Communist indoctrination had taught them in over forty years. The churches of the city were filled with frightened people. The local party paper was forced to discontinue the fictitious reportage, but not until the Communists had added a happy ending to it: They announced in the final installment that just in time the glorious Soviet scientists had succeeded in liquidating the titanic mass. But the central party paper *Sovietskaja Russija* severely reprimanded the hapless author. "Thanks to the author for the liquidation of the titanic mass. However, the question remains whether the earthly satellite with its capitalistic scientists or the author with his titanic nonsense is burning up from shame." No wonder that any themes and descriptions which reminded people of the end or of apocalyptic catastrophes were most unwelcome to the Communists.

The case of Professor Alexander Ossipov aroused considerable attention. This man was born in 1911 in Tallinn, Estonia, and in 1928 as a student came into contact with the Russian Christian Student Movement. In 1931 he began the study of theology at Dorpat. After he had become a candidate for the priesthood he was called, in 1936, to a Russian Orthodox congregation in Reval. During the war he served as a soldier and later became a priest at Perm and again at Reval. In 1946 he applied for the position of professor of Old Testament Theology at the Theological Academy of Leningrad and was elected. He also served for a time as vice-president of the academy. From 1948 to 1950 he also taught history of religions. In 1955-56 he became scientific editor of a new Bible edition. He also published several articles in the magazine of the Moscow Patriarchate. His first wife had gone to Germany with their two daughters during the war and had later divorced him. In 1951 he had contracted a second marriage. For this act he was punished by the patriarch with permanent prohibition from celebrating the Holy Eucharist. Suddenly, on December 6, 1959, Ossipov published in

Pravda a renunciation of religion which began with these sentences: "Yes, I am a full professor of the Old Testament and of the Hebrew language at the Leningrad Orthodox Theological Seminary and a former inspector, a Master of Theology, and an archpriest of the Orthodox Church. Yet I have broken with the church and with religion. After exhaustive studies I confess publicly my conversion to a scientific atheism which is logical and which has been arrived at in a scientific way and to which I have turned after a long and difficult internal struggle and through a revision of my ideology. I have turned my back on a world which I understand now as a world of illusions, a world which is opposed to reality and often commits religious fraud for monetary gains." Ossipov said that since the days when he was a candidate of theology he had entertained doubts. His atheistic conviction was finally confirmed by an honest historical critical study of the Bible, a careful study of religion, the observation of the development of the natural sciences, the personal acquaintance with the depravities of the capitalistic world, and the miserable part which religion was playing in that world. He stated also that he was converted by the study of Marxism-Leninism and its philosophy and finally "through our Soviet reality itself which calls us to follow the right way. All these things," he said, "permitted me to adopt the firm stand that there existed neither a God nor any world beyond and that religion in every form is a delusion, caused by the secrets of nature that have not been recognized and by the deficiencies of our relationships and societies as well as of the psychological and physiological realities of our human consciousness."

This apostasy of Ossipov, of course, was exploited very much in the propaganda especially since two priests, former students of his, also broke with the church. Patriarch Alexei excommunicated Ossipov and his two students by issuing the following declaration which was approved by the Holy Synod on December 31, 1959: "The former Archpriest and Professor at the Leningrad Academy, Alexander Ossipov, the former Archpriest Nicolai Spaski and the former Priest Pavel Dasmanski and other clergymen who have publicly blasphemed the name of God are herewith deprived of their spiritual office and are declared to have lost the communion with the church. They went from us and they are no longer among us (1 John 2:19). Yevgraf Duluman and the other former Orthodox members of their congregations who have blasphemed the name of God are also excommunicated from the church."

As is very often the case with renegades, Ossipov now became an active and radical propagandist of atheism. In 1962 he received a letter from another atheist, E. Spinakin of Tartu, who during his childhood had given up faith in God. The letter by the old atheist to the newly converted atheist was important for the reason that it showed the inner conflicts existing in atheistic ideology. Spinakin wrote: "While I was following the developments of science and theoretical thinking, I came to the conviction that atheism in its present form can have no claim to be scientific, that it does not satisfy the spiritual demands of man and does not correspond to his feelings. Besides, I am surprised that atheism in its present form has abdicated and no longer seeks the truth because it passes over in silence those facts and arguments which are opposed to it. It tries to explain everything; and since it does not succeed, it runs away for lack of power. With such tactics I am not in accord."

What was the numerical strength of the Russian Orthodox Church? According to the figures released by the patriarchate there were about 30,000 priests and 20,000 parishes which were under the jurisdiction of 73 bishops. Besides, there were 67 convents and monasteries with an unknown number of nuns and monks. For the education of the priests there had been for some years two theological academies and eight seminaries (of which one was closed in the summer of 1965). There was apparently never a lack of applicants for the education for the priesthood. The future priests came from all strata of society. Their number was just about sufficient to fill all existing parishes. But since the closing of four seminaries in 1961 there had been a shortage of men for the priesthood which was aggravated in 1965 when an additional closing was ordered by the government. The remaining facilities of the church were able to take care of less than 1,800 students of theology. The course of education usually lasted four years at the seminary level, with another four years added for those who went on to the theological academies.

The question about the number of believers was never statistically settled. In the census of 1937 there had been a rubric concerning religious affiliation. But this rubric was later eliminated on account of, as was stated, "tampering by counter-revolutionary elements." Why? Because, according to the best informed sources, seventy percent of the population still called themselves orthodox Christians after twenty years of Bolshevist rule. In the next national census the rubric "Religious affiliation" did not appear. President Martin Niemoeller of the Church of Hesse received the information from a high Soviet official that sixty-five percent of the Russians still considered themselves orthodox Christians after the Second World War. Some reporters spoke of 50 million believers in a total population of 215 million. The correct answer probably lies somewhere in between. No one will know the exact figures. Therefore any effort of numbering church members statistically has proved most ineffective. From the number of votive candles bought annually by the faithful, one has arrived at the conclusion that there are at least 25 to 30 million *practicing* orthodox church members. That would mean that for each active member of the Communist Party there are at least three active orthodox Christians.

But this should not lead the observer to forget the terrible devastation which the church has suffered. For the 11 million inhabitants in the province of Moscow only 52 churches were available, and the 5 million people within the city limits of Moscow had only 20 churches at their disposal. The city of Leningrad with its 3.3 million inhabitants had only 14 churches. In Kiev with 1.1 million people there were only seven churches. In Nishni Novgorod with 1 million inhabitants two churches were still open. New large cities like Karaganda (400,000 inhabitants), Kaliningrad (Koenigsberg) (200,000), Komsomolsk (177,000), or Angarsk (134,000) had no churches at all. Krasnodor (200,000) and Novorossuisk (400,000) have had no churches since the 1930's. There were numerous other cities and whole areas where there was no organized church life.

In his book *Der Sowietmensch* (Soviet Man) one of the foremost experts on Russia, Dr. Klaus Mehnert, declared: "Religious indifference and lack of knowledge which are the results of atheistic education and deep faith which forgets itself in devotion are living side by side today in the Soviet Union. For the outsider and even for the Soviet citizen it is not possible to say how much weight should be attributed to either attitude. It is certain that among the people whose parents belonged to the Orthodox Church there is a strong loyalty to religious customs. This interest in religious customs is so strong that even the younger generation is yearning for it, because these customs seem to be more colorful and more attractive than the poor Bolshevist substitutes. The Bolshevists, after more than 45 years of rule, have not been able to create new rites which would silence the desire for the old church festivals." On the other hand, Dr. Mehnert indicated that the Soviet people in spite of their tradition of religiosity had to a large extent accepted without contradiction the battle of the Bolshevists against the church and that the end of direct persecutions of the church had not brought about a rebirth of church life as could have been expected. Of the new leading classes, Dr. Mehnert wrote that they had been concentrating completely on material things during the last decades and that they had spent all their strength in the passionate attempt to conquer the material world. They believed that they would be able to solve all the problems of the world with the help of science. The Bolshevists had done everything in their power to further this attitude and had stigmatized religion as an enemy of science. It was true that the Orthodox Church had given reasons for this evaluation since, unlike Roman Catholicism and Protestantism, she had not passed through Renaissance and Enlightenment and had not kept pace with the developments of the natural sciences or the development of the human mind. But in the long run it was to be doubted that the Messiah complex that had been ingrained in the Russians and had been furthered by the czars and the church, namely a faith in the special mission of the Russian people, could be diverted by the Bolshevists into different channels. Not much of the missionary zeal of the early years of the Revolution was left, and it was possible that the apparent evaporation of the revolutionary spirit might benefit the church which had to offer more for the messianic yearning and the metaphysical needs of the Russian people than had the increase of a production quota. Furthermore, Communist ideology had been unable to face the last reality, death. Death did not fit into its contrived optimistic world-picture. Therefore death was mentioned as little as possible and funerals always give rise to embarrassment. Here it was that the gap was being felt most strongly in time of war with all its mass sorrow. Thus the Great War gave impetus to a revival of religious faith among the Russian people.

B. THE ROMAN CATHOLIC CHURCH

At the beginning of the Revolution of 1917 the Roman Catholic Church in Russia was organized into seven dioceses with about 6,000,000 believers. This organization was completely destroyed during the following years; seminaries for the priests were closed, and the clergy quickly decreased as a result of arrest and exile. In the archdiocese of Mohilev with the diocese of Minsk, where there had been 470 priests and 331 churches in 1917, only 16 priests and 30 churches were left in 1932. Of the 200 priests in the diocese of Shitomir there remained only six. In the year 1958 there was no hierarchy left in all of Byelorussia and only very few priests. In their place there appeared many sects. The clergy of the Slavic and the Armenian rites were also arrested, and many of them perished in prison. The rest died of various deprivations and of old age. In 1938, according to a compilation made by the Jesuit G. M. Schweigel, former professor at the Byelorussian College, there were only 500,000 Catholics in Russia proper. After World War II five Catholic churches were still open in Moscow, Leningrad, Tiflis, Shitomir, and Odessa. Mr. Kelly, the English Ambassador to Russia, stated that at the end of 1951 he heard of only two priests who were still saying mass. Thus the Roman Catholic Church had been all but destroyed in the territory belonging to Russia before World War II.

Through the annexations of new territories in the wake of the last war Roman Catholic populations numbering 8 million believers came under Soviet rule. These people were living in Lithuania, Latvia, Estonia, Eastern Poland, and Bessarabia, formerly a part of Romania. They, too, had to face a most difficult future. The destruction of the Uniate Church of Ruthenia through the joint action of the Orthodox Church and the Communist state has been mentioned. In the Baltic countries Roman Catholicism was especially strong in Lithuania. Here two and a half million Roman Catholics were organized in about 800 parishes with 1,600 priests under three archbishops and seven bishops. Four theological seminaries and a theological faculty at the University of Kaunas served the education of the priests. The various orders were represented by 1,000 members. Soon after the first invasion of Lithuania by the Red Army, in June 1940, the concordat with Rome was abrogated, the papal nuncio expelled, and religious instruction in the schools forbidden. The theological faculty at the University of Kaunas was dissolved, schools were completely secularized, and church property nationalized. Many churches were closed and religion was driven underground. In June 1941 the German occupation of Lithuania began. In 1944 the Bolshevists returned, driving the Nazis before them and continued their interrupted war against Roman Catholicism with a new wave of arrests, starting in 1946. All clergymen who did not unconditionally condemn the resistance movement of Lithuanian patriots against the Communists were charged with the crime of aiding banditry. At the end of 1946, 350 priests were liquidated and several bishops were arrested and disappeared without a trace. By the beginning of 1949 about 600,000 Roman Catholics had been deported from Lithuania alone. During the first few months of 1950, 61 Catholic priests and members of religious orders, among them two bishops and 18 prelates, were arrested, as it was announced, "at the urgent desire of a great number of the population" and were charged with espionage, sabotage, and malicious propaganda. In 1954, 513 churches had been closed and 689 were still open. Of the 1,646 priests, 675 were banished, 230 had fled the country and 741 were still active. Only one of the bishops, Kasimir Paltarogas, was still active. With the permission of the Vatican two additional bishops were consecrated in 1955 in the Cathedral of Vilna. In that same year permission was obtained to publish a Catholic calendar and a prayer book. These were signs of a return to normalcy and of a lessening of tensions. But soon enmity against the church of the pope resulted once more in open terror. Bishop Paltarogas was transferred to the interior of Russia and soon died as a result of inhuman treatment which he had suffered at the hands of the Soviets. The last active bishop of Lithuania, Julius Steponavicius, was deported in 1961 because he had refused to ordain four students of the seminary in Kaunas who were dedicated Communists. In 1961 also three priests were killed, one of them through stoning by Communist young people.

Religious instruction even within the churches was no longer possible since the priests were not permitted to catechize young people under 18 years of age. Only small children could be instructed by their parents in the family circle. The propaganda of the atheists was very intensive. On the occasion of the election of people's judges at the end of 1960 about 20,000 atheists were sent into the country. St. Michael's Church in Kaunas was closed in 1962 and converted into an anti-religious museum. The nave of the Regina Pacis church in Memel (Klaipeda) became a dance hall. In the spring of 1962 the rector or president of the seminary in Kaunas, Msgr. Lape, was forced to resign, and the apostolic administrator of the diocese of Panevecis, Msgr. Sidlauskas, was placed under house arrest in a small village in southern Lithuania.

In Latvia the numerically small Roman Catholic Church was deprived almost immediately of her leadership. The bishop of Riga, Antonis Urbbs, was exiled; his auxiliary bishop, Peter Strods, apostolic administrator of Liepaja, died in 1961. The auxiliary bishop of Riga, the last bishop of the Roman Catholic Church in Latvia, was banished in 1962 to Byelorussia where he was employed as a carpenter on a collective farm. The Riga Cathedral was closed in 1959 and used as a concert hall and a branch of the historical state museum of Riga.

C. THE PROTESTANT CHURCHES

Before World War I about 2,100,000 Germans resided in Russia. Of these 1,600,000 were farmers. They suffered heavy losses through war and revolution. The Soviet census of 1926 showed that there were 1,300,000 Germans, of whom 1,100,000 were farmers. For the Volga Germans Lenin had decreed the establishment of an autonomous republic of 20,000 square km. which later received the name

Volga German Republic. Here the number of Germans decreased from 453,000 to 350,000 during the civil war and the great famine. The Bolshevist battle against the *Kulaks* (prosperous farmers) was especially hard on the German-Russian farmers because they had become moderately rich through their own industry and had developed a strong upper middle class. In the fall and winter of 1929 began the expulsions of the *Kulaks* from the Volga Republic toward the north and toward Siberia where most of them died as a result of the difficult conditions of their existence. Similar bad times came upon the Germans residing in the Black Sea region. In addition the purges of 1937 and 1938 led to the arrest of almost the entire male population. When Hitler attacked the Soviet Union in 1941, the Volga Republic was liquidated and the entire population was sent to other parts of Russia. The majority of the male population was sent to concentration camps or shot outright. Also the German groups in the Crimea and in Transcaucasia were deported to Siberia. All these national groups were rehabilitated, but not permitted to return to their ancestral homes, at the beginning of the 1960's. By that time only very few of them were left. On the other hand, during the German retreat of 1943-1944, over 350,000 German-Russians residing in western Russia, in the Black Sea region, and in the Caucasus were forced by the orders of the German occupation authorities to settle in the so-called Warthegau in Poland where the Poles later delivered most of them to the Soviets. About 280,000 to 300,000 of these resettled German-Russians were sent to Siberia.

A large number of the Germans residing in Russia belonged to the Lutheran Church. Thus, for example, the Volga German group before World War I numbered 443,000 Protestants and 110,000 Catholics, while among the Germans in the Black Sea area there were 224,000 Protestants, 195,000 Roman Catholics, and 104,000 Mennonites. In 1917 the Lutheran Church in Russia had 539 parishes with 1,828 churches and 230 pastors. Her organization was destroyed without a trace. The churches were turned into movie houses, clubs, party centers, and stables. Many members of the congregations held firm to their faith and found comfort even in the most difficult times. In the freight cars in which the *Kulaks* were sent to

Siberia there were regular prayer meetings. In 1929 the church was being served by 90 pastors. In 1930, 27 of these 90 were condemned to prison and two of them were shot. In 1935 there were only 14 pastors left who were able to carry on under most stringent regulations. In 1936 the 76-year-old Lutheran Bishop Dr. Malmgren had to leave Russia as a very sick old man, and the Lutheran Church officially was declared dead. The German *Pro Deo* Commission was informed of the fate of the other pastors. The reports were monotonous: arrested, exiled, condemned to forced labor, disappeared, condemned to death. At the end of 1937 it was announced that the last two pastors, the father and son Reichert, had been arrested in Leningrad.

The church as an organization had been destroyed, but the life of faith survived the decades of terror, resettlement, and exile. In the far regions of Asiatic Russia, at the foothills of the Altai Mountains, there were at the beginning of the 1960's still 150,000 German settlers, many of them Lutherans. Sparse news which leaked out after Stalin's death indicated that the Christian faith had survived and was being nourished by means of Bibles, sermon books, prayer books, and hymnals. Parents and grandparents instructed their children in the faith. Lay preachers held services and continued to administer the sacraments, and at the time when external oppression was somewhat relaxed these faithful Lutherans even effected a reorganization of their church. Some pastors, after being released from prison, became active again.

The Lutheran churches of the Baltic countries which were incorporated into the Soviet Union in 1940 and 1944 had been only tolerated churches in the days of the czars. They had never enjoyed the privileged status which the Orthodox Church enjoyed. But when, at the end of World War I, these Baltic countries established their national identity, the independence of the churches was also established. They received an autonomous administration and control of their finances. The need which they had to overcome, however, was great. The destruction of the war, the flight and deportation of congregation members, the expropriation, the impoverishment, and the many other hardships made the church life difficult. In addition, there were all kinds of interferences by the state and other legal limitations. The excesses of atheistic propaganda made the existence of the church precarious.

The Communist government which took over Latvia in 1940 secularized all church property. When the Communists returned after the German occupation this decree was energetically carried out. Local executive committees decided whether a congregation needed a church or not. These executive committees imposed such high rentals upon the congregations that tremendous sacrifices were necessary in order to keep the churches going. In other cases the churches were used for secular purposes. Later things became somewhat easier. Agreements were made for definite times of service, and churches were placed at the disposal of the congregations without the payment of rents. The reconstruction of destroyed churches often became, however, a hopeless undertaking since the population was too poor to carry it out and since there was a great lack of building materials. The state also often interfered and hampered plans for reconstruction with red tape. As an intermediate solution little prayer houses were built of wood. Often small annexes to churches and chapels were built which served as parsonages.

At the end of the German occupation the Archbishop of the Evangelical Lutheran Church in Latvia, Theodor Gruenbergs, was forced against his will to go to Germany. About two-thirds of the pastors, or about 150, went voluntarily into exile. Only 90 pastors, of whom the majority were quite old at the time, remained to serve the 280 congregations in Latvia. Some of these died as a direct result of the war; others were arrested and exiled to Siberia, or condemned to long prison terms. In order to take care of the orphaned congregations in this emergency, students of theology were ordained as pastors, and qualified lay people were licensed as clergymen. Since the theological faculty in Dorpat had been abolished by the Bolshevists the church administration at Riga established theological courses in which pastors served as teachers. When Archbishop Gruenbergs was forced to leave Latvia, he appointed Dean K. Irpa as his deputy bishop. The latter was, however, condemned to several years imprisonment and sent to Siberia. Pastor Gustav Tuurs, who issued a call for the establishment of a new church administration, was now placed at the head of the church. A church constitution was drafted. On March 14, 1948, a general synod of the church was called. According to the new constitution this synod represented the highest authority in the church and was authorized to elect the archbishop for life. Tuurs now became archbishop. With him seven members of the church administration were also elected by the general synod.

There was no possibility to reach the unchurched or even non-churchgoing members outside of the portals of the churches. The church was not allowed to print a periodical. Finally, in 1954, it was permitted to publish a small hymnal in which all stanzas and passages which could in any way be interpreted as directed against Communist ideology were eliminated. Some years later a church calendar was authorized and finally, in 1961, a new edition of the New Testament in Latvian. In 1962 the church claimed a total of 500,000 members, 115 pastors, and 15 deans (provosts).

The Evangelical Lutheran Church of Estonia also accepted a constitution. It corresponded to the Latvian church order. Here too the synod exercised the highest administrative power. Its members were elected by regional synods or deanery (provost) synods which in turn had been formed by representatives from the various congregations. The central synod of the church elected the archbishop for life and also his consistory. The archbishop and six members of the consistory, called assessors, formed the praesidium of the consistory.

Immediately after the war, when the theological faculty of the University of Reval was closed, the consistory formed so-called higher examination commissions which included both the leaders of the church and former teachers of the faculty of theology. Concerning the financing of the church the post-war Archbishop Jan Kiivit reported in 1958: "Everything that the church possesses comes from the love offerings of the members of the congregations. According to the law we are not allowed to raise church taxes. Everything depends on the will of the congregations. They are giving as much as they desire to give. Members of the congregations are asking how much money is needed and the leadership of the congregations on the basis of the need figures out the average amount for each congregational member. Experience shows that the norm is always oversubscribed. People always give more than is necessary."

The congregations in Estonia took care of the salaries of their pastors, of repairs and of the erection of church buildings, and other matters. The administration of the church, which received 15% of the congregational income, took care of the education of future pastors and of rent payments and pensions for the pastors. The spiritual position of the church improved somewhat after the storms of the war had passed. Only active members were enrolled on the membership lists, i.e. those who went to Holy Communion and gave regularly to the support of the church. According to the statistics of 1962 the church had about 350,000 members in 148 congregations with 114 pastors and 27 deacons and lay-preachers. Children were baptized only if at least one parent was a member of the church. Marriage in church presupposed that the young people had been confirmed. Since the Soviet state had set the minimum age for religious instruction at 18, the age of confirmation was of necessity higher than in the western countries. Young women were usually confirmed at 18 or 19 years of age, while young men were mostly in the 21- or 22-year bracket at the age of confirmation. Instruction of confirmands, as all instruction, took place in the family circle or during divine services. From their old catechisms, from religious books, or from hectographed sheets the young people in their homes learned those things which they had to know for the confirmation examination. In most congregations confirmation was held three times a year.

Komsomolskaja Prawda of April 17, 1962, complained that the religious prejudices were "very tough" in Estonia and therefore, as a counter-offensive, the Komsomols established youth days during the summer in which during 1961 about 7,000 boys and girls had been enrolled. Nevertheless the attendance at church services was very good. In 1957 the church was able to publish a church calendar, and in 1958 a hymnal and an organ manual.

In the former state of Lithuania and in Memelland, which Lithuania had annexed from Germany after World War I, there were only about 80,000 Protestants over against 340,000 in the year 1943, the last "normal year." Of the 77 pastors who had served the Protestant Church only 10 were left. Eight of them were Lutherans and two Reformed. Numerous church buildings had been expropriated and secularized. Many churches that had been destroyed had not been rebuilt. Church publications were forbidden and organized training of pastors was made impossible. Yet despite these suppressions there was a very active participation in the services and the various rites and sacraments which indicated that the congregations were still alive. Of great help to the church in this era of crisis was the prayer circle movement that had been influenced by pietistic circles in neighboring former East Prussia. The center of the movement was in Memelland. From there it spread all over Lithuania. The movement brought forth lay preachers who became very active in the church. Older pastors began preparing promising younger men for the ministry. In the Christian family, the mother often became the guardian of religious traditions.

The Methodist Church, which also existed in the Baltic states, was of course completely isolated from her Anglo-American bases. She was permitted for the first time in 1962 to receive a Methodist bishop from Scandinavia, after almost 20 years of isolation. In spite of these hardships she had increased in numbers in Estonia. In Latvia and Lithuania, however, her congregations had been dissolved and transferred to other communions.

There were only few reports coming from the Reformed churches in the territories that had belonged to Hungary and later to Czechoslovakia, and had been taken over by Russia after World War II. According to a report by her bishop, Adalbert Genczy, the church maintained her independence and organized herself along synodical and presbyterial lines. Every congregation had its own presbytery, a Council of Twenty, in whose hands were placed the internal, external, and spiritual care of the congregation and its discipline. Above these presbyteries there were Rayon seniors who with the dean of the district formed a council. The Rayon seniorates were combined into a diocese which in turn was directed by a bishop and his episcopal council. After the very heavy devastations of the war the congregations quickly rebuilt their churches. They reported early in the 1960's that about 90 churches had been rebuilt or re-opened.

A rather surprising development occurred among the Baptists. In 1917 there were about 100,000 Baptists in the territory of Russia proper. At that time they were divided into three major movements and a very large number of unorganized groups. After the Revolution they were combined into the League of Gospel Christians and Baptists in the USSR. As the name indicated, this organization was set up to include many other communions besides the Baptists. According to its constitution, other groups were admitted and at the same time they were assured of a certain degree of autonomy within the League. Besides the Baptists there were Pentecostals, Mennonites, whose 35,000-40,000 members were scattered throughout the far reaches of the Soviet Union, and others. As long as these widely-scattered groups were not able to form legally local congregations of their own—which required a minimum of 25 members— they had a powerful protection through their membership in the League of Gospel Christians and Baptists, while celebrating their own baptism and Lord's Supper and other rites.

As characteristic traits of the League of Gospel Christians and Baptists the following were mentioned: "We proclaim the pure Gospel. Our entire communion holds firm to its basic beliefs. We are preserving conscientiously the purity of the evangelistic and evangelical doctrines. The central theme of our doctrine is the cross of Golgotha with the sacrifice of Christ and his precious blood. We emphasize the divine nature of Christ. We do not deny a single one of his miracles. We do not omit a single one of his words. We emphasize sanctification—spiritual depth, purity, and holiness of life—in our church and among her members. These things are of prime importance in our educational work. It seems to us that in many countries the church is suffering from the restless spirit of Martha. We try to impress upon our members the spirit of Mary, the spirit of a deep, meditating Christian life which she received when she sat at the feet of Jesus Christ. The spirit of primitive Christianity—the simplicity of the ancient Christian church —is our example. We are striving to attain it in our lives and actions. It is our basic idea to carry out God's work in our country with our own resources. The liberality of our members finds its expression in large contributions."

According to statistics published in 1962 the Gospel Christians and Baptists numbered 545,000 members in 5,545 congregations with about as many pastors and 32,313 lay preachers. The high number of preachers indicated a strong missionary activity of the congregations. Besides those congregations which were registered, there were others that were scattered so that the leadership under President J. Zitkov and Secretary General A. Karev had no information concerning them. To those might be added thousands of groups that had less than 20 members and therefore did not have the minimum number required for registration. Only persons over 18 years of age were received into the congregations and only after a long probationary period during which their way of life and the progress of their faith were strictly examined. Thus, for example, someone who smoked and who dressed extravagantly was either not received into membership, or, if he had been received, was again expelled. If to the number of the baptized adult members the children and the young people, plus those who were taking part in the congregational life without, however, having joined the church, were counted then, according to President Karev's statement, the number would be at least 3,000,000 souls. He declared that one could speak today of the greatest revival movement in the history of Christianity in Russia. Foreigners testified again and again that a fire was burning in those believers. At the head of the organization was the All-Union Council in Moscow. The organization was divided into 17 districts, each of which was governed by a district elder. The Gospel Christians and Baptists had their own monthly magazine, *The Brotherly Messenger*, which usually contained more than 80 pages. The association also published a hymnal and Bibles. From the reports in *The Brotherly Messenger* it became clear that numerous chapels and prayer houses were being constructed.

Missionary activity was also evident, for example, in the fact that every Baptist was responsible for several of his fellow-believers. In the larger cities there were for the most part several congregations with houses of worship. Thus there were four in Kiev, three in

Kharkov, six in Mariopol. Only in Moscow there had been only one house of prayer for the 4,500 members. The building held about 2,000 people. In Tashkent the Baptists grew from 700 to 2,000 between 1952 and 1955. Chain letters were used as a method of communication. During the services young girls could be seen copying the sermons which were later recopied on typewriters. These copies were distributed among the old and shut-ins.

On account of their growth and their missionary zeal the Gospel Christians and Baptists came often to the attention of the Party and of the other authorities. They were often attacked in the press. It happened that their evangelists who lived from the gifts of the faithful were sent to work camps for re-education and punishment. They were called parasites. Added to this was the fact that a number of the believers had embraced a Bible-centered pacifism. The organ of the Red Army, *Krassnaya Svesda,* under the heading: "Women Praying to Christ in a Small Garrison Town" reported on December 28, 1958, that several officers' wives had engaged in religious activities. It stated: "The wife of Major Kusnezov used her stay in a sanitarium of the city of Truskovez to win the patients for her Baptist faith. She refused to attend movies and never took part in the reading evenings or in excursions. She preferred to visit prayer houses instead. She read her Bible and propagated her religious ideas among other women. Even being married to a husband who is one of the most active Communists in his unit did not separate her from her faith. Only a few houses from the Kusnezovs lives Colonel Jakovlev. The colonel's wife is an even more fanatical and active Baptist. She too proclaims her faith so patiently and passionately that no propagandist is able to outtalk her. All attempts by their husbands to cure these women of their religious fanaticism have been a failure. Even scolding them and tearing up their Bibles did not help. On the contrary, their religious fanaticism was further strengthened. Also other women in the garrison were influenced by this religious zeal, and their husbands sadly neglected their duty to report to the Party the behavior of their wives. It is completely unthinkable that a leader who during his working hours carries on a constant battle against the religious remnants should be unable at home to bring his wife, no matter how intoxicated she may be by all this nonsense, to her senses." Two months later the same paper reported that at the request of the Party there had been a conference of the commanders and the political leaders which had taken a second look at the status and the task of anti-religious propaganda in the garrison town and had established a seminar for agitators which would operate on a year-round basis. Officers Jakovlev and Kusnezov, however, had been fined by the Party.

The newspaper *Komsomolskaja Prawda* reported in November 1959 about a confrontation with a pacifist. The officer of the military recruitment commission looked with knitted eyebrows at the man in front of him and said: "Are you the recruit Bobrovsky?" Answer: "I am a Christian." Officer: "Are you a citizen of the Soviet Union?" Answer: "No, I am a child of God." Officer: "If you want to believe in God that is your business. But you must submit yourself to the laws of the Soviet Union." Answer: "I submit myself to the law of God." Officer: "Citizen Bobrovsky, according to your Holy Scriptures, all power on earth is given by God. Is that not so?" Answer: "Yes." Officer: "That means that the power of the Soviets is also from God, doesn't it?" Answer: "They have it by God's permission."

D. THE SECTS

In Communist society the care of the individual is entrusted to a functionary. He has to see to it that every person is influenced by Communist thought, that he performs his daily quota of work, and that he complies in his private life with the ethical requirements of the Communist Party and of the collective. The functionary counsels, criticizes, admonishes, and sees to it that the directives of Communist ideologists are put into practice, and he does a great number of other chores. But he cannot be a pastor. He cannot see man as an individual or as a person who has his own intrinsic value. To him man is merely a cog in the apparatus of the collective. A society which is organized in this way must suffer from undernourishment because the human side of the individual does not receive the necessary food. Feeling; love in its many aspects; the desire for human companionship, for belonging, for dialogue—all these are missing. After the first enthusiasm has worn off and the intoxicating hope for the future has been replaced by the sobering and often disappointing realities of everyday life, there remains a vacuum in the souls of people. This is one of the important reasons for the surprising success of the Gospel Christians and Baptists among the Russians. From this dilemma of the Communist society we can also understand the phenomenon of the tremendous increase of Russian sects.

From the very start, sects have had an easier way of carrying on their activities than the organized Orthodox Church. They were able to function without organization. They were able to work unobserved by the state and the party and to adjust themselves with greater elasticity to any situation. The small circles which they formed were able to go underground or to assemble in secret. The fact that they were forbidden and persecuted was a recommendation in the eyes of the Orthodox believers who saw a sign of treason in the rapprochement between their church and the Communist regime. Added to this was the fact that the sects with their teachings of salvation and their often strongly developed apocalyptic theology were able to attract many people who had been disillusioned in their hopes by the Communist message of salvation. Above all, in these small sects, which were drawn together by a common threat, a common faith, and a high sense of mission, repressed humanity was enabled to unfold itself and to develop into an intimate brotherly community. In their active love of the neighbor, their help for the needy and the sick, there was the most important reason for the success of the sects. They filled a vacuum created by Communist society. By proclaiming a confident way of salvation they created the basis for an intensive life of faith and a feeling of community. They became oases of true humanity in the cold climate of the official Communist society.

No statistics exist concerning the number of adherents of these sects. But all observers are agreed that it must be very large. The Soviet author L. Dashenki admitted this fact indirectly when he wrote in an article in *Literaturnaja Gaseta* at the end of 1958: "If we hope that the religious remnants will die of themselves, we are merely working for the sectarians and for those who are fishing in troubled waters. We must declare war without reprieve on them, and they must be battered with all the means of education and propaganda at our disposal." Aurel von Jüchen, who spent some time in 1950 at the Vorkuta concentration camp and lived in other Russian camps during the next five years, reported in his book *Wo die Hunde heulen* ("Where the Dogs Are Howling") that almost all European sects were represented in the Soviet Union. He too was unable to give any figures, but stated: "Everything indicates that not only in the camps but also in the villages and towns of the country they continue to spread without any external form of organization. The men whom I met in the camps did not look upon faith as a pious substitute for their lack of freedom. They had been arrested and sent to the camps on account of their religious convictions. . . . These religious groups are large in number and of many different varieties. It appears as though the individualism which had been banned from public life has found refuge in the sects and the religious groups." Another former German prisoner of war wrote: "In general the sects are enjoying a high esteem among wide circles of people because the congregations and the preachers are completely independent of any control of the state, and they are trying to preserve their independence. The larger denominations, however, have been compromised by their more or less close cooperation with the Soviet government."

In the publications of the party and of the press there had for decades been much talk about the sects. They were considered disturbing and obstinate evils. Through insults in the press and court trials the state occasionally found out something about the types and activities of these sects. For example, *Sovietskaja Rossija* reported on June 2, 1959, about the activities of the so-called "Old Believers" who had been organized as a result of the protest against the reforms of Peter the Great. They were still active in some villages of the district of Makovskoje, in the region of Krasnojarsk. They were even represented on the village Soviets, and one of their members was the leader of a collective farm. The paper reported in detail—with definite polemical intention, which leads to distortion—that a sick woman was not taken to the doctor but was dipped four times into ice-cold water during the winter and that, when this treatment had no effect, she was subjected to four years of treatment for exorcism of the devil until she finally lost her mind. It stated further that a Komsomol member who was engaged to marry the daughter of one of these Old Believers was able to marry her only after he had resigned from the Komsomol and had grown a beard. It said: "The sectarians are working hard to catch the souls of not only these young people who are of Komsomol age, but even those of the children in the lower grades." The report continued to tell that some pupils had left the Young Pioneer organization, had taken off their red neckerchiefs and had hung around their necks crosses made of copper. When the case of the healing of the sick became known, the alarmed comrades sent a group of agitators into the village as a task force to make short shrift of all religious superstition. With great zeal they delivered two or three speeches per day and went away convinced that they had "re-educated" the Old Believers. But the spiritual leader of the sect continued, the report concluded, "as always to drive the children to prayer and was angry with the whole district, saying that no one would be allowed to go to the Young Pioneer or Komsomol meetings." The Moscow paper also wrote concerning the lack of success of anti-religious agitation. It stated: "We assure the functionaries of the regional committee that in the villages of Makovskoje nothing has changed after the visit by their storm troopers. In general nothing can be done with such raids because we need continuous and painstaking work to unmask the religious fanatics and to re-educate the young people."

Another sect, called the Lady Birds (which in Russia means "gentle and peaceloving people"), was also in sharp opposition to the ruling powers. Yet it did not offer active but only passive resistance. The *Moscowskaja Prawda* reported of a growing sect which called itself "Children of God" and found a wide field of activity in central Russia and central Asia. At its head was a Brother Nikolai who forbade his followers to read Communist literature and to cooperate with the Communist Party, the unions and other agencies of the state. He had issued a call for active resistance against the state. His followers in the central Asiatic republics refused to send their children to state schools. His sect was convinced that the end of the world was close at hand and that they were among the elect who would rule the world. The Soviet press accused the members of the sect of polygamy and other abnormal practices. Some of their leaders were condemned to long prison terms.

In the eighteenth century originated the Subbotniki, the "Baptized in the Spirit." They kept their Sabbath on a Saturday and observed the whole Old Testament law. Under Nicolas I they had been exiled to the Caucasus. In its edition of May 31, 1959, *Sarja Vostoka* of Tiflis reported a trial of four presbyters and one "prophetess" of the Subbotniki who came from Batumi and its environment. The accusation was that they had led people astray through their preaching and prophecies as well as through their practices, and that they had undermined their morals. It was alleged that they had spread lies concerning Soviet life. They had called upon the faithful not to recognize Soviet laws and to refuse to do their duty in the armed forces. They had propagated ideas which were against society and had withdrawn their young people from the cultural, political, and social life of the community. They had forbidden their members in the name of God to join the Komsomol and the Young Pioneer organizations; they had forbidden calling a doctor to heal the sick, reading newspapers and literary magazines, visiting cultural and educational institutions; and they had destroyed family life where one member of the family had forsaken the faith. A 19-year-old girl, who had formerly been happy and full of life, had renounced everything that made life joyful. Said *Sarja Vostoka*: "Her heart became petrified, her smile disappeared, she became old. A 19-year-old woman stood before the judge's bench." She answered the question of the prosecutor whether she attended clubs, movies, or speeches by saying: "No, this is sin." He asked her whether she went to a library, and she answered: "Apart from the Bible I read nothing. To read secular books is sin." He asked her whether she had any friends, and she answered: "In the Law of God it is written that friendship with the world is enmity against God."

The Jehovah's Witnesses, too, have made converts in all parts of the Soviet Union. After the Great War they increased considerably through the repatriation of former Russian war prisoners who had been converted to their doctrines by German Jehovah's Witnesses. Prawda complained that "the Witnesses have been schooled in German concentration camps for their evil work in order to undermine the spirit of the proletariat." The paper called them "an anti-Soviet espionage organization." Its leaders were called "former prisoners of war, Fascist collaborators and Gestapo stool pigeons." After 1948 thousands of Witnesses were persecuted, as reported in the book *Jehovah's Witnesses in God's Plan,* published by the Watchtower Society. This Communist persecution was in many respects worse than the persecution that the Witnesses had suffered at the hands of the Nazis. Thousands of those who had returned from the concentration camps of the Nazis three or four years previously were now condemned to forced labor in Russian mines or exiled to Siberia. But their transfer to forced labor camps and concentration camps merely strengthened them in their desire to carry on ever more fervently their religious propaganda. In 1956 the world organization of the Jehovah's Witnesses sent a petition to former Prime Minister N. A. Bulganin which stated: "In the course of the past two years we have heard alarming news from Russia through some reports in the press and through people who have returned home. We have heard that about 2,000 Jehovah's Witnesses are in Camp Vorkuta or have been there; that in the beginning of 1951 about 7,000 Witnesses from the Baltic to Bessarabia have been arrested and have been sent to far-away regions near Tomsk and Irkutsk and into the neighborhood of Lake Baikal in Siberia; that Jehovah's Witnesses are confined in more than 50 camps all the way from European Russia to Siberia and northward as far as the Arctic Ocean to the island of Nowaja Semlja; and that a number of Jehovah's Witnesses, especially among the 7,000 mentioned above, have died as a result of lack of nourishment during their first two years in Siberia." The letter suggested that a conversation should be held between representatives of the Jehovah's Witnesses and the Russian government, and it asked that permission should be given to a delegation of the international organization to come to Moscow and to visit the camps. The Soviet government did not answer this letter.

Like the Jehovah's Witnesses also the Piatidesjatniki ("The Fifti-ers") were forced to carry on their work illegally. They were called by the people Trjasuni ("Shakers") because during their prayer meetings they exhibited signs of an ecstasy which led to violent shaking of the whole body. They were Pentecostals. They were descended from a man by the name of Voronajev, who over 50 years ago had come from Los Angeles to Russia as a messenger of the outpouring of the Spirit. According to Borys Lewytsky, who wrote about them in *Christ und Welt* (November 1959), they were adept at spreading rumors and transmitting messages from God and they prophesied the early doom of the Soviet state. Like the Jehovah's Witnesses they refused to do military duty and were harshly treated for it by the courts.

Among the illegal sects must be numbered furthermore the so-called Adventists-Reformed which were apparently the Russian branch of the Seventh Day Adventists. Their program consisted in part of a strict vegetarian fare and of the prohibition of sexual intercourse. Some Seventh Day Adventists, however, were permit-ted to exist legally. Their center today is the Ukraine where they were almost unknown before the War and where they had only some followers among the German colonists, since then expelled. At present they seem to be growing rapidly.

How much of a problem sectarianism is in the USSR is shown in an article in the Moscow young people's paper *Pionerskaja Prawda* of April 1962 which attacked the sectarians under the headline: "Holy Rats." The paper complained: "The most abomin-able animal is probably the rat. But there are also people whose character has something evil, something ratlike. You have perhaps heard about these sectarians. Under the pretext of believing in God and in the name of the salvation of souls they bring destruc-tion upon our nation by entangling our people in the dark nets of their superstitions. These evil rats also pull their children into these nets so that they begin to tremble with fear." During the past few years an increasing number of cases have been tried before the so-called "People's Courts" which were composed of lay people and which were established especially to deal with the sects whose members were called "corrupters of society."

CHAPTER TWO

POLAND

A. THE ROMAN CATHOLIC CHURCH

In Poland Communism did not have to fight the Orthodox Church, but Roman Catholicism. But in this church it found a formidable adversary which was immeasurably stronger and harder to subdue than Orthodoxy had been in Russia. Furthermore, the Roman Catholic Church, in contrast to the Orthodox Church of Russia, had not been burdened by a former alliance and identification with czarism. When Communists took over Poland, the Roman Catholic Church had been the central rallying point of the people and their protector for almost a thousand years. Catholicism and Polish nationalism had been identical during most of these centuries so that they now were forming a close unity which permeated the whole spiritual life of the Polish nation and united the Poles against both the Orthodox Russians and the Protestant Germans. This spirit had been successful in all the crises through which this nation had to pass up to the German occupation of Poland during the Second World War.

The Roman Catholic Church, deeply rooted in the consciousness of the Polish people, could claim the unbroken and unwavering faith of the great majority of the nation. Some statistics cast a light upon the religious attitude of the Polish people.

Among Warsaw students who were polled in 1957 and 1958 by the Ministry of Education through the Warsaw Institute of Sociology, 66% claimed that they were religious. Most of them (46%) declared, however, that they did not attend church regularly, but 42% said that they were ready to protect their religion at the cost of their lives. Only 13% declared that they were unbelievers and that they never attended church. Three percent called themselves "enemies of religion." To the question: "Are you a Marxist?" only 1.8% gave a definite affirmative answer; 11.8% thought that they were Marxists to some extent and 34.1% said that they were definitely not Marxists, while 33.7% stated that they would rather not be Marxists.

Of 700 young workers at Gliwice (Gleiwitz) who were living in workers' colonies and who were asked, in 1959, by the Katowice (Kattowitz) *Trybuna Robotnicza* about their religious views, 2.6% called themselves zealously practicing Christians, 29% believing and practicing, 28.5% believing but not regularly practicing, 10% believing but not practicing, and only 9.5% unbelievers. Under the theme "My Ideology" the Polish center of public polls in 1959 instituted an anonymous research project among young people aged 15-24. Of 3,000 young people questioned, 2,746 supplied answers. Of these, 82.6% stated that they had very definite ideological convictions. Of these again, 78.3% considered themselves Roman Catholics and 4.3% atheists, while 5.3% stated that they were not concerned about these things, and only 11.9% said that they had no opinion at all.

A poll taken in 1960 among 938 teachers, under the auspices of the Society for Lay Schools, had the following results: 26.3% of the teachers called themselves unbelievers or active atheists; 38.6% stated that they believed and practiced their religion; 45.5% said that they believed but were non-practicing Catholics; and, surprisingly, almost 8% claimed that they did not believe but practiced their religion. The Danzig (Gdansk) Communist paper *Glos Wybrzeza* stated that especially teachers in the cities had been polled. The religious feelings among village teachers were estimated to run about twice as high as those among the city teachers. The fact that according to the report of the Warsaw paper *Trybuna Ludu* only 19% of all Polish teachers have joined the Communist Party seems to agree with these findings.

The figures which have been given show clearly the spiritual influence of the Roman Catholic Church among the Polish people. The church does not have to worry about recruiting men for the priesthood. In 1958 it was reported that the Roman Catholic seminaries were hardly able to take in all those who wanted to study

theology. The Polish church at that time had 44 archbishops and
bishops, 10,912 priests, 5,503 monks, 21,687 nuns, and 3,802 students of theology. The number of Roman Catholics was estimated
at 25,166,000 out of about 28 million inhabitants. These 25,166,000
Catholics were served in 6,484 parishes.

1. Years of Open Church Struggle

In the first three years after World War II the Communists were
not completely in charge of the government of Poland. But their
influence in the coalition government was increasing steadily. On
September 12, 1945, the Provisional Government abrogated the
concordat of 1925. On November 25, 1945, compulsory civil marriage was introduced. Catholic newspapers were not permitted and
church magazines were subjected to rigid and petty censorship.
There were constant political attacks against the Roman Catholic
hierarchy. Priests and even the two Cardinals of the Church of
Poland, Hlond of Warsaw and Sapiaha of Cracow were accused
of being subversives. Bishop Karl-Maria Splett of Danzig (Gdansk)
was condemned to eight years of imprisonment for "anti-Polish
activities during the Nazi rule."

The government also took seriously its initial promise to protect
the rights of all religions. The so-called Polish National Church
received recognition which it had tried in vain to win between
the two wars, and was permitted to take over, in September 1946,
the former Lutheran St. Peter and St. Paul Church in Stettin
(Szezecin). Also Baptists, Methodists, Adventists, and other smaller
religious bodies were recognized by the state. The listing of denominations for 1962 numbers a total of 25 recognized churches or
denominations. The official publication of the Archdiocese of Warsaw warned against "these sects which enter uncalled into Polish
families. For no price, neither gold nor dollars nor any foreign
gifts, should we sell our faith, our immortal soul, our Catholic
honor." The Communist cultural magazine *Kuznica*, however, encouraged all sects working in Poland to "take up a more intensive
activity."

The political opposition to Communism disappeared when the

Peasants' Party suffered a defeat at the Polish elections. Since the flight of its leader, Mikolajczyk, in the fall of 1947, it had practically stopped to exist. In the spring of 1948 the Communist Party and the Socialist Party joined forces, and a one-party rule was established throughout the country. This was the beginning of the absolute dictatorship of the Communists. In 1949 the Communist Party was cleansed of all internal opposition. Gomulka and his followers were forced to resign from the Central Committee and the Soviet military commander of Poland, Marshal Rokossovski, became virtual dictator.

This was the beginning of years of open church struggle. Catholic schools were forced to close their doors. Religious education on all levels was attacked. The activities of religious youth organizations were limited, and a League of Polish Youth was founded in competition with the organization of the church. This League was led by Communists and was heavily subsidized by the state. In the press priests were constantly accused of corruption, immoral life, and enmity against the state. At two show trials at Warsaw and Lodz several death sentences were pronounced against priests on account of their alleged underground work. When, after the death of Cardinal Hlond in October 1948, his successor Stefan Wyszynski was enthroned as Archbishop of Gnesen (Gneizno) and Warsaw (February 6, 1949) the government took no notice of the solemnities.

On July 1, 1949, the Vatican published a decree against Communism. The Holy Office had decided that Catholics who had joined the Communist Party and had supported it or had published Communist books, newspapers, magazines, and pamphlets, or had made contributions for these purposes, or had spread and read them, would no longer be admitted to the sacraments. People who openly professed the Communist doctrine or defended and propagated it were, according to the decree, "*ipso facto* considered apostates from the Catholic faith and excommunicated with the excommunication reserved for the Holy See." It stated that "Communism is materialistic and anti-Christian. Moreover, the Communist leaders show through their ideology and their actions that they are enemies of God and of all true religion and of the Church of Christ even though they claim at times that they are not fighting against religion." The Polish government answered this decree with a *Law for the Preservation of Conscience and Religion* which threatened punishment for everyone who would forbid any person for political reasons to participate in religious ceremonies or who would abuse religious freedom for his own purposes and spread false information. This quick countermove by the Polish government may have been the reason why the Polish episcopate did not publish the papal decree. The interference of the state now became more massive. On August 11, 1949, all birth registers of the parishes were confiscated. On September 21, 1949, hospitals which had been directed by the religious orders were secularized and placed under the supervision of the Ministry of Health. At the same time Roman Catholic associations were forbidden. Catholic clubs and other auxiliaries of the church were forced to register. The bishops declined to do so, and the state at first refrained from enforcing its decree. But at the end of the period prescribed for registration the organizations were nevertheless dissolved. On November 6, 1949, the decrees of the abolitions were announced from the pulpits. All possessions of the organizations, including orphans' homes, homes for spiritual retreats, and other real estate were confiscated.

The only remaining active and influential organization of the church was *Caritas,* the charity arm of the church. Of the 4,975 parishes of pre-war Poland 4,169 had branches of *Caritas.* In addition there were some 900 kindergartens, 300 kitchens, 1,700 vacation retreats or camps, and 1,200 hospitals and first aid stations. Through voluntary contributions, including large sums transmitted by Catholics from abroad, especially in the USA, the *Caritas* organization had been able to carry on important public services. Its renown among the Polish population was correspondingly high. Now the state tried to dissolve the organization. On January 22, 1950, the Breslau (Wroclaw) Communist *Arbeiterblatt* reported irregularities which had allegedly been discovered during an inventory carried out by the state in the Breslau diocesan *Caritas.* It was stated that the leaders of the organization had used a large number of gifts for their own coffers and that they had employed in their offices a large number of reactionaries, German-lovers, former Gestapo agents, and former political prisoners. These disclosures were reprinted in the entire Polish press and were used by the government as a pretext for placing the administration of *Caritas* under government control. On January 23, 1950, the administrative offices of *Caritas* were occupied by new members who were acceptable to the government. By means of censorship the bishops were prevented from defending themselves against the accusations leveled against *Caritas*. In a Joint Letter published at the beginning of 1950 they called upon all priests to stay away from political and anti-church meetings which were being conducted by the new *Caritas* leadership. They were warned not to accept any offices in the organization. Some priests who had placed themselves at the disposal of *Caritas* were removed from their parishes by their bishops. In spite of this warning by the episcopate the government was able to get together 1,000 priests for a rally held at the Institute of Technology in Warsaw. The rally expressed its gratitude to the state for having interfered in the administration of *Caritas*. The bishops now wrote another pastoral letter in which they reiterated their firm and fatherly admonitions to the priests, "for," they said, "the life, the organization, and the unity of the Church of Poland are in mortal danger." In a memorandum written on February 16, 1950, Archbishop Wyszynski and Cardinal Sapieha warned the President of Poland, Comrade Bierut, that they would not be able to renew the church with men who were at war with the canon law of the church. If the state, on its part, should try such a renewal then the whole Catholic community, the large majority of the nation, would be estranged from the state. On May 20, 1950, the Sejm, the Polish parliament, voted on a law which expropriated without compensation all ecclesiastical property and subjected it to the stipulations of the "Law for Soil Reform" passed in 1948. The reasons given for the application of this law to the church were of great significance. They stated that the bishops had used the income for their real estate to carry on activities against the state and had at the same time neglected the essential needs of the church and of the lower clergy. The by-laws stated: "Places used for the exercise of the religious cult as well as buildings, monasteries, and other edifices which serve as residences for bishops and archbishops are exempt from this confiscation." Individual parishes received the right to own land ranging from 50 to 100 hectares depending on the size of the congregation. This exemption included 375,000 hectares (a hectare is approximately 2.47 acres).

The outside world was surprised when in the midst of all this fighting an agreement was reached between the Roman Catholic Church and the Communist state. Consultations which had begun as early as the middle of 1949 culminated in a joint declaration, signed on April 14, 1950, and consisting of 19 articles and its attached protocol. It stated that in order to secure the best conditions for the peaceful development of the nation: "The Polish government, which recognizes the freedom of religion, and the Polish episcopate, thinking of the welfare of the church and the interests of the state, regulate their relationship as follows: (1) The episcopate agrees to admonish the clergy to carry on its pastoral work in agreement with the dogma of the church and to teach all believers to respect the laws of the state and the political authorities; (2) The episcopate agrees to request the clergy to encourage the faithful to increase their activities for the rebuilding of the country and the raising of the living standard of the nation; (3) The episcopate agrees that economical, historical, and religious justice demand that the newly-won territories must always remain with Poland. Starting with the presupposition that the newly-won territories are an integral part of the Polish state, the episcopate agrees to ask the Holy See that the temporary administrators who now carry on the functions of bishops be appointed as regular resident bishops; (4) Within the limits of its influence the episcopate will oppose all activities which are directed against Poland, especially the anti-Polish and revisionist ideas of a part of the German clergy; (5) The episcopate adheres to the basic idea that the Pope is the highest authority in the church in matters of faith, morals, and ecclesiastical jurisdiction. In all other respects the episcopate promises to consider Polish interests first."

In the four articles which follow these basic statements the episcopate agreed to insist that "the clergy should not oppose the development of collective farms" and that it should not abuse religious feelings in order to carry on anti-government activities. The episcopate promised to curb the criminal activities of the underground movement and to make clergymen who were involved in such criminal activities responsible for their actions and punish them according to canon law. The episcopate also promised to support all endeavors to strengthen peace and to oppose to the best of its ability all warmongering in the church.

In return the state made the following concessions: Religious instruction in the schools would not be curtailed in its present scope. School curricula would be established by the school authorities in consultation with representatives of the episcopate. Catholic schools which existed at the time of the agreement were to remain open and would enjoy the same rights and privileges as state schools. The Catholic University of Lublin would be allowed to continue its work as heretofore. Catholic clubs would enjoy their guaranteed rights, provided they fulfilled the requirements laid down in the agreement. The church would have the opportunity to continue her charitable work and to carry on catechetical instruction. The Catholic press and all Catholic publishing houses would be treated like other publishing enterprises. Public divine services, traditional pilgrimages and processions would not be hampered. Religious orders would enjoy complete freedom of action. In the protocol which was added to this document it was stated expressly that *Caritas* would be reorganized into an organization of Catholics interested in assisting the poor and needy. The episcopate promised to permit clergymen to cooperate in the work of *Caritas*. The government on its part promised to take into account the needs of the bishops and of the ecclesiastical institutions whenever it became necessary to carry out needed expropriations. The office in charge of church funds would at all times put the needed sums at the disposal of the bishops.

But this agreement did not lead to peace. On the contrary, it was used as a weapon by the Communists for further attacks upon the church. On the basis of Article 9 the government demanded that all bishops should sign the so-called Stockholm Peace Appeal. When they refused, they were accused of having violated the agreement. They were forced to give in, but added certain reservations when they finally signed the appeal. The news agency of the state, however, did not report these reservations. The collecting of signatures for the Stockholm Peace Appeal, furthermore, gave the state an opportunity to eliminate those teachers of religion who refused to sign it. They were called enemies of world peace. Clergymen and members of religious orders were publicly attacked and often arrested because they refused to sign the Stockholm declaration.

The *Law Concerning the Expropriation of the Property of the Church* had provided that endowments should be established for "meritorious priests" from the sale of such property. This was one of the means which the government used to win over priests to cooperate in its program. Tension between the episcopate and the lower clergy had always been a Polish tradition. In the Polish patriotic songs of the nineteenth century Polish poets had often rhymed the words "prelate" and "magnate," and had contrasted the prelates with the poor local priests who had sprung from the common people. Now the state organized a *Society of Patriotic Priests* which soon numbered several hundred members. It met without the permission of the episcopate and issued calls to Catholics to cooperate with the Communist authorities. It started a great deal of confusion among the Roman Catholic believers. The government took this society under its special protection, granted it release from taxation, and did not carry out any confiscations of property in congregations whose priests were enrolled among the patriotic priests. It also granted a number of other privileges.

Article 3 of the state-church agreement was used by the government to pressure the episcopate to terminate the temporary administration of the church in the newly-won territories. The government considered this article as a promise by the bishops to pay for the favors which they had been granted in the agreement and demanded such payment forthwith. In this respect it was in a favorable position. It was able to mobilize Polish nationalism against the church and to find enthusiastic support among the lower clergy. The episcopate was faced by a dilemma. Either it would be driven to oppose and disobey the express wishes of the Pope or it would have the faithful lined up against it with the government. Furthermore, the non-fulfillment of the promise given in

Article 3 could lead to all kinds of repressions against the church. Also the Vatican was in a most difficult position. If it agreed to yield to Polish pressure, it meant that it was anticipating a state of affairs that had not yet been sanctioned by a formal peace treaty between Poland and Germany. It would legalize the expulsion of millions of Germans and thus cause great resentment among German Catholics. On the other hand, opposition to Polish demands to appoint regular bishops for the newly-won territories might lead to the establishment of a nationalistic rival church in Poland, and this threat was always present. The episcopate might align itself with the lower clergy and separate from the obedience to Rome.

The following areas were included in the territories mentioned in Article 3: The Diocese of Ermland (Olsztyn), the Diocese of Danzig (Gdansk), the Free Prelature of Scheidemühl (Pila), and the larger part of the Archdiocese of Breslau (Wroclaw). Also included were smaller portions of the dioceses of Berlin and Meissen. In the year 1945, when the German occupants of these dioceses and all German priests were driven out, the Holy See had authorized Cardinal Hlond, Primate of Poland, to restore pastoral care by appointing apostolic administrators to take care of the orphaned episcopal sees. But these administrators did not have the dignity and the prerogatives of bishops. As far as canon law was concerned the dioceses of the former East German territories were listed in the Yearbook of the Pontifical See as German dioceses, and continue to be listed in this way until the present day.

The Communist government of Poland applied tremendous pressures on the bishops to change this state of affairs. Patriotic clergymen and Catholic "activists" were sent to them and "spontaneous rallies of the Catholic people" were held everywhere. Resolutions were passed by so-called people's priests. The press implied that the hesitation of the bishops was equivalent to high treason. Wyszynski and Sapieha assured President Beirut that the bishops were willing to submit the question of the newly-won territories to the Apostolic See, but they made it clear that the Apostolic Administrators were not very different from real bishops in the exercise of their functions. The state was not satisfied with this assurance. The conflict quickly snowballed. On November 12, 1950, the episcopate declared in a pastoral letter that the government was guilty of repeated violations of the declaration of last April. It had refused to recognize the ecclesiastical organization of the newly-won Western territories, had suppressed the publication of Catholic magazines and had caused the closing of all diocesan printing shops. It had furthermore ordered the confiscation of the entire properties of the monasteries so that many monks and nuns had been forced to accept jobs as untrained workers. Finally, the government had tried to create a church subservient to its purposes by organizing a society of so-called patriotic priests.

In a note published at the end of October 1950 the State Office for Ecclesiastical Affairs accused the bishops that "the attitude of the church is in flagrant violation of the national and state interests of Poland and encourages anti-Polish elements and oppressors and warmongers." Press and radio announced that the non-recognition of the Oder-Neisse Line by the Catholic episcopate was giving "encouragement to revisionists in Western Germany and to people who were anxious for retribution against the Poles."

On January 27, 1951, the government in a declaration concerning the administration of the church in the liberated areas declared that all attempts to carry out the provisions of Article 3 of the state-church agreement had failed. The bishops, the government declared, had avoided making clear arrangements for the creation of Polish dioceses in the newly-won territories. At the same time all those who hated peace, especially the revisionists in Western Germany, had begun to profit from the provisional status of the church government in the newly-won territories and from the support given to this provisional status by the Vatican. Since the Oder-Neisse Line had been recognized by the Polish People's Republic and by the German Democratic Republic as the unchangeable and final boundary, and since the provisional character of the church administration in those areas was being used to encourage anti-Polish activities and thus threatened the interests of the people and of the state, the declaration continued: "The Polish government has decided to abolish the provisional character of the church administration in the form of Apostolic Administrators in the liberated areas and to separate them from the clergy in the dioceses concerned. By this action the election of vicars for the cathedral chapters and the recognition of all priests as permanent resident pastors becomes possible. By removing the provisional administrators, which have become outdated, the full freedom of exercise of religion guaranteed by our laws is now secured and the religious desires of the believers have been fully respected." The government forced the Apostolic Administrators of Breslau (Wroclaw), Oppeln (Opole), Landsberg (Gorzow Wielkopolski), Danzig (Gdansk), and Ermland (Olsztyn) to resign and to leave the areas of their administration. In their place state commissars were appointed who received the title "Vicar" of the cathedral chapters. But since there were no cathedral chapters in the newly-won territories the election could have taken place only among clergymen who were subservient to the Communists.

This was indeed gross interference in the rights of the church. How would the episcopate and the Vatican react? The Primate of Poland protested orally to the President of the State against these measures. He quoted the provisions of the declaration of January 27. But *ex post facto* he gave his ecclesiastical sanction to the "Vicars" who had been appointed by the Communist authorities. He wanted to save the dangerous situation in this way. Without a doubt these "Vicars" would have assumed their offices even without the consent of the Primate and would have found strong support among the lower clergy. In order to forestall the beginnings of an opposition church, which would have led to a schism, Archbishop Wyszynski legalized the position of Communist-appointed episcopal vicars. Thus they legally became holders of episcopal power. Feeling that he had been authorized to make this decision by the powers that had been given to his predecessor in 1945, the archbishop did not ask the Pope's consent. Some Catholics called this decision of the Primate "one of the most important occurrences in the history of the church in our days." Not only did he accept the *fait accompli* created by the Communist state, but he also tacitly sanctioned the usurpation of ecclesiastical powers by the state in order to forestall confusion in the order of the church. Telling Rome about the difficulties that had arisen was a problem.

The agreement of the episcopacy with the Polish government of April 14, 1950, had been concluded without inquiry and thus without the consent of the Vatican. Therefore the Vatican was not bound to observe Article 3. On April 4, 1951, Wyszynski made a trip to Rome. But his discussions with Vatican officials did not lead to the desired results. The disappointment of this trip was utilized by the state to renew its hostile propaganda in the Polish press against the bishops.

In order to counteract the force of these attacks, Archbishop Wyszynski in December 1951 granted an audience to a journalist. At that time he declared that the priests of all Polish dioceses had worked together in the task of rebuilding church life with great sacrifices and devotion, and this work included the territories, he said, "about which our religious feelings have been concerned during the last 1,000 years." Article 3 of the agreement had been an expression of the feelings of the entire Polish episcopate. The special authorization given to the Primate of Poland by the Holy See in 1945 was proof, he claimed, "stronger than words of the friendly understanding of the Holy Father for the problems of the western provinces." The archbishop also reminded the journalists of a memorandum which he had submitted to Pope Pius XII in October 1950 concerning the life of the church in the newly-won territories. He said: "We presented to him, in accordance with our most sincere convictions, the fact that the return of Poland to the Oder and Neisse meant at the same time the return of the Holy Church to the provinces which had become Protestant. This is especially true in the case of the provinces of Lower Silesia and Pomerania. Today seven million Catholics are living in these provinces. Three thousand priests are working among them. In the diocese of Landsberg (Gorzow Wielkopolski) alone there are now a thousand Catholic churches where before the war there had been less than one hundred. The Catholic Church has thus returned with the Polish people into the territories from which she had been driven during Luther's Reformation. This clear fact is fully appreciated by the Holy Father. The point of view of the Polish episcopate in the question of the western provinces is identical with the point of view held by our government. The Holy Father knows this and agrees with it. The Holy See is not desirous of making these declarations publicly, but there is no lack of actions which are more eloquent than words. It cannot be denied that the Holy See has recognized the reorganization of the ecclesiastical life in the western provinces which were ordered by the late Cardinal-Primate Hlond." Wyszynski said even more: The Holy Father had agreed to the formation of definite ecclesiastical bodies which were a part of the church according to canon law, including the administration of dioceses, the establishments of the courts of the church and of the seminaries for the dioceses. He said: "From this we may see that the Holy See is interested in the development of the life of the Polish Catholic Church in these territories and in the stabilization and completion of the organization of the diocesan structure."

The archbishop turned then to the attitude of German Catholics. He stated that the Polish episcopate shared the worries of the Polish people concerning the mounting anti-Polish propaganda which was directed against the Oder-Neisse Line. He stated: "We have a right to expect that the Germans, and especially German Catholics, should show a different attitude. Catholic ethics demand that the conscience recognize the responsibility for the start of the war. Poland was one of the victims of that war. The German Catholics must recognize this injustice which was done to Poland and to Polish national culture during the war." Therefore, suggested the archbishop, the German Catholics should regard the transfer of the newly-won territories to Poland as an act of justice, while the Polish Catholics have the duty to defend the rights of Poland in the western provinces.

The Polish Primate continued to act in this direction. By a decree of May 26, 1952, he appointed a Polish cathedral chapter for Breslau and a few days later he installed its members personally. From that moment there were two cathedral chapters for Breslau, and the Polish cathedral chapter had been appointed in clear violation of canon law. It was true that the legitimate chapter had been removed by the force of circumstances to Germany. After the death of Cardinal Bertram in May, 1945, it had elected Prelate Dr. Piontek as chapter vicar. The appointment of the new Polish cathedral chapter for Breslau occurred without the knowledge of the Holy See. A permission for Archbishop Wyszynski to appoint canons for Breslau had never been given. But since the archbishop stated that he had the power to do so, it was assumed that he was forced by the pressure of the Communist state to interpret the powers given to his predecessor in 1945 in such a way that the Holy See did not dare to interfere publicly in order not to hurt the interests of the Church of Poland.

But the willing cooperation of the Primate in the question of the Polish-administered former German territories did not pacify the Communist state. It continued its fight against the church. The Communists were interested in organizing a National Catholic Church free from Rome. They openly encouraged the development of the Society of Patriotic Priests, and the membership of this group eventually increased to over 2,000. Its president, Professor Czuj, became the first director of a newly founded Academy for Catholic Theology which opened its doors in November 1954 at Bielany, near Warsaw, under the aegis of the government. The old theological faculties at the universities of Poznan (Posen), Warsaw, and Cracow were abolished; and the Catholic University of Lublin was severely restricted in its activities. Religious instruction in the schools was made very difficult by all kinds of chicaneries. The Catholic press was either choked off or coordinated, and the activities of the Catholic *Caritas* organization were removed from the control of the hierarchy. All these actions by the government were accompanied by violent attacks against the church in the press which constantly accused the hierarchy of subversive activities. In a conversation with the secretary of the Bishops' Conference, Bishop Choromanski of Lublin, held on March 14, 1949, Minister Wolski had accused the episcopate of supporting those priests who were organizing the public against the state under religious pretexts or favoring criminal activities and American agents, and of abusing the right to educate the youth. He had stated that the church had permitted the political resistance movement to enter her ranks, that Bishops Adamski of Katowice (Kattowitz) and Kaczmarek of Kielce, who had been subservient to the Nazis, were now active against the Polish state. In July 1950 a representative of the government declared at a press conference in Warsaw that both foreign espionage and fascist gangsters were using several monasteries as bases for their activities. He accused especially the monasteries of the Salvatorian monks and of the order of St. Bernard. The monastery of St. Bernard at Radecznica, he said, had organized, with the help of its superior, a fascist gang of terrorists who had perpetrated political murders and robberies. This monastery and an academy in Cracow supervised by the Jesuits had hidden a collection of weapons within their walls.

In connection with such accusations, the truth of which was definitely disputed by the Catholics, there were numerous arrests and trials. There were deportations, prison sentences, and even death sentences. In the fall of 1951, 900 priests were arrested. One year later the attacks reached the high water mark. After a campaign by the press six bishops were arrested in November 1952 and in January 1953. A decree issued on February 3, 1953, recognized that the government had the right to issue a general *placet* for all ecclesiastical appointments. Before taking over an office in the church each nominee had to obtain the consent of the government in the case of bishops, or of the district authorities in the case of priests, and had to take an oath of loyalty to the Polish People's Republic. Furthermore, the government claimed the right to remove ecclesiastical appointees from their offices and to put men sympathetic to the regime into the more important positions. A short time later the government vetoed the appointment of two new bishops at Czestochowa (Czenstochau) and Wloclawek. It also brought to trial Bishop W. Kaczmarek, who was condemned to 12 years in prison. Cardinal Wyszynski protested against this verdict and was himself arrested the following day, on September 25, 1953. He was forbidden to exercise his duties as Primate of Poland and was interned in a monastery. Shortly after these occurrences another bishop was sentenced to a prison term.

2. Coexistence with Second Thoughts

For three years the Roman Catholic Church was without leaders. Now the government thought that the favorable moment had arrived when it could separate the church from Rome and organize a national church with the help of patriotic priests. But the surprising thing happened. The government did not follow up its initial success. Apparently it had become clear to the Communists that any attempt to separate the church from the Pope would meet with the determined opposition of the majority of the priests and of the faithful. Furthermore, the government and the party had been weakened by the death of Stalin. The party was confronted by increasing troubles within its own ranks. These tensions finally exploded in the famous Posen revolt of June 28, 1956. The revolt led to a change in government and to a turning away from Stalinism. On August 10, 1956, the Central Committee of the Polish Communist Party restored party membership to Wladislaw Gomulka who had been arrested in 1948. On October 20, 1956, Gomulka was elected First Secretary of the Central Committee and the Russian Marshal Rokossovski was ousted. Gomulka gave a speech in which he declared the end of the Stalinist era and demanded that democracy should be reintroduced in accordance with the spirit of the basic principles of socialism. On October 27, 1956, he announced the release of Cardinal Wyszynski after a collection of signatures had been started throughout Poland and after a meeting of students, held at Breslau on October 23, had ended in street demonstrations at which the shout was heard again and again: "We demand the release and the restoration of our Cardinal Wyszynski." Also the other bishops, five in number, who were still in prison, were released at the same time. The cardinal was greeted by a large Warsaw crowd. In one of the speeches which he gave shortly after his release he affirmed: "I owe my liberation to our Lady of Czestochowa, the Queen of Poland. Poland is Catholic and will remain Catholic!" At the same time he also indicated his consent to the policy of peaceful coexistence which the government was proclaiming, and in his first sermon after his liberation he said: "We are in the midst of an extremely difficult period of our national existence, a period during which it will be necessary for some time to speak less about our rights and more about our duties; and we shall do so because we love our Fatherland."

The government appointed a commission consisting of members

of the state and of the church, which was entrusted with the solution of all outstanding questions. This commission met for the first time on November 4, 1956, and formulated its policies on December 8 in a common declaration. This declaration, which became normative for the future development of the relationship between church and state until the present time, stated: "During the conversations between the representatives of the government and the episcopacy, the government showed its readiness to remove all hindrances which during the past few years have hampered the realization of the basic concepts of religious freedom. The representatives of the episcopate stated that the government and all other authorities of the state had the full sympathy of the hierarchy and of the clergy in their attempt to restore law and order, justice and peaceful coexistence, and to improve the morals of society and to remove injustice. The representatives of the episcopate also assured the government of their support for the plans of the government to strengthen and to develop the People's Republic of Poland. They pledged that they would concentrate their efforts to encourage all citizens to help in this common task for the welfare of the country, to observe conscientiously the laws of the People's Republic of Poland and to help the people to do their duty as citizens of the state."

The joint commission also regulated a number of individual questions. First, it asked the government to rescind the law of February 9, 1953. In an agreement which was to be concluded later the state was to be given a certain degree of influence in the appointment of archbishops, bishops, deans, and provosts. But the right of ecclesiastical jurisdiction was not to be abridged.

Secondly, the government was asked to guarantee complete freedom in the exercise of religion and to permit voluntary religious instruction in the intermediate and elementary schools to children whose parents desired such instruction. But it pointed out that religious instruction was not to be an obligatory course. School authorities were asked to make it possible for the church to offer such instruction by drawing up a definite schedule. Teachers of religion were to be employed by the school authorities on behalf of the ecclesiastical authorities. School administrators were to see to it that the children received unhampered religious instruction.

Both parties in the conversations assured complete freedom and tolerance to both believers and unbelievers and promised to oppose all attempts which would interfere with the freedom of conscience.

Thirdly, an understanding concerning work in hospitals and old folks homes was reached. Fourthly, an agreement was reached to permit priests to carry on pastoral work in prisons. It regulated the position of prison chaplains in penal institutions of the state.

Fifthly, the government promised to permit the return of the nuns who had been expelled from the dioceses of Oppeln (Opole), Breslau (Wroclaw), and Kattowitz (Katowice). Furthermore, it agreed that priests who had been exiled from their parishes during the past few years would be allowed to return to their congregations in western Poland.

Finally, an agreement was reached dealing with the appointment of five bishops who would administer the former German territories as vicars-general.

On the basis of these declarations the government issued instructions to the various state authorities. By government decree of December 4, 1956, the religious care in penal institutions was resumed. On December 14, 1956, the pastoral work in hospitals was restored; and on December 15 religious instruction was reintroduced on a voluntary basis in elementary and intermediate schools.

The decision to coexist was not the result of an enthusiastic reconciliation, but of dire necessity. The church needed her freedom of activity, and the government was dependent upon the support of the Catholics. Both church and government were concerned about the future of Poland. But the ideological tensions continued. They neither decreased nor could they be glossed over. Thus this so-called peaceful coexistence never became a harmonious living together. Both sides had their mental reservations. Both hoped to gain by the armistice which they called peaceful coexistence, and both continued to pursue their long-term goals.

For the Communists certain considerations were important. These considerations were formulated by Taddeusz Pluzanski in the following sentences: "To force atheism upon the people will lead only to a strengthening of piety. Poland cannot be secularized through the efforts of atheists and freethinkers. The activities of these people will only lead to a renewed resistance. Direct anti-religious propaganda creates unrest and does not help secularization but retards it because it provokes the opposition of the faithful. Therefore it is advisable to take steps to isolate the Catholics intellectually. Polish society cannot be secularized in the course of two generations. Therefore we should not expect quick solutions and decisive results. But neither should we be worried about the so-called successes of religion which are deceptive. Religion whose present revival is merely the logical result of Stalin's oppression, will decline again once normal conditions return to Poland. This cooling-off process in the religious area can be developed into a trend by isolating religious problems so that they will become a completely private concern. In an atmosphere of indifference religious fervor will disappear very quickly."

Also the organ of the Polish intelligentsia *Po Prostu,* which was later suppressed, wrote that the reason why the church had increased during Stalinism was to be found in the terror of the Stalinist regime of Poland and in the atmosphere of fear and uncertainty which that regime had created. Under those conditions only the church had been able to satisfy the people's desire for justice, kindness, and love. It wrote: "Fear creates gods. This old materialistic truth has often been confirmed in our country." The paper stated that during the Stalinist period religion had been strengthened. Robbed of the possibility to make decisions about their own life, people had turned to religion. Robbed of their freedom, they had begun to look for freedom in heaven. Now, thought the editor, the battle against religion would need to be carried on not with Stalinist methods, but on a different plane. He stated: "The conditions in our society which strengthen religion need to be eliminated. The battle against religion has to be fought without terror. The development of freedom must bring also freedom to religion and from religion." The Minister of Education, Bienkowski, gave this laconic definition: "Only by supporting indifference can we prepare the way for the decline of the influence of the church. The death of religion does not start with a fight against religion, but with the death of the problems which are favoring religion."

That this reasoning contained a kernel of truth became clear during the following years. The Roman Catholic Church had gained many advantages during the years of struggle against militant atheism. She had been able to appear in this struggle as the spokesman for a great number of people and to enjoy the sympathy even of groups which were not closely tied to her. But now, after the conclusion of the armistice between church and state, she received more freedom and security while at the same time her difficulties developed on a different plane. The Liberals and Socialists, who had been attracted to her during the fight against Stalinism, no longer supported her, since the goal for which they had been striving with her had been reached. The Communists stopped attacking the church directly. Instead they concentrated on criticizing the doctrines of the church, especially Catholic ethics, and proclaimed with the help of all the means of propaganda at their disposal a materialistic ideology which was opposed to her. In this endeavor they were able to count on the support of all the groups which did not like the church and her doctrines. They were even able to infiltrate the very ranks of the Catholics. The complaints of priests about the lowering of morals in married life, about the numerous legal abortions, and above all about alcoholism had become more and more vocal. Especially the young people who, according to the opinions of one priest, threatened to leave the church in large numbers were influenced by this new moral climate. Addressing about one million believers at Czestochowa (Czenstochau) in August 1957, Cardinal Wyszynski attacked the increase of alcoholism and accused the press of publishing pictures of naked women. Said he: "There is freedom for pornography, but it is difficult to get permission to print religious books." On Epiphany 1959 the Lazarist priests of Warsaw's Holy Cross Church declared that while there was no longer open persecution of the church in Poland, there was danger that through the improvement of the living standard religious indifference was spreading.

But did not this return to practical materialism endanger Communism too? Communism is, after all, an idealistic movement despite its materialistic basis because it thrives on the hope of a better life and demands readiness from its followers to fight, and to sacrifice themselves, for the sake of this hope. The cult for a higher living standard was as much opposed to the ideals of Communism as was the demand of the church, "Do not love the world," and all the other principles of Christian ethics. Two and a half years after the conclusion of the armistice between church and state the Catholic writer Stephan Kisielewski stated that "the messianic patriotism which we have eaten like manna for many generations has made room for technological patriotism. Inner and foreign policies, ideological conflicts, all these are considered interesting only from the viewpoint of economic organization, of production, profit, and the rising living standard. Religion fares worst in this climate. Lay people interfere with it. The church is now losing to a great extent the favorable image which the persecutions of the past had given to her. The secularization of society is not the result of the activities of Marxism, but it is a worldwide phenomenon, caused to a large extent by the rise of technology." The Marxist Jan Kott reached the same conclusions as Kisielewski when he said: "For the first time in 130 years a generation is growing up among us which does not intend to save Poland or the world. . . . Probably for the first time in our national history we are surrounded by young skeptics."

These indications of a growing religious and ideological indifference alarmed both the church and the party. The climate of peace was not conducive to either church or Communism. It profited a third force. Perhaps this was the underlying reason why both sides were forced to continue their struggle against each other.

The Roman Catholic episcopate started a large-scale program of action for the renewal of the church. This was inaugurated in 1957. On May 5, 1957, in all the congregations of Poland the vow of loyalty which over one and a half million pilgrims had made at Czestochowa on August 26, 1956, was renewed. It stated: "I promise to do everything in my power so that Poland may become the true kingdom of thy Son." To this general vow were added eight individual promises: To live continually in a state of grace; to be loyal to the church and her bishops; to protect the lives of unborn children; to keep marriage sacred and pure; to educate all children in the love of God and of the neighbor; to live in peace with one another; to fight against all vice; and to increase the devotion to the Blessed Virgin Mary in the whole country. The text of this vow was spread among the Catholic people in every possible way. The celebrations of May 5, 1957, were turned into a fitting start of the preparatory period of the millennial observance of the conversion of Poland to Christianity, which was to culminate with celebrations in 1966. The nine years until 1966 were to be under the sign of the thousand-year jubilee. According to the plans of the bishops, the whole life of Poland was to be renewed systematically. In all parishes missions, spiritual exercises, retreats, and religious weeks were to be conducted. The Holy Image of our Virgin of Czestochowa (Czenstochau) was to be carried from parish to parish during these years and to remain in every church for a period of time.

The state on its part played out the trumps at its disposal to check the progress of the church. For this purpose the state utilized the services of the *Society of Atheists and Freethinkers*. This society stated that it would receive "all those who are ready to fight publicly for an ideology free from superstition and dogma." The leader of the society was Professor Andrezej Nowicki. The membership numbered about 12,000. Since October 1957 it had been publishing the magazine *Argumenty* to which had been assigned the task: "To fight against the growing influence of the clergy, especially in the villages and among the impoverished middle class in the cities, and among women and children." Of greater importance than this society was another group, the *Society for Secular Schools*, founded in 1957, which published the newspaper *Wychowanie* ("Education"). At the beginning it numbered only 19,000 members, but when the state resumed its attacks on religious instruction in the schools, it gained greater influence. Also the Polish National Church which had broken away from Rome enjoyed the support of the state. This church numbered only 35,000 souls and 48 congregations. It enjoyed far-reaching tax reductions, and its Bishop Rode received permission to open a number of shops and small manufacturing plants. There was some excitement when, toward the end of 1957, the large Catholic congregation at Bolesslawik, with its priests and 7,000 members, joined the National Church as a unit.

A still more important means to pressure the Roman Catholic Church was the *Pax* movement. This movement had been organized as early as 1945 by Boleslav Piasecki, a member of the lesser nobility. In the feudal Polish state before 1939 he had been one of the most active leaders of the chauvinist rightist youth movement which was dedicated to a noisy anti-Semitism. During the German occupation, however, he had joined the resistance movement without renouncing his opposition to Communism. His antagonism against the Communists was so well known that when the Red Army occupied Poland he was immediately arrested. While his trial was being prepared by the Reds, he worked out a program of social organization of progressive Catholics which he submitted to the Soviet security police. The officials of the police were so impressed that they released Piasecki immediately and removed all the legal stumbling-blocks that could have thwarted the realization of his plan. They agreed with him that in an overwhelmingly Catholic country like Poland Communism could scarcely hope for success, unless it used as a tool a "Catholic" movement like the proposed *Pax* movement to carry out its objectives.

Piasecki was able to establish a powerful and heterogeneous organization on a sound economic basis, somewhat between a private stock company and a cooperative enterprise. He was given all the advantages which nationalized factories enjoyed. He had access to raw materials, and the insurance rates for his many enterprises were kept at a minimum. The greatest privilege enjoyed by the *Pax* movement was the complete remission of income taxes and of all other payments to the treasury of the state. The *Pax* publishing house dominated the field of Catholic literature. It published, partly as a monopoly, all prayer books, Bible translations, theological and other works, including *belles lettres* and political writings. Important Catholic writers contributed to its success, especially younger authors who were in great demand. The daily newspaper of the *Pax* movement, *Slowo Powszechne*, published in Warsaw, had a circulation of 150,000. Besides this daily paper, *Pax* published several weeklies. Most important among these was the Warsaw *Kierunki* ("Directions"). Besides its publishing house, *Pax* also owned factories, warehouses, and stores, and employed between 4,000 and 5,000 people. It dominated much of the Polish building industry, because the *Pax* enterprises produced a great number of products: tiles, wooden floors, one-family houses, and many other items. In addition, the *Pax* movement controlled schools and hospitals and even owned an insurance company. At the end of 1956 *Pax* had more than 66,000,000 zloty in invested capital and over 100,000,000 zloty in liquid assets. It was said that it made during that year over 100,000,000 zloty in profits of which 30,000,000 was used for "social and political planning."

The movement which had been started by a handful of Polish intellectuals from the beginning followed the Stalinist line and invited the cooperation of the patriotic priests. During the time of the church struggle it was standing firmly at the side of the state against the so-called reactionary clergy. When Gomulka came to power in 1956, Piasecki continued to support the Stalinists in the Polish Communist Party. Although Cardinal Hlond in 1945 had given *Pax* about $2,000 to get the movement off the ground, the church soon began to have second thoughts. She recognized that *Pax* was not mediating the difficulties between church and state, but augmenting them. In June 1955 the Holy Office in Rome put two *Pax* publications, including a book by Piasecki and the Warsaw weekly *Dzis i jutro,* on the Index of Forbidden Books. In July 1957 the Holy See forbade all priests to publish books in the *Pax* publishing enterprises and to write for *Pax* brochures and newspapers or to cooperate with *Pax* in any way. But no newspaper in Poland was permitted to publish this prohibition.

On account of their initial negative attitude toward Gomulka, five members of the directorate of *Pax* were forced, in October 1957, to resign. They founded an independent *Christian Social Institute.* Although Piasecki continued to inveigh against the liberalization policy of Gomulka and hewed to the old Stalinist line, *Pax* was not deprived of its privileges because the state thought to use it as a wedge with which it could destroy the unity of the Roman Catholic Church. The expressed wish that *Pax* should be suppressed fell on deaf ears. When, in the summer of 1957, Cardinal Wyszynski in a sharply-worded article criticized the attitude of the state toward Pax, censorship prohibited the distribution of the article. The only concession made by the government to the church consisted in giving to ZNAK, a group of Catholic parliamentarians which had been formed in 1957 by independent Catholics under the leadership of the deputy Stomma, the permission to open a publishing house. The men of ZNAK represented a middle course between *Pax* and the church and worked for a better understanding between church and state. They enjoyed and continue to enjoy the support of the cardinal.

3. A Continuing War of Attrition

The fight between church and state continued in a number of individual cases. There was, for example, the vexing problem of the limitation of the Catholic press. The Catholic church published 63 magazines, of which four-fifths were controlled by the episcopate. They appeared in a total edition of only 600,000. There was also the refusal of the state to return the property of *Caritas* and to permit *Caritas* to function under the auspices of the church. Until the present day *Caritas* remains under the tight control of the state. By founding a circle of patriotic priests willing to cooperate with the state-controlled *Caritas* (1960) the government made it clear that it possessed the power to organize once more, if need be, opposition groups within the church.

The Catholic University of Lublin, founded in 1918 and closed in 1939 by the Germans, had been opened again in September 1944. It was the only Catholic University behind the Iron Curtain. Its financial needs were met by a society of friends of the university, a society that numbered about 70,000 members, and by collections which were made three times annually in all the parishes throughout the land. The government continued to permit this university to grant academic degrees, but in competition with it the state opened a secular university, also at Lublin. The Catholic University, however, was able to continue its work despite this handicap and at the beginning of 1960 it numbered 1,700 students and 225 scholars. Its central library had increased to over 1,000,000 volumes. At the end of 1959 the state suddenly froze the assets of the university in the amount of one and a half million zloty. The reason given for this action was that the university had not been able to pay an assessment of 3,000,000 zloty in back taxes for the years 1950 to 1954. However, the decree freezing the assets of the university was lifted within 24 hours. The state also postponed the reopening of the faculties of law and of social sciences that the church had requested and which had been closed down before the rise of Gomulka to power. On the other hand, the church was able to get the permission of the government to close the schismatic Polish Academy for Catholic Theology at Bielani in January 1958.

The above-mentioned demand to pay back taxes was the direct result of a secret decree by the government, issued on February 25, 1959, in which all privileges granted to the church after Gomulka's rise to power were abrogated. The decree stated that all income of the church was subject to a progressive tax scale which went as high as 60% of the church's income. Included in this taxation was also money which had been contributed for the support of the poor and for the building of new churches. With the passage of this decree, the church suddenly found herself burdened with a fantastic amount of back taxes. Also the clergy was hard hit, since there were grave material needs, especially in the rural parishes. At the end of 1957 there was a report from southern Poland that the majority of the rural priests were forced to do agricultural work since it was impossible for them to pay the taxes from their regular income and to make a living. Many priests were overworked. Most of them had not been able to buy a new clerical garb for many years. They were not willing to ask their parishioners for help because these parishioners were as poor as they were. According to official statistics, the average annual income of a priest was between 6,000 and 25,000 zloty while a common worker made between 15,000 and 35,000 zloty. The taxation decree was, however, not enforced except in the case of the Warsaw Jesuit Academy. But it remained a powerful threat to the church. The Jesuits conducted a theological school in Warsaw which was financed for the most part by foreign gifts. Now not only the contributions that were sent in were made subject to taxation, but also backtaxes for a number of years were collected. The result was that the Jesuit Order of Poland for all practical purposes became bankrupt. The government confiscated the entire possessions of the Jesuits. The headquarters of the order were taken over by the state, and the priests became dependent upon the mercy of the state.

The properties of the church in the former German territories had been administered by the Polish Catholic Church. Besides church buildings, which numbered more than 3,000—including many former German Lutheran churches—there were parish halls, parsonages, seminaries, convent schools, hospitals, old folks homes and other charitable institutions among them. On the basis of a decree passed on April 23, 1959, also these properties were declared to be the property of the state. The church was forced to conclude agreements with the state authorities permitting her to lease these buildings from the government. The rent which the church now had to pay for these properties was an additional heavy financial burden. Thus in the archdiocese of Breslau (Wroclaw) the priest of one congregation of 5,000 members had to pay 88,000 zloty, or about $4,000, per year for the use of a building which he, his chaplain, his organist, and his sexton were occupying. When he declared that he was not able to pay this sum, the authorities decreed that his private property should be auctioned off. In order to be able to pay this rent the church was permitted to have collections of money, but these collections in turn were subject to further taxation. The result was that in order to collect $4,000 the faithful were forced to give more than twice this amount to pay for the rent of the building. It was quite clear that these were unbearable burdens, and it was understandable that the church insisted that the secret taxation decree should be rescinded. But on July 16, 1961, the Sejm passed another law which declared that the state was the sole legal guardian of all properties in the Polish-administered former German territories.

Another law concerning military service for students of theology gave the government a weapon with which it could empty diocesan seminaries if it so desired. The decree was carried out in the diocese of Kielce where all students of theology were drafted. Bishop Kaczmarek of Kielce was considered an enemy of the state. Another decree placed all diocesan seminaries under the supervision of the Ministry of Education and gave them the status of vocational intermediate schools. Thus the state reserved the right to control these schools and their faculties. Until this time, however, the state has not made use of its right to interfere with the administration of the seminaries.

A violent controversy arose on the question of birth control. In 1955 Poland had had the highest birth rate in Europe, and the great increase in the population presented problems to the government that it could not solve. In order to decrease the surplus of births social abortion was legalized. Every doctor was given permission to carry out an abortion, the costs of which were charged to the state, if a woman declared to him that the expected child would be a social burden. In 1960 about 113,000 women made use of this permission. The actual number of abortions, however, was estimated by government sources to run as high as 600,000. Thus the surplus of live births was reduced from 19 per 1,000 in 1955 to 14.9 per 1,000 in 1960. The Roman Catholic Church rejected this social abortion without compromise. In a sermon which he preached on September 22, 1958, Bishop Kaczmarek said: "The children are being killed in the wombs of their mothers before their births. Mothers who agree to this murder should be called living coffins." In March 1960 Cardinal Wyszynski demanded in a pastoral letter that Catholic doctors should refuse to perform any abortions except those that were justified for urgent medical reasons. He stated that both women and their doctors should resist all pressure to destroy human life. He said: "We shall defend our cradles as our forefathers defended their native soil. The serious crisis in the economy of our country must never be used as a justification for murder." But the state refused to give in and church and state continued to battle about this issue.

Another heated controversy started around the person of Bishop Czeslaw Kaczmarek. In 1956 he had been released after the supreme court had proved that the verdict against him had been unjust. Throughout his career he had been the most aggressive and most outspoken of the Polish bishops. This was the reason for a letter written on June 5, 1959, by the State Secretary for Ecclesiastical Affairs, Jerzy Sztachelski, to the Polish episcopate. After enumerating a number of so-called illegal acts perpetrated by the bishop he informed the episcopate that the government had decided, on the basis of Article 7 of the decree of December 31, 1956, to forbid Bishop Kaczmarek the further exercise of his episcopal functions in Kielce. Bishop Kaczmarek proved that the accusations leveled against him were without foundation.

The Secretary of the Bishops' Conference, Bishop Choromanski, wrote to Sztachelski on June 19: "Neither the episcopate as a body nor the Primate of Poland with his special powers is in any position to appoint a bishop or to remove him from office. They are also not in a position to judge a bishop. The appointment and the removal of a bishop and the authority to judge him are reserved to the competence of the Holy See alone." Furthermore, he informed the Secretary for Ecclesiastical Affairs that the episcopate could not accept the statement that the decree of December 31, 1956, applied to this case. For in that decree the removal of bishops was not even mentioned. On the contrary, it had been agreed, Choromanski wrote, "that in case of clergymen whose activity is detrimental the state shall get in touch with the administration of the church to whom this clergyman is subject." The authority that is set above a bishop is not the Polish episcopate, but the Holy See. Choromanski closed his letter with these words: "The episcopate hopes that the government of the People's Republic of Poland will review its position and will change its decision. Otherwise such a decision would make the cooperation between state and church very difficult and would cause great resentment among the believers and the clergy."

By return mail Sztachelski answered that "the government has no choice but to ignore the contents of your letter which informs it of the decision of the episcopate. . . . I would like to emphasize especially that the government must insist that you carry out the decision which it has communicated to you on June 5." On June 29 Bishop Choromanski sent another letter to the Secretary for Ecclesiastical Affairs in which he stated: "The episcopate is not in a position to change its decision as it was outlined to you in our letter of June 19." On July 1 Secretary Szachelski wrote back: "I do not accept the declaration which you have given in your letter of June 29." Finally, on July 10, Bishop Choromanski lodged an official complaint with the Council of State: "The rescinding of the decision of the government concerning the removal of His Excellency Bishop Kaczmarek is requested since it is illegal and is based on false accusations." Pope John XXIII interfered personally by writing a letter to Bishop Kaczmarek, assuring him of his support. As a result Bishop Kaczmarek did not resign from his office. But he was ignored by the Communist government. The government refused to answer his letters and to give him permission to function as bishop. It withdrew from his diocese the printing permission of the diocesan quarterly and harassed him in many other ways. After a long tug of war, Cardinal Wyszynski found a temporary way out. In February 1960, he persuaded the bishop to take an indefinite leave of absence. The bishop entrusted the work to his auxiliary bishop and took up his residence in the resort town of Krynica in southern Poland in a boarding house run by nuns.

One of the most important and most annoying results of the church-state agreement as far as the Communists were concerned was the reintroduction of religious instruction in the schools which had been sanctioned by the state in a decree of December 8, 1956. The Minister of Education, Bienkowski, called it the most difficult problem in Polish cultural policies. He accused the church of engendering cases of intolerance and anger on the part of the faithful. He claimed that teachers had been discriminated against and maltreated on account of their secular views. The Warsaw paper *Trybuna Ludu* wrote on January 22, 1957, about a school in Zamosc where children refused to sit next to the daughter of the Communist Party secretary because she was, they claimed, "in league with the devil." The paper stated that such discrimination existed in many places. For this reason it could happen that even outspoken atheistic activists were compelled to send their children to attend religious instruction, especially in small towns and villages, in an environment which did not permit atheists to live in peace. In many classrooms crucifixes had been reintroduced by priests and even by zealous students. When school officials tried to remove them, there had been trouble. The communique of December 8, 1956, had permitted parents to indicate whether their children should participate in religious instruction. The result of this stipulation was that in 1957 and 1958 there were only 26 elementary schools out of a total of 23,223 schools, where no religious instruction was given. Of these 26 schools 16 were located in Warsaw. The Communist Party did its utmost to hinder the spread of religious instruction everywhere. The Society for Secular Schools, which had been promoted by the party, arranged lectures and indoctrination courses for young teachers and on a trial basis introduced a course in "Lay Ethics" as an elective in the schools. At the beginning of 1960 this society numbered 50,000 members, among them over 12,000 teachers. In October of the same year the membership had risen to 100,000 and the society had 5,000 local chapters. In the first five months of the year these chapters had arranged for the giving of 2,000 lectures. A so-called Parents' University was organized by the society to "raise the educational standard among parents."

The activities of the society were not without success. In June 1959 the number of schools where no religion was offered had increased to 452 and by October to 1,500. There were a number of schools where no religious instruction could be offered for lack of "qualified" teachers. On September 3, 1959, the bishops had warned in a pastoral letter: "Any limitation of our religious rights in the schools which we notice at this time is, without a doubt, against the will and intentions of the parents." In spite of this protest the number of schools where religious instruction was no longer available continued to increase. At the beginning of 1960 the government announced that over 800,000 students were enrolled in religionless schools. There were 2,700 secularized schools which increased in the following year to about 5,000. In most cases the parents were not even asked for their opinions.

Thus the government did its best to make religious instruction impossible. At the beginning of 1958 Minister of Education Bienkowski had issued a number of directives which, among other things, ordered the removal of religious symbols from the classrooms and forbade prayer before or after school. In August 1958, he had decreed that members of religious orders could give religious instruction only if they were properly qualified teachers. By this decree about 2,000 monks and nuns were disqualified from giving instruction so that it had to be discontinued in many schools. In the late summer of 1960 the government tried by devious ways to eliminate religious instruction altogether. The superintendents of schools were instructed to proceed on their own initiative and not to take umbrage under any specific order of the state. But the bishops noticed that the lists of teachers of religion which they had submitted in accordance with the state-church agreement to the various school superintendents were returned to them with the laconic notation that the schools in question had been "changed into secular schools by the decision of the school board." Bienkowski's successor, Minister Tulodziecki, further alarmed the church by announcing that he was introducing a new course called "Philosophic Propadeutics" which would include such subjects as "lay ethics, logic, and the science of religion."

At this juncture the episcopate decided to protest publicly in a pastoral letter which was to be read from Polish pulpits on September 18, 1960. They stated that they wanted to tell the faithful that the church was threatened by attacks of the godless "whose activity increases from month to month and who fight against the church of God with their inhuman fanaticism. . . . Our faith and our Holy Mother Church are attacked without bounds; and if Catholics defend themselves, they are branded enemies of progress. These tactics are the insincere tricks designed by the godless." The pastoral letter contained protests against the expropriation of the church in the former German territories and the systematic elimination of religious instruction in the schools. It called upon the faithful: "For all of us the hour of witnessing has come." But the pastoral letter was never read. The episcopate was moved to change its mind by an argument which the Minister of Ecclesiastical Affairs, Sztachelski, submitted to Bishop Choromanski. On September 20, two days before the planned reading of the pastoral letter, there was a meeting of the United Nations at which Gomulka wanted to propose peaceful coexistence and to warn against the danger of German nationalism. He wanted to demand the recognition of the Oder-Neisse Line. The minister asked the episcopate whether they intended to undermine Gomulka's position by reading a pastoral letter from the pulpits. The bishops answered that they did not want to do such a thing and, as a patriotic gesture, withdrew the letter from circulation. The state, however, showed no gratitude for this friendly gesture of the church. A short time later, on July 14, 1961, the Sejm decreed the complete abolition of all religious instruction in the schools. The Catholic deputy, Mazowiecki, protested against this decree with great fervor. He argued that the state had forsaken the principle of the secularized neutral school since it demanded that all children should be indoctrinated in the scientific materialistic ideology of Marxism-Leninism. He demanded that a paragraph should be added to the decree which would permit religious instruction outside of the regular school hours. He also demanded a guarantee for the continued existence of Catholic private schools. The Communist deputy, Adrzej Werblan, assured him that no one who desired religious instruction for his children would be hindered in having this opportunity now or later. But he insisted that the Polish school must be a secular school. It must also become a socialist school.

Whether this change-over of the Polish school system to purely socialistic indoctrination will succeed is a different question. The Warsaw correspondent for the *Frankfurter Allgemeine Zeitung,* H. Stehle, prophesied: "The school in Poland will have as little Communist influence as it has had during the past 15 years. On the contrary, it will become an ideological void, as has become the whole public life in Poland. Who nowadays is interested in Marxist doctrines and its empty slogans?" As proof Stehle gave the results of a poll that was conducted in the Cracow high school which indicated that the favorites of young Poles were James Dean and Robert in Hemingway's *For Whom the Bell Tolls,* and that the favorite authors were Steinbeck, Huxley, Sartre, Camus, and Kafka. A poll conducted at the same time in Cracow's intermediate schools indicated that only 0.5% of the girls and 0.8% of the boys called themselves enemies of religion. On the other hand, among these students, whose ages ranged from 13 to 18 years, 80% of the boys and 89% of the girls indicated that they went to church. Of the girls 14.8% and of the boys 8.0% stated that they were "deeply religious and regularly practicing Catholics." Another 69.2% of the girls and

74.9% of the boys called themselves believers who were practicing their Catholic faith in varying degrees.

The constant arguments which, for example, were raised by the question of religious instruction in the schools, were not only fought out among the highest authorities, but very often on the lower level. They created an atmosphere of tension which often vented itself in tumults. It became clear to the state that the Catholics were ready to revolt when provoked. Besides smaller altercations and physical attacks there were some serious rebellions throughout Poland. We shall mention only a few. On Jasna Gora ("Mountain of Light") near Czestochowa (Czenstochau) there stands the Monastery of the Black Mother of God. It is a national shrine and is annually visited by hundreds of thousands of the faithful. It contains a painting of the Black Mother of God by an early Italian master. This painting is alleged to produce miracles. It is unveiled every morning to the sound of trumpets and is put back every evening with the same ceremony. On July 21, 1958, a state prosecutor accompanied by several policemen appeared at the monastery to carry out a search. Not only did his men confiscate the publications of the episcopate which were deposited in the printery of the monastery without permission by the state censors, but they also rifled the private archives of the cardinal and confiscated what they claimed was anti-Communist literature, among it a new edition of a book first published in the 1930's under the title *Acts of Miracles and Grace* in which the miraculous salvation of Poland from the Soviets in 1920 was recorded. The action of the prosecutor caused a demonstration by the pilgrims assembled in the courtyard of the monastery. When the demonstrators showed inclinations to beat up the police, the prosecutor called for a company of the state militia. The latter broke open the gate of the monastery, beat the pilgrims with riot sticks, and liberated the embattled prosecutor and his policemen. This raid was considered an insult to the Black Mother of God. Cardinal Wyszynski ordered that all the faithful should daily ask the Mother of God for her forgiveness. This instruction was faithfully carried out throughout Poland. Through negotiations the controversy concerning censorship was removed. The cardinal ordered that all printing machines and mimeographs must leave the monasteries and other sacred places. Publications of the church were henceforth submitted to censorship, but letters meant exclusively for the clergy remained free from censorship.

In a country which had suffered great devastations through the war and had to cope with a large increase in population and the establishment of numerous new settlements the need for new church buildings had become very great. But the state made construction of churches very difficult, claiming that lack of materials made new constructions practically impossible. But the underlying reason for the refusal of building permits was always ideological. In the district of Oppeln (Opole) two-thirds of all church building projects were abandoned without explanation. In defiance of these orders most priests and congregations continued to build. There were large-scale demonstrations in eastern Poland when a church that had been built without a building permit was torn down. Very serious outbreaks by embittered Catholics occurred in Krasnik near Lublin. For this so-called Socialist Model City, which numbered 11,000 inhabitants and which had been built around a new industrial plant, the state had planned no church building. The Catholics helped themselves by erecting a small altar in a nearby forest. At various times the church warned the authorities that their refusal to have a church erected in Krasnik would lead to serious difficulties. On June 28, 1959, the Catholics of Krasnik expected the visit of a priest. Numerous people had gone to the altar during the previous days, had decorated it and built a temporary roof over it. In the evening of June 28 when several hundreds of the faithful came to the altar to pray, they found the place blocked by ropes which had been strung by the police. The decorations on the altar and the roof had disappeared. The faithful now marched to the city hall and demanded the return of the materials that had been removed. On their way to the city hall they were joined by hundreds of others who had just come from attending a movie. The excitement quickly increased, and suddenly rocks were seen flying into the windows of the police headquarters and of the Communist Party offices. The crowd completely wrecked the interior of these buildings while the members of the state militia were forced to barricade themselves on the top floor. It became necessary to send reinforcements from Lublin, which dispersed the crowds with tear gas and jets of water.

Even more serious were certain occurrences which took place at the end of April 1960 at Nowa Huta near Cracow. Here, too, there was a new industrial settlement with some 100,000 inhabitants who were working in the great iron works. Built as the First Socialist Industrial City it was designed to be a city "without God." But after the October revolt of 1956 a workers' delegation from Nowa Huta had forced Gomulka to give his reluctant permission for the building of a church. The city fathers in cooperation with the church administration selected a fitting building site in the neighborhood of a theater on the Marx-Lenin Square of Nowa Huta, and architects were instructed to submit blueprints for a church seating 4,700 worshipers. The church's tower was to be 83 meters high. The population declared its willingness to bear the costs of the construction through private donations. The blueprint was accepted by the city fathers, but the permission to begin with the building was postponed from week to week. In the meantime a temporary cross had been erected on the building site in 1957 and it had been consecrated by the Archbishop of Cracow. Then suddenly in 1959 the city fathers announced that the church would have to be built elsewhere because the building site was needed for a new school. The pastor of the village of Bienczyce, which was on the outskirts of Nowa Huta, was requested to remove the consecrated cross. He refused. On April 27, 1960, workers were instructed to remove the cross. When they arrived at the building site they were maltreated by irate women who ran out of their houses and made it impossible for them to carry out their instructions. Their machinery was totally destroyed. The women now placed a watch around the cross. In the evening thousands of people came together, sang hymns, and lighted consecrated candles. The city fathers reacted with acts of terror. While the women who were protecting the cross against desecration put cooking utensils on their heads to protect themselves against the police attack and continued to sing hymns, their husbands who had come to protect their wives began singing the Internationale, thus making it impossible for the police to continue their attack. The city fathers now decided to turn off the electric current. But this did not help matters. Juvenile delinquents had infiltrated the excited crowd, looking for an excuse to start a general revolt. They now stormed the police station, burned the places where the Communist papers were being sold, plundered stores, and tried to burn down the building of the National Council. The result was that numerous persons were injured. The damage to property was estimated at over 1,000,000 zloty. But the cross remained standing where it was and was later separated from the building site of the new school by a high fence.

A month later there were grave disturbances in the Silesian city of Grünberg (Zielona Gora). Here the fight broke out in a house that had belonged to the Evangelical Church and was now serving as a Catholic old folks home. The right of ownership of this building was claimed by the state, and the city fathers designated three rooms and one assembly hall for the use of an atheistic society, a musical band, and an association of old-age pensioners. The senior priest of the Catholic congregation, Miehalski, refused to surrender the rooms, organized the signing of petitions, and argued against the city ordinance from the pulpit. The city fathers tried to put the congregation before a *fait accompli* by sending a group of workers to the home who were instructed to renovate its interior. But these workers were thrown out bodily by the angry inmates of the home. When a number of young people became involved in the arguments a general melee ensued. Two police cars were burned and several public buildings were attacked. The disturbances continued throughout the day until evening when police reinforcements were able to subdue the masses with tear gas.

On June 24, 1960, another bloody revolt took place at Gleiwitz (Gliwice). Here, too, it had been the question of erecting a new church. A wooden cross was standing on the building site. When police and Communist functionaries tried to remove the cross, they had the misfortune of arriving at the conclusion of the morning Mass. The priests and a number of the faithful placed themselves in front of the cross. They were attacked in force by the police who used their sticks and were beaten mercilessly until they fled into a nearby church. Here they held a prayer vigil.

Occurrences of this type were stopped by the state in 1960. They had given a warning to Warsaw that there were certain limitations beyond which the state should not go in its fight against the church. If these limitations were not observed, then the faithful were ready to answer force with force. Since the Catholics were in the overwhelming majority, the Communist Party was dependent upon their good will and their cooperation. The leadership of the church, too, for ecclesiastical and patriotic reasons, was not interested in a complete break with the state. Therefore, although there were repeated attacks and always new conflicts between the church and state, the two opposing parties were not interested in carrying their controversies too far. They continued to fight each other, but they always left a way open for reconciliation. They continued to meet around the conference table to help extinguish the fires that had been started. Their war was a constant partisan war, mitigated by the will to coexist. This war may continue until the political and spiritual climate in Poland has changed to such a degree that both the church and the Communist Party no longer deem it necessary to proclaim peaceful coexistence. At that time the battle for survival will start in earnest.

B. PROTESTANTISM

Polish Protestantism had become the victim of Nazi race policies and of the events occurring after World War II. Before the war there had been about a million Protestants within the boundaries of prewar Poland who were members of seven denominations of German, Polish, and Ukrainian provenience. Since 1921 an Evangelical Theological Faculty had been connected with the University of Warsaw. The main struggle of the Protestants before World War II had centered around the desire of the German congregations to remain German. They had resisted all attempts to Polonize them. After 1939 all Protestants, including the German congregations, were suppressed by the ruthless policy of the Nazis against the conquered country, especially in the so-called Warthegau, carved out of Polish territory, which was completely dechristianized. Later the Protestant churches lost heavily through the expulsions of the Germans from Poland and through the surrender of large Polish areas in the Ukraine to the Russians. As a result of the policy of reuniting families who had been separated by the war—a policy that was inaugurated in 1955—the emigration of Protestants continued and led to further decreases in the congregations.

In addition to these 1,000,000 Protestants living in the Poland of 1939, there were millions of Lutherans and other Protestants living in Silesia, Pomerania, and East Prussia who were expelled in 1945 and 1946. This created a great void, and the former Protestant villages and cities were taken over by Catholics who were resettled in the newly-won territories by the government.

In 1957 the Protestants who were united in the Ecumenical Council of Churches in Poland listed the following memberships:

Evangelical Church of the Augsburg Confession	175,000
Polish Catholic Church (Old Catholics)	95,400
Methodists	15,000 to 20,000
Mariovites	33,000
Union Church (including independent congregations, Free Brethren, Decided Christians, Evang. Christians, Pentecostals, Church of Christ)	7,250
Baptists	6,000
Reformed Church	5,000

But in 1961 Bishop Dr. Wantula listed the membership for the Evangelical Church of the Augsburg Confession (Lutheran) as only 115,000 and the other smaller groups as 20,000.

According to these reports the Lutheran Church consisted of 131 congregations divided into six districts. To these 131 key congregations about 150 filial congregations and 102 preaching stations must be added. The church was served by 114 pastors. Her publishing house published religious literature and a semimonthly magazine, *Zwiastun*. The theological training of future pastors was carried on at the Christian Theological Academy of Chylice near Warsaw which had been established after the separation of the Evangelical Faculty from the University of Warsaw in 1955. At this academy also the ministers of the other minority churches, including the Orthodox Church, were trained. There were about 100 students enrolled. The Lutheran Church joined the World Council of Churches and the Lutheran World Federation. She was strongly supported by both agencies and was not hindered in her work in any way. The state even made available to the church the means to take care of the Germans who were still living in Poland. It helped the church to restore some valuable church buildings, e.g. the Christopher Church in Breslau (Wroclaw). Pastors' salaries were very low, because their congregations were poor. The church was suffering from the usual needs of the diaspora, above all, from lack of pastors, from overwork through religious instruction and the great distances between the congregations, from lack of theological training facilities, from lack of literature, and from the problem of mixed marriages. Despite her poverty and weakness, the church maintained her own Deaconess Motherhouse at Dziegielow, four Old Folks Homes and two orphanages.

Polish Protestantism has not been involved in controversies between the state and the Catholic Church. The Protestants are only a small minority without political importance. It was sufficient to them that the state gave them the opportunity to exist as a minority in a Catholic environment. It must be said that over against former centuries when she was suppressed by the overpowering pressure of the Catholic Church, the Protestant church of Poland considered her present condition as a measure of liberation.

At a meeting of the Lutheran synod in 1951, Bishop Karol Kotula had declared that the position of the Lutheran Church was now more favorable than ever since the days of the Reformation. There was no longer a privileged church in Poland as in the past. The church was assured of complete freedom in the administration of her affairs within the laws established by the state. The former suppression of the Protestant minority by the Catholic Church had forced the Protestants to reject Rome and to feel profound suspicion toward her. For centuries the Catholics had equated the terms Protestant and German as they had equated the terms Orthodox and Russian, and this attitude continued after World War II. The Catholics have shown very little inclination to cultivate the good will of the Lutherans. A Polish Lutheran pastor stated the conditions between the churches in one sentence: "The Catholic Church rejects us; the Cardinal treats us with contempt." When the famous Evangelical Trinity Church in Warsaw was destroyed by Nazi bombs in 1939, the Catholic Church promised help. In 1958, when it was rededicated, the Cardinal did not even bother to send a word of greeting.

Only very recently the ice seems to be melting. There are a few Catholic theologians who have contacted Protestant congregations and pastors to engage in a brotherly dialogue with them.

CHAPTER THREE

CZECHOSLOVAKIA

A. THE ROMAN CATHOLIC CHURCH

"In contrast to the Poles only a few Czechs would be willing to mount the barricades to fight for religion, and not even many priests would be willing to do so. This is a fact which has hurt the church's creditability. Therefore, in Czechoslovakia the Communists found fertile soil when they tried to reeducate the church." These sentences written by a reporter for the *Frankfurter Allgemeine Zeitung* made it clear that there was and still is a different spiritual climate in Czechoslovakia as compared to the strong spirituality of the Poles. The Czech Catholic Church had been decaying for a long time when it was confronted by the challenge of Communism.

This weakness of the church was the result of historical developments. There was also a marked difference between the church in Czechia, which included Sudetenland, Bohemia, and Moravia, and the church in Slovakia. The history of the church in Sudetenland, Bohemia, and Moravia had been full of crises. It had been strongly influenced by the work of John Hus and the Hussite Wars of the 15th century, the Reformation of the 16th, and the Thirty Years' War of the 17th. Later it had been deeply influenced by the splendor of Catholic baroque and the ice age of Rationalism, by Josephinism, Liberalism, and the Catholic restoration of the 19th century. It was also influenced by the continuous struggle between the Germans and the Czechs. Around 1900 about 90% of the Czechs had been Roman Catholics and 97% of the Sudeten Germans on the fringes of Bohemia and Moravia professed the same religion. But the activities of the anti-Catholic forces never

came to rest. When the Austro-Hungarian empire of the Hapsburgs was destroyed in 1918, this anti-Roman activity broke forth
with renewed power. A movement of large-scale apostasy got
under way. About 800,000 Roman Catholics left their church and
formed a Czechoslovak National Church. They used the vernacular
in the liturgy, outlawed celibacy among the priests, and even proclaimed Unitarian doctrines; e.g., they often rejected the divinity
of Christ. In the cities and the industrial areas there was a strong
swing to irreligion. Thus a total of about 15% of the entire population of Czechia left the Roman Catholic Church. When the census
of 1930 was taken, only 73.8% of the Czechs and 91.5% of the
Sudeten Germans claimed membership in the Catholic Church.
The expulsion of some 3,000,000 Sudeten Germans after the Second
World War meant a further tremendous loss to the Catholic
Church. Apostasy among the Czechs who remained in the country
continued unabated. But in Slovakia, where the Catholic population had not been exposed to the same indifferentism and anti-
clericalism as in Bohemia and Moravia, the church retained her
strong influence, although she had lost face through her close cooperation with the Nazis. The president of the Nazi puppet government of Slovakia had been a Catholic priest, Msgr. Tiso.

1. The Ascendancy of the State over the Church

During the first post-war years the Communists had been only
part of a coalition government which included many other parties.
But they had occupied a strong position from the very start. Thus
it was inevitable that soon tensions would arise between church
and state. An old law against the abuse of the pulpit for propaganda against the state was exhumed and reactivated. A number
of priests were arrested because they had openly criticized Communist doctrine. A pastoral letter by the bishops complained bit-
terly that under the pretext of national renewal outrageous injustices had been perpetrated against the church. The bishops demanded a guarantee of freedom of religion and the right for
Catholics to live according to the dictates of their conscience. They
stated: "We cannot be silent when our young people are influenced

ideologically and when a one-sided doctrine is proclaimed officially in the textbooks of our schools."

By a *coup d'état* in February 1948 the Communist gained complete power. The Archbishop of Prague, Joseph Beran, in a letter addressed to the Communist Minister of Justice voiced the desire for an agreement between the State and the Holy See, since until that time only a *modus vivendi* between church and state had existed. He wrote: "We thank you for the promise that nothing will happen to disturb the good relationship between church and state. Nevertheless, we must call your attention to grave interferences which we cannot accept. The rights of the church have been violated, especially by the brutal confiscation of church buildings and institutions. Priests, monks, and nuns have been deprived of their work. In the same breath we must also mention that the majority of Catholic publications have been forbidden and that Catholic associations have been hampered in their activities." On his part, the archbishop assured the state that the church would remain aloof from the parties and would devote herself exclusively to religious tasks.

At first the government tried to gloss over these conflicts and to awaken the impression that it was friendly to the church. It accepted chaplain Joseph Plojhar of Budweis, who was not a member of the Communist Party, as Minister of Health and invited the clergy to work together with the state. Repeatedly the state issued reassuring declarations concerning freedom of religion and of religious education, but the actions of the government contradicted these assurances. The *Law Concerning Soil Reform* which was promulgated in March 1948 declared the confiscation of the property of the church, which amounted to about 320,000 hectares. The *Law Concerning Education* which was promulgated on April 21, 1948, prepared the way for the abolition of religious instruction in the schools. The law gave the individual government officers the right to work out details for the application of this law, apparently in a desire to establish the sole authority of the state over the extent of religious instruction. All church schools and Catholic pedagogical institutes were suppressed. A new curriculum for the elementary and high schools based all education on Marxist-Leninist materialistic ideology.

But at the same time the government showed a friendly interest in the church toward the outside. When there was a major church celebration the government was usually represented by a cabinet minister. For example, at the consecration of the Archbishop of Olmütz (Olomouc), Matocha, two government ministers were presented. When the Communist dictator, Gottwald, was elected President of the Republic, the government requested that a *Te Deum* should be sung in the Cathedral of St. Vitus in Prague, and atheist Gottwald himself attended the service. But the bishops were not deceived. At the beginning of 1948 they instructed their priests and catechists that they should keep aloof from political activities and threatened those of the clergy who disobeyed with suspension. On May 21 Archbishop Beran protested in a letter to Minister Plojhar and demanded that he should resign from his government office. Soon after the election of May 30, 1948, open conflict between church and state broke out. Archbishop Beran laid down six basic principles for the attitude of the church and her priests to the state which included not only a fine distinction between loyalty to the state and political non-interference, but also differentiation between the state and the ideology which the state was sponsoring. At the same time Beran announced that Plojhar and two other priests, who were members of the Slovak state government, had been suspended from their priestly office. On June 18 the government demanded that the publication of this letter and of the suspension of the ministers should not be carried out, otherwise, it said: "We shall send our workers into the streets." But Beran refused to capitulate. On June 20 the pastoral letter was read from the pulpits, and the announcement of the suspension of the three disobedient priests was nailed to the church doors.

In the middle of January 1949, the episcopate in a joint declaration to the government declared: "In spite of the promise of religious freedom an attack has been opened against the church and religion which is developing along the same line as the well-known attacks in other countries. The declaration referred especially to the interference by the government with the work of the church administration; the suspicion generated against those members of the clergy who did not participate in political demonstrations; the limitations placed on Catholic schools and charitable institutions, on the Catholic press, on religious organizations, and on public meetings. Finally, it declared that the bishops could not give their consent to the unconditional confiscation of church property in connection with the soil reform because the existence of a number of religious orders was dependent upon the property which had been confiscated.

In a joint pastoral letter written in the middle of May 1949 the bishops again expressed their misgivings. They said that the Catholic press had been gradually silenced and the official church publications, which even during the Nazi occupation were not suppressed, had been forbidden. Every Catholic book had been subjected to advance censorship, even prayer books. In Moravia and Slovakia not a single church school remained open; in Bohemia the secularization of schools had made rapid progress. In several areas the collection of money by the church had been forbidden although the church was completely dependent on the free-will offerings of the faithful after all other sources of income had been dried up. The bishops refused for all future times to declare their loyalty to the government if the occasion for disobedience should arise. Archbishop Beran furthermore protested that the government had recently published an official magazine for the Catholic Church which, he claimed, was the sole right of the church authorities. He told the clergy to pay no attention to it. Anyone who cooperated in this publication was threatened by the archbishop with excommunication. In a letter to the President of the Catholic People's Party, Minister Petr, the archbishop denounced the presumption of the party to call itself Catholic and threatened with excommunication those who supported the measures of the government against the church.

During the Communist Party Congress of May 28, 1949, two government ministers answered these charges. They declared that the state had to insist on its right to educate all children in the doctrine of Leninism. They declared that the state would interpret any attack against education in the scientific materialistic ideology as an attack against the state. The ministers also declared that the government was planning to issue a decree for the establishment of state kindergartens which would become obligatory for all children. Immediately the government began to take an inventory of all church property and other sources of income. Archbishop Beran, on the other hand, instructed the parishes to give no information to the state about their income and property values.

During the next few weeks the attacks against Archbishop Beran began in earnest. On Corpus Christi Day 1949 he took leave of a large crowd at the monastery of Strahov in which he said that he anticipated his arrest. He stated: "I do not know how many more times I shall be able to talk to you in the future. Probably very soon all kinds of slanders will be broadcast about me on the radio. They will tell you that I have made a confession or some similar lies. . . . Whatever may happen, do not believe that I have capitulated. I come before you and I swear that I shall never sign an agreement of my own free will which violates the laws of the church." On June 19 during a sermon in the St. Vitus Cathedral in Prague the archbishop was rudely interrupted. He declared that the demonstrations had been prearranged. He stated that he had received warnings on June 18 from private sources that the Communists of Prague had received orders to leave their factories and go to the cathedral. The government issued a brochure in which it declared that Beran had planned to preach a revolutionary sermon in order to be arrested, because the church needed a martyr. But instead of arresting him the state police had gone to his palace, the government said, "to be at his disposal and to protect him against the wrath of the faithful." This protective custody by the police was the beginning of his imprisonment and of his isolation which continued for almost 15 years. It was only recently removed. Beran was not allowed to receive any visitors. His mail was confiscated, as were also the funds of the archdiocese and the 50 hectares of land that had been granted to the church after the soil reform. A functionary of the Communist Party occupied his office. Despite this supervision the archbishop succeeded in smuggling out a letter from his strictly guarded palace in the Hradcanin Castle. This letter was read in many churches of Prague at the beginning of September. In it he declared that "he who refuses to betray God cannot be a traitor to his country and to his people. Let all the faithful pray that the nation will return to God as the prodigal son returned to his father. We are so insignificant and helpless in the midst of these raging and satanic powers. But even though we are powerless we can help through our attitude to keep the evil from our people."

The government prepared definite charges of treason and treasonable connections with foreign powers against the archbishop. Furthermore, it stated that he had been guilty of preparing actions against the state. The Roman Catholic clergy passed a resolution in July 1949 and rejected the demand of the government that they denounce Archbishop Beran and the Vatican. They declared: "In loyalty we stand with our bishops and our archbishop and we shall continue to do so even if we are persecuted." They stated that their resolution "was dictated solely by our conscience and was not written at the request of the Catholic hierarchy." The resolution was read in numerous churches throughout Czechoslovakia.

The decree which the Vatican issued against Communism at that time was answered by the Czech Communist Party with a circular letter (July 16, 1949) in which it called upon the people to fight "without compromise against our greatest enemy, the church." The directives of the Communists gave three instructions for action: (1) Remove all ties between the clergy and the Vatican; (2) Isolate the bishops and the archbishop from the people; and (3) Incite the population against Archbishop Beran. In a speech given on July 25 Prime Minister Zapotocky declared: "If the pope wants to excommunicate all Communists, he will have to excommunicate the whole Czechoslovak nation. We never considered the alternative Rome or Moscow. If, however, through actions by one side a decision concerning that alternative should be forced upon us, we shall leave no doubt about the answer which our people will give. We will stand up for Moscow, Stalin, and Socialism." The government informed the clergy, the religious orders, and the parishes that there would be reprisals if the decree of excommunication issued by the Vatican were carried out.

In order to split the church a *Catholic Action* movement which was subservient to the state was founded and was given permission to print its own paper, *Catholic News*. A secret pastoral letter by the bishops warned the parish priests not to support this organization. The Minister of Justice, Cepicka, in the middle of July 1949 claimed that despite this letter 2,000 clergymen had joined the Catholic Action movement. The secretary of the Papal Nuncio, de Liva, who was expelled in 1950, later claimed that only 17 to 18 priests belonged to Catholic Action. In 1949 the Holy Office condemned Catholic Action, and the *Catholic News* was put on the Index on July 22, 1955.

State commissars were now assigned to all bishops (June 1949) who were responsible for the administration of the dioceses and who used the official seals of the bishops. In spite of this close supervision, pastoral letters were still being sent secretly to the parishes. Therefore, at the end of June, the government published three new decrees: The clergy were forbidden to hold meetings without the express permission of the government; all pastoral letters and other communications which might cause unrest among the people were ordered to be submitted to the state for pre-publication censorship; and all ecclesiastical punishment which had been ordered by the church for political reasons was declared invalid. Priests who had been disciplined by the church were promised the support of the state.

In violation of the decree by the government that all new bishops had to be approved by the state, two new bishops, Lazik and Probozny, were consecrated on August 19, 1949, by Archbishop Matocha in Tyrnau (Trnava) in Slovakia. The government had tried to make access to the city impossible by stopping all trains and blocking the highways. Despite these efforts, over a hundred priests and about 12,000 lay people participated in the solemnities. Besides Archbishop Matocha, there were ten other bishops present. On the same day they addressed a memorandum to the government in which they declared their readiness to resume negotiations concerning the relationship of church and state and to take an oath of loyalty under the following conditions: (1) complete restoration of freedom for Archbishop Beran; (2) removal of the state commissars appointed by the government for the administration of the dioceses; (3) no more persecution of, and interference with, clergymen who were loyal to the church; (4) refusal by the state to support Catholic

Action; (5) removal of all propaganda publications against the church and the Vatican; and (6) no more arrests of priests who were carrying out the Vatican decree against Communism.

Now Archbishop Matocha, too, was placed under police surveillance. The entrance to his palace was occupied by security police who searched all visitors. He was forced to accept the company of a policeman whenever he drove his car, ostensibly for his own protection. In the meantime the government worked out a law for the control of the church. It was accepted on October 14, 1949, by parliament and became effective on November 1. The first part of the law declared that a State Office for Ecclesiastical Affairs would be established under the direction of a minister. It was to be his duty to see to it that the life of the church and freedom of religion would develop in accordance with the constitution of the state and on the basis of religious tolerance and equality for all denominations. The second part of the law dealt with the economic security of the church and of all religious organizations and made the clergy completely dependent upon the good-will of the state. Article I stated: "The state promises their personal salary to those clergymen of the churches and ecclesiastical communions who are active in the educational institutions of the church." Article VII declared that only such persons could serve as officers of religious organizations as were accepted by the state and had sworn an oath of loyalty. Any appointment, election, or nomination of such a person needed the previous acceptance by the state. Vacant positions had to be filled within 30 days, otherwise the state would take the necessary steps to insure the orderly care of the congregations, the administration of the parishes, and the education of the clergymen. Article IX made it mandatory for all religious organizations to publish a budget which had to be submitted for approval to the State Office for Ecclesiastical Affairs. Article X stipulated that "the state has the supervisory authority over the possessions of the church and of the religious communities." It also stated that ecclesiastical representatives had to submit a detailed compilation of the total property of the church to the state. Article XII declared: "The state is responsible for the support of the institutions for the training of clergymen."

After the promulgation of this law the first important issue to face the church was the matter of the loyalty oath of the clergy. The formula of the oath had the following wording: "I promise on my honor and conscience that I shall be loyal to the Czechoslovak Republic and its People's Democracy and that I shall do nothing that is detrimental to its interests, its security, and its integrity. As a citizen of the People's Democracy I shall honestly and sincerely carry out all duties which are incumbent upon me in the position which I occupy, and I shall support with all my strength the efforts toward reconstruction which are being made for the welfare of the people." The bishops made it clear that they would not swear this oath and would not accept their salaries from the state. They advised the lower clergy to accept the oath, however, but to add the following sentence: "If it is not in contradiction to the laws of God and of the church, and to human rights." Later this reservation was changed to read: "After I have become convinced that the government will not demand anything that is in contradiction to the law of God and to human rights." The administration of the oath then took place. According to *Catholic News* the overwhelming majority of the clergy (95%) added the reservation prescribed by their bishops. The bishops who had refused as a body to take the oath, soon weakened. In March 1951 it was announced that the four bishops of Kaschau (Caslov), Königsgrätz (Kralove), Leitmeritz (Litomerice), and Tyrnau (Trnava) and the two administrators of Kaschau and of the Czech part of the archdiocese of Breslau (Wroclaw) had taken the oath before Minister Fierlinger who had succeeded Cepicka during the summer of 1950. A similar solution was also found in the question of the payment of salaries by the state. In a pastoral instruction of November 17, 1949, the bishops demanded that the priests should be ready to renounce their salaries "if," they said, "anyone should demand a Judas-service as a compensation for the payment of your salaries. Under no circumstances must you become traitors." In a later instruction the bishops told the priests to accept their salaries with the following reservation: "I declare that I am ready to accept the salary because it is the law of the state. But with this acceptance of the salary I do not make any promises which are against my priestly conscience or against the laws of the church. I declare that the spiritual affairs of the church and the complete freedom of my priestly activities are more important than the material security of my personal life."

In a declaration of December 17, 1949, the bishops declared that the law of November 1 was in contradiction to the law of God. They referred especially to the provision that every kind of religious activity by the clergy could be carried out only with the consent of the state and also, they said, "to the right which the state has reserved to itself to make the necessary provision for the continuation of the pastoral care in the church." They pointed out that no priest was allowed to accept a spiritual office from anyone except his own bishop and that the church must insist on the right to organize new spiritual offices and not merely the privilege of being consulted in such cases. The strongest objections were raised against the stipulation of the law according to which the state could assign offices of the church to certain people without consulting the proper church authorities. The bishops stated: "Communist control of the contents of preaching and of religious instruction must be rejected. The stipulation of the decree that priests need Communist approval for the exercise of their religious functions is to be disregarded. Before assuming a new pastorate every priest must obtain the permission of his bishop." Further the bishops insisted that sacred objects like chalices and vestments should not be listed in the inventory demanded by the government. The bishops concluded: "If the government wants to start a new fight in this country of saints and martyrs, a great number of the faithful will be ready to sacrifice everything for the glory of God and for religious freedom."

The request of the bishops that the government should revise the law concerning the churches was rejected in extremely sharp words by Prime Minister Zapotocky. The Office for Ecclesiastical Affairs made use of its extraordinary powers in the field of education, of its control of the clergy, and of the right to persecute infringements against the law, and published a number of new decrees and limiting measures. In March 1950 it expelled the last representative of the Holy See, Ottavio de Liva, from Czechoslovakia. All pastoral letters and the entire correspondence of the bishops with the Vatican were subjected to strictest censorship. All seminaries for priests were placed under the supervision of Communist school inspectors. The *Caritas* organization was separated from the church and made autonomous, as it had been in Poland. It was placed under the direct control of the state and forced to discontinue much of its work. But in 1955 it still had 115 institutions with 9,300 beds. *Caritas* was authorized to publish books for the church and to provide materials for the requirements of church services. The bishops were more and more shoved to the sidelines. Their work was constantly interrupted. The last bishops' conference in Prague was closed by a policeman.

2. Elimination of the Bishops Loyal to the Pope

The episcopate loyal to the Pope was more and more eliminated during the following years and the bishops were replaced by men who had no ecclesiastical legitimacy, but were loyal to the Communist state. The first direct interference in the episcopate took place at Neusohl (Banska Bystrica). Here Bishop Skrabik had died on January 8, 1950. The cathedral chapter promptly elected its former vicar-general to become vicar of the diocese, but failed to ask the government for its approval as required by the law. An admonition by the Ministry for Ecclesiastical Affairs remained unanswered. The ministry now appointed Dean Jan Dechet to act as Ecclesiastical Administrator for the vacant diocese. The Vatican promptly excommunicated Dechet and ordered all believers to break off all contact with the usurper. The latter, however, refused to relinquish his office, appealing to his conscience. He stated: "I have accepted this appointment and I believe honestly and sincerely to have acted as a good priest and a good citizen." The cathedral chapter, which in the meantime had been packed by state-appointed canons, proceeded to elect Dechet vicar of the diocese.

At the end of February 1950 the bishops threatened to excommunicate all priests who without the approval of the church accepted offices entrusted to them by the state. The state answered this challenge to its authority by promulgating still another law (August 1, 1950) which contained the statement: "Everyone who, without the approval of the state, exercises the function of a pastor in a congregation or any other ecclesiastical organization, will be punished with a prison term not exceeding three years. Similar prison sentences will be imposed upon persons who exercise the office of pastor in a place where they have no state approval. Whoever appoints a person to exercise such functions in a church or a church organization without the approval of the state will be punished with a prison term from one to five years."

In March 1951 the state invaded the archbishopric of Prague. On March 8 the cathedral chapter of St. Vitus met, accepted the resignation of its vicar-general, Dr. Opatnry, and elected Canon Antonin Stehlik as Vicar-General. This cathedral chapter, too, had been changed in its composition by the fact that it had been forced to accept four progressive priests who had been appointed by the government. On March 10 imprisoned Archbishop Beran was removed from Prague. The government declared that he had been dismissed from office and expelled from the archdiocese on account of his negative attitude toward the law regulating state-church relationships. At the same time the government declared that the archdiocese was now vacant. When the new vicar-general took his oath, the government left no doubt that it considered him to be the legal successor of Beran. The former archbishop was first imprisoned at Rosalov Castle, but since foreign radio reports had made his place of confinement known, he was sent away to the remote concentration monastery Nova Rise in southern Moravia.

The Vatican again excommunicated all those who had been appointed by the government to administer the archdiocese of Prague and who had had a hand in the removal of Beran and in other anti-church measures. One of the first official acts of the new vicar-general was to remove the excommunication of Minister Plojhar which had been ordered by the former archbishop. Thus Plojhar, who was still a member of the Communist government, was able to celebrate Mass at Easter time. The government appointed Vicar-General Dechet of Neusohl (Banska Bystrica) bestowed upon Plohjar the title of Honorary Counselor for "extraordinary merits in the field of religious consolidation."

In February 1950 the Bishop of Budweis (Budejovice), Msgr.

Hluch, had rejected the appointment by the government of the fellow-traveling Joseph Buchta as his vicar-general. But the government proceeded to appoint Buchta over the protest of his bishop. The reason given for this appointment was that the bishop had neglected his duty to appoint a successor to his former vicar-general who had recently died. Buchta was promptly excommunicated by Rome, but assumed his office as if nothing had happened and, in the spring of 1951, appointed four other progressive priests to serve as canons. At the beginning of April 1952, he got rid of his bishop by instigating a trial which condemned the bishop for his negative attitude toward the law concerning the church. The bishop was expelled from his diocese. Buchta became absolute master of the diocese. When he celebrated Mass a few days after the expulsion of Bishop Hluch, the enraged faithful began to whistle in the church and the Mass had to be discontinued.

Also in Olmütz (Olomouc) the coordination of the church with the Communist state was enforced. Here Archbishop Matocha had at first fought energetically against the policy of the state, but after two years' internment and at the urging of Minister Fierlinger he was persuaded to appoint Joseph Glogar his vicar-general. At the installation of Glogar 11 other excommunicated priests were present to witness the installation of three state-appointed canons. In April 1952 Radio Prague announced that the archbishop had installed six canons who had been appointed by the state. The members of the old cathedral chapter had been arrested. Until his death in 1961 Archbishop Matocha was under strict police surveillance and was not allowed to leave his residence. He was able to communicate with his vicar-general only once a week in the presence of a commissar of the state.

In the fall of 1950 the auxiliary bishop of Spis was arrested, as was also the auxiliary bishop of Olmütz (Olomouc). The bishop of Leitmeritz (Litomerice) was condemned to 25 years in prison. When the bishop of Königsgrätz died in 1956 the state appointed a fellow-traveling priest to direct the affairs of the diocese. In Brünn (Brno) Vicar-General Joseph Kristek took over the government of the diocese as a trustee for the government. His bishop was exiled and detained somewhere in Czechoslovakia, as was also the former

Apostolic Administrator of Königsgrätz (Kralove). The Apostolic Administrator of Roznava in Slovakia, Bishop Proposnik, was deposed in 1953 because he had refused to take the loyalty oath to the government. Subsequently, in 1956, he is said to have declared that he recognized the validity of all Communist laws and received permission to assume his office again. Auxiliary Bishops Eltschkner of Prague and Tomasek of Olmütz were set free again after they had spent some time in concentration camps. A survey of the leadership of the Roman Catholic Church at the close of this period indicated that practically all dioceses were without legitimate ecclesiastical leadership. They were administered by vicars who had been elected under strict Communist supervision by their respective chapters. Each action of these state-approved vicars and each meeting of the diocesan chapters was supervised by government commissars, who were laymen, including former craftsmen and even atheists, who had no training in, or understanding of, canon law. They gave orders even to the highest church officials and directed all church activities, including the liturgy of the church and other matters.

During this period also the fate of the Greek Uniate Church in Slovakia was decided. These Uniates had been organized into the Diocese of Presov with about 400 priests. Like the Uniates of Romania and Carpatho-Russia they were now being incorporated into the Orthodox Church. On April 29, 1950, a council was convened at which the five priests and about 300 lay people present declared that they favored the return of the Uniate Church to the Orthodox Church and the jurisdiction of the Patriarch of Moscow over the church. Uniate Bishop Gojdic was arrested and about a hundred priests were imprisoned with him. The other priests were forced to continue their work and to care for the congregations which had become a part of the Orthodox Church. Any attempt to resign from their offices was interpreted as sabotage.

3. Against Clergy and Monasteries

The Roman Catholic clergy had suffered heavy losses through the expulsion of the German priests at the close of World War II.

Of the 6,000 priests who had been active in Bohemia and Moravia in 1940 over 1,800 were forced to leave the country. After the Communist take-over young priests were often arrested or forced to enter military service and after the promulgation of the law concerning state-church relationships the arrests among the remaining priests still further increased the pastoral shortage. At the beginning of 1951 over 2,000 priests were kept prisoners in eight concentration camps which had been set up exclusively for the clergy, while a number of other priests were lodged together with political prisoners in four other concentration camps. From reports by refugees it became known that another wave of arrests took place in March 1952, especially in Moravia, in the course of which over 300 priests were arrested. During an amnesty which was declared in May 1960, a total of 800 priests were released from prison, but only a few of them—in the archdiocese of Prague, for example, only four—were permitted to return to their former parishes. Most of them were placed in factories as common workers. Thus, at the beginning of the 1960's there were only 1,500 to 2,000 priests to care for the more than 3,000 parishes of the Roman Catholic Church in Bohemia and Moravia. Many churches had been closed or were decaying due to neglect. A reporter for the *Frankfurter Allgemeine Zeitung* reported at the time: "About half of the villages in Moravia and Bohemia do not have a priest, and where they are still allowed to function, they are wearing civilian clothing and are keeping their churches closed during the weekdays in order to keep them from being plundered. They are living with a few of the faithful like outlawed sectarians in a Ghetto. Even in places where there are several thousand Catholics we heard about a church attendance from between 20 and 30 people. Some priests told us: 'This year we had no wedding and no baptism.' Many churches are decaying unless they are being preserved by the government for their architectural value. They are standing empty, and in the church steeples loudspeakers have been installed which broadcast the bulletins of the local Communist Party."

It was not by chance that in these territories where the Catholic Church was declining the sects began to flourish. The Communist Party organ of northern Moravia, *Nova Svoboda,* reported angrily in January 1962, that a number of illegal sects were very strongly carrying on their work in the Czech industrial areas. It alleged that a number of these sects had their origin in the USA. They received most of their material support from abroad. Wrote the paper: "By way of West Germany and other countries large amounts of subversive literature, pamphlets, and messages which are directed against socialist countries, are being smuggled into Czechoslovakia."

Leading members of the clergy were brought to trial. In April 1950 there was a show trial in Prague against 10 prominent members of religious orders, among them two abbots of the Premonstratensians and the father provincial of the Jesuit Order. One of these men was condemned to life imprisonment, the others to long prison terms. They were found guilty of high treason because they had shown greater respect for the Pope than for the government and had not denied their close contact with the Vatican. At the end of November 1950, there was a further trial in Prague of nine high church officials in the dock. It was significant that several of the defendants freely confessed that they had been the tool of Western powers, had carried on espionage against the Czech state, and had committed other crimes worthy of severe punishment. All declared their guilt, and some demanded to be punished. The court meted out sentences that agreed with the self-accusations of the defendants. The Benedictine Abbot Opasek was condemned to life imprisonment, the Auxiliary Bishop Zela of Olmütz (Olomouc) to 25 years in prison, the Secretary General of Catholic Action, Mandl, also to 25 years in prison, two canons of St. Vitus Cathedral to 20 years, the Secretary of Archbishop Beran, Jan Boukal, to 18 years in prison. In February 1951 a show trial was conducted against Bishops Vojtassak of Spis, Buzalka of Tyrnau (Trnava), and the Uniate Bishop Vojtek of Presov. The latter was condemned to life imprisonment and the former to 25-year prison terms. In 1956 they were transferred to the former headquarters of *Caritas* where they remained under house arrest. The former vicar-general of Spis, Joseph Tomanocy, who had taken over the administration of the diocese after the condemnation of Bishop Buzalka, was also arrested. He was accused of having resisted the state-sponsored Catholic Action. Uniate Bishop Gojdic died in prison in 1960.

In order to make those priests who were permitted to remain in their parishes more pliable the State Office for Ecclesiastical Affairs instituted two-week training courses in which four main themes were discussed: "The Theory of Stalinist Marxism," "The Meaning of Christianity in a Socialist State," "The Duties of a Priest in the People's Democracy," and "The Socialist Structure of Czechoslovakia." The priests were assigned to these training courses by Communist district committees. In the discussions everyone was forced to give testimonies. On the basis of these testimonies the director of the institute reported to Prague concerning the attitude of individual priests. If the results of the reeducation were not sufficient, the priests were forced to attend additional training courses.

Also for the seminaries government-decreed courses were established. Future priests were now instructed in "The Bases of the Policies of the People's Democracy." This course was given by state-appointed lecturers. In August 1950 the government had taken over the selection and the education of the candidates for the priesthood. The diocesan seminaries were closed. In their place state seminaries were established at Prague, Leitmeritz (Litomerice), and Bratislava. They were administered by a director appointed by the state. The state outlined the course of studies and insisted that all future priests must do manual work and be instructed in the principles of Marxism. Above all, the state limited severely the number of young men who were admitted to these seminaries. For Leitmeritz (Litomerice), for example, only 25 candidates were admitted annually. Even before this time Bohemia and Moravia had been suffering from an acute shortage of priests. Now only 10% of the number who had been studying for the priesthood in 1939 were admitted to the seminaries. In the year 1955 26 priests were ordained at the Leitmeritz seminary. They were distributed among seven dioceses. The Diocese of Königsgrätz (Kralove) with 850,000 Roman Catholics received only one solitary new priest. In 1957 six new priests were ordained, but 36 died in that same year. In 1960 the number of new priests had increased to 21. The Bratislava seminary during that same year produced 12 new priests who were shared by five dioceses. The lack of candidates for the priesthood became the most pressing problem of the Roman Catholic Church.

The salary paid by the state to the priests was very small indeed. A newly ordained priest received only 680 koruna (crowns) monthly. After three years of service he received a 60 koruna increment and when he became chief pastor of a parish he received an increase of 200 koruna. From these amounts the state taxes were deducted. All these salaries were far below the wages paid to common workers. A priest in his twentieth year of service received 950 koruna or about $75.00 per month, while a worker got 1,000 to 1,300 koruna and a specially skilled worker 1,300 to 1,700 koruna. For this small consideration the state expected a high return. In practice all priests were prisoners of the Communist commissars who administered the dioceses and had to submit to the force placed above them. The Catholic *Schweizerische Kirchenzeitung* reported on May 21, 1959: "The echo of the church among the people is not as strong as in the other satellite countries. While the Slovaks make full use of their freedom of religion, the Czech must forever and again make decisions regarding participation in the life of the church. The Czech clergy are trying to make this decision easy for the faithful by accepting all the concessions which are demanded of them in the political and ideological fields."

The religious orders had to feel the whole brunt of the state's attack against Catholicism. It began in August and September 1949, when the monasteries were accused of activities against the state. When the Communists invaded the monasteries they "found" weapons everywhere. In the show trial against 10 superiors of religious orders in 1950—which was mentioned above—the Communists used all the lies and slanders they could muster. The Franciscan Dr. Jan Urban, one of the best preachers and religious authors of Czechoslovakia, was called "an agent of the Gestapo." After the verdict against the 10 men had been pronounced on April 5, 1950, the monasteries and convents were attacked during the night of April 13-14. Monks and nuns were put on trucks and carted off. They were allowed to take only the most necessary item with them. On April 18 it was announced officially that monks and nuns had committed crimes against the laws of the state. Since many monasteries had been half empty during the years of the worst housing shortage, the monks and nuns were concentrated into central monasteries in which they were allowed to live their religious lives while their former monasteries and convents were used to help alleviate the acute housing shortage of the people. The superiors of the former monastic communities were separated from their former subordinates. The younger and more pliable members of the orders were sent to reeducation centers where they were educated in Marxist ideology. Most of the former monks and nuns eventually became common laborers. They were strictly forbidden to engage in church activities and to communicate with other former members of their orders.

The orders for nuns which had been engaged in nursing were not permitted to recruit new members. Eventually the sisters were removed from all hospitals without any consideration for the needs of the patients. They were assigned to the state-controlled *Caritas* which sent them to old folks homes, to homes for the deaf-and-dumb, to the infectiously ill, and to the mental health hospitals. The state was very much concerned that they should have no contact with young people. They were often moved so that they would not come into close contact with people and influence them.

In order to enlist the clergy in the active service of Socialism the state-sponsored *Peace Committee of the Catholic Clergy* was founded on September 28, 1951, under the sponsorship of Minister Plojhar, the excommunicated but reinstated priest of the arch-diocese of Prague. At the time of the founding the Secretary General of the Peace Committee, Professor Joseph Benesch, wrote: "1,700 priests are meeting in Prague to demonstrate their unchanging loyalty to the church and to our young People's Democracy." He further stated that the commandment of Jesus Christ "Blessed are the peacemakers, for theirs is the kingdom of heaven" had brought these priests together to undertake their important work for peace. In rhapsodic phrases Benesch five years later praised the work which these peace priests had done for the Communist state. Said he: "Urged on by their pure Christian conscience and the sanctifying grace of the whole people, they can now reconstruct their lives upon the two alabaster pillars which are the basis for their spiritual and temporal happiness. . . . Everywhere the new will to live is bubbling over. The whole nation is running a race to find new happiness in a life which is fitting for those who have been created in the image of God." Christians, he stated, could be completely at home in this wonderful era, especially since nobody asked them to compromise the least of their beliefs.

The number of members belonging to the Peace Committee has never been ascertained. From Catholic estimates it appeared that 10 to 15% of the clergy had been organized in the movement and that all influential posts in the church had been taken over by them. According to a report published in the *Frankfurter Allgemeine Zeitung* by its reporter Stehle, nearly all Czech priests belonged to it, either voluntarily or through force of circumstances. The German *Herder Correspondence* reported in 1958 that "an anti-Roman climate is spreading within the church and it is spreading faster than in any other church behind the Iron Curtain." On the other hand, the *Herder Correspondence* warned against the assumption that the peace priests were unreliable. It stated: "Today there is in Czechoslovakia no other way to maintain the minimum care for the souls of the faithful than to accept the conditions laid down by the state." The Peace Committee published its own magazine, the monthly *Shepherd of Souls,* which promoted pastoral and scholarly education among the clergy.

The Peace Committee was very active. It arranged for peace congresses which were attended by large numbers of Catholic priests, in which political speeches were given and resolutions passed against the re-militarization of the German Federal Republic, against atomic tests, for the acceptance of the Polish Rapacki Peace Plan and for other worthy causes. The peace priests were actively working for the socialization of the country. They supported propaganda for the collectivization of agriculture, took part in discussions about the fulfillment of the Socialist year plans, and demanded that all Catholics cooperate loyally with the Communist government.

A further task assigned to the Peace Committee was the spreading of favorable news concerning the conditions of the Roman Catholic Church in Czechoslovakia. For this purpose the government used *The Bulletin of the Dioceses and Apostolic Administrations of Czechoslovakia* which was published "on behalf of the corps of bishops" by Bishop Dr. Joseph Karski of Kaschau (Caslov). This *Bulletin* with its news of church life in socialist Czechoslovakia was sent to numerous addresses throughout the world. In 1955 the Peace Committee also published a brochure in the leading West European languages with the title *God Be Praised*. It gave a survey of Catholic life in Czechoslovakia in which, it said, "our Holy Church can unfold her religious activities in complete freedom." Bishop Lazik of Tyrnau (Trnava) maintained that the state "has great understanding for the requirements of the Roman Catholic Church." He said that the state had given to the clergymen an adequate income and had spent $2,000,000 for the upkeep of church buildings. Bishop Karski emphasized that the clergy was fully conscious of its apostolic mission and that it was faithful to pope and church. He wrote: "In this spirit also the training of priests is being carried on in Czechoslovakia." He stated that the church considered it her duty to "help the faithful to find the right and proper solution for economic, social, and cultural problems and to lend a hand in the abolition of the weaknesses of our society."

In a letter to the Christians in the West, Bishop Lazik reported in 1955 about the church life in Tyrnau (Trnava). He wrote: "The teachings of Christ are proclaimed everywhere without interference, priests are permitted to preach publicly without being hindered, the Catholic press is supporting them in their work so that the life of the church can develop in all its richness and inwardness and that participation in the administration of the sacraments becomes a work of true devotion." Professor Benesch, the secretary-general of the Peace Committee, delivered a speech in the German Democratic Republic (1957) in which he declared: "If some people in foreign countries speak about the decaying religious life in our country, they are in error or are lying. At Christmas and Easter foreign visitors are surprised to see the unexpectedly high attendance in our churches during Mass." The Corpus Christi celebrations of 1957, he said, were a marked triumph for the religious attitude of the people. The pilgrimages were becoming more and more popular from year to year and the number of communions in the archdiocese of Prague alone had increased by 300,000 over 1956. He stated: "The religious life takes on an intensity which has never existed before and was completely unexpected." In glowing colors Benesch described what he called "the marvelous organized work" of *Caritas* and the "generous help of our government."

But not all centers of opposition had been removed through the elimination of the old bishops or the cooperation of the remaining bishops. The supervision of the clergy was not complete, and the religious orders were still very much alive. This became clear in numerous court trials, held in recent years.

Two priests were condemned to long prison terms at Brünn (Brno) in 1955, because they had sent secret reports to foreign countries about the conditions in Czechoslovakia. In June 1957, Father Vojtech Frelich and seven other priests and lay brothers of the Salesian Order were condemned at Mährisch-Ostrau (Ostrava) because they had distributed pamphlets against the state and had conducted secret meetings. In August 1957, Father Vaclav Filipek of the Salesians was condemned to nine years in prison by the Olmütz (Olomouc) court because he allegedly had received orders from the Vatican to engage in activities against the state and had been in the pay of "American intelligence services." His illegal act consisted in the fact that he had tried to keep in touch with his fellow ex-monks after the abolition of the Salesian Order and had written typewritten circular letters. In January 1958 Father Dokubil of Iglau (Jihlava) was condemned to 12 years in prison because he had tried to organize a "fanatically reactionary" Christian Democratic Party. In April 1959 a group of 14 priests, theology students, and laymen was condemned to long prison terms at Neutra, Slovakia, because they had allegedly organized a "secret school of theology" for students of theology who had been expelled from the state-run theological seminaries. They were called by the prosecutor "spies of the Vatican," "religious fifth columnists," and other names. On December 1, 1959, the People's Court in Prague condemned six Knights of the Order of St. Lazarus to from five to nine years in prison because through their religious activities they had tried to prepare a revolt against the People's Democracy of Czechoslovakia. They had allegedly planned to organize a party on the pattern of "Adenauer's Christian Democratic Union and to incorporate the Czechoslovak Republic into a Danubian Federation within the framework of a new Free Europe." The same People's Court also condemned 11 young women and girls to from one to five years' imprisonment because they had become members of the Apostolate of the Third Order of St. Francis which had been abolished by government decree. They had continued their activities against the state by reorganizing as an Association of the Sisters of St. Mary and distributing pamphlets in which the state had been attacked. They were also charged with having recruited other young women for their illegal association. Father Vojtech Zabransky of Rohatek, Moravia, was condemned to three years' imprisonment because he had stated in a sermon: "The lie has become a powerful weapon in this world. You are confronted by lies everywhere in public and private life, in the arts, in science, in philosophy, and in politics." The priest, who, according to the testimony, "was esteemed in his congregation like a saint," had encouraged farmers to procrastinate and not to join the collectives. In March 1960 Father Ladislav Hlad was condemned to five years in the penitentiary because he had "secretly exercised the office of Bishop of Leitmeritz (Litomerice)." In this connection a Prague newspaper wrote that since 1949 there had been a secret Catholic church administration which would take over the functions of bishops who had been hindered in the exercise of their office. It was stated that the last papal nuncio in Prague had given to Father Hlad a letter from Pius XII in 1950 in which he was appointed Bishop of Leitmeritz (Litomerice). He had been consecrated secretly and in turn had secretly ordained others who had not been allowed to finish their studies at the state-run seminaries and had completed their studies under private tutors. This news story indicated that there existed a church in the catacombs. Also a report in the Bratislava paper *Praca* of April 7, 1960, stated that agents of the Vatican had secretly organized two seminaries in the dioceses of Neutra and Neusohl (Banska Bystrica). The same newspaper announced that the police had discovered an illegal religious organization. More than a hundred boys and girls were accused of having seduced others and having them organized "under the leadership of the Vatican." They were alleged to have founded Catholic youth groups which went by the name "The Unfree."

4. Atheist Propaganda

The chief organ for atheist propaganda in Czechoslovakia was the *Czechoslovak Society for the Dissemination of Political and Scientific Knowledge*. At its founding on June 22, 1952, the Minister of Information, Vaclav Kopecky, named three goals for its work: to make people realize that the center of all problems is the problem of the relationship between production and the development of the means of production; to give them an understanding of Czech history and the role of class struggle in that history; and to enlighten them about the role of religion in the life of the nation. He said that among church members two types of people must be differentiated, those who abuse the church for their reactionary purposes and the simple people. The latter must be educated, the former must be eliminated. He stated: "It is a question of liberating our people from their lack of knowledge and of teaching them to see the light of understanding and scientific ideology."

At the end of 1956 the *Society* numbered about 17,000 members. During the first four years of its existence it had held 135,000 meetings at which more than 9,000,000 people had been present. Besides 311 brochures 250 texts and materials for meetings had been published. It had also published two monthlies, *Priroda a spolecnost* ("Nature and Society") in Slovakia and *Veda a Zivot* ("Science and Life") in Czechia. The *Society* was represented in all districts of the country. In almost every district it had organized independent groups of scientific atheists. In its propaganda in the cities and factories it had concentrated on enlightening people concerning the origin and the development of religion, while in the country districts reports had been given on questions of natural science which led people to draw their own atheistic conclusions.

In the following years there were repeated urgent calls for ideological campaigns against religious superstition. The Central Committee of the Communist Party, in its session of June 30, 1957, heard a complaint to the effect that many party members were still influenced by religion. In a resolution dealing with ideological questions it declared that at no time might the party lose sight of the problem of how to overcome religious prejudices. The goal of healing people from their religious prejudices was to be reached by systematic and patient education. The faithful were to free themselves step by step and voluntarily from all religious prejudices on the basis of their own scientific convictions. Atheistic propaganda was to be carried on in close collaboration with the political, cultural, and other aspects of enlightenment.

There were many complaints about the failure of atheistic propaganda. The Communist Party was often accused of laxity and of not putting enough emphasis on atheistic education. In the magazine *Oswetova Prace* ("Work of Enlightenment") a woman teacher complained that in some regions there was still great emphasis on church ceremonies such as baptisms, weddings, and funerals. The local national committees very often participated in the consecration of church bells. She had also noticed that some citizens were spending large sums for the restoration of churches. There was plenty of superstition. In one village a state buyer of eggs failed to reach his quota. He asked the local priest for his help. Everything went well after that. The teacher also mentioned that in a congregation in Prague an active and energetic priest against whom 20 atheistic teachers had been unable to stand up had caused a tremendous increase among those who were anxious to attend religious instruction. The Bratislava newspaper *Pravda* was enraged about a letter to the editor written by three women who were living in the village of Poprad. They stated that their congregation had fulfilled all the prescribed quotas and demanded a new church building in return, since 77% of their children attended religious instruction. The paper replied in cold anger that the government would be willing to build a theater, a swimming pool, or a stadium, but not a church.

In 1959 the Communists introduced a secular ceremony which was to take the place of baptism. At this ceremony the mayor of the town gave a brief address. A lullaby was played on a reed organ and uniformed members of the Communist Youth recited a poem. At the end of the ceremony the parents of the child received a bouquet of flowers. By law religious instruction was permitted in the schools, but in practice it was very often difficult to give this instruction. It was abolished in the first year of school under the pretext that the children were not able to write or read. In the upper grades the usual excuse was that the children were over-burdened with other subjects. Besides, both parents were required to submit a written request to have their child instructed in religion. It was strictly forbidden to make propaganda for religious instruction. The largest school system at Aussig (Usti) had at the end of 1956 only 7% of the children in religion classes. The Prague newspaper *Mlada Fronta* reported in the spring of 1960 that in the district of Prague. the number of participants in religious instruction had been greatly reduced and that in the city districts of Slany, Klando and North Prague religious instruction had been completely abolished.

All teachers were required to sign a statement in which they subscribed to the Communist ideology. But the newspaper *Jihoceska Prawda* complained in March 1960 that teachers with "clearly defined Marxist ideology" were very rare. Many good Communist teachers were getting old. Children who had been influenced by the religious remnants in the family circle and transferred from other schools into secularized schools often influenced others. Said the paper: "Atheistic education of the children of such parents is a difficult and time-consuming task."

There were also difficulties at the universities. At a meeting of the Central Committee of the Communist Party the Slovakian representative for school administration, Vasil Bilak, put the blame on certain influential professors who not only did not lay a good groundwork for atheistic materialistic indoctrination but even attended religious ceremonies. The magazine *Ucitelske noviny* ("Teacher's Journal") stated angrily that in the medical faculty 81.3% of the students still were church members and that 48.7% had indicated that they were active believers. The magazine stated that conditions in the other faculties were not better. At the Third Czechoslovak Youth Congress in the spring of 1959, a speaker complained that the larger part of the students stubbornly refused to give up their religious convictions. As a specially striking example he cited the action of a coed who had received excellent marks when she wrote an essay on the theme "Marxism and Religion," but who told her friends that before taking the examination she had gone to confession.

5. Shrinking Congregations

According to the peace priests' propaganda church life in Czechoslovakia was flourishing. But other reports gave an altogether different picture. *Herder Correspondence* reported from Czechia in May 1958 that while churches were still comfortably filled, there were few young people among the worshipers. It stated: "The great majority of the people become more and more dulled in the face of the many problems confronting the church. The number of unbaptized children is constantly growing. Thus this country in the heart of Europe becomes more and more dechristianized." In Slovakia the story was somewhat different. The Slovak people continued to be basically a religious people and church-oriented. Conditions had changed little in 1959 after more than a decade of Communist rule.

According to the Vienna magazine *Die Furche*, of July 5, 1958, the participation of people in divine services and in the reception of the sacraments had declined in certain areas, especially in Bohemia and Moravia. In the Stuttgart weekly *Katholisches Sonntagsblatt*, of September 18, 1960, it was reported that only 8 to 10% of the city children participated in religious instruction, while in the country districts and in all of Slovakia over 50% of all school children were enrolled in religion classes. In a large parish which formerly had 800 new first communions each year, there were only 60 such in 1960. A study made by the magazine *Otazky marxisticke filozofie* ("Questions of Marxist Philosophy") in 1962 reported on conditions in the district of Kyov-Gaya in Slovakia and admitted that more than half of the population attended "religious ceremonies" on Sundays. Among those in attendance 25% were young people. In the villages of Slovakia the conduct of the priests constituted the most effective counteroffensive against atheism. These priests, coming for the most part from poor families, were loyal to the state and concentrated on their religious duties. They carried on their work briskly, often much better than the average functionary. It stated that even Communists in the Slovak villages had not yet freed themselves completely from religious superstitions.

Very discouraging, on the other hand, was a report by the newspaper correspondent H. Stehle. Said he: "In wide areas of Czechoslovakia religion is at the point of death. It appeared to us as a symbol when we visited the Cistercian Abbey of Osik at the foothills of the Ore Mountains. At the time of the open church struggle this had been the site of a large concentration camp for hundreds of clergymen. Even today the gates to the monastery courtyard are blocked and the church is not open to the believers. After ringing a bell tourists who are art lovers are admitted by a nun who sits under the picture of the Communist Party chieftain Novotny. Every visitor is asked to write his name and address in a registry book. In the monastery there is a home run by the state for feeble-minded children who are taken care of by 50 sisters. When we saw some priests in the corridor we were told that also some Jesuits were lodged here. 'They are taking care of our domestic work,' we were told, 'they are useful in the kitchen and cellar.' Our steps through the quiet abbey church seemed to be a mockery to the exuberant Baroque architecture. Did our steps sound as if we were walking in the quietness of a museum or in a mausoleum?"

The government clearly showed its intention to turn the whole church into a mausoleum. From the new constitution which was published on July 1, 1960 the word "church" had been omitted. This new constitution no longer claimed that it was regulating the relationship of the state to the churches or religious organizations, but was only concerned with the religious freedom of the individual. Article II, paragraph 32,1 stated: "The freedom of religion is guaranteed. Every individual has the freedom to exercise his religious faith or not to belong to a religious association, and to participate in religious services as long as he does not violate the law of the state." This stipulation sounded very magnanimous, but the next paragraph immediately circumscribed its limitations: "Religious faith and confession must not serve as a pretext for neglecting, or refusing, to carry out the duties of citizenship and other duties assigned by the law." According to Article I, paragraph 18,1, "the entire cultural policy of Czechoslovakia is directed toward the improvement of education and instruction in the schools on the basis of the scientific Marxist-Leninist ideology and must be carried out in close relationship with the lives of the workers." This statement denied in practice the promise of so-called "religious freedom," because the Christians were not allowed to oppose the official line of Communist ideology. The Deputy Prime Minister, Vaclav Kopecky, declared that freedom of religious confession had been guaranteed in the constitution, but, he said, "we must state frankly that we consider religion a remnant of the past which is still present in the consciousness of man." He demanded that all cultural institutions serve the ideology of the state. He said: "In the interest of man we shall take care of all souls and shall fight without compromise for the souls of our children." In this sense, he concluded, the constitution and its stipulations about cultural policies had to be interpreted.

B. PROTESTANTISM

Among the more than 12,000,000 inhabitants of the country there were about 1,000,000 Protestant Christians who were members of various churches. Another million believers belonged to the Czechoslovak Church which had been organized in 1918 as a Rome-free Catholic Church. The largest Protestant church was the Slovakian Church of the Augsburg Confession (Lutheran) which had about 430,000 members in over 300 congregations. At its head was the Presiding Bishop of Bratislava. The Evangelical Church of the Bohemian Brethren (Moravians) numbered about 350,000 souls who belonged to about 300 congregations and were served by 300 pastors. The Christian Reformed Church of Slovakia (Calvinist) with 140,000 members in 310 congregations was served by about 170 pastors under a bishop. It was predominantly of Hungarian background. The Silesian Church of the Augsburg Confession (Lutheran) had about 53,000 members. In addition to these larger bodies there was a new Brethren Church (Moravians) that had been founded from Herrnhut and some Methodists and Baptists.

1. Relationship to the Communist State

The Protestant churches had no objection to the law regulating the state-church relationship that was passed in 1949. The synodal council of the Evangelical Church of the Bohemian Brethren declared: "The Church of the Czech Brethren has again and again until the days of the Edict of Tolerance (by Joseph II) experienced the bitter fruits of inequality. Therefore she looks upon the stipulation that all churches are equal with great satisfaction and also accepts the fact that the new law prescribes equal treatment of all churches and promises tolerance to all. The church is determined to accept the assistance which this law offers, not to diminish the spirit of sacrifice among her members, but to provide for her congregations everything that is necessary for the spiritual life of the church. During the discussions with the representatives of the Office for Ecclesiastical Affairs the representatives of the church were assured that the present structure and effectiveness of the church will not be changed and that her freedom to carry out her mission would be guaranteed. The representatives of the church note with satisfaction that the representatives of the government carried on these deliberations in a friendly spirit."

The conference of the *Movement of the Bohemian (Czech) Brethren,* which was endeavoring to win lay participation in the work of the church and in public life and was established to train lay leaders, in November 1949 gave directives for the future work of the organization. In these directives a negative attitude to the state was rejected. The conference stated that the country was passing through incisive changes in its social, spiritual, and moral life as a result of the introduction of Marxist-Leninist ideology and that every Christian had the duty to come to grips with the factors that were operative in these changes. The danger for the church was not only an environment of isolation but also her inactivity and her lack of concern, due in part to the selfishness of her members. The conference stated: "Let us protect ourselves against identifying our attitude with the attitude of the Roman Church and her present battle against the state." The conference considered the fight of the Vatican against Communism and the Soviet Union a political one. It stated that the Vatican was not concerned to preserve the purity of the church of Christ or the genuineness of the apostolic witness. The statement concluded with these words: "Our task is to watch and to pray that we may realize the correct time when we have to speak up, when the world must be made aware of the judgment of God, and when the people who are sick today must receive a word of help, of comfort, and of spiritual healing."

Only the Lutheran Church of Slovakia showed some opposition against the law concerning the relationship of church and state. As a result of this opposition her presiding bishop was imprisoned. His place was taken by Jovan Chabada who was elected by the synod in October 1951. This synod also accepted a new constitution for the church which stated that the church accepts Jesus Christ as her head and that she considers herself to be a part of the Holy Christian Church on earth. It stated that it was her duty to preach the Gospel, to strengthen the spirit of love and of truth and to build the kingdom of God here on earth by helping to bring about permanent peace and brotherhood among all nations. The synod stated: "The Slovak Lutheran Church is under the protection and supervision of the state. She is on an equal footing with other churches. Her rights and duties are described in her constitution of May 9. The task of the church in her relationship with the state is to help the state to build the people's democracy and to support the state through her moral and spiritual education so that a new man may come forth in the spirit of Jesus Christ."

The pastors of the Protestant churches were elected by the congregations. The salaries paid by the state were low and pastors' wives were forced to take jobs in order to maintain a minimum standard of existence. The future pastors were educated in two theological seminaries, called "faculties," which were recognized by the state. The faculty at Modra near Bratislava was a Lutheran faculty, while the Comenius Faculty at Prague educated ministers for all other Protestant churches. Professors and teachers were appointed by the government on the recommendation of the churches and were paid by it. Students of theology received the same kind of state stipends as students in the other fields of learning.

According to the impressions of foreign observers, the activities of lay people in the Protestant churches of the Czechoslovak Republic were especially outstanding. The churches had regular meetings and training courses for lay workers. The most difficult aspect of the work of the church was the work among the young people, especially in the cities; and although participation in religious instruction was, generally speaking, quite good, it was still difficult to carry on the work of religious education. In many congregations 90% or more of the Protestant parents enrolled their children in religion classes.

The Protestant churches took a different attitude toward the state than the Roman Catholic Church. This difference in attitude was determined by the historical development of the non-Roman churches. In Czechoslovakia the Counter-Reformation had had dire consequences. In 1620 Bohemia had been ninety percent Protestant. When the Counter-Reformation came to an official end in 1781—at the time when Joseph II issued his Edict of Tolerance— there were hardly two percent Protestants left. Professor J. B. Soucek of the Prague faculty wrote: "The Catholization was associated with a great defeat for our country and our church. This caused a great number of the Czech population to turn away from Roman Catholicism during the past three or four generations, since about 1860. Unfortunately, it also meant in many cases a turning away from Christianity." The memory of the Counter-Reformation continued to remain very much alive in Protestantism. The Counter-Reformation had been the "time of darkness." Professor Hellmut Gollwitzer wrote in *Kirche in der Zeit* in 1958: "A united front with Catholicism against Communism cannot be established, because the ruthless struggle of extermination against the Gospel that had been waged for centuries by the papacy, a struggle which Protestants had experienced in their own bodies, no longer made Communism look like the beast from the abyss. The Catholic Church which did not repent for the sins of the Counter-Reformation was not considered by the Protestants as the legitimate defender of the purity of Christianity."

Furthermore, it must be remembered that the Bohemian Brethren were the descendants of John Hus and that they had shown throughout the centuries a strong revolutionary pathos which revealed itself in former times in many social and political activities. They never understood grace merely as the forgiveness of sins, but as a call to change the individual and his environment. On the fifteenth anniversary of the liberation of Czechoslovakia, which was celebrated in 1960, the Ecumenical (Federal) Council of Churches in the Czechoslovak Republic published a declaration in which it described the relationship of its member churches to the new state as "sincere and positive." The Council stated: "We are more and more convinced that our state is carrying on the work of great social and welfare activities on behalf of our workers and that it is concerned with the struggle for peace and takes into account the interests of the entire society and guarantees it on a basis broad enough for the individual to realize his hopes and aspirations." It further proclaimed that the socialist classless society "is close to the Christian concept of a healthy society order." The Synod of the Christian Reformed Church of Slovakia declared at that time: "These fifteen years were a time when we became equals with all other churches of our country, something for which we had fought in vain since the days of the Reformation. In the internal and external reconstruction of our church we have attained results which bind us in sincere gratefulness to God and to our People's Democracy through which these gifts have become possible." It stated that justice in the relationship between people and real joy in the life and results of work and the expectation for a happy future have been realized. It continued: "A tremendous growth in the standard of living among our people and its new relationship to work and its fruits, to coworkers and to the common tasks confronting us, make it easier for the church to carry on her principal work which is the proclamation of the Gospel."

The Protestant church leadership did everything in its power to encourage congregations to cooperate with the government in the setting up of a socialist society. Professor Soucek declared that in view of this development the congregations of the Evangelical Church of the Bohemian Brethren faced a real challenge, since they were composed mostly of members of the middle classes. Said he: "We have to fight against the temptation to confuse with Christian concern an aversion which can be logically explained but which is not based on our Christian faith, an aversion which is solely based on our class-consciousness against the socialist order. We must see to it that we do not start our resistance at the wrong place and are using the wrong means, but at the same time we must strengthen ourselves in understanding and loyally carrying out the essential commandments of our faith. I might add that this is a condition which is very difficult to understand outside of our country and which is very often judged on the basis of insufficient and haphazard information. But especially in this respect we must ask for some reticence and some trust in the loyalty and the understanding of the brethren who are working in this country and who are wrestling for its understanding." Bishop Varga reported in 1959 on the attitude of the church to the collectivization of agriculture. This was an especially burning question since 85% of the membership of the Reformed Church were farmers. He said: "In many places there was at first an inner rejection of collectivization. Our church, too, was confronted by the serious question whether she could support socialization of farming openly. But she solved this question after a serious inner struggle in such a way that she can recommend to her members that they join the collective farms. She wants to indicate that Christianity is not bound to any given form of society and that socialism also offers many rich, rewarding opportunities to give a testimony to Jesus Christ and to our faith in him. Among the best agricultural collectives of our republic are our farms, and we know even now that in those places where congregations are alive there is also a strong collective life. The common working together will prove that the spiritual life in a congregation is positive enough to lead people to engage in a common, mutual, and unselfish service."

2. Joseph Hromadka

The most influential theologian who has followed consistently the line of a positive attitude toward the Communist state and has proclaimed his attitude with great conviction was Professor Joseph Hromadka. He was born on June 8, 1889, the son of a peasant in the village of Hodslavice in Moravia. Later he studied theology in

Vienna, Basel, Heidelberg, and Aberdeen. From 1912 to 1916 he was vicar of a Lutheran congregation and until 1918 he was pastor of Our Savior's Church in Prague. At that time he was strongly influenced by reports which returning prisoners brought back from the Soviet Union. He wrote his dissertation on the philosophy of religion of T. G. Masaryk and later became pastor of the Church of the Brethren in Sonov. In 1920 he was called as professor of systematic theology to the newly founded John Hus Evangelical Faculty of Prague. In the summer of 1923 he became acquainted with the theology of Karl Barth, which influenced him decisively in his attempt to find a new point of departure for theology and church which were confronted by a world revolution. As early as 1918 Hromadka stated that socialism would become the outstanding issue in the church. In 1925 he found something good to say about Communism. He said: "Russian Communism creates a good atmosphere for free religious propaganda. It has broken the bonds with which the czarist system of government suppressed the free cultural development of the nation and the true and free religious life of the Christians." He then asked the question whether Soviet Russia with its impact on modern literature and art was not the beginning of a new era in world history. In 1932 he stated: "The Russian Soviet revolution is perhaps the greatest positive influence in the history of religion." On the other hand, as early as 1929, he was very critical of the "so-called Christian civilization" which he saw represented in American democracy. It worried him to see that Christianity separated itself from the basis of its faith and was slowly developing into a program for liberal democracy. He said: "If it does not return to its original destination it will become a little wheel in the cultural and economic life of American imperialism." After 1933 in his articles and speeches he untiringly warned against the dangers of National Socialism. From 1936 to 1938 he was active as secretary of the *Society for a Democratic Spain.* On March 15, 1939, he witnessed the German occupation of Prague, but emigrated soon afterwards. With his family he came to the USA where he served as professor of Christian Ethics at Princeton Theological Seminary for eight years. From the beginning, he cooperated with the *Czech Peace Movement* and the *World Peace*

Council. He was elected president of the Christian World Peace Conference and played an important part in the formation and development of the World Council of Churches.

In many publications Hromadka indicated the place and the voice of the church in Communist society. He understood Communism as something that could not be removed from the face of the earth, as something that had started a new historical era. He felt that the future belonged to Communism and that the old systems were coming to an end. He saw the world involved in a radical and complete change. He challenged the Christians to cope with this fact. Hromadka himself declared that he was not a Communist but a believing theologian, but he also stated: "The prejudices of Western Christians who claim that you cannot lead the life of a believer in a church under a Communist system often worry me. The truth is that I am feeling very well under this system. Under this system we can serve the church faithfully."

Hromadka became one of the most influential advisors to Protestant churches, not only in Czechoslovakia, but also in Hungary and other Iron Curtain countries. His opinions have found a favorable echo in a large part of the ecumenical movement. Within the scope of our report we can give no complete overview of his opinions, but some quotes from him may help to clarify questions concerning his position.

Hromadka was always critical of the Christian West. Said he: "The so-called Christian nations of Europe and America have lost, spiritually speaking, the right to consider themselves the firstborn among the Christian nations. They have played out their role as political leaders in international affairs. The era of the hegemony of the Christian civilization is past. The historical philosophy which was based on the idea of the superiority of Christianity must be given up; we must begin to build again upon the ruins, without self-glorification, without a claim to be arbiters of all moral, cultural, social, and international situations. This does not mean that the great creative qualities and the genuine inheritance of the so-called Christian civilization has lost its validity.... However this inheritance must be freed from the chains of a self-righteous feeling of superiority, from its sterility and from all claims to be the judge of what is right or wrong, just or unjust, and of what is freedom and righteousness."

Toward Communism Hromadka was a great deal less critical. He wrote: "The history of mankind cannot be understood merely as a history of ideas and abstract intellectual values. The history of mankind will be understood in its true impact only if we also look at the presuppositions of human society. Historical materialism wants to help man wrestling in society so that he can gain an understanding of his past and his present and can begin to work toward a better future . . . . Classless society, which is the aim of all human endeavors founded on the actual recognition and the accurate knowledge of the history of society, is a guarantee of all human rights and of full freedom. This is a society without contradictions, without differences, without rich and poor, without exploitation and exploited, without overindulgent parasites and without hungry people."

Concerning Communist atheism Hromadka said: "Let us not forget that Communism with all its atheism is not primarily an ideology. It is a force fighting for the future of man and of his rights, for freedom and dignity, by establishing better and more adequate social institutions, through legal and political forms, and in a better way than was possible under the old forms of society. . . . Atheism of the Marxist variety is nothing new. It is merely a radical expression of modern European revolutionary thinking. Since the days of the Renaissance and of the Enlightenment, everywhere in the depths of the heart of every European and American citizen there has been a *Leitmotiv* of man without God. It has been the motive that accompanied all progressive movements of modern history. Now it has become the official ideology—an ideology which does not permit compromise—of the Communist and radical Socialist movements. It has shocked the traditional Christian churches in all countries. This fact has made it easy for the conservatives, anti-socialists, anti-Communists to win their victories in the hearts of the great majority of Christians during the post-war period. Thus the Christian churches of our time have been hampered in their endeavors to break through to the essential problem facing the post-war period. . . . The thing that we call Marxist atheism is essentially nothing but radical humanism. The God whose existence is denied by the Marxists is nothing but the creation of human fiction. He is a self-deception, an attempt to lead man away from the real understanding of the real deity. It is an idol that man has created for himself and with whom he wants to deceive and intoxicate himself and others. Thus this man-made idol leads man away from his true self-understanding and his true tasks."

About the place and the task of the church in present-day society Hromadka wrote: "If I look at the statesmen and the politicians in our country, I do not have the feeling that they have real power. But I always have the feeling that these people are poor sinners who have taken it upon themselves to shoulder the heavy burden of responsibility, a burden which they perhaps will not be able to bear. What can we do to help these poor people? We should not fight against them, but we should serve them in forgiveness and true Christian love. . . . Communism was a temptation only for a very brief period for some orthodox groups in the Soviet Union who tried to accommodate the doctrines and substance of the church to the new situation. The so-called 'Living Church' of Russia was the counterpart to the so-called 'German Christians' in the Third Reich. But the danger to the church has quickly passed. The situation after World War II cannot be compared to the situation that existed during the German Church Struggle under Hitler. The church has made no attempt to consider Communism as a revelation or as a creative factor in the spiritual realm. As matters stand things are completely clear. The differences between the ideology of Communism and the theology of the Christian Church are clear beyond the shadow of a doubt. The contrasts between the two have been overemphasized by Christian theologians and churchmen who did not always realize that a theology which is based on the Word of God is moving in a different direction and must act differently than the secular ideology of Marxism and Communism. . . . We must take man seriously behind the facade of Communism. It is our task as Christians to look behind the petrified suspicions and prejudices. The growing anti-Communist sentiment, the involvement of Christians in the anti-Communist crusade, and the cultivation of everything that we call by the collective term Cold War is terrible. . . . Our chief task, which no one else can carry out, is to lift ourselves above the present-day tensions and to come down where man is in his agony of sin and guilt, of hope and aspirations, where he is suffering, fighting, despairing, and rising up again in order to make a new beginning. . . . I would like to give testimony of everything our work stands for; our positive attitude toward our present-day leaders and toward our present-day state is not an unconditional submission, but an attitude of serving love born of the Gospel. I have never belonged to a political party and I shall never belong to one. I am free to wrestle for inward freedom, for freedom of responsibility and of service. For you know, my dear brethren, Jesus Christ, the risen Lord, put himself into the place where we are standing now. He did not come to erect human, ecclesiastical, and confessional barriers against the world. . . . Without the doctrine of justification by faith the Gospel cannot be understood. The Lord is not only the justifying Lord, but also the risen Lord. The Gospel is the majestic message of the kingdom of the lordship of Jesus Christ over the whole life of the individual and the people, over the state, and over the church. It is not an abstract rule, but a concrete interference of God through Jesus of Nazareth in the concrete and emperical conditions of man. We must keep this before our eyes today in order to be able to wrestle with the fullness of the Gospel and to help each other to understand it. It is our great task to call our churches to this service. For the difficulties which are threatening to overcome the churches today are much more deeply rooted in the church herself than in the secular world. If the church does not become the divine tool of Jesus Christ, if she does not become free inwardly of all the things that threaten her identity, if she forms false fronts, then she will not be in a position to meet the dangerous challenge threatening her and to continue—humanly speaking—victoriously. The question of forgiveness as a power in the struggle of present-day Europe is a question addressed especially to our churches."

Of course, Hromadka did not meet only with consent, but also with much contradiction. He was asked whether Communism, at least in its present form, really possessed the historical significance which he had assigned to it; whether it was called upon, and able, to take the place of radical humanism which would lift human society up; and whether it could create through its social message of salvation a better possibility for human self-realization; whether, on the other hand, the West was really "finished" and rushing toward its doom; or whether there were not certain principles in the Western order of society which have seeds for the future and which therefore should not be cast aside.

Others questioned the high esteem of Communism voiced by Hromadka. Could one really claim that this materialistic atheism was harmless? Was it not more than merely a perverted image of God? Or did it have more sinister implications? Were Communism and materialistic atheism not necessarily intertwined and were they not one and the same as two sides of the same coin so that they should and could not be separated from each other? Would Communism not lose its foundation if it divorced itself from atheism? Dr. Adalbert Hudak, in *The Theology of Life and the Prague Peace Conference*, wrote: "It could be that behind this atheism there is a new idol. Man, even in his mature life, is not completely without religion. The state is not merely a state in the secular sense of the word. Its doctrine is not an autonomous doctrine, and its secularism is not merely a liberation from, but at the same time a turning toward, the great idols of our century. Therefore church and theology have the task to proclaim the first commandment and to resist any attempt to present atheism as harmless."

From this point of view Dr. Hudak drew certain conclusions for the position of the Christian congregations in and toward the Communist state which were quite different from the conclusions at which Hromadka had arrived and which the Protestants of Czechoslovakia were carrying out in practice. Hudak wrote: "The knowledge of the existence of the church which is not bound to certain economic or social structures does not give the right to our so-called theology of life to eliminate completely the critical function of the Gospel in the Communist society of Eastern Europe as it has been doing to a very large degree." However, even the West recognized that Hromadka and the church in Czechoslovkia were in dead earnest in their attempt to generate a Christian reaction to Communism. The way in which this attempt was carried out may have been wrong, but the Westerner must try to understand it on the basis of the experiences of the church under Communist rule.

CHAPTER FOUR

HUNGARY

A. THE ROMAN CATHOLIC CHURCH

After 1945 the party of the Small Landholders came to power in Hungary. Its leader, Zoltan Tildy, was elected president of the state in 1946. All large landholders were expropriated, and the take-over of the economy began. In the governments of Prime Ministers Dinnyes, 1947 and 1948, and Dobi, 1948 to 1952, the Communists with the help of the Soviet military gained the majority. The parliamentary elections of May 31, 1949, gave the National Front, which was dominated by the Communists, absolute power. All other parties were dissolved. On August 20, 1949, a new constitution was proclaimed by which Hungary was changed into a People's Democracy. The First Secretary of the Communist Party, Matthias Rakosy, who later served as Prime Minister, applied immediately the policy of the "hard course."

1. A Cardinal Who Would Not Compromise

Even before the Communist take-over in 1949 there had been a hard-fought battle between the state and the Catholic Church. That church at the time numbered 6.5 million souls who were organized in three archdioceses and seven dioceses, and were about 68% of the population of Hungary. Her leader from the beginning was Joseph Cardinal Mindszenty. Born on March 29, 1892, at Csehimindszent in Eastern Hungary of a family by the name of Pehm, he later took the name Mindszenty from his native town. In 1918 he was ordained priest, and in 1944 he became Bishop of Vesprehn. In November 1944 he was arrested by the Germans. After his liberation in April 1945, Mindszenty in August of that year was appointed

Archbishop of Eczergom and Primate of the Roman Catholic Church
of Hungary. In February 1946 he was created a cardinal.

Already in his first letter to his diocese, written on October 18,
1945, he made some strong statements. He wrote: "The building
up of our political life can be carried out in the future only on the
basis of democracy. We must say openly and frankly that we are
noticing many occurrences in public life which are contrary to the
ideas of pure democracy. In the new laws concerning marriage there
is incorporated a superficial and frivolous point of view. Some of
the stipulations of the law for land reform are phrased in such a
way that it means the complete liquidation of a certain class of our
society. These laws apparently were written in the spirit of revenge."
Furthermore, the cardinal indicated that the marriage law contained
some ambiguities. He stated bluntly: "We see everywhere that the
basic demands of the law are rejected and that the most useful pillars of human society, morality and justice, are not considered at
all and that those ideals and traditions are trodden under foot which
should be retained to lift up our Hungarian people to new heights,
to noble courage, and to readiness for sacrifices. But you, dear believers, are called upon to think about these our words. Do not be
afraid of threats which the sons of wickedness are uttering against
you. It is easier to fight against and to endure threats, than to follow the path in which irresponsible elements without conscience
want to lead the Hungarian people. Force and power become greater
the less resistance there is against them. Therefore it is in the nature
of these systems that they ask you for your vote today, but tomorrow
they may be pushing you to do their bidding by using threats. They
may force you to slave for them, to wage war for them, and to permit yourselves to be led to destruction."

Those were harsh words. The government answered with a mol-
lifying appeal, but the cardinal refused to be mollified. The controversy quickly came to a boiling point. The refusal of the government
to establish diplomatic relations with the Holy See, the shortage of
Catholic newspapers, the tax on Catholic schools, the abolishment
of Catholic organizations, and other matters became objects of complaints. In a manifesto the episcopate proclaimed, "Not only do all
bishops not oppose the heroic and manly behavior of the Cardinal

in defense of the church, of freedom of conscience, and of justice in Hungary, but they also support him with their whole heart and all their strength." Before a mass meeting of Catholic farmers in Budapest Mindszenty declared in the fall of 1946: "Today we are making a solemn vow, to sacrifice, if necessary, our lives, so that our country of St. Stephen may also be the country of St. Mary."

The controversy between the cardinal and the state continued. At the end of 1947 Mindszenty handed to Prime Minister Dinnyes a list of complaints on the part of the bishops' conference about the persecution of the church by the Communists. On February 18, 1948, he stated in a speech that the big lie was present everywhere in Hungary. Even non-Communist middle-class newspapers now began to protest against Mindszenty's intransigency. When the cardinal heard about the intention of the government to secularize all schools—it was a question of 4,453 schools of which 2,297 were Catholic with a total enrollment of 650,000 students—he issued, in May 1948, three pastoral letters in short order. In the last letter he appealed to the faithful: "The time for a witness has come." When the law of secularization was finally passed, on June 14, 1948, the cardinal ordered the bells to be tolled throughout the country in protest and, on July 3, he excommunicated all ministers of government who had helped to draft the law of secularization. On July 10 he called on the bishops throughout the world: "Announce the above facts to the faithful and to your groups so that as quickly as possible everyone can send telegrams to the Hungarian government and to the Parliament and declare his opposition to the persecution of the church which is constantly increasing in our country.... Today, with the secularization of our schools and with the spiritual and physical suppression, the souls of our young people are condemned to death. If Hungary completely becomes a victim of Marxism, then all of Europe will bury its freedom. He who does not believe this should come to us and see it with his own eyes."

The resistance against the secularization of the schools—all clergymen henceforth refused to cooperate with the schools—led to bloody occurrences, to punishments and arrests of priests. The cardinal ordered that the bells should no longer be rung until the church had regained her complete freedom, and he attacked the government with sharp accusations. In answer to these attacks the press and radio in August 1948, started a so-called spontaneous campaign against Mindszenty. Even the prime minister did not mince any words. He said that the government had to meet the dangerous situation that had been brought about by the cardinal, that the cardinal was making a mockery of Christianity and that he had placed his trust in the outbreak of a new world war. The public agitation against Mindszenty became more and more violent. The Communist Minister of the Interior, Janos Kadar, called him "the most important confederate of the foreign imperialists" and "the head of all reactionaries." Two thousand workers and students demonstrated in front of his palace and shouted, "Down with Mindszenty, the American Agent! We shall see whether he can stir us up and get us to revolt against the government." Letters of protest were organized and the rage of the people soon reached the boiling point. Mindszenty had a premonition of what was in store for him. In a pastoral letter of November 20, 1948, which was confiscated by the government, he once more criticized the political powers of Hungary and then continued: "I shall not be intimidated by artificially aroused waves of protest, and I shall not waver. For where I am standing by the grace of God and the will of the Holy Father the changes of history have been manifold. Two of my predecessors have fallen on the field of battle, two have been deprived of all their possessions. Hogn Vitez was imprisoned. Martinuzzi was killed by the hired assassins of the rulers. Peter Pazmany—one of the most important personalities in our history—was exiled. But I must state that none of my predecessors was as forsaken, as much without means, as I am now, who have been exposed to many intrigues and many traps and have to refute lies every day, lies that have been refuted a thousand times before and yet they are repeated again and again. I have to do this in a measure in which none of my predecessors has done it. Here I stand in the service of God for my church and my fatherland, for I am called upon to defend the faith of the forsaken people of all nations and of Hungary. My own fate cannot change my determination because I am working for the interests of my people."

The cardinal did not everywhere find the support of his clergy and of the Catholic lay people. In Szegedin a mass meeting of Catholic youth and students protested against the cardinal's policy. In Budapest two thousand Catholic students presented a petition to the vicar-general of the primate in which they requested Mindszenty to leave Hungary. In several cities in the provinces there were similar demonstrations. The cardinal on his part dismissed the director of the Catholic college at Pecs because he had agreed publicly with a group of protesting students. The priest Stephan Barlogh was suspended because in his newspaper he had published attacks against the cardinal at various times and had criticized his position in the school controversy. The cardinal excommunicated all journalists who attacked him and the church.

On November 21, 1948, Mindszenty's secretary, Monsignor Zahar, was arrested. On December 17, the cardinal as a precautionary measure sent a letter to all bishops of the country. In it he stated: "I have never participated in any conspiracy. I shall not give up my episcopal office. If you should hear later that I have confessed or that I have resigned, even if it should be admitted over my own signature, consider it a consequence of human weakness. I declare such a confession *a priori* null and void." His sermons during these last days before his arrest sounded like words of leave-taking. He said: "It is midnight, night over Hungary, at the shores of the Danube. Nobody is watching with us. We are without friends and brothers. Necessity drives us to the bosom of the Holy Mother."

2. Arrested, Broken, and Condemned

In the evening of the day after Christmas 1948 the cardinal was arrested, after documents had been found in his residence during a search on December 23. With him 12 other persons were also arrested, among them the professor of canon law, Dr. Baranyai; Prince Paul Eszterhazy; the director of Catholic Action, Nicholas Beresztoczy; two archivists of the cardinal; two Jesuits; and two secular priests. A few days later the Ministry of the Interior published a report about the reasons which led to the arrests. The cardinal was accused of pro-Hapsburg activities. He was said to have been the head of a movement which sought the restoration of the royal throne in Hungary. Documents were alleged to have been found in a metal container which had been buried in the cellar of the cardinal's palace. In this container the secret files of the cardinal were said to have been enclosed, among them hand-written requests to the Western powers in which the cardinal demanded their intervention in the internal affairs of Hungary. The answers of the ambassadors of those powers and copies of reports by the cardinal indicated that the cardinal had suggested that the Western powers should interfere in Hungary. He had also furnished reports on the Russian army of occupation and on the economic conditions in Hungary. All these documents had been "found" by the secret police when they searched the cardinal's palace. Furthermore, on June 27, 1947, the cardinal was said to have had a secret meeting with Archduke Otto of Hapsburg in a monastery near Chicago. They allegedly agreed that after World War III, for which they were fervently waiting, a federated kingdom of central Europe, supported by the USA and including Hungary, should be set up. After his return from the USA Mindszenty was said to have taken up connections with Professor Baranyai, the leader of the secret royalist organization in Hungary. The latter was alleged to have worked out a plan according to which after the invasion by American armies Mindszenty would be appointed provisional regent for Hungary and would prepare the way for the return of the Hapsburg dynasty. For the realization of these goals he was said to have established a close personal contact with the ambassador of a foreign power and to have written to the United States ambassador, on August 31, 1947, that he should try to influence the American authorities not to return the crown of St. Stephen which was then in the possession of the American occupation authorities in Austria.

In spite of the arrest of the cardinal, the Archbishop of Budapest, Bela Vitez, declared at the New Year's reception of the Hungarian president that the church was "ready to arrive at an agreement with the state." On January 4 the first official discussions between the 12 Hungarian bishops and the representatives of the government took place. In a communique they stated: "Despite the existing difficulties, the discussions were carried on in a spirit of mutual understanding. They will be continued within the next few days." But they were never resumed. The Vatican at once interfered. The Congregation of the Consistory published a declaration dealing with the arrest of Cardinal Mindszenty. It stated: "They have dared to lay hands on His Eminence Joseph Cardinal Mindszenty and to deprive him of the exercise of his ecclesiastical jurisdiction. The Congregation of the Consistory declares that all people who have become guilty of the above-mentioned outrage are herewith excommunicated with the special excommunication reserved to the Holy See and in agreement with canon law." In a letter of January 2 to the Hungarian episcopate, Pope Pius XII declared his sorrow over everything that had been done against the rights of the church. He protested solemnly against the grave accusations that had been leveled against the church. He admonished the bishops to carry on their office as shepherds with determination and not to forget that for the freedom and the right of the church one must not only labor with painstaking care, but must also be willing to lose his life.

On January 12, 1949, Prime Minister Doby was informed by the bishops' conference that they were not able to continue the discussions that had begun on January 4. But before the beginning of the Mindszenty trial Archbishop Czaplik of Erlau (Eger) informed the prime minister in the name of the bishops that they would make no effort to interfere in the case of Cardinal Mindszenty and would leave the whole matter to the "wise deliberation of the government.

The trial was quickly and intensively prepared. The methods that were employed to prove that the cardinal was guilty were extremely ruthless and unscrupulous. The government published a Yellow Book of 96 pages. It contained among other things, a facsimile of a "confession" which the cardinal was said to have written about his political activities, in which he declared that he had always been a royalist and therefore had always supported political activities which had as their goal the restoration of the monarchy. He stated: "This goal can be attained only, as far as I know, by the overthrow of the Hungarian Republic with the help of foreign and specifically American arms. For this goal I did everything in my power in order to support the policy of the U.S. against Hungary. My activities were directed against the Hungarian Republic. I wanted America to interfere. For this purpose I gave regular information and carried on espionage. But I did not only turn to the Americans. I wanted to rally all the people of Hungary and of other countries around me, anyone who was willing to overthrow the Republic and to do away with the reforms instituted by the government, as for example the agrarian reform and the expropriation of private property."

This alleged confession of the cardinal and other documents which were used to prove his guilt were not accepted in the West. It was clearly shown that Mindszenty could not have met Archduke Otto of Hapsburg on June 21, 1947, in Chicago, because on that day he was over a thousand kilometers away at the Marian Congress in Ottawa. His co-worker of many years, Count Zoltan de Csaky, offered the cardinal's correspondence to the Hungarian Minister of Justice. This included all the letters that the cardinal had exchanged with Csaky and his other friends, who were now his codefendants, and also with the Vatican. These letters proved that all accusations against the cardinal were without any basis and that Mindszenty had never shown the slightest inclination to restore the Hapsburg monarchy and to overthrow the republic. The French abbé Gau who had declared publicly that he himself would gladly come to Hungary to testify was issued an invitation by the government (January 6, 1949). But when he tried to accept this invitation, he was frustrated at every turn and came to the conclusion that "the Hungarian government is afraid to throw light on this affair. Its refusal to hear me is a confession of guilt in the eyes of all free men."

On February 3, 1949, the trial against Mindszenty and several of his codefendants began. From the very start it was clear that the apathetic man who was sitting in the defendant's dock was entirely different from the one who had spoken so courageously only two months before. What had happened to him after his arrest? The mystery was removed in 1951 when two of his prosecutors fled from Hungary. Both had been appointed by the state to convict him and both had had access to the minutes of the preliminary investigations. They were acquainted with the methods that had been employed in questioning the cardinal. They surrendered to the American authorities in Austria certain documents from which it became clear that the cardinal had at first been starved in prison for 24 days, had been given the so-called cold water treatment with tablets and injections, until he was completely broken both in body and in spirit and was willing to repeat any confession of guilt that was laid before him. The documents which had been published in the Yellow Book were falsifications which the handwriting expert of the Budapest police, Lazlo Sulner, had manufactured at the request of the police. During the trial Sulner had fled to Vienna and had reported his fraud. A lawyer who had been a close associate of the cardinal, Dr. Groh, and who had been asked to be his defense counsel, was disbarred by the Hungarian bar a few days before the trial, and was arrested and condemned to two years' imprisonment. In the spring of 1951 he disappeared completely from sight. The cardinal was convinced by his captors, with the help of sedatives, that the appointment of Dr. Coloman Kiczo as his defense counsel would be a wise move. Kiczo was a Communist. His defense merely echoed the accusations made by the state prosecutor. Before the beginning of the trial the cardinal was visited in his cell every day by the president of the court who rehearsed with him his part in the forthcoming trial.

The trial came off without a hitch. It was conducted exactly as the stage managers had hoped it would be. At the beginning of the trial the president of the court read a letter by the cardinal to the minister of justice in which Mindszenty admitted his guilt and begged the government to stop the trial, promising that he would temporarily resign from his office as prince-primate of Hungary. He stated that he wanted to give a free hand to the bishops of the country to carry on their discussions with the government. He stated that he had had ample time to think about the accusations against him and about the future relationship of church and state. Therefore he now wanted to confess his guilt. He concluded: "I shall do my very best to help bring about a general peace and therefore I am asking you to stop this trial." The cardinal then arose from his seat in the dock and declared that he had written this letter voluntarily and in his own handwriting. During the trial he stated among other things: "I feel that I am guilty insofar as I have committed the actions imputed to me and I do not object to the details of the accusation." On the second day of the trial the cardinal was asked about the letter to the bishops which he had written shortly before his arrest and in which he had declared that any admission of guilt he would make under duress should be considered null and void. He declared that he had written that letter when he did not fully realize the consequences of his actions. He stated: "My true point of view is not contained in that letter which I wrote to the bishops, but in the letter which I wrote to the Minister of Justice and which was read yesterday. My letter to the bishops no longer has any validity."

The prosecutor demanded that the court should pass a judgment which would represent the "harsh and irrevocable defense of the cause of the people." On February 8 sentence was passed. Mindszenty was declared guilty on all counts and was condemned to life imprisonment, confiscation of his property, and loss of civil rights. Professor Baranyai and Prince Eszterhazy were condemned to 15 years' imprisonment and Mindszenty's secretary, Msgr. Zahar, to six years.

The trial had been followed by the whole world with breathless suspense. The sentence aroused sharp reactions which went far beyond the boundaries of the Roman Catholic Church. Governments, parliaments, leading statesmen, diplomats, and political conventions discussed it. Protests were sent to Budapest. A plenary session of the United Nations at the request of Bolivia and Australia put on the agenda the trial against Mindszenty and also a trial which had been conducted against a number of Protestant pastors in Sofia, Bulgaria. The request demanded that the United Nations require Hungary and Bulgaria to abide by the clauses of the peace treaty and to respect the basic freedoms and human rights, including religious and civil liberties. Yugoslavia, Poland, and the Soviet Union called this request "a clumsy attempt to interfere in the inner policies of Hungary and Bulgaria." Nevertheless, the plenary session of the United Nations passed a resolution in which it expressed "serious anxiety" about the trials of churchmen in Hungary and Bulgaria. It also expressed the hope that measures would be taken which would lead to a greater respect for human rights and the basic freedoms in those countries. But the resolution had no effect at all on the Communist governments.

In a letter to the bishops of the world Pope Pius XII asked that the day of his Golden Jubilee as priest, which took place on April 3, be celebrated as a day of penance for the crimes of godless people. He stated: "The battlelines between good and evil rarely have been drawn as clearly as today. We are filled with sorrow and worry that the abomination of the unjust has reached a degree of godlessness which is unbelievable and unexampled." In a secret consistory the Pope referred to the hasty and suspicious course of the trial and to the physical condition of the cardinal "which was the result of the use of methods that can not be mentioned." The Vatican excommunicated all people who in any way had been responsible for the condemnation of the cardinal. The cardinal's trial before a secular court was declared illegal. The primate had been deprived of the application of the provisions of canon law. On February 20, 1949, over 200,000 Romans assembled in St. Peter's Square and declared their loyalty to the church. Pope Pius XII addressed them in person.

The opinions among non-Roman Catholics and among Hungarian Protestants were quite different. In a common declaration issued by the Reformed, Methodists, Baptists, and Adventists of Hungary it was emphasized that "Mindszenty did not fight for religious freedom because there was no need for such a fight. He fought for political aims. No matter what opinions the church and the world at large may have about such a fight, we Hungarian Protestants do not condone any attempts by the Catholic Church to restore the rule of the Hapsburg—a dynasty which is remembered without affection—and of a feudalistic regime, which would be the necessary byproduct of such a restoration. We ask the leaders and members of our sister churches abroad to believe that they can serve the cause of the Hungarian church best by helping her to keep the Affair Mindszenty apart from the interests of the church." This position was also shared "with joy"—as they put it—by the bishops of the Lutheran Church. (At that time Bishop Ordass was in prison.) The Lutheran bishops stated: "Our pastors are in no way hindered from carrying out their spiritual office which is an essential part of the life of the church."

World Protestantism reacted in different ways. The President of the United Lutheran Church in America, Dr. Franklin Clark Fry, called the trial "alarming for the whole Christian world." The Anglican Archbishop of Canterbury and the Lord Bishop of Chichester declared their solidarity with the imprisoned cardinal. Others, however, emphasized that they did not agree with the political methods which the Catholic Church was using in her fight against Communism. There were warnings that the church should not consider the battle between East and West as a battle between evil and good men; that while Catholics and Protestants may be united in their resistance against totalitarian government, there should be no doubt that they were not allied in a holy war against Communism; that Protestants generally sympathized with all the oppressed, not only those in Hungary and Bulgaria, but also those in Spain.

Concerning the further fate of the cardinal there were reports that he had been transferred to a hospital in Budapest's central prison where he was kept under strict surveillance and was not allowed to see visitors. He was constantly attended by Communist doctors. In the fall of 1949 he was taken to a villa near the headquarters of the political police to recuperate from the aftereffects of his treatment. Here he regained the use of his memory. Afterwards he was returned to the central prison of Budapest where he continued to live a life of repentance with two days each week set aside for special penance. Once a week he refused to sleep in his prison bed and insisted on sleeping on the floor. Apart from a half hour's walk daily he was occupied exclusively with prayer and meditation.

3. After the Breaking of the Dam

While the Roman Catholic Church, from the Vatican to the lowliest parish, was filled with anger and resentment, the Roman Catholics of Hungary remained silent. There was never any reference to steps being taken by Hungarian bishops or by the faithful on behalf of the cardinal. Where were the 500,000 peasants who had come to Budapest two and a half years before to pledge him their support? Why this silence? Was it due to the realization that they were unable to do anything for the imprisoned primate? Or had the Catholics of Hungary changed their minds about Mindszenty? Or did the Roman Catholic Church lack leadership? The latter seems to have been the reason for the strange behavior of Hungary's Catholics. The church had lost her steely perseverance and stubborn center of resistance when the cardinal was imprisoned. None of the other bishops was able to take his place. The bishops of Hungary were not activists. They showed a marked lack of determination. The government, in which the Communists now had sole control, did not have any trouble when it established its hegemony over the Hungarian Catholic Church. At least there was no opposition visible to the eye of the outsider.

Article 54 of the constitution, which was passed on August 20, 1949, did not indicate any radical change in the definition of religious freedom. Paragraph 1 stated: "The Hungarian People's Republic guarantees to its citizens freedom of conscience and also the free exercise of religion." In paragraph 2 it was said that "in the interest of maintaining freedom of conscience the church is separated from the state." But what the Communists meant by "freedom" was explained in the following article of the constitution, Article 55: "The Hungarian People's Republic guarantees freedom of speech, of the press, and of association as long as this freedom does not interfere with the interests of the working masses." Freedom became synonymous with submission to the decrees of the party and of the state. This interpretation led to numerous interferences in the affairs of the church which continued to increase as time went on.

In 1949 instruction in the Marxist-Leninist ideology was introduced in all schools as a required subject. Religious instruction was changed into an elective. But almost all parents registered their children for religious instruction, especially in the villages. In the cities the majority of the parents insisted that their children should receive religious instruction. But they were put under pressure by the Communists with the result that by 1952 only 11% of all school children were registered for religious instruction. Teachers of religion were subjected to a decree by the Minister of Education which stipulated that they must submit their lesson plans for approval, that they could no longer participate in any other school activities, and must leave the school buildings as soon as they had finished their classes. They were isolated from the rest of the faculty. Persons who showed anti-Communist bias, or who infringed in any way upon the decrees of the state, could be removed from their teaching position without recourse to higher authorities. Students were not to be given grades in religion and were not to be disciplined in any way by their teachers of religion.

Shortly before Christmas 1949 all nuns working in hospitals were ordered to remove their habits if they wanted to continue in the nursing profession. In protest against this decree Catholic sisters resigned from 15 large hospitals. Christmas cards which had been sent to wish friends and relatives a blessed Christmas were stamped by the postal authorities with the inscription: "Christmas is your festival. The First of May is ours. Christ is your superstition. Socialism is our faith."

In February 1950 the Central Committee of the Communist Party called upon all members to fight against "the black enemies of the state." Readiness to sign the Stockholm Peace Appeal was considered proof of loyalty in Hungary. The Catholic Bishops' Conference on April 27, 1950, made a confession to peace but at the same time declared that it was making this confession also in the name of all priests and members of religious orders and that therefore their signature to the Stockholm Peace Appeal was not necessary. Under the leadership of a few pro-Communist clergymen a Peace Movement was organized which at first did not have a large following. About 20 clergymen were arrested when they refused to sign the peace appeal (summer 1950). The Communists launched an attack against monasteries and convents, following the pattern set by the Czech Communists. It began with a violent propaganda war. The Minister of Education, Ravai, incited the people by saying: "Hundreds and thousands of monks and nuns are walking through our country and are doing the work of agents of imperialism." The government took a firm stand against the orders. On April 15, 36 leading members of the religious orders sent a memorandum to the government stating: "In recent months we have suffered great injustices. There have been attacks against our living in religious communities. This interference is not only against the feelings of the masses of the Hungarian workers but disregards outrageously the promises of freedom of religion made in the Hungarian Constitution.... We are forced to live in our monasteries and convents, which have been built by the sacrifices and self-denials of the faithful, as in a ghetto, and some of us have been forced to leave them. By invoking the decree concerning the confiscation of Catholic schools, parts of our buildings which had never been used for school purposes have been taken away from us. We declare that these buildings belong exclusively to our orders. In many cases our chapels, our houses for spiritual exercises and cultural activities, and our print-shops have been taken from us. We are constantly being hampered in our spiritual ministry. Our seminaries, novitiate homes and theological schools have been confiscated."

They were speaking to the wind. Minister Ravai answered in a speech on July 5, 1950, that in a people's democracy there is no room for monks and nuns, because their very existence is sabotaging the purpose of a people's democracy. He stated that it was high time that these parasites should "be deprived of the possibility to hurt the interests of our people's democracy." He declared that the 63 orders and religious communities of Hungary with their 11,538 members and 636 monasteries and convents would be liquidated. They were no longer needed since a people's democracy had no room for beggars. In the night of June 9-10, 1950, 300 priests and 700 nuns were informed by letter: "I have ordered your expulsion. You are commanded to leave your present place of residence and to move to internment camp X. Reason: Your stay in your present residence is undesirable for reasons of public order and safety. There is no appeal against the order, and it must be carried out immediately. You are not allowed to leave your place of internment." During the night trucks appeared at the front gates of the monasteries and convents to cart away the monks and nuns who had thus been expelled. They were permitted to take only five kilograms of baggage with them. The Hungarian people were told that ammunition, radios, and espionage materials had been found in the houses of the religious orders. Archbishop Grösz of Kalocsa, who, after the imprisonment of Cardinal Mindszenty, had assumed the presidency of the Bishops' Conference, called the other bishops together to discuss this action by the government (June 20). In order to put the assembled bishops under pressure the government expelled an additional 2,000 members of the religious orders during the night of June 18-19. It urged the bishops to begin consultations with the government so that they might arrive at an understanding. These consultations were begun on June 28. To bring them to a quick conclusion, the government expelled a third batch of monks and nuns until 3,500 had been interned. Furthermore, on July 4 Catholic Action was ordered to stop all its activities. Finally, a pro-Communist Priests' Convention was held at Budapest (August 3) which condemned the attitude of the bishops and demanded the conclusion of an agreement with the state. This meeting was attended by 300 Catholic priests.

On August 29, 1950, the agreement between church and state was concluded. It was clearly the result of extortion. It proclaimed as its goal "the peaceful cooperation between church and state and contribution to the peaceful development of both." The first part dealt with the duties of the church in the Communist state. The Bishops' Conference recognized the government and the constitution of the Hungarian People's Republic and declared that "it will take action in accordance with canon law against all persons who sabotage the order which has been established by the laws of the People's Republic and who oppose the work of our government." The bishops stated: "We condemn every activity that is directed against the government and we shall not permit that the religious beliefs of the faithful are abused for anti-state purposes. We appeal to the faithful to cooperate as citizens and patriots to the best of their ability in the great work of raising the living standard of our people and to give them social justice. We ask the clergy not to oppose the collectivization of agriculture. We support the peace movement and condemn all warlike activity and the use of the atomic bomb. We will condemn any government which uses this bomb for the first time, and accuse it of crimes against humanity." In the second part of the agreement the government guaranteed the freedom of religion and the free exercise of it, as had been promised in the constitution. It also guaranteed freedom of action for the church. It agreed to the reopening of eight Catholic schools, six for boys and two for girls, and gave its consent that monks and nuns could stay in their religious communities in sufficient numbers to carry on the work in these eight schools. In agreement with the stipulations arrived at with other denominations concerning the payment of subsidies, the government promised to pay subsidies during the first 18 years until the church would be able to take care of her own needs. The subsidies were to be decreased every three or five years and were to be used primarily for the remuneration of the lower clergy.

In a letter to the Minister of Education, Archbishop Grösz voiced the hope that "the difficulties in the relationship between church and state can be solved in the spirit of mutual understanding and that this solution be arrived at in the spirit of sincere humility, especially in the case of those members of the religious orders whose work is considered necessary for carrying out the assignments given to them in the agreement, so that they may be able to continue their work undisturbed." At the same time the Bishops' Conference declared that it did not want "to infringe in any way upon the rights of the Apostolic See." But the hopes of Archbishop Grösz were not realized.

On September 7, 1950, the government promulgated Decree No. 14, which, at one stroke of the pen, dissolved all religious orders. Paragraph 1 stated that members of religious orders would no longer be permitted to carry on their work except those who were actively engaged in teaching students in the eight Catholic schools. They were not allowed to recruit novices, except those needed to continue the work in the above-mentioned schools. Paragraph 2 stipulated that all members of the orders must immediately stop all their activities and leave their houses within three months and to find secular employment. The houses of the orders were declared national property together with all their inventory. In a joint pastoral letter the bishops protested against this decree (September 10). After lengthy discussions between government and church authorities, 1,422 priests of the religious orders were licensed to work as secular priests in the parishes. The remainder were forced to work in factories, in agriculture, and as minor officials in various offices. Those who were unable to work were sent to socialist old folks' homes. A number of the sisters were employed as nurses in hospitals. The Benedictines, Piarists, and Franciscans were permitted to conduct two Catholic boys' schools and to ordain two or three priests every year, for the care of the boys' schools, while the sisters of Szeged received permission to conduct two girls' schools. In order to make the church dependent upon the state also in her inner administration, the government encouraged the movement of so-called Peace Priests. The leaders of this group were first Franz Varga and later Stephan Barlogh, but surprisingly, in 1949, the prelate and canon Nicholas Beresztoszy, who had belonged to the intimate inner circle of Cardinal Mindszenty, was appointed its leader. He had been condemned to prison and was said to have suffered inhuman treatment at the hands of the Communists. Suddenly he was released and entrusted, not only with the leadership of the Peace Priests, but also with the leadership of the cathedral chapter. In June 1950, the vicar-general of Cardinal Mindszenty died. The cathedral chapter elected the legitimate chapter vicar to become vicar-general of the archdiocese. He was to administer the archdiocese "during the absence of the Cardinal." Two days later he was arrested. The chapter now elected Msgr. Meszlenyi to take the place of the arrested vicar-general and charged him with the same duties as the former. Meszlenyi was arrested 12 days later. In order not to endanger any more priests, the chapter felt compelled to elect Beresztoszy. As a counter-measure the Vatican appointed Bishop Hamvas to act as Apostolic Administrator of the archdiocese. But Beresztoszy remained as its vicar-general. His place in the chapter was taken by another pro-Communist peace priest, the Cistercian monk, Richard Horvath, who was given the title protonotary of the chapter.

On April 8, 1951, the collecting of signatures for the Peace Appeal began in earnest. Numerous priests signed willingly, but the bishops refused. The government called them "enemies of the people" and accused them of violating the agreement of August 20, 1950. Thereupon all bishops signed the appeal, with the sole exception of Archbishop Grösz. The latter was arrested on May 15, 1951. On that same date a State Office for Ecclesiastical Affairs was established. It was charged, first of all, to execute the agreement between church and state; secondly, to supervise all personnel of the church; thirdly, to work out detailed regulations for the administration of the church; fourthly, to regulate all questions touching upon matters of religious life and freedom of conscience; and fifthly, to see to it that all government decrees pertaining to the church were faithfully obeyed on the part of the church administration. Thus the bishops and their representatives in the administration of the church became subject not only to the control, but also to the legal power of the state over the church. All self-administration within the church had ceased.

In the meantime Archbishop Grösz and eight others were brought to trial. The accusation strangely resembled the accusation against Mindszenty. They were accused of having organized a conspiracy to overthrow the People's Republic and having planned a war and the formation of a new government. The archbishop was alleged to have been in charge of this conspiracy and to have been slated to become provisional Head of State until the Hapsburgs could return. The other men accused with Grösz were accused of having made a list of ministers proposed for the new government and having given this list to the ambassadors of hostile powers. They were also accused of illegal financial manipulations. They were said to have smuggled out of the country objects of art in order to provide funds for the organization of the conspirators. They were accused of having organized armed bands, of having hidden persons who were sought by the police, and of having had a hand in the dissemination of illegal brochures and other sabotage actions. The prior of the Paulist order, Ferenc Vezer, was accused of having formed after the beginning of the Russian occupation terror bands consisting of *kulaks*—landholders—and of having sworn an oath that he would assassinate members of the Soviet army and of having killed a Russian soldier from ambush.

The trial began on June 22, 1951. The prosecutor and the presiding judge were the same persons that had tried Cardinal Mindszenty. A reporter from the Vienna *Arbeiterzeitung* wrote about this trial: "This is no longer a show trial. It is a surrealistic play performed in an insane asylum. . . . The accused repeat the words which they have been taught; and when one of them stumbles, the presiding judge prompts him that he can continue, adding from time to time an encouraging 'Good,' 'Very Good,' and prodding the self-accusers to implicate themselves, although they are trembling with fear." The defendants confessed to every crime that had been imputed to them. The Paulist abbot—whose order had been abolished with the other orders in 1950—outdid his fellow-defendants in self-accusations by trying to accuse his whole order of immoral practices and of having run a notorious night club in Budapest. He declared that every monk had a mistress. On June 28 the verdict was passed. Archbishop Grösz was condemned on all counts and was sent to prison for 15 years. The Paulist Ferenc Vezer was condemned to death. The others received prison terms of from eight to 14 years.

This trial was the second breaking of the dam after the Mindszenty affair. On the day after the verdict the National Peace Committee of the Catholic Clergy published a peace appeal, in which prelates who were loyal to Rome were called "criminals against the Catholic Church" and in which the committee declared that except for purely religious questions the Vatican had no authority over the Hungarian Catholic Church. The signers of the appeal promised that they would without reservation follow the goals of the Communist government.

On July 3 the Praesidium of the Hungarian People's Republic issued a decree concerning the occupancy of ecclesiastical offices. Archbishops, titular bishops, bishops and their coadjutors, superiors and abbots, provincials of religious orders, and other prelates, might be appointed only with the previous consent of the Praesidium. This decree was made retroactive to January 1, 1946. In the explanation the praesidium stated that the appointment of high church officials had always been a privilege of the government of Hungary and that historically the church had never been able to make an appointment that had not been approved by the government. Even in the twentieth century appointments to the most important ecclesiastical offices in every case had to be submitted to the government for approval. But since 1945 the Vatican had unilaterally done away with this traditional practice and had not asked the government for its consent. The State Office for Ecclesiastical Affairs must see to it that all bishops are assigned vicar-generals who are loyal to the state. In the residence of each bishop was placed a commissar appointed by the Office for Ecclesiastical Affairs. Without the permission of this commissar not a single act of administration was permitted. He alone decided who was allowed to speak to his bishop. The pastoral letters for the most part were written by the vicars-general and signed by them. The Office for Ecclesiastical Affairs increased its authority more and more. For example, it decreed that all church festivals that fell on a weekday had to be celebrated on the Sunday following the festival, so that production would not be hampered. The saying of Masses on Sundays was not to conflict with demonstrations and meetings of the Communist Party.

As in the case of Cardinal Mindszenty the Catholic Bishops' Conference refused to support Archbishop Grösz during his trial and, under its new president, Archbishop Czapik, assured the government of the Hungarian People's Republic of its complete loyalty (July 3, 1951). Whether this declaration was entirely voluntary and whether it expressed the genuine feelings of the Hungarian bishops could not be ascertained. The bishops declared: "We confess that the Hungarian People's Republic is our beloved fatherland and we shall observe its laws. In accordance with this assurance we condemn all activities of terror and illegal methods, especially the activities of priests whose sinful actions have recently come to light. We promise to start disciplinary actions in agreement with canon law against any priest who has become guilty of any infringement against the laws of the People's Republic." At the end of their declaration the subservient bishops expressed their wholehearted support of the World Peace Movement.

On July 21 all Hungarian bishops took the oath of loyalty to the state. At the ceremony Czapik said among other things that with this oath the bishops wanted to give an expression of their sincere intention "to help with all our strength to realize the peaceful goals of our country and of our people in the great undertakings which are being begun for the welfare and the raising of the living standards of our people. We shall support the peace policy of our people and our state." But at the same time they claimed: "We shall confess the faith of the Catholic Church and obey her discipline and shall not be shaken in our loyalty toward the church."

In September 1952 seven seminaries were closed. Now the church had only four seminaries left and the theological academy in Budapest which formerly had been the theological faculty of the university had been changed into an academy by the state. The seminaries of the various orders had been abolished earlier. In the four seminaries which were still permitted to function strict control was maintained by the state. Decisions concerning the matriculation of candidates for the priesthood, the filling of the quota, and the ordination to the priesthood were made by the Office for Ecclesiastical Affairs. Marxism became a compulsory course of instruction in all seminaries. Professors were chosen preferably from among the peace priests. As much as possible, the latter were also placed into all administrative positions.

4. The Lessening of Tensions and the People's Revolt

Beginning with 1953 there was a noticeable lessening of tension between church and state. The cause could be found in the great economic and social difficulties with which the government was forced to cope. In this emergency Archbishop Czapik promised loyal cooperation of all Catholic people. The moderate government of Imre Nagy, in power since July 1953, declared that it would correct certain "errors" and would change things that had been done wrong. It promised to do away with all excessive interference in the affairs of the church. Nagy showed marked reticence to interfere in the affairs of the Catholic Church and Archbishop Czapik together with the Reformed Bishop Bereczky was elected to the National Council of the People's Front which had been recently organized. Even after Nagy had been removed from the office of prime minister on the charge of rightist deviationism there was no change for the worse under the new government of Andras Hegedüs. On June 16, 1955, it announced: "In accordance with the request of Cardinal Mindszenty and of the bishops and in consideration of the health and the age of the prelate, the Ministry of Justice has interrupted his imprisonment. It has assigned to him a place of residence suggested by the bishops." Shortly before this announcement, the Holy Office in Rome had placed on the Index two magazines, *A Kereszt* ("The Cross") and, *Bulletin Catholique Hongrois,* because they had tried to give a false impression concerning conditions in Hungary. They had declared that Catholics in Hungary were living in peace with the Communists and that the church was enjoying full freedom. In spite of the ban by the Vatican the magazines continued to be published.

On April 25, 1956, Archbishop Czapik died. On May 11, Archbishop Grösz was pardoned. Prime Minister Hegedüs received him in audience on May 12 and informed him that the government had no objection to his resuming the administration of the diocese and to his taking over the presidency of the Bishops' Conference. Archbishop Grösz, according to Budapest news reports, thanked the government "for its noble gesture," which made it possible for him to become part of the reconstruction of the nation. He spoke of a very happy change in the relationship between church and state which was proof for the correctness of the way in which the Bishops' Conference under the leadership of Archbishop Czapik had worked. He was willing to continue on this road and to strengthen the relationship to the state. He said: "I want to be a loyal and devoted son of my fatherland, the Hungarian People's Republic, and I want to educate those who are entrusted to me that they may work and be ready to sacrifice as citizens of the Hungarian fatherland. They must take their duties as citizens of the state seriously. Finally, I pray to God for his blessings upon our common task."

In the meantime the political developments climaxed in the bloody revolt of the fall of 1956. Here we can give only a brief account of the revolt: Imre Nagy had been deprived of his office as prime minister in April 1955 by the Stalinist Secretary of the Communist Party, Mattyas Rakosy, because he had shown liberalizing tendencies. But the criticism that had been leveled against Stalin at the Twentieth Russian Communist Party Congress, combined with the condemnation of the cult of personality and with a tendency to permit freer development of democracy, found a fertile soil in Hungary. Rakosy became the best-hated man in Hungary. The chief promoters of this protest were writers who belonged to the writers' union. They demanded freedom for their work and the leading man of the Petöfi Club, which had been organized in the spring of 1956, the sociologist and literary historian George Lukacs, attacked those who insisted on keeping the dogmatism of the old-line Communists alive. On June 27, at a meeting of the club, which thousands attended, Rakosy was harshly criticized. In July 1956 he was forced to submit his resignation. He admitted the mistakes of the past "committed in the interest of the cult of personality and in an effort to uphold the socialist law." At the end of July the Communist leaders who had been executed during the earlier purges were rehabilitated, among them also the former Communist Party chief, Laslo Rajk. In the meantime there was an increase of resistance among the young people, especially the university students, against the régime. In the middle of October 3,000 students of the university of Szeged left the Hungarian Youth movement. Students at three universities in the form of an ultimatum demanded more freedom for press and literature, permission to travel to the West, better living conditions as well as discontinuance of compulsory courses in Marxism-Leninism. If nothing was done, they threatened to strike and to demonstrate in the streets.

On October 23 the students of Budapest carried out a demonstration which soon swelled into a meeting of hundreds of thousands. They demanded that Hungary should follow the example of Poland and should permit greater freedom and that Imre Nagy should be restored to his former position. The new Secretary of the Communist Party, Ernö Gerö, explained in a radio address that Hungary would never give up her friendship with Soviet Russia. The demonstrating students answered him during the night of October 24 with calls: "Get rid of the Russians! Hungary belongs to the Hungarians! We demand a public trial for Rakosy!" Demonstrations increased, and there were acts of violence. The monument of Stalin was toppled, the radio station taken over, and other public buildings were attacked. During the night Prime Minister Hegedüs was replaced by Imre Nagy. In the bloody battles in Budapest and other cities throughout the country the revolutionaries, who represented all classes of the people, seemed to be victorious. Nagy replaced Gerö with Janos Kadar as Secretary of the Communist Party and promised a coalition government if the Russian troops would withdraw. When new Russian troops invaded the country, Nagy announced on October 31 that Hungary was withdrawing from the Warsaw Pact and would be a neutral nation. On November 3 the revolt was suppressed by Russian divisions. Nagy was arrested and later, in 1958, was executed. With him many others lost the freedom or their lives, and 20,000 Hungarians were deported to Russia while a host of refugees fled the country. Janos Kadar formed the new government.

When the revolution started, the peace priests went into hiding and their leading men fled to Czechoslovakia. On October 30 Cardinal Mindszenty was liberated from the country home in northern Hungary where he had been interned and was brought by government car to Budapest. Imre Nagy declared that the cardinal had been released because his condemnation had not been legal. Janos Kadar, the Secretary-General of the Communist Party, in a radio address gave the consent of the party to the liberation of the cardinal. The cardinal's return to Budapest was a triumphant procession. In a message to all bishops of the world he begged that they should call upon the faithful to be active in their love for the neighbor and to send their gifts to the Hungarian *Caritas* organization. Pope Pius XII in a telegram to the cardinal declared his joy over the liberation of the primate: "May this be a good omen for the beloved Hungarian nation that through your efforts and the efforts of all the bishops and the faithful, Catholic life may be renewed after the dangers and the bloodshed, so that the devotion of your ancestors toward the church and the apostolic see may shine forth forever." The cardinal received a delegation of the government. He expressed his sympathy for the foundation of a Christian party in Hungary, but declared that the church had no intention of having him join the government since his work was of a different nature.

On the evening of November 3 he spoke on Radio Budapest and sent a message to the whole world and to the Hungarian people. At the beginning of his speech he stressed the fact that he was the same as before his imprisonment. He said: "Let every man know that this battle is not a revolution, but a battle for freedom. In 1945, after we had lost the war, a régime was imposed upon us which is now branded by its heirs with the hot irons of contempt, condemnation, and antagonism. These heirs do not need proof. The régime was wiped away by the entire Hungarian people. It was a battle for freedom the like of which the world has never seen before. Our young people were the leaders in this battle. The battle for freedom was fought because the nation wished to arrange its way of life in freedom. In freedom the nation now wants to decide about its government and about the way in which it will carry on its work. Our people do not want to be used for secret aims. We need new elections in which every party can take part. These elections should be held under international control. I am and shall remain independent of every party affiliation on account of my office. On the strength of my authority I warn every Hungarian to stop his quarrels during these wonderful days of national solidarity. . . . The successors of the fallen régime have made disclosures about the past which show that it is necessary to make a clean break with the past. This should be done in every area and by independent and impartial courts. Private vendettas and retaliation should not be tolerated. Those who were part of the régime that has just been removed must be made responsible for their actions, omissions, mistakes, and other detrimental measures."

The church would not resist, the cardinal stated, the things that had been accomplished. She would respect the progress that had been made and would not obstruct any future healthy development. But every trace of terror and all the marks that were typical of the fallen government should be removed. The church was waiting for a speedy restoration of her right to give religious instruction and for the restoration of the institutions and organizations to her that had been taken away from her. She was expecting to see her right to publish restored to her, because she wanted to see whether actions would follow the promises made by the new government. The radio speech of the cardinal was broadcast at a time when the revolt was already breaking down. On November 4 Mindszenty was forced to take refuge in the American Embassy in Budapest where he has lived ever since. He was given two rooms on the third floor of the embassy. Both rooms were wired with a special alarm system, and American marines were placed there for his protection. At night there always remained one diplomat in the building of the embassy. The cardinal continued to take his daily half-hour walks to which he had become accustomed in prison. He had no contact with the outside. He spent his days in prayer, in reading, and in writing his memoirs. On Sundays he celebrated Mass in his living room. The Hungarian government, in spite of all the changes that had taken place since 1956, steadfastly refused to negotiate with the Americans concerning a settlement of the Affair Mindszenty.

5. New Restrictions

After the suppression of the revolt of 1956 the new Prime Minister, Janos Kadar, was dependent upon the military might of the Russians since the Hungarian Communist Party had been all but destroyed during the upheaval. In order to secure the position of the government and to build up the shattered economic life he was forced to compromise. This became clear in his relationship to the church. The Ministry of Education ordered that pupils should be permitted to participate in religious instruction without the written request of their parents. The periods of religious instruction were even included in the regular school schedule if more than half the pupils in any given grade desired to participate in it.

In January 1957 the government announced its policy toward the churches in the following four-point declaration: "The revolutionary workers' and peasants' government in the spirit of the constitution respects the freedom of conscience of all citizens, and in regard to religion it is of the opinion that this is the private affair of every individual citizen. Therefore, in the same spirit, the government guarantees, supports, and defends the freedom of the church and of all the cults; it recognizes and honors the agreements which have been concluded between the People's Democracy and the church and guarantees voluntary religious instruction in the schools and participation in this instruction. At the same time the government expects that priests, clergymen, and the members of the various churches in view of the present conditions will honor the stipulations of the agreements in the interest of lessening present tensions and of helping in the social consolidation. Conscious of its legal responsibility, the government cannot permit that any organ or activity of the church be put into the service of political reaction which is against the legal order of the Hungarian People's Republic. The government considers it inadmissible that any servant of the church should be discriminated against on account of his progressive views in the exercise of his functions and his activities. Such discrimination violates the laws of the country. The government desires to do away with any future arguments in the relationship between church and state by way of discussions and mutual agreements."

The question was how the stipulations against political reaction within the church would be applied in practice. Did the church have the freedom to discipline her peace priests? Cardinal Mindszenty had suspended 36 peace priests or had them transferred to other parishes. This procedure was later implemented by a decree of the Conciliar Congregation of the Curia which stated that all priests who did not receive their offices from the regularly appointed ecclesiastical authorities, whose conduct was not in accordance with the laws of the church and who had been suspended or dismissed by their bishops, could be absolved only if they would unconditionally surrender their offices and submit to the legal ecclesiastical authorities. Otherwise they would be automatically excommunicated with the excommunication reserved to the Holy See. But the Hungarian bishops had been unable to enforce this decree. On September 7, 1957, the Holy See forbade by a further decree any political activity of the Hungarian clergy. When Richard Horvath, Miklos Beresztoczy, and Janos Mate, who were members of the Hungarian parliament, did not resign from their offices, the Roman Congregation announced on February 15, 1958, that they had been excommunicated. The controversy in the question of the peace priests did not lead to an open conflict between the government and the episcopate, but it remained a latent source of irritation. The period of the lessening of tension was soon replaced by a new frost.

On December 3, 1957, began the trial of the former secretary of Mindszenty, Msgr. Egon Turcsanyi, and 15 other priests accused of counter-revolutionary activities. The public was not admitted. During the revolt Turcsanyi had taken to himself certain documents from the Office for Ecclesiastical Affairs and had spirited them away. The other defendants were accused of having published the radio address of the cardinal and the letter of Pope Pius XII to the Hungarian people. The prosecutor asked the death penalty for Turcsanyi which was commuted to life imprisonment. He died in the penitentiary at the beginning of 1959. The other defendants received sentences up to 10 years in prison.

While this trial was going on, the government bestowed the Order of the Banner of the Hungarian People's Republic upon Archbishop Grösz on his 70th birthday on December 9, 1957. The President of the Praesidium, Istvan Dobi, declared that the archbishop had done great work for the peace and the betterment of relations between church and state. This was the same Dobi who had been the president of the court that in 1951 had condemned Grösz to 15 years in prison. At that time the archbishop had been called an "infamous beast," an American spy, a friend of fascism, a criminal, and a traitor. Two days after the presentation of the order to the archbishop, the man who had freed Mindszenty from his prison was condemned to death and immediately executed.

The Peace Priests had been discredited during the revolt. Their treacherous acts had come to light when Turcsanyi spirited away the documents from the Office for Ecclesiastical Affairs. These documents revealed how the Peace Priests controlled the attitudes and the behavior of individual priests. The task of the Peace Priests' movement had been to split the church. In order to prevent the revival of this movement and at the same time to pacify the state, the Hungarian bishops organized the *Opus Pacis* movement (May 1957) in imitation of the Polish *Pax Christi* movement. In a proclamation they announced that they had followed the directions of the "Vicar of Christ on earth" to work at the threshold of the atomic age for the preservation and the salvation of mankind. They stated that they were supporting "the endeavors of the World Peace Council and other endeavors which would serve the cause of universal peace. Therefore we expect that our priests will absorb the thoughts of peace into their hearts in ever increasing measure. They must join with all the believers in an attempt to find a solution for the small and big problems, both external and internal, by way of peaceful negotiations." The bishops made an agreement with the national peace council. They declared that in cooperation with the council they would organize a Catholic Committee for the National Peace Council under the presidency of Bishop Endre Hamvas, and would supervise all Catholic peace activities within the framework of the church in cooperation with the National Peace Council through their *Opus Pacis* organization which they placed under the chairmanship of Archbishop Grösz.

But the Peace Priests were not eliminated that easily. They infiltrated the *Opus Pacis* movement which became clear when the membership of the various committees was drawn up and included the excommunicated priests Beresztoczy and Bela Mag. The bishops could not avoid working together with these excommunicated priests and appearing with them in public. Moreover, the *Opus Pacis* movement proved less than a success. The Peace Priests reorganized as a separate movement. One of their speakers declared that it was their task "to conduct the peace movement according to the program of the general peace movement, so that the peace work of the clergy can be done more effectively and can be developed more successfully." Beresztoczy, who on behalf of the Office for Ecclesiastical Affairs reorganized the Peace Priests, published a monthly magazine, *Katolikus Szo*, which was edited by the excommunicated Richard Horvath.

A very serious interference took place at the beginning of 1959 in the seminary of Budapest. The students had been asked to participate in a peace meeting, but 88 of the 90 students had refused.

Thereupon the seminary was closed and when it was reopened the Office for Ecclesiastical Affairs refused to readmit 14 students who had been responsible for the "lack of discipline." Another 18 students resigned in protest. The other 60 declared in a letter to the episcopate that they desired to live in peace with everyone and that therefore they wanted to participate "only in meetings which are arranged by our bishops, but will refuse to participate in meetings which are conducted by persons with whom we do not wish to have any dealings." The signatories of this letter were ordered to write a recantation. Only 10 obeyed. The other 50 were dismissed. The spiritual director of the seminary, Dr. Imre Papp, was replaced by the ex-Franciscan Priest Franz Kiraly. Two years later a similar incident led to a renewed interference by the state. The senior students at the seminary of Györ (Raab) had refused to appear at a rally of the Peace Priests. Several of the students were dismissed and the director of the seminary was also fired.

At the beginning of April 1959 the government published orders for the implementation of the decrees of 1951 at which time the administration of all ecclesiastical offices had been placed under state control. Now in addition it was decreed that if church offices were not occupied within 60 days—in the case of bishops within 90 days—the state would take the necessary measures "in the interests of continuity, of pastoral care, of ecclesiastical administration, and of the education of the priests." This order made it possible for the state to appoint bishops to places where the regular bishops had been banished or interned.

On June 2, 1959, Karoly Olt was appointed the new head of the Office for Ecclesiastical Affairs. In the previous years he had been one of the most prominent representatives of the hard line of Rakosy. Between November 1960 and March 1961 about 150 active Catholics, among them many priests, were arrested. They were accused of having given illegal religious instruction. House searches had led to the confiscation of catechisms. In a letter written to Prime Minister Münich, Archbishop Grösz took the side of the arrested priests. He wrote: "These men have been my co-workers for years, and I personally take responsibility for everything that has been done. If these arrested priests are condemned, then I should be condemned too. Please arrest me and imprison me with my friends." In June 1961 a public trial was conducted against 12 of the arrested, including eight priests and monks. In this trial the former Secretary of Catholic Action, Father Odön Lenard, who was also the spiritual advisor of the Catholic School Association, showed marked courage. Once before, in 1948, he had been condemned to six years in the penitentiary on account of his protest against the closing of Catholic private schools. When he had been released after an amnesty in 1953, he had been forbidden to carry on any priestly activity, especially the education of young people. For a time he had worked as a factory worker. In the evenings he used to gather young people around him, especially students, to instruct them in the Catholic faith. It was for this activity that he had been re-arrested on February 6, 1961. He was the only defendant who pleaded "Not Guilty" in court. Since the court trial was being broadcast over the radio, a large number of people were witnesses to a dialogue that took place between the judge and the defendant. Judge Istvan Bimbo asked Lenard why he had not obeyed the orders of the government. Lenard answered: "I accept orders only from my archbishop, but he was in no position to give me orders at the time." Judge: "You admit, then, to having engaged in illegal activities. Have you instructed young people in the Catholic religion?" Lenard: "If it is permitted to give private music instruction, I see no reason why I should be forbidden to give private religious instruction. In the materialistic society in which we are living each individual is under strong pressure. Some people who are exposed to this pressure in a special way are unable to send their children to religious instruction openly. These children I have instructed privately." Judge: "Have you hidden theological books in a couch?" Lenard: "I do not know of any law that forbids me to keep theological books in a couch." Judge: "What do you think of students of theology who refuse to participate in compulsory lectures on Marxism-Leninism?" Lenard: "There are also Marxists who refuse to go to church." Judge: "You have subjected 300 young people to your influence against the state." Lenard: "I am aware of only 70 whom I have taught the Gospel in my off-duty hours." The court condemned the courageous priest to seven and a half years in prison. The other defendants received prison terms up to 12 years because they "had conspired against the state." In July 1961 a second trial opened against a number of prominent Catholics, but this trial was conducted behind closed doors. The men of this group, too, were accused of having given private religious instruction and thus having become guilty of counter-revolutionary activities.

In June 1961, the Office for Ecclesiastical Affairs issued new regulations for the registration of children whose parents wanted them to participate in religious instruction. According to these new rules, schools could give religious instruction only if at least 10% of the children desired it. At the time of registration both parents had to be present and had to address a special request to the director of the school. When Archbishop Grösz asked the Office for Ecclesiastical Affairs to permit the showing of religious films and slides for the purpose of religious instruction, he was informed: "Catholic religious instruction has been carried on without slides and films for 2,000 years and shall continue in this way." As early as the beginning of 1960 the archbishop had publicly protested at a meeting of the Patriotic People's Front in Budapest that the authorities were "suppressing religion in our country with unconstitutional acts of terror." On October 3, 1961, Grösz died at the age of 74 years. On October 6, 1961, the Bishop of Csanad, Dr. Endre Hamvas, who had been friendly to the government, was elected to become presiding bishop of the conference. But conditions did not change.

B. PROTESTANTISM

Hungarian Protestants are divided into Reformed and Lutherans and a number of small sects. The Reformed Church, which has always been strong among the Magyars, numbered at the end of the war about 2,000,000 souls. The 1,200 Reformed parishes with their 1,500 pastors were organized into four dioceses and into 27 seniorates. The Lutheran Church, which originally had been strongly German, had suffered great losses through deportations and expulsions after 1945 and numbered about 450,000 souls organized into 323 parishes with 430 pastors. Her two—formerly four—dio-

ceses had each eight seniorates and were administered by two
bishops and two district inspectors, while the general church body
was administered by an inspector-general and the senior bishop of
the church.

That Protestantism took a different attitude toward the changes
that had taken place since 1945 and that it rejected the fight of
Cardinal Mindszenty against the state became clear in a declaration issued by the Protestant church leaders at the time of the
Mindszenty trial. The reason for this attitude could be found in
the differences between the doctrines of the Roman Church and
the Church of the Reformation, especially their ecclesiologies. In
addition, there were deep historical wounds, never healed, which
had been inflicted on Protestantism during the Counter-Reformation. The country, which had been almost completely Protestant
at the end of the 16th century, had been re-Catholicized by the
Hapsburgs in close alliance with the hierarchy of the Catholic
Church and her religious orders. This work had been carried out,
especially after 1673, with bloody terror. Churches had been
closed and taken away from the Protestants, their pastors and
teachers had been accused on the basis of falsified letters, they had
been sold into slavery or to the galleys of Naples. All Protestant
officials had been deprived of their offices. Protestant families had
been driven from their homes, their schools and their children had
been taken away from them, and they had been tortured by all the
means at the disposal of church and state. Breaches of promise and
revolts with their underlying social and national motives characterized the bloody battle between the churches. During the Blood
Trial of Eperies in 1687 a large number of Protestants were executed on the basis of testimonies which had been obtained by
means of torture and false accusations, and their property was
confiscated. Even during the 18th century this pressure continued.
Not until the Edict of Tolerance, issued by Joseph II in 1781, was
there a letup. The year 1884 brought equality under the law. But
even during the pre-war years the Catholic Church had pushed
the Protestants around wherever she could do so with impunity. In
the minds of the Protestants the history of these 350 years left a
deep distrust toward the Catholic Church. Thus they felt a certain

satisfaction when the predominance of Rome was broken after 1945. Full equality under the law was given not only to the two major Protestant denominations, but also to the small Free Churches. Formerly the churches of Hungary had been divided into three groups: The accepted Roman Catholic Church, the recognized Lutheran and Reformed Churches, and the tolerated churches. This inglorious division had now become a thing of the past. The President of the Baptist Church, Dr. Imre Somogyi, stated joyously: "One of the first noble gestures of the new democratic government was the recognition of the rights of those small denominations and communions which during the war had been forbidden by the government and by the extremists." The activity of the Association of Free Churches was sanctioned by government decree. Pastors and evangelists received papers entitling them to carry on their work unhampered. All buildings used for divine services were exempted from confiscation, and the Ministry of Education established a special section for the Free Churches.

1. The Reformed Church

Towards the end of 1947 it was reported that the Reformed Church was not persecuted in any way. The state spent large sums for religious purposes and the work of the schools of the church continued unhampered. There was freedom of speech in the pulpit, and the work of evangelization in the congregations was not hampered. Yet the church felt somewhat hemmed in. She knew that the leading men of the state were not kindly disposed toward her. Karl Barth, who traveled in Hungary in the spring of 1948, said many things in praise of the inner condition of the church. During his last visit in 1936 he had found the same persons and circles, with whom he visited now, engaged in feverish nationalistic activities which seemed to him to put into shade even the things he had seen in Nazi Germany. But all this had changed after the war. National pride, hatreds, and aspirations had been toned down. He realized that the Reformed Church was not completely in favor of the socialist system of government. But she had shown a positive attitude toward soil reform, while reserving for herself the right to reject other measures of the government if the necessity should arise. Barth was impressed by her attitude, and stated: "I did not see a church preoccupied with the differences between East and West, nor with the memories of the Russian terror, nor with questions of right and wrong, but with the positive task of the church, not in a way in which things were moving in Germany toward new confessional and liturgical restrictions, but with a concern for proclaiming the old Word in a new way and a new environment, a way that was based on thorough theological heart-searching. She was concerned about evangelization, especially within the Reformed congregations, as a presupposition for her future work and attitudes. If only Germany had started at this point with united efforts."

a. Willing Bishops

In spite of the apparent inner calm which Karl Barth believed to sense in Hungary, the crossbeams of the church edifice were cracking. In May 1947 Dr. Laszlo Ravasz resigned from his office as Bishop of the Danubian Diocese and in his last report gave vent to the wish that the church would be permitted to be free and that the state would remain neutral ideologically. When the church schools were secularized in 1948, the Reformed Church surrendered without protest her 1,079 schools, while the Lutheran church leadership stated that the church "was suffering the secularization only because she had to bow to the dictates of the state." The result was that the state showed greater favoritism to the Reformed than to the Lutherans. The Reformed Church received more paper for her publications, and in marked contrast to the Lutherans her representatives received permission to travel abroad and to attend the organization meeting of the World Council of Churches in Amsterdam. Pastor Albert Bereszky was elected as successor to Bishop Ravasz. He was a man completely devoted to the Communist régime and stated that he was in favor of a thorough house-cleaning like that which had taken place in the Catholic Church. He wanted to rid the church of all people who were opposed to the government. When the government requested the removal of all those who were holdovers from before 1945, the Reformed lay leaders resigned as a body. Roland Kiss was elected moderator of the Reformed Church of Hungary. He had been a charter member of the Communist Party and had served five years in the penitentiary because he had taken part in the Bolshevist revolution of Bela Khun in 1919. He now was serving as member of Parliament and was also a cabinet officer. Ferenc Erdei became moderator of the Trans-Tiszian Diocese. He was the son of a small landholder and was now serving as Minister of Agriculture.

On October 8, 1948, an agreement was signed between church and state. In it the state guaranteed the free exercise of religion in divine services and the unhampered work of the church in religious instruction in the schools. In return the church recognized the seizure of the schools of the Reformed Church by the state. She was permitted to conduct six intermediate schools and her theological seminaries. Until 1954 she would continue to receive full subsidies from the state, but after that the subsidies would be reduced until by 1968 the church would be on her own.

The Bishop of the Cis-Tiszian Diocese, Andor Enyedi, resigned on January 7, 1952. In his place Janos Peter was elected, and he promptly announced in the church's paper: "In agreement with the ideology of the People's Democracy, I am planning to dismiss a number of higher and lower church officials. Whoever cannot accept wholeheartedly the agreement between the People's Democracy and the Reformed Church is not fit to occupy a responsible position in the church." Similar changes in personnel were carried out in the other dioceses. The new leadership of the church insisted that all the property of the church should be surrendered to the state. But even where the church did not own income-producing real estate, resistance against these orders was so strong that Bishop Bereczky at various times had to urge the presbyterial boards to comply.

b. "Prophetic" Theology

What was the reason for this excessive zeal of the church leaders? The reason was based on a twisted theological attitude toward

Communism. Reading the numerous sermons, reports, and manifestos which Bereczky, Peter, and others produced in those years, we must conclude that the Reformed Church was suffering from an overpowering guilt-complex. The church had been identified too closely with the former feudal system and had been the chief guardian of a small group of rich people. She had preserved the injustices under which the impoverished masses had been suffering for decades. Then the revolutions after 1945 had changed all this. The church considered these changes as the judgment of God. She confessed that she had deserved to be destroyed, but God in his mercy had given her a new beginning. Now it was the task of the church to understand the hidden meaning of the occurrences in Hungary after 1945 and to take notice of them in her proclamation.

Thus it happened that the Reformed looked upon the Communist rise to power not merely as a political fact, but as a religious experience. They considered the establishment of the People's Democracy a new beginning in history. They compared the achievements of Communism with the injustices of former days and saw in these achievements a decisive progress in the development of man from his former estate of poverty and servitude. They condemned the past and welcomed the new era. The Reformed theologians were suffering from an overdose of sin-consciousness. They demanded of all their followers that they should do penance for the past sins of the church. The essence of this penance was complete surrender to the socialist society of the future. In doing so the church leaders felt that they were heeding the call of God which had come to them during the historical breakthrough of 1945 and later.

This clamor to do penance led to strange results. The proclamation of the church was no longer satisfied with the spiritual sphere. The church refused to retire into political neutrality. Bishop Peter, in a speech dealing with the duties of pastors, declared: "The church cannot be silent at a time when decisions are being made whether a system of exploitation of man by man shall be perpetuated or liquidated. The church must clearly express her view that she will say 'No!' to the continuance of exploitation and 'Yes!' to its abolishment. Our nation is confronted by the great problems of war and peace, and we are fighting side by side with the Soviet Union, because the Soviet Union champions the cause of peace. For us in the church this is not merely a noncommittal statement, but it is a concern which we shall remember in our prayers and in our divine services."

In a resolution passed in January 1952, the seniors of the Reformed Church stated: "We recognize the efforts to break down the harmful inheritance of the past and to build up a truly new and great society. This is part of the service of those among us in the church who are entrusted with her leadership. The liquidation of all forms and opportunities for exploitation and the construction of a new society which makes this exploitation of man by man legally impossible must be dear to a church which wants to remain faithful to her calling, because such measures are God-pleasing and profitable to man. Therefore our place in this change-over is at the side of those who, freed from centuries-old oppressions, are building with courage and expectation a new, just, and more humane society." At a general conference of his diocese Bishop Peter said that the church was obeying the Word of God when she looked for opportunities to participate in the building of socialism. When Bishop Bereczky was given an honorary degree from the University of Prague, in neighboring Czechoslovakia, he gave a speech in which he waxed enthusiastic about the church which had so clearly understood the gracious will of God. Said he: "This is a question that is shaking the foundations of my whole personality. It is the prophetic service which we are trying to carry out. We are taking our place in the church in a radically changing world, we accept the service that is entrusted to us, we become obedient to the most pressing tasks of the church. Is this not a service which the whole church on earth should render to the Christian religion?" All questions of humanity and of justice, he continued, are waiting for the "prophetic word from the church." The past decade had shown the way to the solution of all social problems. The Soviet Union had led humanity to a brighter future by showing man how to coexist peacefully. During that academic act Professor Hromadka praised the bishop as a person who "in a wonderful way has shown clarity of theological thinking, truth in his preaching, a desire to be a shepherd and a fruitful writer, and who combines with all these a clear, penetrating look into the past and present conditions."

Karl Barth was increasingly worried about these theological outbursts which were coming to him from Hungary. On September 16, 1951, he wrote a letter to Bishop Bereczky in which he asked him whether he had not become victim of a grave theological heresy. "You are at the point," Barth wrote, "of making an article of faith of your agreement with Communism, of making it part of the Christian message. . . . You are at the point of wandering into an ideological Christian wonderland which formerly under quite different conditions had been the ideological frame of mind of the Nazi German Christians. . . . I find a great number of statements in the Hungarian church press that are almost identical with what we rejected in the first sentence of the Barmen Declaration of 1934. . . . How do you know what the Lord, who directs human history, wants to create on earth by means of socialism? We know something about these great world-shaking events even if we are no prophets. We know about them from quite different sources. We know a great deal about false prophets. There was, for example, a similar witness by members of the German Church who attended the ecumenical conference in Oxford in 1937. They too felt called to play the part of people who were misunderstood and to whom the future belonged, and with their 'witness' they helped to lead Europe into war and the German people into the abyss."

Barth declared that the Hungarian Church Press Service reminded him of the official information which he received weekly from the Soviet Union. It proclaimed that Hungary was the true paradise where the wolves were lying with the sheep (Isa. 11). "You see, my dear Bishop," Barth continued, "I must always think of my first trip to Hungary in 1936 when I was amazed to see to what extent the Reformed Church was able to use the Crown of St. Stephen to fight against the Treaty of Trianon and for the Hungarian rights against Czechs and Romanians, how she claimed to have a historical mission as an outpost of the Christian West, and to what extent she was able to look upon this mission as the *causa Dei et ecclesiae* (God's and the church's cause). I asked myself then: Is there no other way in which the Reformed Church of Hungary can act than always to be 100% in agreement with the ruling powers? How is it that you put socialism on your banner as if it were the perfect thing? How can you dare to put it on the banner of Jesus Christ? How can you claim in your propaganda that socialism is heaven on earth and is thus identical with what you find in reality in the Hungary of today and throughout the countries of the Eastern bloc? How dare you proclaim, either voluntarily or involuntarily, an optical illusion, namely that we in the West are the slaves of capitalism and imperialism? Are you not forgetting that even in 'dark America' there was the 'social Gospel' at the beginning of this century, at a time when your Hungarian Reformed Church as far as I know had not the slightest idea of what that term meant? She did not know at that time that there could possibly be a relationship between Gospel and socialism. Why do you have to get mixed up in this business of Eastern propaganda of painting everything black and white? Why do you accept the dubious Stockholm Peace Movement, with its dove that shows its claws, as a genuine peace effort? Why do you bestow upon it your ecclesiastical blessing without any reservation?" Barth concluded: "I can explain your attitude only from that theological, or let me call it philosophical, presupposition of which I spoke above. I am very much concerned about this and ask you to rethink your theology radically."

c. *Goal and End of the Confessing Church*

The objections of Karl Barth did not change the internal and external course upon which the Reformed church leadership had embarked. The Reformed leaders remained uncritically optimistic. They accepted the aims of the Communists as part of the church's proclamation and loyally carried out all the commands of the state. Therefore it was not surprising that opposition should arise within this church. This opposition movement called itself the Confessing Church and included pastors, presbyters, and other lay members of the Reformed Church who, on the basis of the Gospel and Protestant theology, showed that they were opposed to the twisted theology and practices of their church's government. Their opposition was expressed in a confessional pamphlet which was published in the summer of 1956 by the Theological Academy of Budapest. The basic ideas and the aims of the opposition were laid down in four points: First, they declared that Christians must object to the idea that the history of salvation is always clearly apparent in the work of the government. They declared: "Any soteriological sanctioning of such an optimistic faith in the progress of salvation is opposed to the Word of God. Also opposed to the Word of God is a philosophy of history which is cloaked in a theological dress. The official church administration sees in the present order of society a positive historical development which leads toward salvation. It makes this ideology a part of the church's proclamation. We are of the firm opinion that the perfection of the new creation takes place within the church which renews herself daily, and not in a change of certain political and economic factors. Salvation is not found in secular history. History cannot establish the kingdom of God. Salvation is found in the redemptive work of Jesus Christ."

Secondly, the Confessing Church objected to the eagerness of the church leaders to do away with the retreats that had been traditional in the church, and to forbid mission work by lay people. With the elimination of this important missionary activity among children, young people, heathen, gypsies, and alcoholics, the church leadership had "supported the planned interference by the government and had misinterpreted the government's attitude as a renewal of the church's real missionary task. We do not agree with this interpretation and in spite of all prohibitions we shall remain faithful to the command of Jesus Christ to carry on our missionary work with courage. This applies to every member of the congregation and especially to the pastors."

Thirdly, the Confessing Church took issue with the position of the church leaders toward secular government and declared that according to Romans 13:1 also the present political government is no more than "an authority given by God." Opposition to this government is not automatically political reaction. The leaders of the Confessing Church declared: "We reject all attempts to restore the conditions of the past through counter-revolutions. We promise to do our duty as citizens with a joyful and sincere heart. We confess that the social order of the past has been judged by God's righteous judgment. But we also confess in the light of the Word of God that the present order of society, like any other order of society, is under the sign of sin and therefore is showing many traits which the church cannot condone." They stated that the "prophetic service of the church demands of her that, on the one hand, she should encourage the higher powers to do good by consenting to their actions—as long as these actions are in agreement with the welfare of the citizens and with justice—and that, on the other hand, she should point out mistakes, omissions, and sins of the government. The present church leadership has carried out only the first part of this prophetic service and has been completely silent on the second part." The Confessing Church felt that "the serving church" had become "a servile church" in Hungary and thus had lost her *raison d'être*. The leaders of the Confessing Church concluded: "Therefore we deem it necessary to admonish our brethren that in dealing with the church authorities they must obey without fear the will of our Lord and must be ready to confess by word and deed what they believe."

Finally, the Confessing Church sharply criticized the dictatorial cliques within the church. It accused the church authorities of having used "intimidation which is customary in the world and of having forced pastors upon congregations, in spite of the objections raised by the congregations. This has been in violation of the heritage of the Reformation. On the other hand, the church administration had also removed pastors from their parishes because these pastors did not agree with the way in which the church administration was conducted and had criticized it. These things have been done by force and on trumped-up charges." The leaders of the Confessing Church stated that the present church administration had always assumed that its decisions were above criticism. Anyone who dared to disagree with the church leaders was branded a sectarian, a troublemaker, and an enemy of the state. This was not merely dictatorship within the church, but also an attempt by the church administration to introduce novel, questionable theological positions into the church, positions which it claimed had validity alone within the church. It forced these positions upon pastors, and made the continuation of the ministry by pastors dependent upon their acceptance of these positions. They also stated that the church administration had monopolized all contact with churches in foreign countries to such an extent that the impressions which Christians abroad received of the Reformed Church in Hungary reflected the opinions of this clique of church leaders and not the witness of the whole church in Hungary. Therefore foreign visitors did not understand the true conditions of the church in Hungary. The document by the Confessing Church closed with these words: "Therefore we are not bound to be blindly obedient, but we are obliged to state that unconditional obedience to our church leaders might in many cases mean disobedience to our Lord Jesus Christ."

It seems that the church administration began to have second thoughts about the course which it had followed. At least there was a plan to carry out certain reforms. But the revolt of 1956 interfered with these plans. It set the spark also to the powder keg that had accumulated in the Reformed Church. On November 1 a number of Reformed pastors met with lay people in the Theological Academy in Budapest and organized the Administrative Council of the Hungarian Reformed Church which took over the government of the Danubian Diocese and of the whole church. On the evening of that day the Dean of the Academy, Professor Laszlo Pap, read over the radio a message by the Administrative Council of the Reformed Church which requested Albert Bereczky and Janos Peter to abdicate. Bishop Bereczky, who was sick at the time in a foreign country, communicated his abdication through his daughter. It was accepted by the diocesan council on November 16. In his place former Bishop Laszlo Ravasz was called to serve again. Bishop Peter had resigned from his post as early as October 31.

In a radio speech which he made in the evening of November 1, Bishop Ravasz supported without reservation the people's revolt. "The Reformed Church of Hungary," he said, "expresses its deep admiration and esteem for the students, soldiers, men and women, for the heroes of the revolt who with their blood have sealed the victory of our national liberation. The church is mourning for the heroes who have fallen and sorrows over them as a mother would sorrow. She is mourning for all Hungarians who have given their lives in this struggle and who by their blood have won the precious freedom of the Hungarian people. Let us kiss their wounds, let us decorate their graves with flowers. There were students of theology among the fallen. They were killed near their Alma Mater. The church is proud of the dignified and fine progress of the revolution which has restored the honor of our nation. We would pray more fervently that this purity of the revolution may be preserved. The church confesses and is truly sorry that in the past, as a representative of Christ on earth, she has been influenced by force, by persuasion, and by a policy which has turned out to be her mortal enemy. This is the reason why the church has not fully carried out her spiritual duties." Bishop Ravasz called upon the pastors to become the living conscience of the people. The congregational councils were to be examples of national unity, social justice, and brotherly love. Ravasz stated: "Our revolution has two enemies, reaction and anarchy. Let no one believe that the system of the past period can be restored. We look upon the acceptance and the further development of the aims that have been reached in this revolution. But we must do away with the mistakes and must restore the things that have been unjustly abolished."

The breakdown of the revolt had grave repercussions in the church. Nine pastors were arrested as politically suspect. Two of them were allowed to return to their congregations. One pastor, Istvan Ban, was condemned to five years in prison. Nothing is known about the fate of the others. The changes in personnel were not accepted by the government. The seniors and the moderators of the dioceses, on March 22 and April 12, 1957, asked Albert Bereczky and Janos Peter to return to their offices. The recall of Bishop Laszlo Ravasz was declared null and void. Bereczky assumed his office again on November 14, 1957, after his health had been restored. However, Janos Peter refused to return to his bishopric. He became a member of the Praesidium of the Hungarian People's Republic, President of the Office for Cultural Relations with Foreign Countries, and, later, First Deputy Foreign Minister. Bishop Laszlo Ravasz, who was involuntarily retired from office, was at first given unlimited permission to preach, but this permission was withdrawn, because on April 14, 1957, he had allegedly preached on Psalm

13:1-2: "How long, O Lord? Wilt thou forget me for ever? How long wilt thou hide thy face from me? How long must I bear pain in my soul, and have sorrow in my heart all the day? How long shall my enemy be exalted over me?" The Dean of the Reformed Academy in Budapest, Laszlo Pap, was at first given a furlough and then removed from his office. Finally he was assigned a small refugee congregation at Murga. The theology professor Barnabas Nagy was deprived of his office. He found work with the university library. His successor was Pastor Benö Bekefi, who, as the right-hand man of Peter, had been largely responsible for the terror regime in the church. In the year 1957 the Cis-Tiszian Diocese was reorganized, and Pastor Lajos Daranyi was unanimously elected its bishop. He was a product of the revival movement and had tried during the years preceding the revolt to arrive at a better understanding with the Communists. In the beginning of 1958 Pastor Dr. Tibor Bartha became the successor of Janos Peter in the Trans-Tiszian Diocese. At his induction into office he said among other things: "We are firmly convinced that the orientation which has been given to the church and the decision of our church to follow these directions is a gift of the justifying Word of God, and that the justifying and life-giving Word will bear rich fruit. What shall we say after the occurrences of the fall of 1956? The validity of the decisions of ten years ago was defined by certain church leaders and by some illegitimate church organizations." To counteract this development Bartha declared: "We must take seriously the decision which our church made in principle ten years ago with all its consequences." At the beginning of March 1959, Istvan Szamos-közi, who had been unanimously elected Bishop of the Diocese of Budapest, was inducted into his office. On this occasion he stated: "The truth of socialism is no longer strange and frightening to our church. We have proof for the humanity and moral strength of socialism. We have experienced the fact that we, if we live in this new order as a church, can carry on a free ecclesiastical service in her." Finally, on January 16, 1962, Pastor Benö Bekefi was inducted into his office as Bishop of the Trans-Danubian Diocese.

In order to regulate the relationship to the state, the Council of the Synod on December 31, 1956, appointed a permanent council. Through discussions with the Office for Ecclesiastical Affairs the work of the church was regulated in a more complete way. The Office gave guarantees that divine services, Sunday school, and other activities could be carried on freely and that confirmation instruction could be regulated by the church according to her own laws. The general prohibition for meetings was not applied to parish pastors who held religious meetings in their parishes. But they had to obtain the permission of the police, so that church meetings could not be abused by irresponsible elements for agitation and revolt against the existing order of the state and society.

d. The Day of Reckoning

The voices of those who had been able to speak in the days of the revolt were now silenced. They were missing also in the evaluations by the church of the occurrences that had taken place during the revolt. These reactions consisted in recriminations and confessions of guilt, in renewed vows of loyalty toward the state and in sharp polemics against the World Council of Churches in Geneva. The chief object of these accusations was the movement for church renewal. The seniors and moderators in the Cis-Tiszian Diocese declared on March 22, 1957, that human passions had predominated in the life of the church. They said: "These passions have appeared in the way in which our church has been driven to take part in the political developments and has espoused political action which was directed against our society. Therefore we must separate the true service of the church from the so-called movement for renewal and from all other counter-revolutionary movements." Janos Peter made the following statement before a general meeting of the diocese: "The so-called renewal movement led to a revolt against the trust that had been given to the church. It turned the church away from the straight path and subjected her to the yoke of the counter-revolution, even though the majority of her members did not want it. For the sake of the church all remnants, representatives, teachings, and temptations of the reaction must be removed and rejected. Those who are still worshiping America must be liberated from America."

In a book published in 1958 by the former Director of the Hungarian Church Press Service, Imre Kadar, entitled *The Church in the Storms of the Times*, the occurrences of 1956 were called a mutiny of about thirty to fifty people. He stated that these had been "people who had been aggrieved and now tried to win more influential positions in the church. They had been supported by helpers who had come from the West. . . . They had prepared themselves for the day of open revolt for many years." Kadar called Bishop Ravasz the chief perpetrator of the revolt and defamed him as best he could. He accused him of chauvinism, of espousing a theology of war during World War I, of the propagation of a war of revenge, and of Greater Hungarian expansionism. He also accused him of antisocialist attitudes, blind anti-Semitism, glorification of the dictators Horthy, Hitler, and Mussolini with Bible verses, deification of the Hungarian people as a people chosen by God, and other theological perversions. Bishop Bereczky declared in one of his reports to the Reformed Church that "the church has sinned in a special way." At the same synodal meeting the director of the Office for Ecclesiastical Affairs, Janos Horvath, accused the Reformed Church of having served the counter-revolution. He stated that it was now up to the church to initiate steps for the improvement of church-state relationships. A conference of the seniors of the Danubian Diocese on April 12, 1957, promised: "We recognize the agreement which has existed between church and state with all its implications. We shall keep this agreement and shall see to it that those who are entrusted to our responsibility will also keep it. All members of this conference promise to give a testimony that they consider the Hungarian People's Republic, which is building up socialism, as their beloved fatherland. Therefore they condemn and denounce all open and hidden attempts which are being made to disturb, overthrow, and change our Hungarian People's Democracy." As early as April 3, 1957, the bishops and other representatives of the two major Protestant churches had met at the request of the National Peace Council in order to consider which service the church might render to the cause of peace. They organized an Evangelical Church Committee for the National Peace Council which was charged to function within the framework of the national organization as the official peace arm of the church.

The sharp polemic against the World Council of Churches in Geneva continued. During the days of the Hungarian revolt, Dr. Visser 't Hooft, then Secretary General of the World Council, had sent the following message to the Hungarian member churches of the Council: "At the time when, God willing, a new beginning is being made in the churches, I would like to send to you in the name of the World Council of Churches the expression of our most cordial hope that the work of the churches of Hungary may experience in this new era God's richest blessings. We have known about your difficult spiritual problems which so many of you had to face during the past few years. We rejoice that you have remained faithful to your Christian witness and have stood firmly with Jesus Christ. We are especially happy that persons have taken over the reins of the church who have shown that loyal perseverance in the Christian faith is more important to them than anything else. The new conditions under which we are living will open up many new opportunities, but there will also be many new problems. We would like to assure you that we shall help you to the best of our ability to use these opportunities and to overcome these problems. May the Lord God be with you in the coming weeks and months."

This message and the close telephone contact between Visser 't Hooft and Professor Pap during the days of the revolt were used against the latter. The director of the Ecumenical Institute in Budapest, Bohuslav Pospisil, stated that the relationship of the Reformed Church to the World Council of Churches was "influenced by the occurrences of the last few months and not advantageously. Therefore it is necessary to clear up our relationship with the World Council of Churches and to find an answer to the questions which have arisen in the course of the recent developments." Bishop Bereczky said about the message of the World Council of Churches that it went beyond loving interest, which the Geneva agency may show to an independent member church responsible to God alone, and that it looked very much like an uncalled-for interference in Hungarian affairs.

In his last speech before the general conference of his diocese
Janos Peter declared that one of his greatest mistakes had been
that he had invited the Central Committee of the World Council
of Churches to hold its meeting in Hungary in August 1956. He
said: "I do not want to insult the honorable occupation of small
shop keepers by comparing the busybodies of the World Council
with them. But a village storekeeper can answer questions concerning the political life with greater understanding than Visser 't
Hooft, Laszlo Pap, and Laszlo Ravasz have answered problems
of Hungarian history, world politics, and the political situation of
the church." Peter stated that what had happened at the meeting
of the World Council of Churches at Galyetetö in the summer of
1956 had formed "an organic part of the psychological preparation
which led to the counter-revolution; and while the counter-revolution began its tragic role in the life of the Hungarian people, Laszlo
Pap and Visser 't Hooft telephoned each other day after day rejoic-
ing about the things which were happening in Hungary and looking
forward to what was going to happen to our people in the future.
When God is judging, he hardens the hearts and takes away sight
and hearing so that seeing they cannot see and hearing they cannot
hear."

Voices that were as sharp as Peter's fortunately fell silent during
the next few years. But to demonstrate with what furor the Reformed leadership could react to admonitions coming from foreign
countries, it might be well to consider the following exchange of
letters between the Hungarian Reformed Church and the Reformed
Alliance of Germany. On September 25, 1957, the Moderator of the
Reformed Alliance of Germany had written a letter to the pastors
and seniors of the Reformed Church of Hungary in which he stated:
"Permit us to communicate to you in a brotherly way a concern
that bothers us. When during the summer of last year representatives of our congregations were in your country and came into contact with your congregations, they felt immediately that not all
leaders of your church were enjoying the trust of your congregations. This fact led to the situation that after the occurrences of
last fall your church lost her leadership and that now she has no
leaders who are accepted by the congregations. We have heard

that some of you are of the opinion that the church can get along without her bishops. Thank God that this is the case, if the church follows with determination the one and only bishop of our souls, our Lord Jesus Christ. But the things that God has entrusted to us, the immediate care for our congregations, should not be accepted as something that is self-evident. It is our task to do something so that the church may have a good leadership. That is also your task, beloved brethren. Therefore we are asking you that you call the right men to become your leaders. How helpful it would be for your congregations if you had people at the head of your church who do not use their ministry as a pretext for carrying politics into the church, but who call upon congregations to return to the Word of God. How important it would be for your government if such people would lead the church. They would no longer present to your government a politically colored picture of the church, but would be able to tell the government what is the real concern of the Christian citizens of your nation. Therefore, dear brethren, take the decisions which you are facing seriously, as in the presence of God. See to it that the church remains the church! A church which merely says and does what the state says and does is, according to the Word of God, useless salt in this world. She does not serve the people and the state. She does not bring salvation closer to the people and does not help to preserve peace, but disturbs and confuses the relationship between church and state. Therefore you should order your church in such a way that she will call men to leadership who have the confidence of the believers and who are strengthened by their prayers, men who do not want anything but that the church remain the church and that she become more and more a church and be able to carry out her ministry to your people for which your nation is looking. May the Lord give you joy and strength in making this decision."

The executive committee of the general convention of the Hungarian Church called this letter a "serious violation of the fraternal relationship" between the churches. It stated: "We reject this interference because we want to retain the fraternal relationship between the churches." On November 25, 1957, Bishop Bereczky answered the letter in detail which, he said, "was addressed strangely and which had contents that were even stranger." He stated that there were still some people who tried to teach the Reformed Church of Hungary from abroad what kind of leadership she needed and what kind she did not need. He said that it was not the aim of the Hungarian church to reorganize her life on the basis of the "Western point of view. We do not need leaders who are acceptable to the leadership of the World Council of Churches, but leaders who can work for our congregations, for our own Hungarian Reformed Church. Brotherly counsel which is based on knowledge and good will is certainly not rejected. But the leadership of the German Reformed Alliance does not show such knowledge, for goodwill is clearly absent from your letter. You are trying to interfere in the centuries-old constitution of our church, and you are making statements which according to the letter of St. Peter are a judgment in strange matters." Bereczky was referring to 1 Peter 4:15. He continued: "You venture to judge us and to declare the leaders of our church who have been elected by the congregations, who are devoting their lives to the service in these congregations, to be untrustworthy people. I cannot keep from marveling that the moderator of the German Reformed Alliance would send such a libelous letter, not to his own pastors and presbyters, but to the pastors and presbyters of the Hungarian Reformed Church. What would you say if a Hungarian church leader tried to tell the pastors and presbyters of the German Reformed Church what type of church leadership they needed?"

2. The Lutheran Church

a. The Condemnation and Rehabilitation of Bishop Ordass

In the first years after World War II the Lutheran Church of Hungary had shown greater strength in maintaining her spiritual autonomy than the Reformed Church. This was due largely to the leadership of Bishop Lajos Ordass. Therefore the state struck at him with greater vehemence than at any leader of the Reformed Church. On September 9, 1948, the government announced that Ordass and the Secretary-General of the Lutheran Church, Varga, together with her Inspector General, Radvansky, had been arrested on the charge of illegal manipulation of funds. The latter two men were forced to resign, and Varga was condemned to three years' imprisonment. Also the senior pastor of Budapest, Dr. Andres Keken, who had been closely associated with Ordass, was arrested. The bishop himself, who refused to resign from office, was condemned to two years in prison because he had accepted a gift from Lutherans in America in the amount of $5,000 without registering it in the prescribed way with the government. Statements by the Lord Bishop of Chichester and by the National Lutheran Council of America showed the absurdity of these charges. The Lutheran World Federation and many personalities and individual groups of World Lutheranism protested to the Hungarian government. The government, at the beginning of 1949, offered a pension to Bishop Ordass for his family during his imprisonment, but he refused to accept the offer. He became a symbol of upright convictions in the face of persecution by a totalitarian state.

The church leadership, however, surrendered. Its representatives visited the imprisoned bishop and asked him to resign temporarily from his office. Ordass refused. Therefore, at the demand of the Ministry of Cults, a special court of the church was set up which, on April 1, 1950, demoted Ordass and stated that henceforth he would be considered a common pastor. The court stated: "The difficult conditions which were caused by the condemnation of Bishop Ordass are hurting the interests of our church. For this reason he is declared removed from the office of bishop of the diocese."

On April 14, 1950, the Inspector General of the Lutheran Church, the surgeon Dr. Ivan Reök, submitted a request for a pardon to the government. The request was accepted, and on May 30, 1950, Bishop Ordass was freed. He made his home as a pastor in retirement, first at Budapest and later near Lake Balaton, but remained under constant surveillance.

After the removal of Ordass a complete change in the leadership of the church took place. Persons who were friendly to the regime were elected to leading positions. In 1948 Lajos Vetö became Bishop of the Tiszian Diocese and, on May 2, 1950, the former student pastor, Laszlo Dezsery, became Bishop of the Southern Diocese. Dezsery had been a Communist in 1948 and had attacked Ordass in an open letter. Inspector General Reök was replaced in 1950 by the former Minister of Education, Joseph Darvas, who in turn was replaced in 1952 by the Undersecretary for Education, Ernö Mihalyfi, a pastor's son. At the time when he was inducted into his office, Mihalyfi stated that he was devoted to the People's Democracy and said: "I consider it my noblest task to support and to make secure the carrying out of the agreement between church and state. I will eliminate those dangerous situations which are threatening the church and which can originate only within the church." His reference to the state-church agreement was to a document that had been signed on August 19, 1949.

In the spring of 1952 the other two bishops, Turoczi and Szabe, resigned under pressure of the Office for Ecclesiastical Affairs. They had been elected before the Communist revolution. Thus Vetö now became the ranking bishop of the Lutheran Church. With Turoczi pietism in the church lost its leader. He had formerly been director of the Deaconess Home in Györ and had worked for a revival of the church. But the state had hampered his work severely when it introduced an ordinance which made it necessary for pastors to obtain a license from the state before they were permitted to speak outside of their congregations. The new party-lining bishops attacked pietism because it allegedly showed lack of political responsibility

Through the removal of Ordass and Turoczi and the defamation of pietism, groups of pastors and congregations were driven underground in their opposition against the new leadership of the church. But the tension within the church had been removed to a large extent before the revolt of 1956, because after lengthy discussions which the Lutheran World Federation had carried on with the Hungarian government in August 1956—during the meeting of the Central Committee of the World Council of Churches of Galyetetö it had been announced that Bishop Ordass would be rehabilitated. It had been agreed that he should formally resign from his bishop's office and, until he was rehabilitated, take the office of professor of theology.

Bishops Vetö and Dezsery did not agree to this and were criticized for their attitude by the pastors. A protest of the clergy was drawn up on August 31, 1956, which demanded the reintroduction of the work of evangelism in the church. Furthermore, the dissident clergymen stated: "For the renewal of our church a broad ecclesiastical self-examination, a confession, and a cleansing from the mistakes of the last few years are absolutely necessary. We must examine the answers of our church to the questions of today and her whole policy to determine whether she is willing to listen to the Word of God in her essential work. On October 5 Bishop Ordass was rehabilitated by the government in a letter written to the inspector general of the church in which the church leadership was informed: "The Praesidium of the Supreme Court of the Hungarian People's Republic on October 5, 1956, has absolved. . . . Lajos Ordass from the accusations made against him on the basis of the absence of criminal intent." The church was informed that the verdict of 1948 had been declared null and void. The inspector general was ordered "to undertake the necessary steps for the rehabilitation of the bishop." In answer to this order the Disciplinary Court of the Lutheran Church declared on October 8 that "the verdict passed by the special court of the Evangelical Lutheran Church in 1950 . . . is declared illegal on account of its formal and material violation of the laws of the church and is herewith declared null and void." On the same day Bishop Ordass formally resigned from his office as bishop with the understanding, as he indicated, that "unless I have lost the confidence of the congregations belonging to my dioceses this provisional abdication loses its validity as soon as my return to active service is made possible."

On October 9, 1956, Bishop Lajos Vetö announced an over-all reorganization of the church in order to erase mistakes that had been committed. He admitted that "in several areas of our church things have developed in a way which cannot lead to desirable results." In his program of reform he envisioned the dissolution of the so-called Preliminary Committee which consisted of a number of important church functionaries and had sole control over decisions concerning the work of church organizations. He promised the re-examination of all cases where people had suffered injustices through the church leadership and a stronger emphasis on, and utilization of, lay conferences as well as permission for pastors to invite guest speakers without having to check with their bishop. Also included was the permission for retired pastors to officiate, unless they had lost the permission of the state, and to exercise their spiritual ministry. On October 14 Bishop Ordass preached for the first time since his release, to a congregation of 1,600 people.

The revolt, which began on October 23, accelerated this development in the Lutheran Church. On October 30 Bishop Dezsery resigned; on October 31 Bishop Ordass took over the leadership of the Southern Diocese. On November 2 Bishop Vetö too resigned from his office; and Ordass took over the direction of the entire church. When he resigned, Bishop Vetö made a confession of guilt which contradicted his former arrogant behavior. He stated that he was in complete agreement with the aims of the revolt. He wrote: "Our Hungarian people and especially our heroic youth have broken their chains in a way that has surprised the whole world, and they are now independently and freely arranging the future of our fatherland. We too have unchained ourselves from the chains of slavery with which we have been tied during the past decade. . . . The rule of the demonic forces among our people and in our church has been stopped during these days. I thank my God with all my heart. . . . At the same time I feel that it would make no sense for me to participate in the further direction of our church. I shall do all I can to make it possible for our church to develop freely in this new era. Therefore I am resigning from the office of bishop which I have held in the Northern Diocese and into which I came as bishop of the former Tiszian Diocese, into which office I had been installed on December 22, 1948. At the same time I also resign from all ecclesiastical functions which are connected with the episcopal office. The office of presiding bishop is in any case the office that belongs to our oldest bishop, Dr. Lajos Ordass. For my errors I ask God for his forgiveness. I pray him that he will send his richest blessings upon the renewal of the life of the church in our Northern Diocese, upon our fatherland, and our nation."

On November 2, Secretary-General Grünvalsky and the other leading lay members of the church government also resigned. On the evening of that day Bishop Ordass by way of Radio Budapest addressed an appeal to the foreign countries to help in this emer-

gency. To the representative of the Lutheran World Federation he stated: "We do not want to act politically. All we want is our freedom, and we shall insist on it even if they shoot us tomorrow"
On November 3 Turoczy was reinstated as bishop and took over the leadership of the Southern Diocese. The two lay presidents and 16 seniors of the church were asked to resign so that the congregations could elect their own representatives. After the Russian attack on November 5, Grünvalsky attempted to regain his office. But he did not succeed. Bishop Ordass stated: "We do not intend to give up our offices until we are put in chains." Inspector General Mihalyfi had fled with his family as a refugee to Austria. On November 16 Bishop Ordass reported to the President of the Lutheran World Federation that the church had regained her freedom and that church life in Hungary was unhampered. He stated that it was possible again to take up pastoral work in the hospitals and to give religious instruction. Also the charitable work did not encounter limitations. The Executive Secretary of the Lutheran World Federation, Dr. Carl E. Lund-Quist, confirmed this report when he was permitted to visit Hungary on January 30, 1957.

For a while the church now had rest. Bishop Zoltan Turoczy, who had taken over his office provisionally, was elected to the office of bishop by the overwhelming majority of his congregations and was inducted into his office by Bishop Ordass on February 6, 1957. In his inaugural address he declared: "I accept the People's Democracy as the frame for my work and life, which has been given to me by God himself who is the ruler of the world." He also stated that he considered the agreement between church and state as something that could close or open doors. Said he: "I shall obey the higher authorities in the spirit of Romans 13:1, but I shall also bear witness that when the will of the higher authorities contradicts the will of the highest authority one must obey God rather than man. I am convinced that a loyalty of citizens which is built upon the foundation of the Word of God is at the same time the strongest foundation on which the state can be built."

At the end of March 1957 the Lutheran church paper *Evangelicus Elet* was permitted to appear again. Bishop Ordass was listed as its publisher and Dr. Andres Keken as its editor. In an Easter message the bishop declared that the church must participate in a fitting way in those endeavors which have as its goal the external and internal peace among nations. For this purpose a committee of the church for the Hungarian Peace Council had been organized. In the message it was also stated that both bishops saw the highest calling of the church in the proclamation of, and the instruction in, the Gospel message because they were of the opinion that the goal of all peace on earth was reconciliation with God. They stated: "We accept in obedience to God the fact that the church must fulfill her mission in a Hungary which is on the road to socialism. The church as a church cannot take any position in politics because this would endanger the universal character of her ministry. But she is convinced that the fruits of faith which are brought about by the proclamation of the Word, namely love of fatherland and of man, respect for law and readiness to sacrifice, are the human virtues without which no socialist order of life can exist. Therefore the church asks the leaders of the Hungarian people in brotherly responsibility that they do everything in their power to advance the inner pacification of the minds, to strengthen the rule of law, and to develop patriotic virtues. We are firmly convinced that only in this way can a new, healthy, and just order of society and life built on honest work be most quickly developed. In this spirit the church supports all efforts of the revolutionary workers' and peasants' government."

b. Dismissed Again from Office

In November 1957 the breathing spell which had been granted to the church came to an end. In consultation with the representatives of the Lutheran Church, the President of the Office for Ecclesiastical Affairs, Janos Horvath, whose life had been saved during the days of the revolt by Bishop Ordass personally, demanded that the church should rescind all changes that had taken place during the October revolt. In an interview with the *London Times* which he granted on November 12, Horvath declared that the government had started negotiations with the church to eliminate the attitudes which had been influenced by the illegal changes during the October revolt. These discussions had been broken off two weeks previously because of the unchanging and stubborn attitude of the representatives of the church. Horvath stated that while Bishop Ordass certainly was not a reactionary he had been pushed into the position by his advisors. He stated: "Ordass also seems to receive negative advice from foreign countries, especially from the Lutheran World Federation." Horvath stated that the Praesidium of the Parliament had investigated the circumstances accompanying the resignation of Bishop Vetö on November 2, 1956, and had noticed that he had acted under duress. Therefore his resignation could not be accepted and he would take over his diocese immediately. Also Inspector General Mihalyfi had been removed under similar circumstances and would take over his former post again.

After the breakdown of the consultations, Lajos Grenak, an official in the Office for Ecclesiastical Affairs, was appointed Commissar for the Lutheran Church. On November 29, 1957, Horvath called together 60 Lutheran pastors and declared to them in a long speech the actual situation of the church. The decisions of the state were soon recognized by the leaders of the church. On December 19, 1957, the Council of the Northern Diocese stated that "Dr. Lajos Vetö must be considered Bishop of the Northern Diocese. This does not imply a judgment on the legality of the election and of the service of Zoltan Turoczy until December 4, 1957." The council expressed its gratitude to Bishop Turoczy for the faithful work he had done in his office. On December 23 the council declared that Ernö Mihalyfi had not resigned from the office of inspector general during the revolt as had until now been erroneously assumed. Mihalyfi immediately took office again. The council also stated that Bishop Vetö was now again the ranking bishop of the Lutheran Church because Lajos Ordass had begun his active service as bishop later than Vetö and had not yet obtained the recognition of his episcopal rank from the Praesidium of the Hungarian People's Republic. The Council of the Southern Diocese was asked to announce all changes that had taken place since October 4 in the actual exercise of the episcopal office and in the office of diocesan inspector, and to obtain the approval of the government as was required by the law. Karoly Grünvalsky was reinstated as secretary-general of the diocese.

Thus the change of guard that had taken place in the fall of 1956 had been rescinded. Ordass was henceforth confined in his activities to the Southern Diocese. Together with 23 other public personalities Bishop Vetö at the end of the year received the Order of the Banner of the Hungarian People's Republic, Second Class. The citation stated: "These clergymen remained loyal during the counter-revolution against the People's Republic and were active in the interests of the Hungarian people. They are now working again for socialism and for peace." At the beginning of 1958 Vetö and Mihalyfi asked that the commissar of the state should be recalled because all necessary changes had been made in the government of the church. The Minister of Cults answered on January 13 that Krenak would be recalled from the Northern Diocese and from the general administration of the entire church, but not from the Southern Diocese because there his services were still needed. At the request of the church for the continuation of state subsidies, Horvath answered on January 20 that the request would be honored. He also stated: "At the same time we must indicate that the Bishop of the Southern Diocese has refused to participate in the solution of important questions. Therefore we do not see any possibility of giving sufficient state subsidies to the Southern Diocese because the leadership of that diocese had not been willing to start discussions on questions of burning interest to state and church." After this announcement salaries of pastors, organists, and others in the Southern Diocese were reduced by 25%.

On January 20, 1958, Vetö and Mahalyfi continued their discussions with the state that had been broken off previously. On January 21 these discussions were concluded. In a declaration consisting of five points both parties expressed their agreement to regulate the relationship between church and state according to the agreement of the year 1948. The agreement stated: "The Lutheran Church recognizes it to be the will of God that she proclaim the Word and administer the Sacraments within the framework of the political, economic and social order of the socialist state. She desires to declare that our state in the spirit of its constitution guarantees the undisturbed activity of the pastors of our church and the free exercise of religion in our congregations, and she maintains that both state and church are interested in good mutual relationships. The above-mentioned theological point of view of our church also includes the fact that she recognizes in the revolutionary government of the workers and peasants the higher authorities which are appointed by God and that she will educate her members to be loyal to the state and obedient to the higher authorities. At the same time, through the activities of her responsible leaders, pastors, and church members, as well as through her faithfulness in her calling, she tries to advance the efforts of our people and our government for the building of socialism. We consider the advancement of unity, cooperation, and well-being; the raising of the living standard of our people; the education for patriotism; the maintenance of external and internal peace and order in our fatherland; and the furthering of the good reputation of our nation in the world our special task. We are satisfied with the foreign policy of the government of the Hungarian People's Republic which expresses the interests of our people and of our church members and which insists on the promotion of the peaceful coexistence of our nation and the solution of all controversial questions by way of negotiations. We shall cooperate in the realization of a lasting peace which will serve the welfare of the whole world." In the final part of the declaration the church thanked the government for its support: "We want to show our gratitude by supporting, in the way which we have outlined above, the efforts of our government for peace and for the welfare of the people."

The pressure against Bishop Ordass was now increased systematically. On January 24, 1958, President Horvath called together the pastors of the Southern Diocese and addressed them for two hours. Ordass was present, but did not take the floor. After a discussion among the pastors, which was held without their bishop, a delegation called on the State Office for Ecclesiastical Affairs and on Bishop Ordass and asked them to find a way for the solution of the unsettled questions. Horvath wrote to the executive committee of the Lutheran Church that Ordass had "a closed mind against the settlement of existing problems." On February 21 the Lutheran bishops of Scandinavia asked Horvath to create conditions which would make it possible for the faithful workers in the church to carry on their work. In his answer Horvath attacked the Lutheran World Federation whose "unfounded, often brutal attacks in press and radio had fed the mills of Western propaganda." He stated that the Hungarian Church would solve her own problems without any help from the outside.

In the beginning of April 1958 the pastoral convention of the Southern Diocese passed a resolution which read: "We see with regret that many measures of the leadership of the church during the past year coincided with the counter-revolution. The time is past when we can solve our problems by a vote of confidence. For this would hardly help our church government to carry on its duties, but would make the solution all the more difficult." At another meeting in the middle of April the pastors assured Ordass of their love for him and declared their desire that he would remain bishop of the diocese also in the future. But they said: "At the same time we must ask you to reexamine your present stand and to contribute to the security and the peaceful life of the diocese in its relationship to the state, to the presiding bishop of the church, and to the inspector of this diocese." A part of the pastors, however, did not take part in this vote but declared in a separate statement that they had severed their connections with Bishop Ordass.

Against the will of Bishop Ordass the council of the Southern Diocese was called together on May 27 by its lay inspector, Joseph Darvas, who had not been active in his office since the revolt of 1956. He asked that the council should insist on a clarification of the legality of the leadership of the diocese. On June 24 the council met again without Bishop Ordass, but this time in the presence of Horvath, and announced that the state did not recognize the resignation of Bishop Dezsery during the revolt of 1956. Therefore the council felt constrained to declare: "The real bishop of the Evangelical Lutheran Diocese South according to the status of October 31, 1956, is Dr. Laszlo Dezsery. This diocese asks him to take over the episcopal chancellery and to exercise again his episcopal functions. The council asks retired Bishop Dr. Lajos Ordass to surrender the chancellery and wishes to thank him for his past services. It asks God's blessings upon him." Dezsery accepted the council's decision, but immediately declared his intention of resigning from his office. After Dezsery's resignation the deputy-bishop, Koren, became provisional bishop. Horvath now announced that he was satisfied with these developments and recalled the state commissar from the Southern Diocese. The state resumed the full payment of the subsidies to the congregations of the Southern Diocese. Dezsery attacked Ordass once more before he retired completely from the affairs of the church. He said that Ordass, in the year and a half in which he held office, had not been able to rehabilitate himself politically. He had not given any indication of a change of heart to the pastors of his diocese and had caused a great deal of unrest by his actions. Dezsery even went so far as to say that Ordass did not have the ability to be a bishop. The pastors and the congregations, however, did not give their assent to this harsh judgment. They stated that if they had asked Bishop Ordass to resign they had not done so on their own accord, but because they had been forced to do so under pressure.

At the beginning of October 1958 Zoltan Kaldy was elected successor of Bishop Ordass in the Southern Diocese of the Lutheran Church and was inducted into his office by Bishop Vetö on November 2, 1958. Kaldy promised: "I shall do my best to further develop the good relationship between church and state so that we can remain faithful servants of our country." At the end of February 1959 Kaldy announced that several pastors had been transferred to positions where they could no longer do harm to the church. Such forced transfers included the former Senior of Budapest, Danhauser, who had been a trusted co-worker of Bishop Ordass; Dr. Andres Keken; the former President of the League of Pastors, Scholz; and the former director of the church press, Istvan Botta. On May 29 Kaldy declared at a meeting of the Southern Diocese: "We want to educate our members to love their home on earth as much as they love their heavenly home, so that they can help with their hearts and hands in the rebuilding of the world for socialism. We shall work and live in the faith that we in our church are on the road which God has charted for us. That means, we want to be a church that can work within the framework of socialism." He stated also that all contacts with the state had been in the spirit of mutual trust and respect, but that among the leaders of the church there were still some political reactionaries. Said he: "Many church councils and congregations cannot adjust themselves to the total task of the church. They are trying to work against important and decisive orders in the church on the local level." He furthermore declared that the relationship to the Lutheran World Federation had been normalized.

In March 1960, Kaldy reported at a pastoral conference that he had asked 20 pastors by telegram to submit their sermons. After reading these sermons he had become convinced that they were poor preachers. Besides theological shortcomings he criticized the pastors because they could not make decisions concerning problems which they should have learned to understand during the past 15 years. They were not communicating with the congregations and were keeping political problems out of their sermons. Thus their sermons had no real relevance. Kaldy showed that he was in favor of following the party line. Whenever he spoke on political questions his point of view showed no difference from the Communist point of view. For example, he stated that for the defense of democratic Berlin and for the interests of peace the building of the Berlin Wall on August 13, 1961, had been a necessity. Said he: "These justified measures prepare the way for clarification and therefore are promoting the peace of the world." He criticized the position of the leaders of the Protestant Church in Germany because their position was increasing political tensions. In his statement he said: "We request that the Council of the Evangelical Church in Germany should raise its voice in the interests of unity against the militarism and the spirit of revenge which exists in Western Germany. It should thus help to bring about the conclusion of a German peace treaty." The Hungarian Lutheran magazine *Evangelikus Elet* was enlisted so completely in the propaganda effort of the state that some observers felt that the Lutherans were cooperating more fervently with the Communists than the Reformed. Kaldy, however, objected to the suspicion that had arisen in certain church circles in the West that the Lutheran Church of Hungary was repeating the mistakes of the German Christians under the Nazis.

He stated that his church was not interested in mixing theology with Marxist-Leninist ideology and in asking her believers to undergird the objectives of socialism with Christian faith. There could be no talk, he said, about combining socialist ideology with Christian theology.

The relationship of the Protestant churches to the state was thus determined by the fact that they emphasized in theory the differences in ideology, but in practice followed the official line of the Communist government. The Reformed Bishop Szamosközi wrote in the Scottish paper *Life and Work* that the Hungarian Reformed Church saw her task both in the proclamation of the Christian message and in the participation in the life and the conditions of her fellow men. He stated: "At present this means that we must all help to realize true socialism in our country as soon as possible. This does not mean a subjection to any special ideology. No one is asking us in Hungary to submit. We are taking part in the reconstruction of our homeland for the sake of our faith." The Reformed church paper *Reformatus Egyhasz* on February 15, 1960, discussed the task of pastors in the socialist reconstruction of agriculture: "We welcome socialism and consider it and collectivization as an opportunity which the Lord has given to our generation so that our material and moral progress may be secured. . . . Whenever we follow the intentions of the Lord of the world in obedience, the influence upon the life of the congregation is fruitful and enriching."

D. ANTIRELIGIOUS PROPAGANDA

1. Atheistic Enlightenment and Communist Substitute Rites

There could be no illusion that the acceptance of socialism by the churches would lead to a friendly cooperation between Communism and the churches. This became clear from the anti-religious propaganda that was continuing full force in the Communist papers. The Communist Party organ *Somogiy Neplak* in August 1960 attacked those church circles that were hoping to secure the future of the church by cooperating with the regime. It stated that these circles spoke of their conviction that in a socialist society the fight against religion had lost its meaning. The paper insisted: "These defenders of religion are no longer able to fight openly against the Marxist ideology. Therefore they are trying to accommodate themselves to the changed conditions and to proclaim the dogma of an alliance between religion and socialism. But it is a deception to expect that an understanding between socialism and religion can help the churches to regain their lost prestige." The article stated that the revolutionary development would lead to the complete elimination of all religious concepts and prejudices.

In Hungary too, as in other Communist countries, a Society for the Dissemination of Scientific Knowledge was founded which, with the support of the Communist Party, inundated the people with antireligious pamphlets and speeches. But also here the complaint about a lack of impact of this propaganda and about the toughness of the religious remnants was heard again and again. The daily paper *Nepszabadsag* complained in February 1958 that there were still numerous Communist functionaries who attended church regularly, who spent their money for religious purposes, and who sent their children to religious instruction. The Györ newspaper *Kisalfoel* reported in December 1958 that it was unbelievable that "teachers who give instruction in materialistic ideology during school hours are going to church during their off-duty hours." The ideological monthly of the Communist Party, *Tarsadalmi Szemle*, of November 1959, stated that during the first phase after the take-over of the Communists the atheists had imposed upon themselves certain restraints, but that now was the time for every member of the party to reject all false religious ideas. The party demanded of her members that they should give up their idealistic concepts. Party members who disseminated religious views inside and outside of the party were to be expelled from the party. The most important field in which each Communist was to begin his work of enlightenment was the family. Unfortunately this propaganda effort often meant a heavy burden to the family. But the guilt for this state of affairs was to be attributed exclusively to a faith which rejected conversion to atheism and thus caused conflicts within the family. The paper said: "Religious errors endanger and destroy the happiness of the family." The paper demanded that the fight against religion should be carried on with changing methods and should show variety in order to incite the imagination of religious people. In every situation the propagandist should turn to the faithful in order to stimulate their interest and to awaken them from their religious sleep.

The secretary of the Central Committee of the Communist Party, Gyula Kallai, in an essay in the magazine *Kommunist* (No. 15, 1959) discussed the relationship of Communism to religion and stated: "Religion still exercises a very great influence in the consciousness of our people, especially among the workers in the villages. This is true especially of the Catholic religion. Unfortunately the opportunistic interpretation of the relationship between state and church in the last five or six years has led to a slackening-off in our ideological battle against religion. The position of religion has become stronger and has increased the political role played by the church. . . . The behavior of clergymen, especially of priests of the Roman Catholic Church, in the days of the counter-revolution has proved once more that clerical reactionaries in the churches are at this time the only enemies of the socialist state who are operating legally and who, supported by the convictions of the backward masses, can harm the constructive work of socialism. Within the churches there are many who are fighting against our People's Democracy. There is the clerical reactionary who, under the leadership of the reactionary forces in the World Council of Churches, and, in the case of the Roman Catholic Church, of the Vatican, makes no secret of his reactionary aims. The actions of men of this type combine more and more with the espionage activities of the American imperialists against our People's Democracy. Clerical reaction is political reaction. In the fight against this reaction we must act in the same manner as in the fight against any other political groups which are opposed to the People's Democracy. In the battle against religious ideology our party must take account of the actual circumstances and must watch closely the development of the cooperation between church and state, but must not lose sight of the fight against clerical reaction and against religion as an expression of an idealistic reactionary ideology. But during the process of building socialism in our country churches will of necessity continue to exist." Kallai emphasized that every Communist should start with the presupposition that the religious ideology of the masses of the faithful does not disappear overnight. Therefore the state had to see to it that the churches would not hinder the socialist construction. It was necessary to establish cooperation between church and state within a framework determined by the state. The churches, Kallai thought, were interested in such cooperation, not only because the workers had the power but also because most of the faithful were in accord with the principles of socialism and wanted to support the party in the socialistic state in the work of socialism. But this cooperation, he said, "does not exclude an active atheistic and materialistic work of enlightenment among the masses. This work of enlightenment must be done with great care. It must not violate the feelings of the faithful, but must explain to them the truth of our scientific views in a logical and impressive way."

In April 1960 it was announced that orders had been issued to all leaders in factories that they must enlighten their workers about religious questions. In the intermediate schools, circles of atheists were organized. But the organ of the Writers' League *Elet es Irodalom* criticized the mental level of this propaganda and its methods which were often too primitive. The new materialistic magazine *Vilagossag* (Light) was founded not only to support the Hungarian atheists in the dissemination of "light," but also to spur them to greater efforts. But its mental fare seemed to find little response in spite of all the improved methods of dissemination. The director of the House of Education in the community development of Szolnok complained in the spring of 1962 that "in the cities interest in speeches dealing with science is constantly decreasing." Another functionary called it extremely difficult to win listeners for an ideological meeting of minds. The director of another institution stated that there were 300 visitors to his institution which was located in a city of 24,000, and that among these 300 there were very few people who had intelligence.

On the other hand, dangerous results of atheistic propaganda were also noted. Laszlo Dezsery, former Lutheran bishop, warned against the error of assuming that those who rejected religion would automatically profess the ideology of dialectic materialism.

Said he: "We should not believe for one moment that they are all interested in Communist ideology. There are circles among our young people where contempt for religion goes together with contempt for Communism. Besides these, there are many young people who have not yet made a decision. For example, someone might say: 'I cannot imagine how the world could have developed for such a long time by evolution, but I also do not believe that it has been created by someone who is above all others.' Thus neither science nor faith has given a satisfactory answer to these questions. Where should the young people turn? Between the limits which we have established in church and state there is a dangerous vacuum. We are responsible for the filling of this ideological vacuum because the attitude that nothing matters or that all is the same is open cynicism, and cynicism is our greatest enemy."

Since 1959 the state has established Communist substitute rites. In the summer of 1960 the People's Council of the county of Csongrad established a Committee for the Observation of Family and Community Celebrations which had three subcommittees. The first subcommittee was charged with the arrangement of national holidays and government celebrations; the second subcommittee was made responsible for the publication of programs for family celebrations; and the third subcommittee was assigned the task of eliminating from the Christmas and Easter festivals all "superstitious mysticism" and of restoring to these festivals their original popular character.

The organization of these Communist substitute rites was regulated by a decree of the Ministry of Education. It stated that the arrangement for such rites was, in the first place, the task of the people's councils. But they could also be arranged by other committees of the state, by factories, by organizations of the society, and by labor unions. The Council was to make available suitable places where these celebrations could be held.

There were also other proposals for substitute rites. Thus the Labor Union paper *Munka* in January 1960 issued directives for atheistic funerals. It said: "If possible, there should always be an important functionary to give the funeral oration. The oration itself should have a personal appeal. It should deal with the family and with the deceased and should move the hearts of those present. It is wrong to make trite, impersonal speeches at the funeral of a progressive citizen. After the funeral oration a procession should be formed which carries the coffin to the grave in good order. On the way to the grave a choir should sing and a band play a funeral march. At the grave a close friend or colleague of the deceased should give a brief farewell address and the coffin should be lowered to the sounds of a funeral march."

The Kossuth Publishing House published a book in 1960 entitled *The Organization of Family Celebrations by the Community*. It proposed the following vow which parents were to take at the name-giving ceremonies of their children: "We, the parents and sponsors, promise solemnly that we will educate our child, to whom we are giving the name N.N., to become an honest, hard-working, and loyal citizen. We will use our whole influence to educate our child to become a worthy member of the socialist society and to turn him into a loyal and devoted citizen of our state." In a sample speech for the name-giving ceremony the speaker was to say: "Today the birth of a little baby means great joy. This joy only our government can bestow. In the past the protection of the family was proclaimed, but nothing was done for the development of our children." The Communist paper in Győr indicated that probably the author of this sample speech had been confused about the aims of socialist name-giving ceremonies since he was writing "seminary speeches instead of making this occasion an intimate family celebration."

2. Living Congregations in All Churches

The monthly magazine *Tarsadalmi Szemle* wrote in March 1960 that numerically the overwhelming majority of the students, even members of the Communist student movement, had not yet broken with religious ideas. Especially strong was the influence of religion among students who came from the rural areas. Many students subscribed to the idea that without religion there is no morality. Sandor Szerenyi, a member of the Central Committee of the Communist Party, wrote in the same paper in October 1960: "In very important parts of the intelligentsia there are deep-rooted idealistic and religious ideas from which the intelligentsia can be separated only slowly and with great difficulty." The Eger paper *Nepujsag* reported at the beginning of 1961: "The activities of the churches, especially the Catholic Church, are increasing in an alarming measure."

Indeed, atheistic pressure was unable to weaken religious and ecclesiastical life in any decisive degree. In the Catholic Church it was estimated in 1955 that in the cities about 30% of the children took part in religious instruction and in the country about 75%. Over 90% of the newly-born were baptized. The percentage of the first communicants was high too. Concerning the type of people who attended church it was reported that women predominated, but the participation of men had also increased in comparison with that in former years. In the same year a visitor reported concerning the daily life of the church in Hungary that the first thing he saw was the surveillance of the church, and that nobody knew what his neighbor's reaction toward the church was. But whoever was dependent upon the favor of the Communist Party as an official of the state, as a soldier, or as a member of the professions, avoided as much as possible being visibly connected with the church. Therefore many pastoral acts were performed in great secrecy.

Six years later Georg Kaldi wrote in *Stimmen der Zeit* of November 1961 that it was impossible at the moment to give a generally valid picture concerning the status of religious life in Hungary and that the manifestations of religious life were different in different parts of Hungary. He said: "We can only state that the majority of the population, now as before, rejects Marxist atheism, although the Communists are trying more and more intensively to find substitutes for the sacraments and the rites of the church, for baptism, communion, confirmation, weddings, etc., by establishing secular and atheistic celebrations. Atheistic propaganda is rarely believed because the Communists have been lying in the past. The general distrust of them is so strong that most of the Hungarians do not even believe in the space exploits of Gagarin. This spiritual resistance does not mean, however, that the Hungarian soul is completely at peace because resistance against the Marxist system does not make the Hungarians immune against their propaganda."

Concerning the life in the Reformed Church, Dietrich Ritschl reported in *Junge Kirche* on June 10, 1960, about first-hand impressions which he received in 1958 and 1959. He wrote that there was a relatively great number of young men and women at the church services, and that there was no serious lack of pastors because the academies of the church were well attended. There was much serious Bible study. Prayer probably had a greater weight in the life and thinking of the Christians in Hungary than in the life and thinking of the Christians in the West. This fact was emphasized also in many other reports.

During the war one-fourth of all the church buildings had been destroyed, either partly or completely. A tremendous work of reconstruction was awaiting the congregations. Bishop Bereczky wrote: "Christians have started with great willingness to sacrifice in order to rebuild their churches. I have experienced consecrations of churches that had been rebuilt in villages where half of the private homes were still ruins blackened by smoke. Churches have been restored before private dwellings were rebuilt. But this is not the decisive thing. The decisive thing is that our church has come to a new understanding of the Word. The divine service has become a real experience for many people. This experience has meant more for us than the fact that we have rebuilt more than 450 churches."

The Lutheran Church, too, had no lack of pastors. The number of pastors in relation to the number of members in the congregations was twice as high as in the Lutheran Church of Austria. There was one pastor for every thousand members of the congregations. This made it possible to carry on an intensive program of spiritual care. Statistics which Bishop Vetö gave in his report to the church in 1961 were impressive. In the Northern Diocese, which numbered somewhat more than 136,000 souls, there were held in 1959-1960 over 70,000 services and 35,000 Bible study classes; 4,268 children were baptized, and 187,158 people went to Holy Communion. The number of hours devoted to religious instruction exceeded 20,000 per year; the number of hours given to confirmands was about 8,000. More than 74,000 pastoral calls were made, and the number of occasional services was about 6,000. This work was carried on by about 170 pastors and 40 institutional chaplains. According to a survey made by Oberkirchenrat Hanfried Lange, religious instruction in Budapest reached only 20% of the children, but in the smaller towns and villages from 70 to 80% were being taught. The figures for confirmation instruction were even more favorable: In the cities 70 to 80% of the children were being taught, in the country almost 100%. The formerly flourishing Christian schools had disappeared with the exception of a few that were permitted by the state to operate, but the Lutheran Church no longer made use of the permission to operate at least one church school because she was financially unable to do so. The Reformed Church still had a large *gymnasium* at Debrecen. Publishing activity was lively. The Lutheran Sunday paper *Evangelikus Elet* had a circulation of 10,000; her theological magazine *Lelkipasztor* of 1,000. In 1959 the Lutheran Church published four religious textbooks for elementary schools and three for secondary schools in a total edition of 40,000. Church calendars and devotional books appeared in issues of 10,000 each. It was remarkable how strong the diaconate was continuing in the Lutheran Church. She was operating 14 institutions in 18 buildings in which 578 people were being cared for. Since there were no longer any deaconess houses, the congregations were willing to take over the work. In 1963 there were 122 people active in the work of the diaconate, among them 34 former deaconesses. The property of the church, with the exception of the church buildings and a garden lot for each parsonage, had become property of the state for which the church received a generous compensation. The state continued to pay about one-third of the pastors' salaries. These salaries ranged from 1,600 to 2,000 forints. For retired pastors they were 900 forints. In comparison, a good suit of clothing cost 1,500 forints and a good pair of shoes from 300 to 400 forints. The methods used for raising pastors' salaries in the congregations were different. Salaries were raised partly through collections and offerings in the services, through free-will gifts, or through assessments arranged by the elders. About 10 to 20% of the believers participated in the church services in the cities. In the country the participation was between 20 and 30%. These figures were reported by the representative of the Lutheran World Federation, Pastor Paul Hansen, who had visited Hungary: "These figures give an indication of the lively interest in the church. Still more important, however, are the impressions which one receives through the sermons and the conversations with pastors and members of the church's administration. These conversations give a clear indication that there are Christians in Hungary whose chief concern is to hear the Gospel of Jesus Christ and to bring it to the people, who are trying seriously to be witnesses to the Lord in the conditions under which they are living today."

3. Remnants Ready for the Museum?

The outsider must understand these reports and statistics in the right way. They do not come from a church that lives in peace in a friendly environment. They come from an embattled church. The congregations are surrounded by an atmosphere which is explosive. Under the cover of tolerance which is granted only reluctantly there continues the old enmity of the ideological conformists and the all-powerful political apparatus. The drums of atheist propaganda are being beaten without pause throughout Hungary. The temptation is there for everyone to forsake the church. The atheist propaganda uses not only the soft but also the harsh arguments which always have the same refrain: "Deny your God." It is the same way in Hungary as in the Soviet Union, Poland, Czechoslovakia, and all the other countries of the East bloc.

Every Christian is placed before a decision. His decision is not made easy for him by his church. For the churches have been pushed from one crisis to another, in Hungary as well as in other Communist countries. Christian congregations heard their bishops and pastors defamed and saw them removed from office, and they witnessed the spectacle of the new church leaders bowing down before the throne of the government. They heard how they argued with each other and tried to discredit each other, and how many of their fellow members followed the current party line, how they tried to make a good impression on the government, and how they covered up their squabbles with beautiful spiritual words and theological formulas. In many areas the clergy have been compromised. The church in her organized form certainly is no longer a Mighty Fortress, a refuge, a haven of peace, or a guide to a Christian life. The church has become a battleground, torn by dissension and full of questionable practices. Yet the congregations have remained alive.

The propaganda of the godless assails the members of these congregations daily; yet they continue to believe in God. They reject all enticements and accept scorn, insults, and threats and continue to believe. They are suspect as political reactionaries; they are treated as second-class citizens, as people who are backward and regressing, as stupid fools; and yet they continue to believe. They are exposed to many other spiritual temptations; yet they continue to believe. Whatever is sacred to them is being torn down and dragged into the dirt, and yet it remains sacred to them. They have become witnesses to confusion and weakness in the church; and yet they remain unshakably loyal to her. They meet in their houses of worship and pray to their Lord; they confess that they believe in this church which is not spotless; they increase their sacrificial giving; they care for the souls of their children and give a witness to their faith in a world that has turned against them.

Not all the people are doing this, but many, surprisingly many. We would like to sing the praises of the "unknown Christian" whether he be Orthodox, Roman Catholic, Reformed, Lutheran, Baptist, or Mennonite, who lives his daily life quietly according to his faith and proves himself in word and action. He is the one who carries the church through her crises. The Communists may look upon him as a remnant of religious superstition that is ready for the museum, but grudgingly they must admit that there is a power in him, which to this day they have not been able to break. Is he merely the last remnant of a past era, or is he the light in the darkness and the messenger of the Lord who holds the future in his hand as he held the past and who will also continue his work as the supreme ruler of the universe in the atheistic era?

CHAPTER FIVE

EAST GERMANY

A. PRELUDE

1. The Political Changes in the Soviet-Occupied Zone

After the German capitulation of May 8, 1945, the power of government was taken over by the four allied powers which organized, on June 5, the Allied Control Council. The Soviet Zone of Germany included 107,431 square kilometers and 17,180,000 inhabitants (with East Berlin 18,355,000 inhabitants). According to the Potsdam Agreement of August 1, 1945, the German population in all zones was to be treated equally, as far as it was practical, but in the Soviet Zone the Soviet Military Administration (SMA) at Karlshorst near Berlin changed these directives from the very beginning.

Very early the SMA started with the organization of central governmental authorities for the Soviet Zone. In July 1945 it established 11, and later 16, German central administrations. In June 1947 it formed a German Economic Commission. In February 1948 this commission was given government powers to rule the states and communities. On March 20, 1948, the Soviet Union left the Control Council of the Allied Governments and blockaded Berlin, beginning June 24. The Airlift of the Allies forced the Soviets to lift the blockade on May 12, 1949. But even before that date the political split of Berlin into a Communist sector and a Western sector had taken place. On November 30, 1948, Berlin had received two separate administrations. On October 7, 1949, the German Democratic Republic was proclaimed.

In these four years the Soviet political apparatus had been built up. According to the Potsdam Agreement several political parties had received permission to organize: First the Communist Party, later the Social Democratic Party, finally the Christian Democratic Union and the Liberal Democratic Party. In 1946 the Communist Party forced the Social Democratic Party of the zone to enter a union with it. This new party was called the Socialist Unity Party (SED). It was a party of a new type. The leaders of the other parties who were not willing to follow the Communist line were dismissed. Thus the Christian Democratic Union lost its two presidents, Jacob Kaiser and Ernst Lemmer, and was given new leaders in the persons of Otto Nuschke and Georg Dertinger, who were amenable to the wishes of the Soviet Military Administration. Most of the Christian Democratic cabinet ministers and other high officials were dismissed in the following months and years. The new Secretary-General of the Christian Democratic Union, Gerald Goetting, in 1951 developed a program of "Christian realism for progressive Christians." These 21 Theses on Christian Realism were accepted by the party in 1952.

The Liberal Democratic Party was also coordinated. In 1948 there were established also a Democratic Farmers' Party of Germany and a National Democratic Party, the latter serving as a party for former Nazis and members of the armed forces. Both parties were under the control of the SED.

A great number of organizations sprang into being which were placed directly under Communist influence. There were the Free German Labor Union, founded on June 14, 1945, the Free German Youth (FDJ), founded on March 7, 1946, a Democratic Women's League and a Union for Mutual Farm Assistance and several others. The Communist Party controlled everything, including sports. All these organizations fought for the so-called Peace Movement of the Communist Party and adopted the motto: "Union of all Honest Germans! Fight for the Unity of Germany and the Signing of a Peace Treaty!" But after 1955 this motto was more or less discarded.

Elections were held after the pattern of totalitarian states. A so-called "Unity List" was drawn up by the SED, which included members from all the shadow parties. On this list were elected, on November 6, 1947, the members of the "German People's Congress for Unity and a Just Peace." Their motto was: "All Germans Around

One Table!" They considered themselves the legitimate representatives of the German nation. The Congress appointed a People's Council which drafted the constitution of the German Democratic Republic, which was accepted by the People's Council on March 19, 1949. On May 16, 1949, the Third German People's Congress was elected on a unity list on which all anti-Fascist parties were represented and which had only the alternative of voting *Yes* or *No*. In spite of intensive propaganda only 61.8% of the population gave their consent. The 1,523 members of the Third People's Congress elected the 323 deputies for the German People's Council, which accepted the constitution. On October 7, 1949, the People's Council established a Provisional People's Chamber and accepted the elected members of the provisional government. Thus the German Democratic Republic (DDR) came into being. Later there were elections in 1950, 1954, 1958, and so forth, which all followed the totalitarian pattern. The Unity List, dominated by the Socialist Unity Party, was forced on all voters.

According to Article 50 of the Constitution, the People's Chamber became the highest organ of the government and supervised the functioning of all government agencies. But a law dealing with the Council of Ministers of the German Democratic Republic, passed on November 16, 1954, established the separation of the powers of the executive branch of the government. Since then the government is no longer subject to parliamentary or legal controls.

On July 23, 1952, the state governments of Brandenburg, Mecklenburg, Saxony, Saxony-Anhalt, and Thuringia were abolished, and the last federal elements in the German constitution were eliminated. In place of the five states 14 districts were established which were ruled directly from Berlin.

Also the legal branch of the government was deprived of its independence. The career judges were replaced more and more by so-called People's Judges, who were appointed presidents of the various courts. These judges of "a new type" were no longer allowed to be objective, but were faithful members of the party as prescribed in a law of October 2, 1952, which read in Paragraph 2: "The administration of laws in the German Democratic Republic must serve the victory of Socialism, the unity of Germany, and peace." Disagreement with government policies was punished severely. Article 6, Paragraph 2, of the Constitution was applied to the penal code. It stated: "Boycott against the constitution and democratic institutions, incitement to murder of democratic politicians, propagation of hatred in matters of faith, race, and nationality, military propaganda, incitement to war, and all other actions which are directed against equality, are crimes according to the penal code." This penal code was also applied to German citizens who did not live in the territory of the German Democratic Republic and were tried *in absentia*.

A further decisive interference in the structure of the Soviet Zone was the confiscation of private property. Beginning in September 1945, the SMA expropriated all agricultural holdings of over 500 hectares and all factories that had been owned by war criminals and former Nazis. The farmers were forced to elect soil commissions which would determine the scope of the expropriations. The former owners were driven from the farms, and the new owners had to pay their debts. Until January 1, 1949, about 11,300 farms with a total of 2,024,000,000 hectares were expropriated by the state. These expropriated farms were parceled out among 119,930 workers who had owned no land, to 85,989 expellees, and to 80,444 farmers who did not have enough land and a great number of renters, workers, craftsmen, and others. About 550 large farms were transferred directly to the state. The factories which were expropriated amounted to about 40% of the total productivity capacity of the Soviet Zone. In the following years more and more of the remaining private property was expropriated.

2. The Church Under Soviet Occupation

In the year 1945 the churches in all zones of occupation were faced with very difficult tasks. At first the SMA was trying to respect the Potsdam Agreement in regard to the churches. The Administrator for Religious Questions of the SMA, Captain Jermalajew, showed marked understanding for the churches. Bishop Dibelius later testified that the Soviet Government had loyally carried out the stipulations of the Potsdam Agreement. There were eight regional churches in the Soviet Occupied Zone: Berlin-Brandenburg,

Province of Saxony, Pomerania, and Silesia, which were members of the Old Prussian Union (later called: The Church of the Union); Thuringia, Saxony, and Mecklenburg, which in 1948 became members of the United Evangelical Lutheran Church of Germany (VELKD); and the Church of Anhalt, which was an independent Union Church.

But the whole climate was different in the Soviet Zone than in the other parts of Germany. According to Decree No. 2 of the SMA the reconstruction of organizations and clubs was forbidden. But since a large number of Protestant and Catholic young people were represented in the Free German Youth, the Protestant churches were permitted to gather their young people in the "Young Congregation" *(Junge Gemeinde)*, which was a free organization without membership lists and was permitted to discuss religious questions. A difficult problem arose when the SMA abolished religious instruction in the schools. Yet within a few years the church was able to train 12,000 catechists, who took over the instruction of most of the young people outside the school buildings or at times even within the schools.

On June 4, 1946, the SMA published a law aimed at the "democratization" of the German schools in which it declared that the state alone had the right to educate children. Private schools were no longer permitted. Since a large number of teachers had been dismissed in the process of de-Nazification, new teachers were being trained in a crash program containing special courses. These new teachers were recruited from the ranks of "democratic" workers and were educated in the new "democratic" spirit. As early as October 25, 1945, Bishop Dibelius had warned the parents of the children of Berlin that the secular unity school which was being established was not a religiously neutral school. He stated: "There can be no neutrality concerning the ultimate questions of human life."

The church also did not accept soil reform in silence. Expropriation without compensation was not considered an act of justice, but the result of class struggle. The Westphalian Provincial Synod, on August 3, 1946, condemned both the heartlessness that was being shown to the expelled farmers and the expropriation of private property. It stated that stealing did not become right by being made the law of the state. The Mecklenburg Church, on October 31, 1945, accepted the necessity of soil reform, but opposed strongly unjust expropriations. It admonished the new occupants of the farms: "The soil which you are taking over has been looked after in a different way by different people before you. Many of them have done their best to produce on this soil what they could produce. We want to thank them and ask God that he will give them grace." The Confessional Synod of Berlin-Brandenburg demanded that all soil reform should be carried out according to the laws of God.

The more the German governmental authorities were established in the Soviet Zone, the stronger became the opposition to the church. The SED, however, at first assured the church of religious tolerance.

The President of the SED, Wilhelm Pieck, who later became President of the German Democratic Republic (DDR), stated at the Luther Memorial Celebration in Eisleben in October 1946: "The Socialist Unity Party is very much interested in close cooperation with the churches, in the interest of the democratization and the reestablishment of the national unity of Germany." Bishop Dibelius gratefully accepted this declaration in the name of the church.

But as early as 1947 dissonant voices were heard. There was a hostile suspicion in a circular letter of the SED of Magdeburg which was sent to all information centers of the party on January 11, 1947. They were asked to participate in church services and to find out whether the sermons of the pastors were purely religious and whether they agreed with the democratic intentions of the people, or whether the pastors were trying to influence the churchgoers through various arguments which were opposed to the democratic orientation of the people. It stated: "We are interested in finding out whether the sermons clearly indicate who is guilty in the present condition of the people. We are asking you to pay special attention to this question." On January 24, 1947, President Kreyssig of the church of Magdeburg asked the writer of this circular letter: "Do you really think that by this method of the supervision of the church by a political party the new democratic orientation of the German people is advanced, or do you not rather propagate an adverse reaction by destroying the trust in public life and by interfering with the most personal relationships?

When the district of Pirna ordered the destruction of a monastery church in the summer of 1948 in order to obtain building materials for new farms, the Mayor of Gunnersdorf near Pirna, who was a member of the SED, stated that every person would agree to this plan. He stated that sooner or later all the symbols of the church had to disappear. In the following year, 1949, many of the leaders of the new state and of the communities left the church.

In a letter to the congregations of the diocese of Berlin and Brandenburg on Pentecost of 1949 Bishop Dibelius protested against the political methods which were being used by the Socialist Unity Party. He compared the methods used by the SED and by the People's Police to those used by the Nazis and the Gestapo. He complained that the People's Judges had been instructed to judge according to their political convictions and not objectively. He complained about the many lies and breaches of promise. He concluded his letter with the following statement: "Say your courageous *No* to everything that is against God's law and thus free yourself even though you may at first encounter great difficulties in doing so."

3. The First Conflicts After the Establishment of the German Democratic Republic, 1949-1950

In 1946 the Protestant population in the Soviet zone without Berlin numbered 14,132,174 souls or 81.6% of the population. In all sectors of Berlin there were 2,228,108 or 70.4% Protestants. These Protestants of the Soviet zone were organized into about 8,000 congregations. Thus the German Democratic Republic (DDR) became the only Communist country where the majority of the population was Protestant. The membership of the individual regional churches was as follows:

Berlin-Brandenburg, Bishop Dr. Dibelius	4,535,432
Saxony, Bishop Dr. Hahn, later Dr. Noth	4,413,432
Province of Saxony, Bishop Dr. Mueller	3,465,951
Mecklenburg, Bishop Dr. Beste	1,177,034

Thuringia, Bishop Dr. Mitzenheim 1,678,260
Pomerania, Bishop Dr. von Scheven, later
    Bishop Dr. Krummacher 637,334
Anhalt, President Dr. Schroeder 385,034
Silesia, Bishop Dr. Hornig 230,214

The Roman Catholic Church in the DDR increased through the numbers of refugees and expellees from 1,205,144 to 2,110,507 and thus included, at the founding of the DDR, 12.2% of the population. But it decreased again during the following years. In 1962 there were only 1,939,000 Catholics in the DDR and West Berlin, of which 1,640,500 lived in the territory under Communist control.

Since the formation of the Evangelical Church in Germany (EKD), which took place at Treysa in 1945, the eight Protestant territorial churches of the DDR had belonged to this body. Previously they had been members of the German Protestant Federation of 1922 and of the *Reichskirche* of 1933. The membership of these churches in the EKD was not contested by the Soviet Military Administration. On July 30, 1948—during the blockade of Berlin—the church convention at Eisenach accepted a constitution for the EKD, and the representative of the SMA, Major Eichenwald, wished success to the church leaders assembled in Eisenach.

At the founding of the DDR in 1949 the chief of the government was the former leader of the Socialist Unity Party, Otto Grotewohl. Otto Nuschke, the nominal leader of the Christian Democratic Union, became one of the deputy prime ministers. He was also entrusted with the Office for Church Affairs. The veteran Communist Party leader Wilhelm Pieck became President of the German Democratic Republic (October 11, 1949). The constitution of the DDR was to all outward appearances completely democratic. Article 9 stated that all citizens had the right to voice their opinions freely and that this freedom could not be abridged. Article 12 promised all citizens the right to form their own associations and societies. Article 16 protected Sundays and holidays and the first of May as days of rest. Article 31 gave the parents the right to educate their children. Article 34, Paragraph 1, stated that the arts, the sciences, and all teaching were free. Article 37 gave the parents the right to help with the education of their children in the schools, and Article 40 stated that religious instruction was the affair of the religious denominations and that this right and privilege was guaranteed.

Concerning religious denominations, Articles 41-48 made the following stipulations: Every citizen was to enjoy complete freedom of faith and conscience; the institutions of religious organizations, religious actions, rites and instruction were in no way to be abused for political and anticonstitutional purposes. The articles also established the freedom of those who dissented from religion; they affirmed that there was no state church and that each religious organization had the right to order and to administer its affairs autonomously. Article 48, finally, gave the parents the right to decide the religious education of their children until they reached the fourteenth year of their lives. From then on the child was to decide whether he wanted to belong to a religious organization or not.

But there were many tensions. In October 1949 Bishop Otto Dibelius wrote an open letter to the President of the DDR, Wilhelm Pieck, in which he protested against the pressures that were being placed upon the church to participate in the elections. He asked the new President to see to it that the elections would be conducted honestly and decently and that the German population of the East Zone would be able to express its opinions. The elections, as we have seen, took place in October 1950, but they did not give the people the opportunity to express their political ideas.

In practice the liberal stipulations of the Constitution of the DDR were soon abridged. On July 1, 1949, the government issued a decree concerning announcements of meetings which made it necessary for the church to obtain the permission of the police for all assemblies outside the regular, scheduled church meetings. This led to a great number of interferences. The enmity of the Communists was felt in the daily life of the church in many ways. Thus, for example, a Communist mayor forbade the playing of the organ on Sunday morning, because workers should not be disturbed in their sleep.

At the beginning of 1950 censorship was introduced for all German church publications. Many West German church papers were forbidden with the curt explanation: "There is no demand for the paper in the DDR." Thus the fourteen million Protestants were permitted only a few church papers, and these had a limited circulation. The Catholic Bishop of Berlin, Cardinal Preyssing, complained in a letter to Nuschke that the Roman Catholic dioceses and commissariats had no official paper of their own. He stated: "Our faithful are waiting for their church papers and are waiting in vain." The West Berlin *Petrus Blatt* of the Diocese of Berlin had been banned from the DDR by the "German Economic Council" in April 1949.

Many hindrances were placed in the way of catechetical instruction. In Mecklenburg the use of school rooms for this extracurricular activity was forbidden. In Saxony, however, the authorities were more accommodating. In Thuringia they were vacillating. The Young Congregations were attacked in many quarters. They were called snakes, and the youth pastors were called reactionaries. The leader of the SED in Thuringia, Hauschildt, declared that any participation of the church in the education of the youth was undesirable. He stated: "We shall not permit pastors to influence our young people. . . . The youth belongs to us, and if anyone dares to poison our youth with outmoded ecclesiastical concepts, we shall smash his knuckles."

On March 16, 1950, the SED surprisingly announced that there would be no more youth dedications as they had been practiced by freethinkers and atheists. It stated that these youth dedications were no longer necessary because the churches were loyal to the state. But this sudden change in attitude was prompted by the desire to win pastors over to join the National Front.

More difficult to cope with was the atheistic education in the schools. A number of books were published, some of them by Russian authors, which had to be studied by all students. Young people who were not willing to give a clear testimony of dialectic materialism and against the church were not permitted to enter high school.

The charitable work of the church was a thorn in the flesh of the Communists. The Communist paper *Tägliche Rundschau* complained that hospital patients were being abused. It wrote: "We cannot bring into agreement with the basic assumptions of our democracy the fact that deaconesses and nuns are trying to monopolize our hospitals with their Christian ideology. This does not agree with the expressed desires of our patients. Therefore we must object to divine services being held in our hospitals."

At the twenty-seventh Bach Festival, held on the occasion of the two hundredth anniversary of Bach's death in 1950, the tendency to dechristianize the life of the nation became especially apparent. When the Bach Society, which had been organized in 1900, prepared the festival program during 1949 it was informed by the District Court of Leipzig that it had lost its charter and could continue to work only as a member of the Cultural Society for the Democratic Renewal of Germany. But even after the Bach Society had joined this Communist organization it was informed that its program was too churchly, and another Bach Committee was appointed. This committee emphasized that Bach had secularized church music and had written parodies of it. It stated that the Cantor of St. Thomas Church had had no choice but to write church music since he had been employed by the church.

The open enmity against the church became more and more pronounced. The Thuringian SED leader Hauschildt declared: "He who becomes dangerous to us must be eliminated. Every district chairman is in duty bound to denounce the black clergy (*Pfaffen*) who are reactionaries. We shall do the rest. All sermons must be supervised. We must organize regular church visitations by reliable Communists." The Thuringian Prime Minister Eggerath declared at a meeting of district councilors that the political influence exerted by pastors was worrying the SED. All party functionaries who had not yet resigned from the church before May 1, 1950, were ordered by the Politburo of the SED to resign from their offices. On the other hand, the party tried to win pastors to enter the National Front and to enlist the church in political propaganda.

Most of the pastors, however, refused to join the National Front. In order to make them more pliable, the Communists encouraged the organization of a very small group of "progressive pastors." Sometimes this group placed the names of pastors who had not agreed to join the National Front under its manifestos without the permission of the pastors concerned. Those who resisted these overtures were threatened with punishment as boycotters. On March

23, 1950, Pastor Aurel von Juechen, of Schwerin, was arrested because he had become obnoxious to the SED through his youth work. He disappeared for five years in the Soviet Union.

The church was forced to take action against these attacks by the state. In February 1950 the church of Berlin-Brandenburg informed her pastors that all the bishops of the Soviet zone had asked the Soviet commander, Sokolowski, to support their contention that the church should not be forced to take a definite position in questions of public life. At the same time Cardinal Preyssing instructed the Roman Catholic clergy that: "It is irreconcilable with honor and truth for a Catholic priest to cooperate with the National Front." Otto Nuschke, the Communist fellow traveler of the Christian Democratic Union, accused the Cardinal of playing the game of Western propaganda and defended the work of the National Front. Bishop Dibelius had asked on April 11, 1950, for an interview with Prime Minister Grotewohl. But the interview was not granted. Therefore, on April 20 Bishop Dibelius wrote a letter to Grotewohl in which he stated: "The church cannot be silent when this ideology which militates against the Christian faith is forced upon our people through the power of the state." On April 22, Cardinal Preyssing also sent a memorandum to Grotewohl.

On April 23 in all the Catholic churches of the DDR a declaration was read from the pulpits although the state had warned the priests against reading it. This declaration said in part: "Higher authorities do not have the right to force anyone to accept an ideology which is contrary to his faith and conscience. We call upon the members of our congregations to confess with determination and joy where their faith is directly and indirectly attacked that Jesus Christ is our Lord and that we belong to him body and soul."

The Christian Democratic Union, in keeping with the role which the Communists had assigned to it, protested that this declaration of the Catholic bishops was an attempt to introduce politics into the church. Prime Minister Grotewohl stated that the attitude of the church was in conflict with the Constitution of the DDR. But at the same time he sent greetings of Bishop Dibelius through Nuschke and his best wishes for the success of the EKD, which was meeting in Berlin-Weissensee April 21-23.

On April 28 a discussion took place between government and church representatives. This discussion lasted for almost six hours. On the part of the state Grotewohl and his three deputy prime ministers as well as Minister of Education Wandel and Minister of State Security Zaisser and two state secretaries took part. On the part of the church Bishops Dibelius, Hahn, Mueller, Hornig, Beste, and Oberkirchenrat Schroeder and the Superintendents General Krummacher and Braun, Presidents Kreyssig of Magdeburg and Scharf of Berlin, and two Catholic representatives, Auxiliary Bishop Weskamp and Prelate Adolf of Berlin, were present. In a joint communiqué the discussants stated: "The representatives of the church assured the government that they were concerned about the reconstruction of German national life in peace and freedom, and the representatives of the government stressed that they were concerned about assuring the churches that they would be able as in the past to develop their work within the framework of the DDR and on the basis of the Constitution of the DDR. Both parties declared their readiness to continue the discussions in the near future."

B. ATTACKS AGAINST CHRISTIAN UNITY

1. Attempts to Split the Church with the Help of the Association of Progressive Pastors, 1950-1951

In view of the forthcoming election of October 15, 1950, the Central Committee of the SED had secretly instructed all school authorities: "In view of the coming elections the impression that the state is opposed to religion must never be given to any captive audience. Principals and teachers must give the impression of religious tolerance in religious matters, but in the workers' and peasants' faculties the well-known viewpoint of the Party must be continued. In schools, anti-religious themes must be presented as a personal viewpoint of the teacher. This order remains in force until the elections."

Also strictly confidential were the instructions to the commanders of the People's Police that they were personally responsible for a wise and unostentatious managing of church resignations. It stated: "In principle Party members serving in the People's Police should be encouraged and even ordered to leave the church." But in carrying out this policy the People's Police must under no circumstances leave the impression that these resignations from the church were ordered by their superior officers. A few meetings of the youth of the church were still permitted in June 1950. For example, the Evangelical Youth of Saxony-Anhalt met on the Petersberg. Four thousand young people took part in this meeting. But the Saxon Youth Congress, at which about five thousand were expected, had to be canceled at the last moment because the City Council of Leipzig, where the meeting was to be held, claimed that the meeting was not in the interest of public welfare. Yet a number of other meetings could be held without interference.

During those months the atheist instruction in the schools continued unabated. In an article published in *Die Welt* Bishop Dibelius reported that among the secret political grades which were given to the high school students, there were the following: "He believes what his parents tell him." "He listens to the church." "He is a hopeless case." Even Otto Nuschke voiced a word of criticism at the Saxon Party Congress of the Christian Democratic Union (July 1950). He admonished the government not to use too much police power against the church since such a course would violate the constitution.

The printing of Bibles was made impossible by the fact that the government refused to allocate paper for that purpose. The Catholic St. Benno Publishing House in Leipzig was not licensed as Grotewohl had promised in the discussions of April 28. The 127 meter high tower of St. George's Church in Berlin, which had been bombed during the war, was dynamited in spite of the fact that the church had been given expert opinion that the tower was not a hazard to public safety. In a sermon of August 6, 1950, Dibelius demanded that all people should be able to live according to their convictions and should not be cast into prison on account of them. He was referring to the persecution of Jehovah's Witnesses during the summer months of 1950.

The official paper of the SED, *Neues Deutschland*, on May 14, 1950, published an article concerning the present conditions and tasks of the SED. It also dealt with the church. It contrasted the millions of church members who with hundreds of pastors belonged to the National Front with certain church leaders who had always defended the rule of the monopolists and Junkers and had agreed with the terror of the Nazis by blessing Hitler's armaments. The writer stated: "Many hundreds of pastors have courageously confessed that they are on the side of the people and have joined the National Committees of the National Front for a Democratic Germany. We must support these pastors and must organize protest meetings within the church so that these members of the churches and their pastors can fulfill their national duty." The article was referring to the small group of so-called "Progressive Pastors," whose leader was Professor of Theology Dr. Emil Fuchs, father of the atomic spy Dr. Klaus Fuchs, who had been imprisoned in England. Other leaders of this group were Professor Hertz of Leipzig; the Mecklenburg Pastor Heinrich Schwarzer, a member of the SED; the Cathedral preacher of Schwerin, Karl Kleinschmidt; the Dresden Pastor Dr. Karl-August Busch; Pastor Helmuth Mehnert, who had demitted the ministry; Pastor Gerhard Kehnscherper of Freienwalde; and others. Their proof for "progressive attitudes" was membership in a Communist organization or in the National Front, and the signing of the Stockholm Peace Appeal.

Bishop Beste of Mecklenburg answered all these appeals to join the National Front in these words: "The peace of God is the peace Christ has given us and which he is giving us even now again and again. To proclaim this peace is our business; this is the ministry of the church to the world." The church also published a "word of Peace of the Synod of the EKD," when the synod met in Berlin-Weissensee. In it she stated: "As people who believe in the peace of God for the world, we are called to seek peace with all people and to work together for the peace of all nations who seriously and honestly desire it. Therefore we admonish all people of our country as we have done in Eisenach in 1948 . . . and call upon all members of our nation in the West and the East: Do not promote a war of Germans against Germans. . . . God is our Lord. He alone has the right over the life and the whole existence of man. Only if the state recognizes this holy right of God is it honoring the dignity and the freedom of man."

The SED paper *Neues Deutschland* called this appeal of the EKD hazy. Pastor Schwarze criticized the message for not identifying itself with the fighters for freedom and the goal of the National Front: "This means that under the present conditions the church is encouraging those who try to interfere with our work of socialist reconstruction." When the church leadership of Berlin-Brandenburg had the appeal printed and mailed to its churches, it was removed from the church doors and from parish halls and parsonages by the People's Police.

The Progressive Pastors continued their propaganda war for the World Peace Movement of the Communist Party. They arranged so-called peace conferences in various places. These conferences were poorly attended. In Thuringia, for example, only 15 pastors accepted the invitation of the state peace committee. In Potsdam only 17 out of over 800 pastors of the church of Berlin-Brandenburg followed the invitation. Of the 420 pastors of Mecklenburg over 400 did not bother to answer the invitation. And church leaders everywhere refused to participate in any of these meetings.

A Catholic pastoral letter, written on August 6, emphasized that the church of Christ should not fight for a true peace with political means. In a similar vein, on November 11, the Evangelical Church of the Province of Saxony declared: "It is a question whether the peace which Jesus Christ has promised and which works through the Holy Spirit can be harmonized with the peace which the World Peace Movement is trying to impose upon us."

In order to force the resisting pastors to sign the Stockholm Peace Appeal, the state applied various pressures. The pastors were labeled "enemies of the state" and "war mongers and agents of the American imperialists." There were mass meetings. At Zittau, Saxony, Superintendent Johannes Mueller was called an enemy of the DDR because he refused to sign the Stockholm Peace Appeal. The Zittau Communist paper wrote: "The members of his church and the entire public demand that he should be removed from office." Also the Saxon Bishop, Dr. Hahn, was attacked by the SED because he did not sign the Appeal. The "progressive" Cathedral Preacher Kleinschmidt published "An Open Letter to Bishop Dibelius" in the *Berliner Zeitung* and offered him the alternative either to sign the Stockholm Peace Appeal or to admit that he had refused to sign it because he did not want to lose the sympathy of the American imperialists. But even these methods did not help much. The number of so-called Progressive Pastors remained discouragingly small. Dr. Busch of Dresden stated that there were on the average 30 Progressive Pastors in each regional church. Bishop Dibelius, however, estimated that only about one-half of one percent of all clergymen belonged to this group.

The results of this whole effort to recruit support for the Stockholm Peace Appeal were most discouraging to the Communists. In addition, many Progressive Pastors had been tainted by their past. Thus, for instance, a certain pastor, Dr. Cristiani of Trebnitz, a member of the SED, had been removed from his office because he had participated in a parody in baptism in which he had baptized a Communist actor in the name of the Father, of the Son, and of *Schnaps*. But the *Berliner Zeitung* stated on June 17 that Cristiani had been popular in his congregation and demanded his reinstatement. A very violent controversy also raged around the person of Pastor Heinrich Schwarze. The Mecklenburg Church Consistory had recalled him because certain irregularities had appeared in his parish and because he no longer possessed the confidence of his people. But Schwarze, like Cristiani, was a member of the SED; in addition he sat in the state parliament and held several offices in the National Front. The newspaper *Neues Deutschland* called his removal an attempt to discipline a pastor who was without reproach in doctrine and behavior and who was removed because he had participated in the democratic reconstruction and the battle for peace. These controversies continued until the state realized that the church would not capitulate.

On June 17 Grotewohl declared that the government henceforth would protect every pastor who was persecuted on account of his positive attitude toward peace. The Catholic chancellory of Berlin answered this challenge laconically: "All our tensions are being caused by the constant interference of the state."

At the next SED Congress, Bishop Dibelius was exposed to massive attacks and to slander. He had just returned from a meeting of the World Council of Churches in Toronto, Canada, and during his trip he had been received by President Truman. The *Tägliche Rundschau* reported that Bishop Dibelius and Truman had discussed common policies against the DDR with a view of the coming elections in October of that year. Grotewohl declared: "We know from church circles that Truman asked Dibelius how the church would react in case of a war in Europe." Grotewohl further accused Dibelius of having blessed the weapons of Hitler's war. He stated that Dibelius, denying this act, had offered 100,000 marks to anyone who would prove that this had actually happened. But Grotewohl felt that Dibelius had given encouragement to Hitler by consecrating the Thousand Year Reich in the *Garnisonkirche* in Potsdam in 1933. He also quoted from an "Evangelical Church Service Book in Times of War," by Gerhard Kunze, which seemed to endorse Hitler's war, and asked Dibelius whether he would be willing to pay the 100,000 marks into the SED treasury.

On July 29 Dibelius answered these charges. He admitted that he had been in Toronto and that he had been received by Truman in Washington. He stated: "The interview, which lasted less than 15 minutes, was concerned with affairs of the World Council of Churches. Nothing was said about the DDR or elections or the possible attitude of the church in case of a European war." As for his sermon at the Nazi inauguration in 1933, Dibelius stated that Grotewohl had omitted the most important passages of his sermon, which had made the Nazis furious. He admitted that there had been some so-called "German Christians" who had blessed Hitler's arms and "who are now members of the SED. These are the people who prayed for Hitler's success." But he declared that it was a lie to state that responsible church leaders were involved in this travesty.

Grotewohl gave up. But the Christian Democratic Union continued the attacks against Dibelius. At a CDU Convention in September of 1950, which met under the motto "Christians, Fight for Peace!" Nuschke expressed his profound regret that the churches were not fighting for peace.

The elections on October 15 went according to plan. The motto had been: "Vote Openly!" and it was observed by most who went to the balloting places. But many Christians had an uneasy conscience about the whole matter.

The church of Berlin-Brandenburg, divided between East and West, was the special target for Communist attacks. Grotewohl complained that the church leadership was living in West Berlin. Said he: "We shall not permit that certain leaders of the church who are itching for a fight shall be able to disturb the peaceful reconstruction in the DDR." The government decreed: "First, beginning with January 1, 1951, subsidies will be paid to the church leadership of Berlin-Brandenburg only if it moves to Brandenburg. Second, the government will not recognize any measures taken against certain pastors on account of their activity in the National Front for a Democratic Germany. Third, the government will continue to pay those pastors who have been dismissed directly from the funds available for church subsidies."

Prime Minister Jahn of Brandenburg now asked all Progressive Pastors to unite against the church authorities in West Berlin. But the Synod of the Old Prussian Union, to which Berlin-Brandenburg belonged, rejected this scheme of the state and expressed its thanks to the church leadership that it had preserved the freedom of action within the church. It stated: "First, there is no so-called West Berlin leadership of the church. We have only one leadership. . . . Second, the desire of the Brandenburg State Government to have a representative of the church government residing in the DDR was taken into account when, in 1946, the church appointed the Superintendent General of Mark Brandenburg to reside in Potsdam. Third, a special department to handle East German subsidies has been appointed for the Democratic Sector of Berlin and is charged with the handling of financial transactions in that part of the church which is located in the DDR."

2. A Milder Climate, 1951-1952

In the years 1950 and 1951 the East German government developed a plan which called for the organization of a so-called Council of Germany in which both German states would be represented. In order to create a better atmosphere for carrying out this plan

Grotewohl tried to establish contact with the West German Federal Chancellor Konrad Adenauer. The church profited by these attempts of the Communists to come to an understanding with the West German authorities. On New Year's Day, 1951, Grotewohl even sent his best wishes to Bishop Dibelius.

There were many signs that a thaw was in the making. Meetings of the young people of the church were again permitted. Funds were made available for the restoration of historically important churches. Even a referendum concerning remilitarization did not disturb this good relationship. The church, as a whole, supported this referendum. Dean Heinrich Grueber, since 1949 the representative of the church with the government of the DDR, received the cordial best wishes of the government on the occasion of his 60th birthday and was given a tea service by President Wilhelm Pieck. The German Evangelical *Kirchentag* was permitted to meet in both parts of Berlin from July 11 to 15. Its motto was: "And Yet We Are Brothers!" Pieck and Otto Nuschke, the latter in his capacity as leader of the East zone Christian Democratic Union, took part in the opening and closing services. From the West over 120,000 visitors had come to Berlin and from the East over 100,000. During these months also new regulations were introduced, which facilitated the study of theology at the state universities; and theological students received state stipends on the same basis as other students. The church was also allowed to publish more than before. At a press conference on August 23 Grotewohl said that the government would take no further steps to change the relationship between the churches or to interfere with the education of the children of the church. In a review of the year 1951 President Scharf of the church of Berlin-Brandenburg recognized that the relationship between the government and the church had improved. At least 70% of the members of the SED still belonged to the church.

Of course, there were also some dark spots in the picture. Since the middle of 1950 gifts by charitable organizations could no longer be imported without a license. A courier of the church by the name of Born was condemned to two years in prison and the confiscation of his property because he had taken the Hamburg *Sonntagsblatt* to Cottbus in the DDR. In East Berlin a Catholic book dealer,

Ursula Mocni, was condemned to 18 months in prison because she had sold publications of the West Berlin Morus Publishing House. Furthermore, the atheistic education of the children in the schools continued despite Grotewohl's promises. On September 9, 1951, Minister of Education Wandel gave instructions for the school year 1951-1952. President Dr. Heinemann reported to the Synod of the EKD that dialectic materialism not only was taught in the schools, but was also required as a confession from all students. Pastors who opposed this requirement had been called enemies of progress, of peace, and of national liberation.

The people of the DDR also suffered greatly under the one-sided application of the laws of the state. On September 18, 1951, Bishop Dibelius wrote to Stalin that the good neighbor policy with the Soviet Union was being endangered by the way in which justice and law were being abused in the Soviet zone. He cited examples of secret trials that had been conducted against young people who had been sentenced to 10, 20, or even 25 years' imprisonment and who had been treated in the most inhuman manner. He wrote: "For this reason I am turning to you, dear Mr. President. We believe that you agree with us that you cannot rule contrary to the understanding of justice of a people without at the same time turning the people against you."

But at this time the church was enjoying a comparatively quiet life. In Thuringia 2,000,000 members were being served by about 700 pastors in about 1,400 congregations; there was a shortage of about 80 pastors. The number of church choirs had increased to 620, which was a larger number than before the war. Of the 300,000 children belonging to the church over 240,000 were in catechism and confirmation instruction classes. Catechists to teach these children were being trained at seminaries in Eisenach, Jena, and Altenburg. The church paper *Glaube und Heimat* had a circulation of 27,000. In Saxony 1,705 people attended the Evangelical Academy of Meissen in 1951. A large number of new trumpet choirs had been organized. Men's Clubs existed in 40 congregations. Catechetical instruction was given in almost all congregations. About 1,250 catechists instructed the children of Saxony. An increasing number of young people participated in the work of the Young Congregation. Similar reports were received from the Province of Saxony where the giving of the people had increased and was now exceeding 1,000,000 marks per year. In Brandenburg 100% and in Berlin 80% of all children received catechetical instruction. In the DDR a total of 5,334 pastors were serving 6,100 parishes. There were also about 15,000 catechists, 653 male deacons, and about 13,000 deaconesses.

The Roman Catholic Church had no seminary of her own and urgently needed one. The government did not permit the opening of a seminary in the DDR until June 1952, when a seminary was established at Erfurt.

The major crisis of the year arose when the Synod of the Old Prussian Union wanted to meet in Goerlitz from May 11 to 15, 1952. The government informed the church leadership on April 5 that this synod could not meet on the territory of the DDR because the Synod of the Old Prussian Union was no longer identical with the church that had been in existence at its founding in 1922 (the territories East of the Oder-Neisse Line were under Polish and Soviet administration) and because the name "Old Prussian" gave rise to the suspicion that the synod wanted to preserve the tradition of Prussia which had been abolished. As a consequence, the Synod of the Old Prussian Union changed its name to Evangelical Church of the Union.

C. ATTACKS AGAINST THE YOUNG CONGREGATION

1. Open Church Struggle, 1952-1953

Many things happened in 1951 that were to have important consequences. The Federal Republic of Germany joined the European Community and declared its alliance with the West. The Soviet Union had done its utmost to hamper this development. On May 15, 1952, Federal Chancellor Adenauer signed a treaty by which the Federal Republic became a member of the European Community. Now also the DDR started to recruit citizens for a national army and established a zone boundary at the Iron Curtain with a five-kilometer wide forbidden zone. The church remained the last remnant of former German unity and thus was suspected of being the center of all Western influences in the DDR. In July, 1952, the SED, therefore, decided to increase the speed for the building up of socialism in the Soviet zone. The first object of the attack was the Young Congregation.

The Communist youth organization, the Free German Youth, had been suffering from the passive attitude of its functionaries and the lack of interest on part of the members. In many communities over 60% of all confirmed young people were members of the Young Congregation while the Free German Youth never gained much support among the population.

The opening shot against the Young Congregation was fired by Walter Ulbricht, Secretary General of the SED, who declared on Pentecost 1952 at the "Parliament of the Free German Youth," meeting at Leipzig, that he would henceforth tolerate no other youth organization than the Free German Youth. He accused the Young Congregation of having abused the Christian message to mask its reactionary tendencies and the clergymen in some communities of having supported forces which were opposed to the DDR.

The result of this speech by Ulbricht was soon felt. On June 8 a *Kirchentag* of the Young Congregation could still be carried out without interference. But beginning with June 14, the organization of the Young Congregation was hindered in many ways. It was not permitted to hold meetings in the open since it was considered an illegal organization. Its members were not permitted to travel to meetings, and trains that had already been allocated were withdrawn.

The paper of the Free German Youth, *Junge Welt*, became the leader in the attack against the Young Congregation. On August 3, 1952, it wrote: "This is not an association of young Christians, but an organization of hypocrites who are using Christianity as a veil to undermine the unity of the German youth in the DDR. There were many other attacks against the Young Congregation, especially since the church had asked her young people not to follow blindly any mottoes which were against Christ.

There were also attacks on other levels. On July 24 the Central Committee of the SED demanded that all property of the church should be expropriated in line with the liquidation of private property. Also an attempt was made to abolish the theological faculties at the universities. On August 14 Prime Minister Grotewohl wrote a letter to Bishop Dr. Dibelius in which he indicated that the education of the clergymen was the private affair of religious organizations. The Progressive Pastors supported the suggestions of the Communist government because they felt, as they said: "At some universities theology is in danger of becoming the bondwoman of the hierarchy, of losing the pure Word of God, and of robbing it of its power which is effective in history." The theological faculties rejected these libels. They stated: "We are bound in our work by the Word of God alone. We are serving without reservation and bondage to outside influences." Grotewohl quickly dropped the proposal. He probably realized that there was a dangerous side to it, namely that an organization of theological seminaries under the sole responsibility of the church would remove the future theologians from the effective control of the state.

Ulbricht now demanded that the connections between the churches of East and West Germany should be cut. The government did its utmost to carry out this demand by Ulbricht. President Pieck had promised 5,000 interzonal passports for the meeting of the Lutheran World Federation (LWF) in Hanover, July 25 to August 3, 1952. These permissions were now withdrawn, allegedly because Chancellor Adenauer was scheduled to be one of the speakers at the convention. Also the participation of many thousands of Soviet zone citizens at the Evangelical *Kirchentag*, which met in Stuttgart from August 27 to September 1, was made impossible. Only 40 representatives from the German Democratic Republic were permitted to go to Stuttgart. The same measures were taken against the Catholics who had planned to attend the German *Katholikentag* in Berlin. The city government of East Berlin withdrew all permission to use public places, schools, and industrial plants for the lodging of the participants.

During a conversation between church leaders and Grotewohl which was held on July 25, the Prime Minister called the political situation very serious and told Bishop Dibelius that he hoped that the next trip abroad would not lead him into an enemy country. Bishop Dibelius answered this threat on July 26, 1952, by declaring to his pastors: "No state has the right to touch the unity of the church of Jesus Christ. . . . We can never consent to the demand that the boundaries of the state must also be the boundaries of the church."

Bishop Dibelius' next trip to America, in December 1952, on which he attended a committee meeting of the World Council of Churches in Denver, caused a new violent reaction in the DDR. Dibelius was alleged to have told the National Council of Churches of Christ in the USA that "God has made Germany the battleground between Christianity and the spirit of materialism." This, it was alleged, showed that Dibelius was looking for a new world war sponsored by America. He was called a warmonger and an enemy of the state. Atheists even accused him of blasphemy.

At the beginning of 1953 it seemed that the state wanted to bring the conflict with the church to a head. The three government officials responsible for relationships with the Catholic, the Protestant, and the Free Churches fled in January 1953 to West Berlin. The Catholic *Petrus Blatt,* published in West Berlin, was forbidden in the East sector. The Protestant matins services which had been broadcast regularly were turned over to Progressive Pastors. In addition, there was a wave of new arrests. On January 23 Pastor Erich Schumann in Zwickau, who had been active in Saxon evangelistic circles, was condemned to six years in the penitentiary for having incited a boycott against the DDR. He was accused of having told the story of a rich Englishman, who, after his conversion, had given his money to Christian youth work. This was called a glorification of capitalism. A Catholic priest, Franz Busch, who had been arrested at the end of 1952, was punished with five years' imprisonment for boycott and for mistreatment of children. A great number of other clergymen of both churches were also condemned to imprisonment and penitentiary.

The thrust of the Communists was directed mainly against the youth work of the church. The youth magazine *Die Stafette,* which had a circulation of about 50,000 and was indispensable for the work of the Young Congregation, lost its license.

At the beginning of 1953 a school diary was introduced in all schools, in which each student had to report concerning the work he had done during the day, including also the time spent outside of school and his membership in various organizations. Thus the school principals had easy access to information about activities of their students outside of school. In one school the young people were asked to write on the theme: "The Young Congregation Is an Organization of Criminals." A large number of students were expelled from school because they were members of the Young Congregation. The Thuringian church paper *Glaube und Heimat*, in which Bishop Dr. Mitzenheim had defended the Young Congregation, was confiscated by the government.

At the same time there were violent attacks against the student congregations at the universities. The Secretary of the Central Committee of the Free German Youth, Kurt Turba, found a poster by a student congregation which read: "Chemistry is important, but God is more important" and stated that the student congregations were leading young people to conflicts of conscience and thus were keeping them from studying. He demanded that they should be outlawed.

In connection with these attacks a number of arrests took place. The East Berlin student pastor, Reinhold George; the student pastor of the University of Halle, Johannes Hamel; the Traveling Secretary of the Evangelical Student Congregations, Vicar Karl-Johannes Althaus of Brandenburg; Deacon Herbert Dost of Leipzig; Pastor Juergen Winterhager of Hohenauen; the student leader of the Evangelical Student Congregations, Gisela Schwan; Deacon Fritz Hoffmann of Magdeburg, who served as District Director of the YMCA in the Province of Saxony; and many others were put into prison.

According to statistics of March 1952, 28 pastors were in prison. Among them were quite a number who had been condemned to five, 10, 20, and even 25 years in the penitentiary and in work camps. At the beginning of March 1953 the number had risen to 49. These arrests caused Karl Barth to write a letter to the Minister for State Security, Wilhelm Zaisser, in which he stated that he had constantly been accused of being friendly to the Communists since 1945, but that he could no longer be silent in the face of the occurrences in the East zone. He stated that the freedom of the church was seriously jeopardized and demanded that these attacks be stopped.

On April 20 Bishop Dibelius as President of the Council of EKD wrote a letter to the Prosecutor General of the DDR, Dr. Mehlsheimer, in which he stated that the attacks against the Young Congregation and the entire youth work of the church centered in the magazine *Junge Welt* and were libelous. He declared: "I demand that you take action against those who are responsible for these attacks, especially against the editors of *Junge Welt*." On May 2 the Evangelical Consistory of Berlin-Brandenburg also demanded that a lawsuit should be started against the Free German Youth. On May 19 Dr. Mehlsheimer stated in a curt reply: "The organization Young Congregation is not registered with the State Secretariat of the Interior of the DDR. Therefore the Young Congregation is not permitted. And so I see no reason why I should comply with your demand for criminal prosecution." The Evangelical Consistory answered on May 1 that in 1946 Bishop Dibelius and Colonel Tulpanov, the representative of the SMA for Germany, had agreed that the church should not carry on her youth work in the form of a formal organization but through a free association of young people on the basis of the local congregation. It stated: "You admit yourself that the Young Congregation has never been registered with the state. But it is difficult to accept your claim that any organization could have existed in the DDR for these past years and carried on its work without being properly registered."

The SED now mobilized all organizations of the party and of the factories to pass resolutions of opposition to the Young Congregation. The Secretary General of the Christian Democratic Union, Gerald Goetting, said at a meeting of his party at Leipzig that the Young Congregation had committed over 130 acts of violence against the DDR. The Christian Democratic Union of Brandenburg issued a call to young Christians to leave the illegal organization of the Young Congregation. The principal of the Olmuetz High School led his student body in front of the St. James Church of Olmuetz where they dismantled the bulletin board of the Young Congregation from the church door. The leader of the Free German Youth, Honecker, demanded the liquidation of all groups of the

Young Congregation and declared that this was not a fight against the church as such, but against the Adenauer clique and the warmongers within the church. Children in the elementary schools were given the choice whether they wanted to attend catechetical instruction or whether they wanted to be expelled from the Young Pioneers of the Free German Youth, and thus be barred from entering high school.

The main battle against the Young Congregation was fought on the high school level. This battle often took the form of terror. In numerous meetings of school students, meetings that lasted up to 10 hours, an intensive investigation of the students took place. High school students were asked to sign papers in which they declared their readiness to leave the Young Congregation. They were threatened: "Either you sign or your parents will be held responsible." Not a single school administrator protected these young people.

Many of the young people gave in to these pressures and threats, but others resisted. By the middle of May about 3,000 young Christians, of whom 50% had planned to graduate that year, had been expelled from school. Many of them fled to West Berlin and to the Federal Republic. A bureau which was established by the EKD helped them find new homes and new opportunities to continue their education.

At the same time there were measures against the charitable organizations of the church. In March the Railroad Missions were expelled from railroad stations and their work was assigned to the Red Cross. A great number of charitable institutions of the church were taken over by the state. The students were sent home and their leaders arrested. Many of these homes, like the Pfeiffer Foundation in Magdeburg, had a long and respected history. The staff of the Pfeiffer Foundation was accused of having sadistically tortured the mentally retarded and of having thus made a mockery of the dignity of man. When Bishop Dr. Mueller tried to protect the institutions, *Junge Welt* wrote: "If Bishop Mueller believes to have license to fight against our republic, he can go to hell and we shall demand that another take his place, a person who is willing to fight as a Christian for the peace of the people."

Other institutions of the church were also taken over by the state, including some Roman Catholic homes. Nuns and deaconesses alike were accused of having maltreated young children who had been entrusted to them. The institutions at Lobethal, which were under the direction of the famous Bodelschwingh Institutions in Bethel, were isolated from the outside and investigated by seven control commissions of the state. The commissions took depositions from the feeble-minded, asked them how they had been treated and fed, and tried to put into their mouths accusations against the management of the institutions. One of the state investigators told a feeble-minded boy: "Beat your educators if they demand anything from you!" He received the answer: "You must be crazy if you think that you can turn us against them!" An 18-year-old epileptic patient jumped out of the window when he was questioned by the Communists and drowned in a nearby lake. President Dr. Scharf complained to the president of the People's Chamber, Dr. Dieckmann, and even Nuschke demanded that the state should pay more attention to the bad results of such attacks against the church.

The Communists also arranged meetings with the inhabitants of numerous villages where they forced members of the local churches to denounce their own pastors. In some cases such pastors were expelled from the communities or were kept from entering their own churches. The leader of the City Mission of Magdeburg, Meidam, was expelled from that city because he had written to his fellow pastors: "Now is the time when we must love the godless until they leave their godlessness behind."

There were also increasing incidences of disturbances of church services. On April 19 the church services were interrupted in two churches of Quedlinburg by whistling and jeering young people. The meeting of German theologians, which included all German theological faculties, and had been scheduled to meet in East Berlin in April, was forbidden three days before the beginning. Bishop Dibelius was not permitted to attend the *Kirchentag* in Brandenburg; and the Paderborn Archbishop, Dr. Lorenz Jaeger, was not permitted to visit the seminary at Halberstadt which belonged to his diocese.

The state even interfered in the most intimate life of the congregation. In Goerlitz Bible classes in the homes were forbidden. Bishop Hornig of Silesia asked the congregations to pay no attention to this prohibition. In Mecklenburg Bible classes were forbidden because the trend of the discussions could not be controlled. In Lusatia any type of church activity, outside of church services and occasional Bible classes, was forbidden. Also the practicing sessions of church choirs, meetings of women's and young people's societies, pastoral conferences, and meetings of church councils were made dependent upon the special permission by the police.

Surprising in all this was the behavior of the so-called Progressive Pastors. Professor Dr. Leipold boasted at a meeting in Karl-Marx-Stadt (Chemnitz) that "No government has given us as many opportunities for development as the government of the DDR." But when Grotewohl invited pastors to meet with him in East Berlin at the end of May, only 10 men showed up; and even these 10 criticized the behavior of the state toward the church. Grotewohl informed them that he had called a mass meeting of pastors for June 15 to meet in Leipzig and that he expected the attendance of 3,000 pastors to plan an advisory council for the churches.

Neither the Protestant nor the Catholic Church left the state in the dark about their attitude. On April 20 the Bishops' Conference of the United Evangelical Lutheran Church in Germany (VELKD) issued the following declaration: "The pressure which is being put upon the members of the church in the DDR in matters of faith and conscience is beginning to become unbearable. . . . We have heard of unbelievably severe punishment in cases where the accepted justice of civilized nations would judge completely differently. We declare that we think that these methods used against our young people are inhuman. As Christian brethren we assure our persecuted brethren that they are in the hands of God and we encourage them not to forsake their Lord Jesus Christ."

On April 28 Bishop Dibelius wrote a letter to the members of the Young Congregation and their parents in which he stated: "We thank all those who, in the school assemblies, in the factories, and in vocational schools, have given a courageous confession to their Lord. The church will be able to weather this second battle by the gracious will of God as she has weathered the first. The Lord is stronger than all his enemies. The work of the Young Congregation will continue. I salute all those who have been loyal in this difficult hour." Also Bishop Dr. Mitzenheim addressed the young people of his church. Said he: "Do not be led astray by threats; do not act from fear. Take all your power from the Word of God and come to the Table of the Lord. He who carries his burden looking up to the crucified Lord will be blessed by God. He will be kept from hatred and bitterness even though he has to suffer injustice. He will forgive and keep good courage." Similar letters were sent out by the Council of the EKD.

The Catholic bishops in the DDR in a letter written to their young people declared: "As all of us, you have the inalienable right to freedom of conscience and of faith. No one should dare to persecute you on account of this. You have the right to be Christians and to remain Christians."

Prime Minister Grotewohl had said in Erfurt on April 23 that there was no church struggle in the DDR. Bishop Dibelius answered by telling him: "You cannot constantly arrest pastors and expel members of the Young Congregation and student congregations; you cannot forbid the printing of church publications; you cannot close one institution of the church after another and then declare that there is no church struggle. . . . The church has not looked for this struggle which you have forced upon her, but she also has not tried to run away from it. A church which is afraid of a struggle and of suffering would not be a Christian church."

The church tried various means to bring the state to its senses. As early as the middle of March Bishop Mitzenheim had written to Deputy Prime Minister Nuschke and had asked him to mediate. But the letter was never answered. On April 10 all bishops of the DDR wrote to General Chuikov, the chief of the Soviet Control Commission. On April 30 President Dr. Martin Niemoeller of the Church of Hesse visited Russian Orthodox Archbishop Boris in Karlshorst. Mediation of the latter made it possible to arrange for a two hours' discussion with the advisor of the Soviet Control Commission for Religious Affairs, Pavel Judin. The first indication that the state was changing its attitude became apparent at the end of May. At a meeting of pastors who had invited Grotewohl, he admitted that the state had gone too far when it expelled members of the Young Congregation from high school. But this error could be corrected, he stated. A few days later Ulbricht in a speech to the communist intelligentsia warned against excesses in the fight against the Young Congregation.

What prompted the government to change its course? Certainly the resistance of the church was one factor. But this was not all. On March 5, 1953, Stalin had died. His successor spoke about a new course of peaceful coexistence with the West. Ulbricht sought at first to keep the "thaw" away from his bailiwick. But the increasing number of refugees since the beginning of 1953—the total number rose from 182,393 in 1952 to 331,390 in 1953—and the international wave of protest against the terror of the government did much to bring the persecution to a halt. The Archbishop of York, Dr. Garbett, even suggested that the church struggle in the DDR should be placed on the agenda of the United Nations. Last, but not least, the increasing economic and interior difficulties, which had been caused by the propagation of socialism, forced the Politburo of the SED on June 9 to decide on a new course which led to considerable changes in various areas.

2. Quiet After the Storm? (1953-1954)

On June 5 the church leaders of the Protestant churches in the DDR met in Berlin and took action concerning the intention of Grotewohl to call a mass meeting of pastors at Leipzig. Dean Grueber was instructed to give the Prime Minister a resolution, stating first that the tensions between church and state must be solved by direct negotiation between the church leadership and the government; secondly, that state and church leaders should appoint representatives who would be instructed to bring about an understanding through joint discussion; and, thirdly, that this should be arranged by the responsible leaders of the church and not by the Progressive Pastors and that it should include all points of view.

The unexpected happened. Grotewohl accepted the proposal of the church leaders, and the discussions took place on June 10. On the part of the state, Grotewohl, Nuschke, Minister of Education

Dr. Wandel, Minister for State Security Zaisser, and the State Secretary for the Ministry of the Interior Goetschel took part. The agenda for the discussion was the reexamination of the relationship between church and state in the German Democratic Republic. In a joint communiqué the participants stated: "During the conversations, which were carried on in the spirit of mutual understanding, the restoration of normal relations between state and church was discussed and far-reaching agreements were reached. It was the unanimous opinion of the participants that the restoration of the unity of our Fatherland and the creation of a peace treaty are the most important concerns of all Germans today and that this goal requires the overcoming of controversies which militate against this development. Therefore the state declares its readiness to guarantee the life of the church in accordance with the stipulations of the Constitution of the DDR. The representatives of the church on their part declare that they will renounce all interference and influence in the economic and political life of the country which is against the Constitution."

On the basis of these general presuppositions the discussants agreed that there would be no further measures against the Young Congregation; that the students who had been expelled from high school on account of their membership in the Young Congregation would be readmitted immediately; that students who had been expelled from universities on account of their membership in student congregations would be reexamined before June 23; that the Ministry of Education would work out rules and regulations for the religious instruction in school buildings. Any limitations that had been imposed since January 1953 would be reexamined and eliminated.

There were also a number of additional stipulations, such as the return of church institutions to the churches and financial compensation for homes that had been expropriated. In a letter which was read from all pulpits of the Protestant churches the Council of EKD, which met on June 11-12 in Berlin, spoke of remarkable changes. A few days later, on June 17, the revolt took place, followed breathlessly by the whole world. Only the active intervention of the Russian armed forces preserved the DDR from collapsing. The revolt probably cost some 400 lives and as many as 1,700 wounded. Over 100 people were executed and between 1,100 and 1,200 participants were condemned to a total of 6,000 years in prison. On June 19 Bishop Dibelius asked the Soviet High Commissioner, Semjenov, to take into consideration the concerns of the working man. He also asked for the release of those who had been arrested.

The promises which had been given to the church had not in all instances been formulated clearly. But on the whole they were carried out. The number of those who were imprisoned decreased considerably, from 72 to 38 by July 1. During the following months further pardons were issued. Most members of the Young Congregation and members of student congregations were permitted to continue their studies. However, members of the Young Congregation were received back by their principals in a very unfriendly way. Over 2,000 of them preferred to remain in the West because they did not want to return to a school where they had been treated so hatefully. Also numerous teachers who had been disciplined were permitted to resume their work. State subsidies were paid once more, but in 1953-1954 only 11.8 million marks instead of the full sum of 19.9 million marks was made available. On July 3, 1953, after a long discussion with the state authorities, the work of prison chaplains was regulated. This new regulation showed some very serious defects. Pastors were allowed to speak to prisoners only in the presence of policemen. Prisoners who were still under interrogation were not permitted to see their pastors at all.

Church officials now received inter-zonal passes again. The Evangelical *Kirchentag* which met in Hamburg from August 12 to 16, 1953, was attended by 10,000 guests from the DDR. The Council of the EKD was able to meet once again in the DDR. It convened in Dresden and participated in the installation of the new Saxon Bishop Dr. Noth, on October 21. Young theologians from the Soviet zone who had studied in the Federal Republic and who had been employed as vicars were now permitted to return to their homes and churches. The papal nuncio, Dr. Aloisius Muench, was permitted to travel to Erfurt and to participate in the St. Boniface celebrations of May 23, 1954, and to address 80,000 assembled Catholics.

For the Leipzig *Kirchentag* of 1954 over 10,000 people from West Germany were given travel permits. This *Kirchentag*, which perhaps was the most impressive and the most spiritual of all these assemblies, counted 60,000 permanent participants. At its final meeting, on July 11, over 650,000 visitors from all parts of Germany participated under the motto: "Be Joyful in Hope, Patient in Tribulations, Constant in Prayer!" It was the greatest meeting for all of Germany since 1945, and it was also the last *Kirchentag* to be permitted in the DDR.

Three Protestant church papers were permitted to be published again, and were authorized to be distributed in their former circulation. The Eastern sector of the Catholic diocese of Berlin was permitted its own magazine, *St. Hedwigs Blatt.* Yet church publications were still being discriminated against. In the fall of 1953 all church papers in the DDR had only a combined circulation of 305,320 while in the Federal Republic church publications had a circulation of 12,800,000. That meant that in the Federal Republic every fourth Christian and in the DDR every sixtieth had a religious magazine. The publications in the DDR were permitted to print without previous censorship the following items: Mottoes for the church year; hymns; announcements of divine services and of religious meetings; and rites administered by the church. However, the printing of addresses was still not permitted. Sermons, discussions of church history, articles which served the edification of the faithful, and similar editorial contributions had to be submitted to the licensing authorities. There were many other restrictions.

A discussion was held on July 11 to regulate the relationship of the Young Congregation to the Free German Youth. Both Dean Grueber for the church and Erich Honecker for the Free German Youth took part in it. On the whole, it was an amiable discussion. In the official communiqué the participants stated: "The discussions took place in a spirit of mutual understanding. Agreement was reached concerning all important questions. We are agreed that the most important concern of all young Germans is the restoration of the unity of the Fatherland and the signing of a peace treaty and that all misunderstandings must be solved."

During these years the church was plagued by an increasing lack

of pastors. In the winter semester 1953-1954 there were only 931 students of theology enrolled at the six state universities, and this number was not even sufficient to fill the quota which the state had allotted to the study of theology. Also the number of catechists had decreased, e.g., in the Province of Saxony from 720 to 540. Their salary was extremely low, from $50 to $100 per month.

The Young Congregation, too, passed through a crisis. Parents were now afraid for the future of their children. Furthermore, decrees by the Minister of Education, issued on March 20 and April 5, 1954, stated that every teacher was an employee of the state and therefore had to consider himself as a functionary of the workers' and peasants' state. In violation of the promises made on June 10, 1953, every teacher and every student was forced to accept the materialistic ideology.

There were other indications that the state was not in earnest in its professed desire to permit complete freedom of faith. In the newly constructed city of Stalinstadt church buildings were forbidden. The Gossner Inner Mission Society sent a mission trailer with 28 seats to Stalinstadt, but this trailer was not permitted to enter the city limits. After the revolt of June 1953 permission had been given for the use of a church barracks, but the idea of using school rooms for divine services and for Christian instruction was rejected. At Christmas 1953 Bishop Dibelius preached in neighboring Schoenschliess to 700 visitors from Stalinstadt, but he was not allowed to speak in Stalinstadt. Only when President Dr. Martin Niemoeller of Hesse arrived in 1954 was he permitted to speak in the House of Culture of Stalinstadt, and a few weeks after Niemoeller's visit the Ministry of Reconstruction permitted the church to erect a barracks chapel.

A new family code which was published on June 30, 1954, by the Minister of Justice was attacked by the church. The East Conference of the EKD declared: "We cannot consent to a law which sees the only reason for the existence of family and marriage in the political propagation of socialism. Political ideas like democracy, socialism, patriotism, peace among nations, do not belong in the Law for the Protection of the Family." The church especially opposed Paragraph 4 of the law which read: "Parents can fulfill their responsible duty for the education of their children only when they work together in close cooperation with the school and youth organizations."

Other events of 1954 which led to sharp controversies were the question of the referendum of June 27 concerning the peace treaty and the removal of the forces of occupuation, and the election of October 17. The leadership of the church of the Province of Saxony demanded that secret booths should be provided for the voting and that the ballots should be returned to the judges in closed envelopes.

D. THE YOUTH IS TAKEN OVER BY THE STATE

1. Youth Dedication or Confirmation? (After 1954)

The discussions of June 10, 1953, had led to a limited armistice. As a result, the SED started its fight against religion on a different level. In place of a frontal attack it tried to undermine the worldview of Christianity in order to win the young people over to materialistic atheism. A survey of SED members indicated that 75% of its members still belonged to the church, and among the women and children even 90%.

On June 17, 1954, a Society for the Dissemination of Scientific Knowledge was founded, which had as its goal "the unmasking of all types of superstitions and prejudices which have been inherited from the old order and which are a hindrance to the solution of our tasks." More than 500 houses of culture were placed, on May 1, 1954, at the disposal of the Free German Unions and were endowed with millions of marks to propagate cultural programs. In its first year of operation the Society held 11,000 meetings, which were attended by 640 people, and it published 35 brochures.

In the fall of 1954 the Central Committee of the Free German Youth published a brochure entitled *Communist and Religious Morality* by the Russian candidate of philosophy, P. F. Kolonitzki, in which he attacked the church and Christianity in the DDR. The first sentence of the brochure read: "Communist morality is opposed diametrically to religious morality. It cannot be reconciled with it, just as freedom and slavery, truth and falsehood, light and darkness cannot be reconciled with each other."

A Central Pedagogical Conference, which met in Halle on October 18, 1953, clearly defined the ideological basis of the school. It stated: "The ideological basis for the entire course of instruction in the schools of the DDR is dialectic materialism. . . . The principle for which we are fighting is opposition to all reactionary ideas." Among these reactionary ideas the statement mentioned especially "mysticism," which had been defined as follows in the *Communist Dictionary of Foreign Words* (Berlin, 1953): "Mysticism is faith in something supernatural, divine, transcendental. It is a firm part of all religions, and an enemy of science, and it is used by the reactionary ideologists for the confusion of the masses in their battle against the scientific ideology."

On December 3, 1954, the East Conference of the EKD protested that the schools were becoming more and more confessional schools where students were forced to accept the materialistic ideology of the state. It criticized especially the texts which were used in the schools and stated that materialism was giving a lopsided picture of reality. The protest remained without effect. In October 1954 the press demanded the reintroduction of Youth Dedications for all 14-year-old children.

The answer to these press appeals was prompt. On November 14 the press published a statement signed by 22 prominent persons who were outstanding teachers, professors, poets, heroes of labor, Nobel prize winners, and high state officials, which called for the reintroduction of Youth Dedications in 1955. Four and one-half years before, in March 1950, Youth Dedications had been abolished by the Politburo of the SED. But now the changing situation demanded a reintroduction of the rite. With lightning speed an organization was built up, consisting of a Central Committee for Youth Dedications; and before November 30, some 30 district committees had been established, each of which was headed by a secretary. Parents were asked to announce their intention of enrolling their children in the courses leading up to the Youth Dedications of 1955. These announcements were to be made before January 15. The preliminary plan called for 10 weekly youth lessons to be taught in preparation for the dedication. Each lesson consisted of 10 double periods. Their topics were: (1) World and Universe; (2) The Origin of Life on Earth; (3) The Development of Man; (4) The Domination of Nature by Man; (5) The Development of Human Society; (6) The Creative Power of the Masses and Their Struggle for Social Progress; (7) The New Era in the History of Society; (8) The Relationship of People to Each Other, Especially the Position of Woman in Society; (9) The Meaning of the Arts in the Life of Our People; (10) Summary and Preparation for the Youth Dedication.

Those young people whose parents had announced them were given a "Bible," called *Universe, Earth, Man,* which they could keep in remembrance of the day of their dedication. Its preface was written by Walter Ulbricht. In it he asked the young people to fight against superstition, mysticism, idealism, and other nonscientific remnants of the past.

The churches immediately took action against these Youth Dedications. Bishop Dibelius declared: "Our church orders state very clearly that children who participated in an action which is opposed to confirmation cannot be confirmed. We shall hold fast to this stipulation with all the determination at our disposal. . . . Children who participate in Youth Dedications are separating themselves from the communion with those who are entitled to participate in Holy Communion and are permitted to become baptismal sponsors." Similar positions were taken by Bishop Mitzenheim of Thuringia, Bishop Noth of Saxony, and other Protestant church leaders, as well as by the bishops of the Roman Catholic Church, who emphasized that "Youth Dedications are not neutral school celebrations, but a solemn vow to accept the materialistic ideology which has been taught. Therefore a Christian who participates in these dedications is denying his faith."

The initiators of Youth Dedications were indignant about the sharp rejection of their rite by the church. They turned furiously against the church and accused her of pressuring the consciences of believers. But they completely ignored the fact that their ceremony was basically anti-religious, anti-Christian, and materialistic and atheistic. The church, on her part, rejected the rebuke that she was violating Articles 41 and 42 of the Constitution of the DDR if she refused confirmation to children who had participated in Youth Dedications. On February 15, 1955, the Saxon church paper *Sonntag* wrote: "The church alone must decide whether any celebration or rite is against the order of the church. This has nothing to do with the freedom of the individual." Pastor Fritz Schulte of Dresden, who had proclaimed in the Communist press that cooperation between Youth Dedication and Confirmation was possible, was removed from office. Bishop Noth declared in a pulpit announcement: "More than church order has been violated. Let no one become confused by this attempt to make Youth Dedications seem like harmless acts in order to undermine the position of Christian parents."

All kinds of inducements, pressures, and force were being used to advance the cause of Youth Dedications. Factories gave money to those who participated in this rite. But only from 5% to 10% of all 14-year-old children participated in the Youth Dedications during the first year. As a result, teachers and leaders of the Free German Youth and of the SED visited parents and discussed with them for hours on end the disadvantages which their children would have to face if they did not participate in the rite.

In April 1955 the first Youth Dedications were held. There were about 1,100 celebrations in all. They were clearly an imitation of the rite of confirmation. There were music and recitations, and the young people were greeted with bouquets of flowers by Young Pioneers of the Free German Youth. The vow, which was the heart of the dedication, stated: "Are you ready to devote all your strength to the building up of a happy and beautiful life, to progress in economy, science, and the arts? Answer: Yes, we promise! Are you ready together with all patriots to devote all your powers to the battle for a democratic, peace-loving, and independent Germany? Answer: Yes, we promise! Are you ready together with all peace-loving people to devote all your powers to defend the peace of the country to the end? Answer: Yes, we promise! We have heard your promise. You have set yourselves a high goal. We, the community of workers, promise to help you and to protect you. Let us go forward with united strength to victory."

On September 21, 1955, the Central Committee for Youth Dedications declared that a total of 60,000 young people had been dedicated and that 500,000 visitors had attended these dedications. It was clear that in the figure of 60,000 all those children were included whose parents did not belong to any church at all. In spite of this discouragingly small number of children who had been dedicated, the press declared that the Youth Dedications had become a necessity to society. The period of preparation for the 1956 dedications was considerably lengthened. The instruction began in early October. The Central Committee for Youth Dedications declared that participation would be on a voluntary basis, and if anyone wanted to go also to confirmation instruction there would be no objection. Nevertheless, the church continued her resistance to Youth Dedications.

There were several incidents during that year. Minister of Education Paul Wandel accused the church of having pressured parents and children. He said: "We can show you letters in which 14-year-old boys were threatened with punishment by the church if they participated in Youth Dedications." But despite the concerted efforts by the SED only 5% of all the graduates from elementary school announced themselves as candidates for Youth Dedications by the end of 1955. The Central Committee once more organized all "progressive" forces in order to get a better showing. Otto Nuschke, however, warned the fanatics that they were doing a disservice to national unity if they applied high pressure methods and threatened Christian teachers. In the area of the Saxon Church only 2,000 children who had been enrolled in confirmation instruction dropped out and went over to the Youth Dedications. An additional 3,500 children of church members had not participated in confirmation instruction. In the territory of the DDR over 90% of all Protestant children were confirmed that spring (1956).

In 1957 the goal of the Central Committee for Youth Dedications was to win at least 40% of all graduates of the elementary schools for Youth Dedication. Prizes were promised to every district, and a general convention of boys and girls was arranged for those who enrolled in youth classes. A special collection of clothing was started for those who went through with the Youth Dedication. Also dances, including waltz and rhumba, were planned for them. They were also instructed in etiquette, how to behave in company of others and during cultural performances. Every district planned a grand ball for them. Louis Firnberg, a Communist composer, wrote a special oratorio for them. And many other events were planned in order to attract young people to the Youth Dedications.

The ideological bases for Youth Dedications were somewhat veiled by new instructions, which emphasized the accomplishments of the workers' and peasants' state of the DDR. The themes were the following: (1) What does Youth Dedication mean? (2) How do the workers of the DDR work and live? (3) In what way are the workers and the peasants the basis for our society? (4) How has man developed in the history of human society through his work? (5) How has man learned to dominate nature and to overcome superstition? (6) How can we better enjoy our work? (7) How does art make our lives more mature and more enjoyable? (8) How do we arrange our personal lives? (9) How can we show our love for our DDR? (10) How can we fight for peace and be the friends of all peace-loving and progressive people? In addition, the vow was changed somewhat, and in the place of the controversial book *Universe, Earth, Man,* a new book, *Our Germany,* was given to the young people as a present of the state. It contained 150 articles on German cultural history and portraits of important Germans from Goethe, Beethoven, Schiller, Herder, to Ernst Thaelmann, Klara Zetkin, and other leading lights of Communism. Marx and Engels were praised as the saviors of mankind. The German national development was reinterpreted on the basis of the idea of class struggle. This time the preface was written by Wilhelm Pieck.

Despite this attempt on the part of the DDR ideologically to neutralize the Youth Dedications, the church continued to reject them. Bishop Noth declared: "No matter how hard they may try to make Youth Dedications as attractive as possible for young people, this rite cannot be reconciled with confirmation. Two worlds are clashing which exclude each other. The goal of Youth Dedications is a pledge to an ideology without God, even if the opposition to God and to religion is not clearly expressed." Bishop Mitzenheim and other church leaders followed the same line.

The Youth Dedications in the spring of 1957 were held in the presence of outstanding speakers, artists, heroes of labor, and important functionaries of the state. In Dessau Walter Ulbricht was the speaker. He attacked the church as a power of reaction and the faithful ally of the Bonn Junkers and of Hitler before them. Said he: "By participating in these Youth Dedications you are giving a pledge—not a pledge to an ideology—but a pledge to our state of workers and peasants and to peace and humanism." Concerning the total participation in the Youth Dedications of 1957 the Central Committee did not furnish any figures. It merely announced that 1,500 celebrations had taken place in the cities and villages of the DDR, and that on the average 5% more children had participated in the Youth Dedications than during the previous year.

In addition to the Youth Dedications, there had been started since the fall of 1955 a number of other socialistic-materialistic ceremonies which were meant to wean people away from the churches. There were now Name-Giving Dedications which took the place of Christian Baptism. There were Marriage Dedications which were meant to take the place of Christian weddings. And there were, finally, Funeral Dedications which were to take the place of the Christian funeral and at which prominent people delivered flaming eulogies.

2. Further Restrictions Imposed on the Church, 1955-1956

At the meeting of the Central Committee of the SED in 1955 Walter Ulbricht declared: "Religious ideology is a hindrance to progress. . . . The fact that the state is trying to maintain a normal relationship with the church and also through the SED is honoring the religious customs of our citizens does not excuse us from fighting against religious prejudices and from fighting against them in our own party." Members of the SED were again asked to leave the church. Bishop Dibelius announced that the People's Police and state officers and other organizations were pressuring their members to leave the church. He anticipated 20,000 resignations from the church. In Leipzig it was announced that from 800 to 1,000 people were leaving the church every month. In 1955 the Saxon Church registered 51,782 resignations.

There were also a number of new brazen attacks against the church. For example, during the Mardi Gras of 1956 in the city of Brandenburg, the Central Committee of the Free German Youth published a *Guide to Carnival Celebrations* in which it was suggested that young people should dance in the mask of St. Peter. But an actor by the name of Peter Geisberg, who was a member of the Central Committee for Youth Dedications, parodied Christ. In a long white garment he appeared with beard, a red paper nose, and a crown of thorns; in one hand he held the Bible, in the other a bottle of whisky from which he drank from time to time. He was assisted by girls of the Free German Youth. On February 12, 1956, the *Maerkische Volksstimme* of Potsdam reported that during the carnival celebrations figures could be seen representing everybody from Lorelei to the Lord, who had come down from heaven in order to teach sinful people, but who could not get along without "booze."

The church protested against the blasphemy and asked people to do penance.

Atheist propaganda was constantly using the word "superstition" *(Aberglaube)* as an antonym for "faith" *(Glaube)*. Thus Paul Froehling, secretary of the Leipzig SED, declared in March 1956 that two hundred propagandists had given 1,400 lectures to teach people that their superstition could no longer coexist with faith in socialist progress.

The protests of the church against this vicious propaganda of the atheists did not influence in the least the Free German Youth and the Communist labor unions. They continued their violent attacks. Even the Communist fellow-traveler Professor Emil Fuchs, the father of Klaus Fuchs, began to criticize these tactless attempts to discredit religion.

The state, in the meantime, started to put the screws on the church. Members of the church administration of West Berlin were permitted only occasionally to enter the DDR. In June 1955 censorship of church papers was intensified. Since December 1, 1955, bulk mailings to pastors and congregations were forbidden. At the end of 1955 the state secretary for university education restricted the Evangelical Student Congregations and forbade them to use university quarters, including the use of the bulletin board for announcements. There was no improvement in the policy restricting public collections. Yet the sacrificial contributions on the part of individual Christians increased to such an extent that by 1955 they had surpassed the collections of 1953. On June 18, 1955, divine services, Bible studies, and the celebration of Holy Communion in old folks homes were forbidden, and pastors could visit the residents only upon request. Pastoral care in hospitals ceased to exist for all practical purposes.

As early as 1952-1953 numerous stations of the Protestant Railroad Missions had been closed. At the beginning of 1956 fourteen leading members of the organization were arrested in the larger cities of the DDR. They were accused of having abused the work of railroad missions for purposes of espionage on behalf of the allies stationed in West Berlin. By decree of the state the railroad missions were forbidden to have any connection with West Berlin and West Germany. The leader of the railroad mission at Potsdam, Eva Louise Schneider, was accused of having confessed that she favored the West and that she had broken the laws of the DDR.

The East Conference of the EKD protested against the allegation that the Railroad Missions had broken the laws of the DDR and committed espionage. Bishop Dibelius declared in a letter to Prime Minister Grotewohl: "The accusation that the Railroad Missions have carried on espionage must be rejected in the strongest possible terms."

A trial of the accused was never held. The accusations which had been leveled against the Railroad Missions were never proved. The arrested were released in February, March, and April. But the separation of the Railroad Mission of East Berlin and the DDR from the missions in West Berlin and the Federal Republic remained in effect. Of the 122 stations in the DDR only eleven were permitted to continue on a limited basis.

On February 15, 1956, the East Berlin city government issued orders which made it very difficult to continue religious instruction.

In order to protect the health of children and to guard them against exploitation the time allotted for religious instruction was restricted as follows: "All extracurricular activities of the pupils can take place only after the close of the regular school hours. Between the close of school and the beginning of extracurricular activities there must be sufficient time for the children to recuperate physically and mentally. There must be an interval of at least two hours between the end of regular instruction and the beginning of extracurricular activities."

Also the selection of catechists who were permitted to instruct these children was subjected to the control of the state. The same decree regulating religious instruction also stated: "If there is any religious instruction at all, it must be concluded at the end of the eighth year of school." This eliminated all religious instruction in high school. The leadership of both the Protestant and the Catholic churches protested against this decree, but their protests were not heeded. The children were forced to participate in many activities of which the church did not approve. The admission of children of Christian parents to high school was made increasingly difficult by regulations which made the registration of children in middle and high schools dependent upon their active participation in the work of the Young Pioneers.

On April 5, 1956, in spite of the violent protests of the church, the ruins of the Ulrich Church in Magdeburg were dynamited. The beginnings of this church went back to 1023. From its pulpit Nicholas von Amsdorf, Luther's good friend, had preached in 1523. The church had been damaged heavily by air attacks on January 16, 1945, but its steeples had been preserved and the bells had been restored. The reconstruction of the church had been planned for the near future. But the Magdeburg city council insisted on dynamiting it in order to make room for the building of modern business houses and dwellings. In the first "socialist street" of Magdeburg no Christian church should be allowed, the council said.

A few months later there were also attempts to dynamite the ruins of St. James Church in Rostock. Professor Holtz, an outstanding architectural expert, declared that the church had great cultural value and stated publicly that it was an indication of the cultural level of a nation if it preserved old monuments and protected them. But he was speaking into the wind. The majority of the public voted for the elimination of the church.

On the credit side, however, there were a number of restorations of important churches.

The Synod of the EKD, which met in June, 1956, received a comprehensive report about the conditions of the church in the DDR. It contained the account of a great number of limitations imposed by the state and concluded: "The impression that there is a planned impediment to the church becomes more and more clear. . . . Many people are suffering from conflicts of conscience. Fear and distrust have been sown, and large numbers of our Christian population have lost their faith in the government."

In 1956 the state subsidies to the church had been decreased by about forty per cent. Also the income from church taxes had decreased. By a decree of the Minister of Justice, Dr. Hilde Benjamin, on February 10, 1956, the churches were practically denied the right to tax.

At the meeting of the Synod of the Silesian Church, Bishop Hornig indicated that the finances of the church had become very critical. The Church of Mecklenburg had about one-tenth as much money at her disposal as a church of comparable size in West Germany had. Thus the eight regional churches in the DDR were able to count on only 46,000,000 East marks in annual income. This covered less than half of the most urgent needs. Therefore the church was forced to reduce her work radically and to give up her traditional function as a "People's Church" (Volkskirche). This meant the closing of a number of parishes, the reduction of religious instruction and a strong cut in the charitable work of the church which at that time included 98 hospitals, 38 homes for the mentally and physically handicapped, 28 homes for mothers, 28 convalescent homes, 122 homes for educational projects, the maintenance of 1,317 deaconesses, and numerous other activities. But the active help of the West German member churches of the EKD kept the church in the East from suffering a financial catastrophe at that time.

Some unpleasant incidents took place during the seventh German

Kirchentag, meeting at Frankfurt-Main from August 8 to 12, 1956. Twenty-five thousand Christians from the DDR had been permitted to attend. Among the guests were also several members of the People's Chamber, some state secretaries, and some mayors of East German cities. Deputy Prime Minister Otto Nuschke and the President of the People's Chamber, Dr. Dieckmann, were also present. The leadership of the *Kirchentag* was not able to remove from the meetings the odium of the Cold War. Members of the East German government were separated from members of the West German government, and there were some heated discussions. Dieckmann complained that the Bonn politicians had staged the separation. Finally, however, in a conciliatory gesture during the last session of the *Kirchentag,* Nuschke was asked to sit together with the Bonn ministers and was officially recognized with the ministers of the West German government.

E. ATTACKS AGAINST THE NATO-CHURCH

1. The Army Chaplaincy Agreement and Its Consequences, 1957

At the Synod of the Evangelical Church in Germany (EKD), which had been scheduled to meet in Halle in the DDR from March 3 to 8, 1957, the chaplaincy agreement between the Federal Republic and the leadership of the EKD was to be discussed. This agreement had been concluded on January 18. A few days before the scheduled beginning of the meeting, the news agency of the DDR announced that the territory of the DDR would not be available for supporters of the NATO policy of the West German government. Nuschke prohibited the meeting of the synod in the DDR.

On February 8 Bishop Dibelius wrote to the DDR Minister of Defense, Willie Stoph, that the question of the role of the church in the National People's Army of the DDR should also be discussed. Stoph replied curtly: "The activity of the church in the National People's Army is not an object for discussion. According to my opinion there is no necessity to talk about the role of the church in the National People's Army." He added that the army was composed entirely of volunteers and had been created for the protection of the DDR against the West, while the West German army was based on general conscription and was serving the aggressive intentions of North Atlantic Treaty Organization of the Western Powers. He concluded: "At this opportunity I would like to tell you that as far as I know not a single soldier of the National People's Army has shown any desire for pastoral care of chaplains."

On March 8 the Synod accepted the chaplaincy agreement with the Federal Republic with a majority of 91 to 19 votes and five abstentions. The reaction of the government of the DDR was extremely violent. It felt that as far as the church was concerned the EKD might well consider itself the unifying force between the two Germanies, but that as far as the government of the DDR was concerned, the DDR was definitely a separate state. In the eyes of the DDR the Federal Republic was a foreign country. Now, after the Synod of the EKD had accepted a chaplaincy agreement with a foreign, and hostile, country, the government of the DDR worked with great determination toward a division of the EKD.

The members of the synod who had voted for the chaplaincy agreement were defamed by East German propaganda. The President of the Church of Magdeburg, Kreyssig, who as the only representative of the forty-four member delegation from the DDR had participated actively in the discussions at the synod, was now called an "atomic-war ideologist." An all-out attack was directed especially against Bishop Dibelius. The old stories about his sermon preached in the presence of Hitler and Hindenburg on March 21, 1933, were revived. In a brochure entitled *The Black Lion and the Military Church* the DDR Committee for Ideological Enlightenment stated about Dibelius and his life's work: "In the name of Christianity this monarchist (Dibelius) drove the Germans to the battlefields of the imperialists (in the First World War). He advised the Germans to accept the death of the Krupps as a blessed death. . . . It is not surprising that this same Dibelius who later became Superintendent General of Brandenburg greeted the Thousand Year Reich of Hitler with enthusiasm." The fact that at the end of April Dibelius and all the bishops of the DDR signed a declaration against the use of atomic weapons, which had been prepared by the deans of the various theological faculties, did not help at all. Pictures were published which showed Dibelius walking side by side with Kaiser

Wilhelm II and Adolf Hitler, holding a bloody ax, and of Federal
Chancellor Adenauer holding an atomic bomb. A large poster in
Berlin's Stalinallee showed Dibelius with the superscription: "From
Heaven Above to Earth I Come." On the left side of the poster
was the bishop in the form of an atomic bomb, with his wings spread
wide and flying toward heaven, while on the right side the same
bishop came down from heaven with folded hands to blow the world
to bits.

From that time on Bishop Dibelius received permission to enter
only the East sector of Berlin. He could no longer enter the territory of the DDR proper. The speeches which he had promised to
deliver at Dresden and other places had to be canceled. The Synod
of Berlin-Brandenburg rejected all these untrue allegations against
its Bishop and declared: "We shall not be separated from our Bishop
whom we have called to be the leading pastor of our church." Also
the Saxon Synod declared that it was standing by the side of Bishop
Dibelius and that it supported the EKD. The East Conference of
the EKD expressed the hope that Dibelius would not be hindered
in doing his work in Berlin-Brandenburg and in the other member churches of the EKD. But in spite of all these declarations
the Bishop was never again permitted to enter the DDR. On April
1, 1957, the Office for Religious Affairs, which had been directed
by Otto Nuschke, and the Office for Church Affairs of the Ministry of the Interior were combined into the Office of the State
Secretary for Questions of the Church and was entrusted to the
old-line Communist Werner Eggerath. He invited all the bishops
of the DDR, but omitted Dibelius and Dean Grueber, the official
liaison man between the church and the government of the DDR.
Under these circumstances the bishops refused to accept the invitation and suggested to Eggerath to discuss matters with their
appointed representatives. But Eggerath did not agree, and the
meeting never took place. When Dean Grueber tried to call on him
personally, he was informed that members of the NATO-Church
could no longer be received by the DDR government.

At the Eighth Evangelical *Kirchentag*, which was scheduled to
meet in several cities in Thuringia in 1957, the renewal of the Cold
War came into the open. Minister of the Interior Karl Marohn

declared in a letter which he wrote in the middle of April to Dr. von Thadden-Trieglaff, the president of the Kirchentag, that the signing of the chaplaincy agreement and other occurrences had made it necessary to require "certain guarantees for church meetings to be held in the territory of our republic." The *Kirchentag* leaders were asked to promise (1) not to support the NATO policy; (2) to permit no one who is in favor of the NATO policy to speak at the *Kirchentag*; (3) to disavow in a public declaration the occurrences that took place during the 1956 *Kirchentag* in Frankfurt; (4) to guarantee that representatives of the government of the DDR would be permitted to explain in the meetings the peace policy of the DDR. On April 14 Dr. von Thadden-Trieglaff regretfully rejected these conditions as unacceptable because some of them would contribute to the abuse of the *Kirchentag* for political purposes. He stated: "The microphone of the *Kirchentag* belongs to the congregations of the Lord. The message of the church cannot be silenced."

2. Fire From All Directions, 1957-1958

When Bishop Dibelius predicted that the church was heading for stormy weather, he was right. In the fall of 1957 the ideological offensive of the SED against the church was intensified. The beginning of this campaign was a speech by Walter Ulbricht, delivered at the opening of the instruction courses for Youth Dedications at Sonneberg on September 25, 1957, in which he indicated that he wanted to enforce the acceptance of Youth Dedications, because without them the young people would not be able to know the things which they needed to know later.

On October 4, the leadership of the United Evangelical Lutheran Church of Germany (VELKD) took note of this speech "with grave anxiety" and declared: "In September 1956 Prime Minister Grotewohl declared to the Evangelical Bishops of the DDR that Youth Dedications were to be completely voluntary. . . . In contrast to this promise the recent speech by Ulbricht indicates that all children, including Christian children, will be forced to participate in these anti-Christian ceremonies." The bishops protested in a letter to Grotewohl and, on October 20, had a declaration read from the pulpits of the DDR. They stated once more: "The child participates either in Youth Dedications or in confirmation . . . . To combine the two is an impossibility." They also stated that Ulbricht, in his speech at Sonneberg, had made it quite clear what he considered the function of Youth Dedications.

The letter of the bishops to Grotewohl and the announcements from the pulpits called forth a massive counterattack by the Minister of the Interior, Marohn. He accused the bishops of having slandered the state and having completely misrepresented the conditions in the DDR. He called them allies of the fascists in the Federal Republic who were preparing a war of revenge. In addition, the vow for the Youth Dedications was now changed again. Instead of the text, which the government felt was too general, the young people were asked to make a more precise promise. The three questions asked of them at the ceremony now were: "Are you ready as loyal sons and daughters of our workers' and peasants' republic to work for the happy future of the whole German nation and to fight for it? Are you ready to place yourselves with your whole strength at the disposal of the great and noble cause of socialism? Are you ready to work for friendship among the nations and, along with the Soviet people and all other peace-loving nations of the world, to fight for peace and to defend it?" To all three questions the young people had to answer: "Yes, we promise," and were accepted with the following words: "We have heard your promise and accept it. You have placed before yourselves a noble and high goal. You have become partners of millions of people who fight for peace and socialism. We accept you into the community of all working people of the DDR, and we promise you support, protection, and help."

The Secretary for Culture and Education of the Central Committee of the SED, Paul Wandel, had recommended that some concessions be made to the church. He was removed from office because he had not been tough enough.

In the Youth Dedications of 1955 only fifteen percent of all young people, including those who were unchurched, had taken part. In 1956 the number increased to about 25%, in 1957 to 34%, and in 1958 to 47%. The main task of winning parents and children for Youth Dedications was assigned to the teachers. The government decreed: "The support of Youth Dedications is the task of all schools and all institutions of training." In consequence, many teachers suffered conflicts of conscience. The Minister of Education, Fritz Lange, had said in November 1957 that it was the task of the school to develop a socialistic conscience. In March 1958 Lange declared that no one could serve two masters. All teachers were forced to support Youth Dedications actively.

In June 1958 the famous Protestant *Gymnasium*, the Gray Cloisters of East Berlin, which had been founded in 1574 and where Leibnitz, Bismarck, Schleiermacher, and many other famous men had studied, was converted into a Communist school. It was renamed Socialist High School Number Two. Its teachers were given the motto: "He who wants to educate for socialism must himself be a socialist." In all schools teachers who were members of the SED and at the same time also of the church were asked whether they still desired to belong to the church. In Frankfurt-Oder of eighty such teachers a total of thirty-five declared that they wanted to remain church members. They were asked immediately to declare their resignation from the church because to remain in the church was irreconcilable with the position of a socialist teacher. This procedure was repeated in other districts of the DDR. Also teachers who were not members of the SED were subjected to the same pressure. The result of this campaign was the declaration by 5,779 Christian Democratic teachers and educators in the DDR in which they disavowed the NATO-Church. Their statement was published in *Neue Zeit* of April 26, 1958. Teachers who continued to show Christian convictions were treated roughly. The *Lausitzer Rundschau* of April 2, 1958, declared that a teacher named Wunsch in Weisswasser had not given his pupils mottoes based on patriotic sentiments and the love of fatherland, but had written in their autograph books such things as: "Without love and without God the human being is subhuman." The paper declared that whoever followed such an ideology had no place in institutions of socialist learning. It demanded the dismissal of Teacher Wunsch. A woman teacher was dismissed without recourse because she had written a Bible verse in an autograph book. She was accused of having confused the issue of the separation of church and state. A teacher by the name of Mietzner, who had been teaching in the eighth grade at the Pankow school, had refused to congratulate his pupils after they had participated in Youth Dedications. When asked to explain his strange silence he declared that he could not reconcile Youth Dedications with his conscience and with his Christian faith. The school board demanded that he should be fired. A great number of other teachers were attacked in newspapers of the DDR and many of them were dismissed.

Also at the universities and other institutions of higher learning great pressures were applied to transform them into citadels of socialism and atheism. When Ulbricht addressed the faculty of the University of Halle on April 21, 1958, Professor Mothes made a long speech in which he denied that socialism was identical with atheism. At the end of his long speech he said: "You may crucify me for what I have just said, but you should be thankful that you still have professors at your universities who have the courage and the strength of character to say the things they ought to say." Ulbricht assured the professor that he knew how to distinguish between scholars who disagreed with his views but were honest and decent, and the enemies of the state who were trying to sabotage the work of the DDR. As a result of these pressures 2,171 teachers and 122 university professors fled to the West during the first eight months of 1958.

Ideological incompatibility was also accepted as a reason for granting a divorce. A Decree Concerning Marriage and Divorce of December 4, 1955, protected Communist functionaries and other SED members whose wives were still "reactionary" in their beliefs. As early as 1951 a district court in Stralsund had declared null and void the marriage between a Communist economist and his wife who had been a former deaconess. She had permitted her children to be baptized, had taught them to pray, and had sent them to an Evangelical Kindergarten and to Sunday school. The court declared: "In a healthy marriage the interests of the marriage partners must agree with the interests of society."

On March 5, 1958, the politburo of the SED passed a resolution concerning the task of propaganda for the socialist education of the masses. It formulated a great number of themes to be discussed and made available fifteen million marks for ideological enlightenment. The official party publishing house, Dietz in East Berlin, offered atheistic books at tremendous savings. A book concerning religion, which contained 360 pages of views on religion by Marx and Engels, and commentaries concerning these views, bound in leather, sold for $1.25. A book of 900 pages entitled *Scientific Ideology* sold for $2.00. Small brochures were sold for less than ten cents, including such titles as "Is There a Life After Death?" "Sputnik and the Almighty," "The Cross and the Federal Eagle," etc. Other publishing houses too issued a number of inexpensive anti-Christian books.

The radio was also pressed into the service of propaganda. In 1958 the radio network of the DDR promised that every Sunday at 9 a.m. there would be an atheistic broadcast which would deal with religious idealism and superstition. On December 25, 1957, the TV stations in the DDR for the first time televised a solemn Name Giving Dedication held for three children in Altenburg. This ceremony was complete with the *Largo* by Handel and a homily by the registry official. It was held in a beautifully decorated room. The presentation of a savings account, congratulations by the mayor of the city, and the presentation of a certificate by the SED district committee and of flower pots by the Young Pioneers concluded the ceremony. On February 23, 1958, the City Council of Suhl arranged for a mass Name Giving Dedication for the whole district. These dedications were complete with the ritual requirement of sponsors and "dedication vows."

The government of the DDR even tried to establish a counter-church year with a number of socialist celebrations. It established the Day of the Great October Revolution; the Day of the Founding of the DDR; the Birthdays of Marx, Engels, and Lenin; the International Women's Day (March 8); the First of May; the International Children's Day (June 1); and others.

The magazine *Freiheit* commented that the Ten Commandments did not come from God, but had been invented by slave owners. At the fifth Party Convention of the SED Ulbricht issued his own

Ten Commandments of Socialist Ethics. They read: (1) Thou shalt work for international solidarity of the working classes and of all workers, and for the union of all socialist countries. (2) Thou shalt love thy Fatherland and shalt be ready to use thy whole strength and ability for the defense of the working masses. (3) Thou shalt help eliminate the exploitation of man by man. (4) Thou shalt accomplish good deeds for socialism, for socialism leads to a better life for the working man. (5) Thou shalt act in a spirit of mutual helpfulness and comradely cooperation in building socialism and shalt respect the collective structure and thwart its criticism. (6) Thou shalt protect the property of the people and increase it. (7) Thou shalt always strive to improve thyself and shalt save and establish discipline among socialists. (8) Thou shalt educate thy children in the spirit of peace and socialism to become well-rounded, firm, and strong people. (9) Thou shalt live cleanly and decently and honor thy family. (10) Thou shalt declare thy solidarity with the nations who are fighting for national liberation and for the defense of their national independence.

The director of the German Theater in East Berlin, Wolfgang Langhoff, declared about these commandments: "Moses tried to instill a new ethical attitude in his people, but the difference is that Moses claimed to have received his commandments from God himself while our Comrade Ulbricht received his laws from his experience in the class struggle to which he had dedicated his life."

This renewed anti-religious agitation led to a great increase of resignations from the church. The number of people who had left the church since 1946 passed the one million mark. Of course, there were also some people who rejoined the church, but their numbers were not enough to offset the losses. Did the SED succeed in winning the great masses of those nominal church members for their dialectic materialistic ideology? Figures indicate that it was able to lead at least part of these people away from the church. Whether they did, however, become true confessors of dialectic materialism cannot be shown in statistics. On the other hand, it is surprising that only a small part of the nominal church members have been moved by this intensive propaganda to leave the church.

More alarming was the decrease in baptisms, confirmations, and marriages. In one congregation in a large city, in which until 1945 about one hundred children were baptized annually the number had decreased to 61 in 1956 and to a mere 16 in 1960. Later, however, it increased again to 37 in 1961 and to 40 in 1962.

In contrast to the attacks of 1952 and 1953, the actions against the church in the late 1950's showed very few direct interferences. The organization of the church as such was hardly disturbed. There were, however, some dramatic exceptions. In the fall of 1957 three trials were held of leaders of the church: particularly the trial of the Leipzig student pastor, Dr. Siegfried Schmutzler, was conducted as a show trial. He was accused of having influenced young people against socialism by defending the thesis that religion is not opium, but a vitamin. The trials began on November 18, 1957, in the district court of Leipzig. Dr. Schmutzler was not able to stand up against the aggressive attitude of the judge. In his final word he said: "I have recognized the weight of the charges against me." He was condemned to five years in the penitentiary for boycotting the state. On December 7 and 8, two students of theology, Andreas Jentsch and Wolfgang Wohlleben, were condemned to one and a half and two and a half years in the penitentiary. The church of Saxony protested against this show trial. Schmutzler was kept in the penitentiary of Torgau until February 1961 when he was released by the government.

A second trial was concerned with money exchange. On October 25 the East German news services announced that large sums had been discovered in the offices of Dr. Gruenbaum and Dr. Klewitz of Magdeburg, members of the Magdeburg consistory. Both were arrested. The press accompanied this announcement with wild charges that NATO was involved in these transactions which were directed against the workers and the peasants of the DDR. The paper *Neues Deutschland* wrote that Bishop Dibelius had received 250 million German marks from American sources, to be used to support refugees from the DDR and war criminals. The result was that a number of high-ranking German church leaders were forced to flee to the West.

The trial took place from February 22 to 24, 1958, at Magdeburg.

President Scharf was present as representative of the church, and the state prosecutor asked that he too should be tried. But the request was denied. The verdict itself was very mild compared to that in similar cases in the past. The prosecutor asked that Dr. Gruenbaum be condemned to two and a half years in prison and ten thousand marks in fines and Dr. Klewitz to a one-year imprisonment, and that their pre-trial imprisonment should be applied to their prison terms. Both defendants were released on parole.

The third trial was the trial of the 59-year-old Dean Otto Maerker of Pampow, Mecklenburg. He had been arrested on October 29, 1959, because he had refused to bury a 19-year-old girl who had participated in Youth Dedications. He had even tried to interfere when permission was asked to bury the girl in the Pankow cemetery. Without a doubt, the Dean had gone too far and was reprimanded by Bishop Beste and the Mecklenburg Consistory for his lack of charity. On September 19 Maerker was condemned by the Schwerin district court to two and a half years in the penitentiary.

Strong personal attacks were directed against a number of individual pastors in the various regional churches. Letters to editors by so-called "enraged readers" were published in almost all East German newspapers in ever-increasing numbers. These letters all gave the impression that they had been pre-written in the SED Party headquarters. On December 3, at the meeting of the Synod of the Evangelical Church of the Union (the former Old Prussian Union), President Dr. Scharf declared: "We are at a loss to see how some of our brethren are attacked by the East German press on account of their actions and decisions. . . . Our practice in regard to confirmation is very old and very uniform. Only the reaction of our adversaries is surprisingly recent and also surprisingly uniform."

During the three months after October 1957 a great number of catechists had been attacked by the press. A number of arrests took place. The number of arrested and condemned pastors and lay people, which in 1957 had declined to 7, increased again until in May 1958 there were 24, among them 11 pastors, 6 students and 7 catechists and others. At the end of 1957 the church decreed that pastors could not leave their East German congregations unless they were expelled. This decree became the subject of much public discussion. Pastors had generally remained with their congregations, and only a few had fled to the West. By the end of 1957 not more than 100 of the 6,000 pastors in the DDR had left their congregations with or without the permission of their church governments and had gone to West Berlin.

Now at the end of 1957 two pastors, Hans Gerber and Erich Frommel, had fled to West Berlin. Gerber had been denounced to the Communists because in his Reformation Day sermon he had spoken against Youth Dedications. The Communists had called a meeting where Gerber was forced to give an account of himself. Frommel had accompanied him to that meeting. Gerber had defended himself manfully, and his congregation had supported him. Now the attacks were intensified. Pamphlets, articles in the press, resolutions by factories, and caricatures appeared everywhere, and a new meeting was called. On December 16 the district court of Bernau had scheduled a trial of the two pastors. But before it could take place they had fled to the West. Since they had left their parishes without the permission of their church government, the consistory of Berlin-Brandenburg started disciplinary action against them. On March 26, 1958, they were absolved of the charge of cowardice. But on March 3, 1959, the Evangelical Church of the Union issued a decree concerning the leaving of parishes in which it declared that if a pastor leaves his congregation without permission and does not return within a certain time, any claim of the pastor for support and salary will be invalid as long as he refuses to take his residence within the boundaries of his former parish.

The Catholic Church too was attacked by atheist propaganda. In a pastoral letter of April 15, 1958, the bishops complained that the conditions had become very difficult. They told their people: "You must permit many things to happen and remain silent. But watch out that you observe the boundaries of your conscience. If you are asked to send your children to Youth Dedications, say 'No' emphatically. If you are asked to resign from the church, say emphatically and clearly: 'No!'" In the spring of 1958, Bishop Dr. Julius Doepfner of Berlin was refused permission to enter the DDR.

There were also renewed difficulties concerning the construction of new churches. The Catholic church had obtained property for a new church at Kayna near Meuselwitz, but the Council of the District of Zeitz, to which Meuselwitz belonged, forbade the members of the congregation to enter the church and sealed it. When the congregation held services in front of the church, they were forbidden to enter the property. The village of Kayna took over the church and made it into a social hall. The same kind of harassment happened at Naumburg, where the city council had given permission to the Catholics to build a new church; but in the midst of the building program construction was stopped. However, sharp protests by the Catholic episcopate caused a return of the church at Kayna for church use and the permission to continue with the building of the Naumburg church. There were also arrests of Catholic priests, who were accused of antagonism against the Soviet Union, Youth Dedications, the Young Pioneers, and of being warmongers. Hundreds of books were confiscated, among them *The Cardinal* by Robinson, *Dogmatic Literature* and several volumes of the Bible commentary, *The Old Testament in German,* and other important books from Catholic and Protestant publishers.

On August 15 and 16, 1958, the German *Katholikentag* was able to meet in both sectors of Berlin. Visitors from the DDR were allowed to attend these meetings. At the beginning there had been between fifty and sixty thousand guests from the DDR, but later the *Petrus Blatt* of the Diocese of Berlin complained about the treatment that they had received when they returned home to their communities. They were sharply questioned on the trains and were searched two times by the People's Police. Young people were treated especially harshly. Their New Testaments, hymnbooks, missals, breviaries and printed matter were taken away from them. The People's Police threw the prayer books out of the windows of the trains.

In December 1958, two new trials were held. The first one was for eleven Catholic men from Rathenow who had been arrested in July. They were accused of having spied for the so-called "Catholic Emergency Help for Men in the Zone" which was called a veiled espionage net of the West. This so-called Emergency Help, which in reality did not exist but had been invented by the court, was al-

leged to have trained people for action against the DDR. All eleven
men were condemned to long prison terms.

On July 26 four Jesuits, Robert Frater, Wilhelm Rueter, Joseph
Menzel, and Joseph Mueldner, were arrested. The district court
of Frankfurt-Oder accused Frater of having worked for the Federal
Republic's counter-intelligence. The other three were accused of
having helped people flee from the DDR and having imported
chauvinistic literature from the Federal Republic. Frater was condemned to four years in prison and four months in the penitentiary.
The others received prison terms from one year three months to
four years three months. No members of the Jesuit Order or representatives of the bishop were allowed to attend the trial.

F. COLD PEACE

1. Loyalty Declaration by the Church? (1958)

Since 1945 the church had taken a stand on many questions, not
only questions that concerned the church directly, but also questions of a political nature, such as soil reform, the so-called "People's
Elections," the perversion of justice and the ideological self-interpretation of the state, and similar issues. She had not been eager
to take these positions, but they had been forced upon her.

The government of the DDR had reacted violently against these
criticisms by the church. It had accused the church of political mo-
tivation. The result was that in the eyes of the public the church
gradually became a religiously motivated political opposition to
the Communist state. She did not desire to be seen in this light,
and attempts were being made to come to a better understanding
with the DDR.

Added to this there was the problem that the division of Germany into two parts in 1945 had been considered a provisional parti-
tion. The church was now confronted with the question of declaring
her loyalty to a state which she did not consider permanent.

On February 10, 1956, the Minister of the Interior, Marohn, and
several representatives of the church had met, among them Bishop
Mitzenheim of Thuringia, Bishop Krummacher of Pomerania, and
President Scharf of Berlin-Brandenburg. The discussion turned soon

into a one-sided harangue by Marohn. He centered his accusation on the fact that the church in the DDR was open to Western influences and was opposed to the DDR. He pointed out to his visitors that he had made the following declaration at the installation of Bishop Jaenicke in Magdeburg: "I would like to assure you at this point that the government of the DDR is very much interested in guaranteeing the right to full freedom of faith and conscience which it had promised in the Constitution of our Republic. . . . But the government of the DDR expects that the church should respect the authority of our state."

In an interview which Bishop Dibelius gave some time later to the Evangelical Press Service he stated that the church in the DDR respects "the reality of the state in which she works." Bishop Dr. Beste declared in an article in the Mecklenburg *Kirchenzeitung*, April 8, 1956, that the church was not unaware that in the DDR there had been progress in many areas of economic and scientific life. But he also stated: "On the other hand, the church is opposed to those phenomena in the life of the people which are based on theoretical and practical materialism and are worshiping it."

At the convention of the SED, Grotewohl declared that the church had the right to take a position, but this confession should not be misunderstood to mean that the church could now engage in activities against the state. He summarized his views as follows: "We are ready to live with the church. The church shall have the things that are of the church and the state the things that are of the state."

Bishop Dr. Mitzenheim of Thuringia reacted to the definition of Grotewohl in the *Thueringer Tageblatt* of May 4, 1956. He stated: "We of the church are ready to render to the state the things that belong to it. We think that we are supporting it by advising our people against flight from the DDR and by telling them to stay where they have been called. But we are asking for the freedom that has been promised to us in the Constitution, so that the church can permit the power of the Gospel to become effective in the lives of our people by giving a clear testimony of her faith."

At a special meeting of the Synod of EKD which met in Berlin from June 27 to 29, 1956, Superintendent General Dr. Guenter Jacob spoke as follows: "We can only tell the state what kind of freedom we expect in the service of the Gospel, because we are bound to the Gospel in obedience to our Lord. A state that limits such freedom and forces the church into a narrowly confined space does not cease to be higher authorities in the sense of Romans 13."

Nuschke, however, was not satisfied with these statements. He felt that the statement that the church could work under various systems of government was not exactly a declaration of loyalty to the DDR. On the other hand, Dean Grueber pointed out that the confession of the synodal meeting to Romans 13 went far beyond any loyalty declaration that could be required. In a letter to Grueber Nuschke wrote that he agreed that the church could not give her official sanction to any one order or society. But he stated: "A declaration of loyalty to our state should be nothing but a declaration that we want to follow Romans 13 in our relation to the state. This the synod has done. But, secondly, we should affirm that we are opposed to the Western propaganda which looks upon the church as the only center of resistance against the reorganization of society in the DDR. This the church has not done."

On September 1, during the 77th *Katholikentag* in Cologne, Dr. Otto Spuelbeck, Bishop of Meissen, described the Catholic concept of church-state relationship in the form of a conversation which he had often carried on on the highest level in the DDR: "The conversation always begins with the stereotyped form: 'Mr. Minister, you are a Marxist. I am a Catholic. Therefore we have nothing in common in our ideologies. There are no bridges between you and me. We are completely separated people. But we are both living in a house, the foundation of which was not laid by us and the foundation of which we think is somewhat shaky. If we live in this house at the present, our conversation can only concern the question of who is going to clean the stairway. . . . We shall gladly do our part to make this house more inhabitable and we shall live in it as Christians. But we shall not build another story on top of it since we are convinced that the foundation is not very solid."

On December 14, 1956, discussions between Grotewohl and Nuschke, on the one side, and all Protestant bishops, including Dr. Dibelius, on the other, took place. But no agreement was reached concerning the loyalty declaration of the church to the state of the workers and peasants. Grotewohl understood loyalty to include both the proclamation of the church and the claim to totality of the SED. State Secretary Eggerath undertook an attempt in this direction when, in April, 1957, he asked Bishop Mitzenheim to support the demand for outlawing atomic weapons in Germany. He asked him to recommend to his fellow-bishops and to pastors to mention in their Easter sermons the responsibility to the people and to the nation and to demand that atomic weapons should be banned from Germany. But nothing was done about this demand.

After the agreement concerning the military chaplaincy had been reached with the Federal Republic, the discussions became acrid. The church was accused of open support of the Bonn regime. At the same time, however, within the districts and smaller administrative units of the church the state tried to enter into a dialogue with the church. Pastors were invited by district officers to hear what the thinking and the wishes of the state were.

The church on her part was trying to rid herself of some of her old prejudices and to find new ways to exist in a Communist environment. The former student pastor of Halle and now a professor at the church's seminary in Naumburg, Dr. Johannes Hamel, made important contributions in this direction. In his book *The Christian in the DDR* (Berlin, 1957) he stated that the church had been less concerned about the spreading of the good news than about the problems confronting Confirmation and Youth Dedications. She had been too much concerned about her prerogatives and the preservation of church customs. He wrote: "Is the Christian attitude different from that of the people who have the power in this aeon?" Hamel interpreted the Pauline injunction: "Be subject to the higher powers" as telling Christians that they should establish a personal relationship, and not a battlefront.

The Synod of the EKD met in Berlin from April 26 to 30, 1958. Its chief topic was "The Church in Education." The meeting was under heavy pressure. Dr. Ulrich Kramer, the director of the Institute for State Law and Administrative Law at the University of Leipzig, had prepared an opinion which condemned the chaplaincy agreement with the Federal Republic. He stated that this agreement had turned the church into a militaristic church which supported

NATO and its policy and thus had made her an enemy of the socialistic state. Therefore, he stated, the authorities of the DDR should no longer recognize the leadership of EKD as legitimate and should demand that the member churches of EKD in the DDR should leave the parent organization. He furthermore asked that the member churches of EKD in the DDR rescind their previous consent to the chaplaincy agreement. The government, on its part, threatened to take action if the church would not pass the desired resolutions.

On April 30, however, Dean Grueber supported Bishop Dibelius, who was under heavy fire, and declared to the synod: "Bishop Dibelius did not stay in a foreign country in 1934 as he could easily have done. But he came back to Germany and gave a clear testimony. He was in the same prison with Ernst Thaelmann, the Communist leader, and visited him there. This should be mentioned and also that Bishop Dibelius did not deliver radio speeches from a safe port for or against Hitler as many others did." These courageous words, which indirectly attacked Ulbricht and comrades who had gone to Moscow during Hitler's Reich, brought upon the dean the wrath of the politicians of the DDR.

Concerning the chaplaincy agreement itself, the synod had finally come to the conclusion that the individual member churches in the West should regulate this matter and stated: "The chaplaincy agreement has no validity for the member churches in the DDR." Also concerning confirmation it was decided that all member churches should regulate the requirements for this rite anew. Three members of the synod, who were residents of the DDR, were asked to seek an interview with Grotewohl in order to convey to him the anxiety which Christians feel for the education of their children.

The reaction in the political circles of the DDR remained negative. When the Lutheran Synod was called to meet at Eisenach from May 31 to June 5, the Council of the District of Erfurt, in which Eisenach is located, rejected the proposed list of participants. It stated that it included persons who were representatives of NATO policy. Bishop Hanns Lilje of Hanover asked Eggerath for an interview. Eggerath answered that he was not in a position to receive the bishop. The synod was forced to meet in Spandau in West

Berlin. Individual synods of the DDR member churches which met a week after the general meeting of the church were put under pressure to support the forces of peace.

In the meantime, on June 2, after the anti-church propaganda had subsided somewhat, the requested interview of the three members of EKD, Superintendent General Fuehr of East Berlin, Dean Johannes Hoffmann of Nordhausen, and plumber Gerhard Burckhardt, accompanied by two members of the Council of EKD, Bishop Dr. Mitzenheim of Thuringia and Bishop Dr. Krummacher of Pomerania, took place. Grotewohl did not permit Dean Grueber to participate. He said he wanted to speak only to citizens of the DDR. On July 21 a communiqué was published by the press office of the Prime Minister in which he stated that on June 2 and 23, and on July 21 there had been consultations at the request of the church in order to remove certain obstacles disturbing the relationship between state and church. The communiqué furthermore declared that the chaplaincy agreement which had been signed between the EKD and the Federal Republic in 1957 and its political and legal aspects were an important part of the discussions. It stated: "After a lengthy discussion of this problem, the representatives of the churches declared that the churches in the DDR are not bound to the chaplaincy agreement and that it has no validity for the churches in the DDR and her clergymen. The representatives of the Evangelical Church in the DDR declared that the church was serving the cause of peace with all the means at her disposal and therefore was in agreement in principle with the desire for peace in the DDR and with its government." The government, on the other hand, promised again that "each citizen would enjoy complete freedom of faith and conscience. The unhampered exercise of religion is protected by the republic." Both parties declared their willingness to remove through clarifying discussions any abuses in the relationship between state and church.

Thus the discussions concerning the loyalty declaration of the church had found their temporary conclusion. The church had not been forced to pledge her loyalty. The result was a compromise. The state promised certain things and the church also promised some things in return. In the meantime the "Progressive Pastors" had attempted to reorganize themselves on a new and broader basis. In February 1958 the National Council of the National Front had invited 150 theologians and lay people to discuss the topic: "The Responsibility of the Christian at the Threshold of the Atomic Age." This meeting took place in the *Lutherhaus* in Wittenberg. The conference issued an "Appeal from Wittenberg" in which it demanded the establishment of an atom-free zone in Central Europe and the the confederation of the two Germanies. One of the leaders at the Wittenberg meeting, Dr. Wolfgang Caffier of Weichsdorff near Dresden, on June 5 directed a letter signed by 11 pastors to all other pastors in the DDR calling on them to participate in the founding of a "League of Evangelical Pastors in the DDR."

The formal founding of the League took place in Leipzig on July 1. The preamble of the constitution of the League stated the political goals of the new organization: "The League will work for a peaceful democratic reunion of our people. It supports the efforts of the government of the DDR which serves these goals. It feels obligated to cooperate in a special way in the renewal of our society as it takes place in the DDR." But in spite of intense propaganda the League at first had only 70 to 80 members. When it convened its first Evangelical Pastors' Conference in May 1959 at Erfurt, it announced that its membership had doubled. But the great majority of pastors stayed away from it.

2. Coexistence with Aloofness, 1958-1961

Although the communiqué of July 1958 was not quite satisfactory to either church or state, it provided at least a basis for coexistence. It was not a friendly coexistence. A state that embraces an ideology that works for the destruction of the church can at best grant an armistice, but cannot be at peace with her.

The SED had reasons why it did not insist on an open battle. There were the concerns of foreign policy. The SED realized that a large percentage of the population rejected the ideology of the state. The government was embattled, it had to fight against all kinds of difficulties and had to stem the flight of refugees. Between 1955 and 1958 about one million people, of whom roughly one-half were under 25 years of age, had left the DDR. Another reason was that the world was full of political tensions. On November 10, 1958, Khrushchev had declared that it was time to abrogate the four-power status of Berlin, and on November 27 the Soviet Union stated that it would abrogate it unilaterally after six months. The Western powers left no doubt that any attempt to drive them out of West Berlin would start another World War. The government was faced by the possibility of a terrible catastrophe. The Berlin problem remained an open problem despite the consultations of the foreign ministers of the various countries. For the government of the DDR this meant that any indication of consent to its policies on the part of the church was of high value. This was the real basis for the attempt of the government to coexist with the churches.

On October 9 and 10, 1958, the Council of EKD considered the ramifications of the communiqué of July and also the discussions that had been carried on after the issuing of the communiqué between Bishop Mitzenheim and the government. It came to the conclusion that in spite of all the efforts to normalize the relationship, there still existed pressure on the consciences and restrictions on church life. At the same meeting Dean Grueber was regretfully relieved of the office of plenipotentiary of the EKD to the government of the DDR.

In 1959 relations between church and state deteriorated. The SED was not ready to change even one iota of its atheistic beliefs. The East Berlin Mayor, Friedrich Ebert, declared at the beginning of 1958, when he opened the new school year, that people who had been brought up in the unscientific dogmas of the church and who believed in mysticism and superstition were not ready to accept their new responsibilities. He said: "Therefore, we must educate them to believe in themselves, to have faith in the power of the working class, faith in the strength of the working people to change the world."

Worse than that, a speech by Grotewohl given before the artists of Berlin on April 1, 1959, partly contradicted the text of the communiqué which he himself had signed. Grotewohl celebrated socialism as the rising of the human race to true humanity. He stated that all people should be freed from prejudices, from superstitions, and from false ideas of the world. He said that the state would fight against the monopoly of the church in the workers' and peasants' state. He demanded that the moral education of the people should go hand in hand with materialistic dialectic ideology. He concluded by saying: "Our state offers to its children an education which corresponds to the interests of all working people. Therefore the state has the right to demand of parents that they should exercise their duty to educate their children in the home in such a way that this education is in harmony with the education which they are receiving in the schools."

The Council of the Evangelical Church of the Union protested against this speech because it was violating the agreement between state and church. On April 20 Bishop Dibelius wrote an open letter to Grotewohl, stating that his address had aroused much apprehension among the Christian population of the DDR. He compared Grotewohl's speech and his claim that only such things as serve socialism are moral with the Nazi claims. He stated that Christians must insist that their children be educated in the faith in Christ and in obedience to his command. Grotewohl did not answer this protest and other protests. However, *Neues Deutschland,* on May 1, 1959, discussed the letter of Dibelius. It stated: "This letter is filled with bold accusations against our republic. It is no accident that on the eve of the Geneva Conference Dibelius is interested in taking the limelight of publicity with such attacks."

The thoughts which Grotewohl had developed in his speech were put into practice in two laws—the *School Order,* promulgated on November 12, 1959, and the *Law Concerning the Socialist Development of the Schools in the DDR,* which was passed on December 2. There it was stated that all children must be educated in the Antifascist democratic school. A school league was organized which was to take care of the activities of children outside of regular class instruction and which was to coordinate its work with the Free German Youth. Especially important was Paragraph 6 of the *School Order,* which stated: "Students may be involved in extracurricular activities only after two hours have elapsed between the regular classes and other compulsory meetings." This meant the total "confiscation" of the children by the school. Religious instruction was made all but impossible.

Also in the daily work of the church there were many small chicaneries. Women's groups were not permitted to use steamers on the Elbe; a bus that had been hired for a church group to transport a choir to a mission festival was withdrawn; couples who had been married in the church were forced to use horse and buggy because cars were available only to people who got married according to the socialist rite. The reason given was: "The central traffic office cannot make cars and busses available for religious purposes."

The people were being swamped with atheistic literature, but Christian publications were restricted more and more. No Christian calendars for 1959 could be printed. The circulation of the Catholic devotional book *The Year of the Lord* was reduced from 70,000 to 40,000 in that same year. When packages from West Germany arrived in the DDR, Bibles and theological books were removed by the postal control authorities and were destroyed, since they represented literature of an anti-democratic character. Newspapers were not allowed to print religious sentiments in the regular death notices.

The Evangelical Church of the Union was amazed at certain occurrences in Halberstadt and Wittenberg. The city council in Halberstadt had decided to withdraw from the congregation the right to use the cathedral. From Wittenberg it was reported that efforts were under way to remove the museum of the *Lutherhalle* from the control of the church. The Socialist Unity Party paper *Freiheit* published a letter by a reader who insisted that the church should have no voice in the running of the *Lutherhalle*, which was a museum of the DDR, because the church could not evaluate critically and scientifically the personality of Martin Luther and of the work of the Reformation. He complained that the *Lutherhalle* in Wittenberg showed nothing about the historical background of the Reformation, about Muenzer, etc.; that the social importance of the Ninety-Five Theses was nowhere mentioned in the museum, neither was the connection of the Reformation with the revolutionary peasant wars nor Luther's betrayal of the peasants and his pact with the princes. Thus the person of the Reformer was either exalted too highly or not given proper credit. The Mayor of Wittenberg, Mrs. Teichmann, declared that both the castle church and the *Lutherhalle* were property of the state and that there had been good cooperation between the church, the state, and the city council.

The protest of the church preserved the *Lutherhalle* in its original state, and also in Halberstadt the city council withdrew its decision to take the cathedral away from the church.

There was another valuable result of another protest. On June 24, 1959, the East Conference of the church complained about the difficulties which were put into the way of evangelical publications. Bishop Dr. Mitzenheim and Secretary of State Wendt held a conference on July 10 in which they discussed these matters. Wendt declared that a limitation of Protestant publications was not in the interest of the state, and certainly there should be no attempt made to apply the measuring stick of historical and dialectic materialism to Protestant theology. Bishop Mitzenheim also reached other agreements with the state concerning the preparation of young people for confirmation and the participation of 1,000 guests from the DDR in the Evangelical German *Kirchentag* in Munich in 1959. There were other signs that the state was willing to meet some of the requests of the church. At a conference in Weimar in June 1959, which was attended by theologians from both parts of Germany, Secretary of State Eggerath declared that the difficulties between state and church were in part due to the fact that the present conditions were not considered permanent. But the state and the SED would try to remove the conditional character of the state.

Reports by the church reflected these changes. Bishop Krummacher greeted the Pomeranian Synod of 1960 by stating that the doors had been opened for a lessening of tensions. Bishop Dr. Jaenicke on March 21, 1961, stated before the Synod of the Province of Saxony that since October 1960 the church had found willingness on the part of the state to listen to her. He stated: "They are really anxious to come to an understanding with the church." There was talk about the "Great Thaw." The list of intercessory prayers for arrested Christians, which had been quite long, was getting smaller, until finally only a few names were left. The newspapers again permitted Christian symbols and religious sentiments to be printed in family notices. Massive anti-Christian attacks were all but absent in the public media. But side by side with the thaw there was also a new coldness. The accommodation was tempered by harshness. Thus there was clearly an attempt to cut off the church of the DDR from the churches of the West. Eighty-one young people who wanted to participate in a European Youth Conference in Lausanne were not permitted to go. A delegation of student congregations which wanted to attend a student conference in Strassburg was also not permitted to go. The efforts of the Bishop of Berlin, Cardinal Doepfner, who in July 1960 tried to arrange for representatives from the DDR to attend the Eucharistic World Congress in Munich, were also doomed to failure. When the apostolic nuncio in Germany, Archbishop Conrad Bafile, wanted to speak in an East Berlin church in September 1960, he was prevented from entering the East sector.

In the fall of 1960 two world-renowned men left their posts and fled to West Germany. The director of the Wartburg, Siegfried Asche, asked the Federal Republic for asylum and wrote to Prime Minister Grotewohl that he had been forced to separate himself from his life's work for the sake of his family and conscience. He protested against all the denunciations, supervisions, and other controls which he had been forced to endure during his years at the Wartburg. In the middle of November the organist and choirmaster of the *Thomaskirche* in Leipzig, Prof. Kurt Thomas, resigned from his office. He was prompted to do this, he wrote to Walter Ulbricht, because trips of the choir to the USA and the Federal Republic had been forbidden, the tradition of Joh. Sebastian Bach had been perverted, and the Thomas Choir had been deprived of its churchly character.

The government tried everything in its power to win the consent of the church for the Soviet proposal and for a peace treaty with East Germany. Was the church ready to give in to this suggestion? If she had done so, she would have followed the road of other churches in the Communist bloc and that of Protestant church leaders in Poland, Czechoslovakia, and Hungary during the past years. But the church in the DDR refused to go this way. On January 27, 1959, the bishops of the DDR addressed the following request to the governments of the four powers and to the two German states: "Do not forget the most important issue. . . . It is a question of people, millions of them, who, as a consequence of the division of Germany, must live their lives in great external and internal need. . . . Do not forget that when you consider the questions before you."

The Synod of the Evangelical Church of the Union also directed an emergency appeal to the German people and to the great powers which closed with these words: "Finally we ask that the reestablishment of the legal guarantees promised to all Germans be made a condition for the conclusion of a peace treaty. Any political reunion must be preceded by a human reunification."

The situation was very discouraging for the government of the DDR. There was no one in a responsible position in the church whom it could use as a tool for its propaganda. Then suddenly Prime Minister Grotewohl got help from an unexpected source. He had written a letter to Chancellor Adenauer asking for a united front of both governments during the Geneva conference. He had suggested that a commission from both German states should work out the German point of view. He repeated this proposal. On April 13 Bishop Mitzenheim of Thuringia wrote to Grotewohl that he wanted to thank him for taking the initiative in the question of the peace treaty and the reunion of Germany. In his letter the bishop went far beyond anything that the church had been willing thus far to concede to the leaders of the DDR.

Mitzenheim was attacked as a collaborator with the SED. He participated in the 10th anniversary celebration of the founding of the DDR on which occasion he thanked the government for the work of reconstruction, which had helped to improve conditions after the catastrophe of 1945.

But the expectation that Mitzenheim would become a spokesman for the progressive pastors fortunately did not become true. When he was attacked by his fellow Christians he was very much hurt. He defended himself before the synod of Thuringia on May 8, 1959. He said that he felt that Grotewohl had tried to bring about a dialogue. This he had to acknowledge in spite of the fact that he had often criticized the government. He stated, "I merely recognized what should be recognized."

The government also tried to win the Catholics for its policy. There were meetings at Bautzen, at Worbis, at Magdeburg, but no representatives of the episcopate participated in them.

The government now turned its full wrath against Bishop Dibelius, who had written a brochure, *On Higher Powers,* in the fall of 1959. This was meant to be a private and personal gift to Bishop Lilje on his 60th birthday. Only 500 copies of the brochure existed. Without the permission of the bishop, Dr. Helmut Gollwitzer of West Berlin had the brochure reprinted. It quickly became a best seller, selling close to 1,000,000 copies. Its contents were provocative and controversial. Dibelius stated that the word "Higher Powers" could not be applied to the East German state because that state did not recognize the existence of God. It had two sets of laws, one for the average citizen, another for leaders; one for Christians, another for atheists. Dibelius felt that "Higher Powers" in the sense of St. Paul could be recognized only if they agreed with the Christian understanding of what is good and what is evil. But if so-called Higher Powers decided autonomously what is good and what is evil, then the basis had been removed from them and what was said in Romans 13 did not apply to them. Dibelius was following the thoughts advocated by Karl Barth in 1938.

The brochure of the Bishop, if it was misinterpreted, could have dire results for the relationship of the state and church in the DDR. The church leadership of his own diocese immediately disassociated itself from it. On October 1 the leaders wrote a letter to all the pastors of Berlin-Brandenburg and told them that they had arranged a meeting with Bishop Dibelius. Later the church leadership declared: "Some of the misunderstandings have been cleared up. Above all, it has become clear that Bishop Dibelius did not want to incite people to disobedience."

But the tumult which had been stirred up was not pacified by this declaration. The acting Mayor of East Berlin, Waldemar Schmidt, declared: "As long as Dibelius maintains this point of view, he will be prohibited from appearing in East Berlin." Nevertheless, on Reformation Sunday the bishop crossed the sector boundary and preached in crowded St. Mary's Church. On November 8 he visited the Young Congregation in Pankow and continued his regular visitations in his diocese until the building of the Wall on August 13, 1961.

In the meantime the theological controversy over the brochure continued very heatedly. A circle of 14 professors and pastors, among whom were Heinrich Vogel and Martin Fischer, published a very critical letter in the magazine *Potsdamer Kirche*. It closed with the sentence: "We are forced to tell you, not without regret, that we must reject your ideas not only on the basis of the Scriptures, but also in view of their possible consequences to the congregations and the individual Christians in the diocese which is entrusted to you as *pastor pastorum*." Various other protests also registered against Dibelius' thesis, including a letter by Johannes Hamel and a set of counter-theses by a group of Saxon pastors.

When the synod of Berlin-Brandenburg met on January 25, 1960, the controversy concerning the brochure broke out full-blast. On the eve of the meeting Martin Fischer and Gerhard Gollwitzer published a booklet entitled *Documents on the Question of Higher Powers, Prepared for the Synods of 1960*, in which Dibelius was indirectly asked to resign from his office. A compromise in the controversy was not reached at this synod. But Bishop Dibelius, who had declared his willingness to step down from his offices in the WCC and the EKD and who had presented a deeply moving ecclesiastical testament, took the edge off the discussions. Concerning the brochure on the Higher Powers, he declared: "I can change nothing in principle. But the examples which I have used as illustrations I can change at any time. I wanted to help. When brothers and sisters tell me that these examples are not helpful, but a burden or even a danger, then I ask them cordially to forget these examples and to erase them from their memory. If they have a copy of my brochure, they should strike them from it." The synod applauded when a reconciliation between Dibelius and Vogel was announced. In a resolution it explained that the differences had their origin in a varying understanding of Scripture and that the bishop was willing to observe all the laws of the DDR.

But there were questions regarding which the church had to take a definite stand. Such an occasion arose in the first month of 1960 when agriculture was collectivized and when the state was exerting tremendous pressures on the peasants. The expropriation, which had begun in 1945 with the collectivization of large land holdings, was extended to the small farms. The number of small farms with 20 to 50 hectares had decreased during the fifties from 43,304 to 16,765 and the farms with over 50 hectares from 4,253 to 684.

In the early months of 1960 a final attack was launched against all remaining small farms. The peasants were forced to join the collectives and to turn over their property to the state. In these dark days Bishop Krummacher wrote to the president of the district of Rostock that the Christian faith was not concerned with economic forms, but with human beings. He described the anxiety, despair, and resignation that were evinced when the peasants were forced against their will to collectivize their property. On March 11 all bishops sent a joint letter to Prime Minister Grotewohl. They reported incidents of terror and declared: "People are being violated in their human dignity, and their conscience is being forced. . . . " Other church authorities, including the Catholic bishops, also wrote letters of protest. But secretary Eggerath answered on behalf of Grotewohl that a large number of church officials were in favor of socialization. This was clearly a lie.

In spite of the fact that the entire church leadership asked for a change in the methods of collectivization, the church was unable to obtain any concessions from the government. All she could do was to offer pastoral help to the victims of collectivization. On February 29 Bishop Krummacher asked the pastors of his diocese to help these people in sympathy. He said: "Our members in the villages should feel especially now that the pastor has an open heart and open door for them. Visit them, counsel with them, my brethren, this is your foremost task right now."

After all these occurrences it was somewhat astonishing that Walter Ulbricht in his speech before the Eighth Convention of the SED asserted: "The new thoughts took hold not only of the peasants. In many villages pastors at the head of their congregations helped from a sense of Christian responsibility to prepare the way for our socialist future." A few weeks later he declared that no one would be hindered from praying and following his religious convictions even on the collective farms.

This line of friendly and at the same time silent treatment was continued when Ulbricht became chairman of the Council of State on September 12, 1960, and thus took over the office of president of the republic. On October 4, 1960, he said in a policy declaration that the members of the churches were able to follow their religious convictions in the DDR. He opposed the NATO politicians who were still in leading church positions, but he stated: "The church leaders in the DDR have become more and more convinced of the correctness, the love of peace, and principle of true humanitarianism with which the policies of our government are being carried out."

Nobody will claim that these explanations made much sense, and it is not quite clear why the chief representatives of Communism should have used collectivization as a basis for establishing a new relationship between church and state.

In view of the continuing flight to the West—in 1960 alone, 199,188 people fled to the West, 55,000 more than in 1959—the synod of the Evangelical Church of the Union issued two declarations, one for the member churches in the Federal Republic and one for the member churches in the DDR, which were read from the pulpits on December 4, 1960. In the declaration to the congregations in the DDR, Christians were asked to remain in the East and not to flee. It stated, "Even in the DDR God has given to each of us a place of work, and we should serve there and be bound to it." *Neues Deutschland,* on December 4, 1960, called this statement hypocrisy and a gross interference in the affairs of the state. The pulpit declaration, it said, "libels our peace policy and our concern for the national development of the German people."

As a high point in the development of the relationship between church and state, the state celebrated the occurrences of February 9, 1961. On that day Walter Ulbricht received a delegation of theologians, church leaders, and Christian citizens who were led by Prof. Dr. Emil Fuchs. The delegation submitted to him the signatures of 32,000 Christians who claimed to speak "as representatives of the overwhelming majority of all Christians in the DDR." They said: "We feel that we can best show our gratitude to you by continuing in the work of Christian love, of peace, and of unity." In a speech which he made at the presentation, Dr. Fuchs praised the DDR as the first peace-state in German history.

Walter Ulbricht responded to the speech by Dr. Fuchs in a similar vein. He stated that he wanted to express the thoughts of a follower of the materialistic ideology, of a pure socialist and Communist. He said that feudalism and capitalism had used Christianity as a façade for their own selfish purposes, but that socialism would lead to a realization of the Christian hope. He stated: "I am getting more and more convinced that socialism, Communism, and the Christian church must work together for the formation of the life of our society and the securing of peace on earth. The Christian who takes his humanistic and social obligations seriously, who frees his head from prejudices, cannot be anything but a socialist." He also stated that the circles who were ruling West Germany had captured the churches and had made them their servants in the preparation of war. He said he was ready to reexamine his attitude toward the West German church leaders if they would definitely renounce their NATO policy. He concluded: "God knows that we would like to live in unity with the theologians and church leaders and Christian politicians of West Germany in order to secure the happiness of the future of our people."

This exchange of speeches, which State Secretary Hans Seigewasser, who on November 15, 1960, had replaced Eggerath, judged to be of timeless importance, took place three days before the beginning of the Synod of the Evangelical Church in Berlin. Seigewasser had told Superintendent General Fuehr that the government was not ready to give the representatives of NATO policy the opportunity to carry on NATO propaganda on the soil of the capital of the DDR. The synod met in West Berlin, but the opening service with a sermon by Bishop Noth was held in East Berlin's St. Mary's Church. At the synod the bishops of the DDR churches declared their unity with the EKD. They said: "We member churches in the DDR state that we are united with all member churches of the EKD in the indissoluble unity of service and of intercession."

Professor Dr. Fuchs's speech of February 7 was criticized by a number of church leaders, including President Scharf, Bishop Krummacher, and others. Prof. Fuchs answered these attacks in a long letter written on April 19. To the reproach of Dr. Krummacher that he had not mentioned some of the important things that divided Christians and Marxists he stated that his main concern had been to make a new beginning and to clear the atmosphere between church and state.

This exchange of letters made clear the great abyss between the official church leadership and the ideas of the so-called "progressive pastors." Dr. Fuchs stated that "socialism is doing things that I had always hoped the Christian church would do."

The government continued its negative attitude toward the EKD. In February 1961 President Scharf, who was a citizen of the DDR, became president of the council of the EKD. He asked Prime Minister Grotewohl for an interview. But he was not received. The government was angry when, at the next election of the EKD, Bishop Krummacher was elected in place of Bishop Mitzenheim, who was also on the ballot but did not receive sufficient votes. The president of the CDU spoke of intrigues. Also Bishop Mitzenheim complained in a circular letter to the pastors of his church: "I am not so sorry that I have not been reelected. But I am sorry about the methods that were used at this election, methods which should have no place in the church."

The government ignored Dr. Krummacher in his capacity as president of the East Conference of the church and chose Bishop Mitzenheim as the recognized spokesman for the churches. The latter was ready for discussions, but he wisely did not accept the part of a spokesman. When he celebrated his 70th birthday on August 17, 1961, he was honored with highest government honors. The Central Committee of the SED sent most cordial congratulations. At a reception on the eve of his birthday at the Castle of Niederschoenhausen, the president of the Council of State presented him with the highest decoration of the DDR, the Patriotic Order of Merit in Gold, and in a speech praised him as a representative of all peace-loving Christians in the DDR.

3. The Wall and the Splitting of the Church, 1961-1963

The tenth German *Kirchentag* met July 19 to 25, 1961, under the motto, "I Am With You Always." The meeting was held in Berlin. At that time no one suspected that only a few weeks later the last gate between the two parts of Germany would be closed. Since the government had forbidden the meeting in East Berlin, the *Kirchentag* finally decided to meet in West Berlin. This *Kirchentag* was to be the last great meeting of Christians from the East and the West. The president of the East Berlin police, Eichenmeyer, had forbidden the *Kirchentag* in his sector because he considered it a tool of the cold war. Dean Grueber wrote to Eichenmeyer and called this prohibition an insult and slander.

But *Neues Deutschland* stated that no Christian citizen of the DDR could participate in this "military" *Kirchentag*. The bishops were called "Atom Bishops" and the professors "Nato professors." When Bishop Krummacher tried to reach Berlin to participate in the meeting of the council, he was stopped. His passport was taken from him, and he was told to return to the council of the district of Rostock to be informed about the goals of the *Kirchentag*. He did not accept this invitation, and his papers were returned to him the very next day because Bishop Mitzenheim had protested in a telegram to Grotewohl. With the exception of the Silesian bishop, Dr. Hornig, the DDR bishops were unable to come to the *Kirchentag* since they wanted to remain at their posts. In trains and on highways there were strict police controls. In spite of that, 11,000 Christians from the DDR came to West Berlin. Smaller *Kirchentage* were held at Greifswald, Magdeburg, Naumburg, and other places in the East zone.

Through the building of the wall on August 13, 1961, not only the city of Berlin, but also the whole organization of the church was divided into two parts. A symbol of this division was the Church of the Conciliation on the Bernauer Strasse, where the wall was built in front of the church portal. The bells were silenced and the clock on the church tower showed five minutes to 12. On the west wall the motto "We are all brethren" was still to be seen. On October 12 the parsonage and 16 deaconesses, who were being trained in

the *Burckhardthaus,* were evacuated by the People's Police. Of the
6,992 members of the congregation about 6,500 were living west of
the wall and were separated from their church. Twenty-five other
churches of Berlin were thus divided by the wall. Thirteen churches
were separated from their cemeteries. These conditions made it
necessary to establish church administrations in both parts of the
city, and members of the West could no longer pass to the East.

On August 14, 1961, the President of the EKD, Dr. Scharf, and
Bishop Dibelius sent a message to the congregations in the East
and the West in which they called upon them not to succumb to
bitterness and hatred. They asked them: "Do not throw away our
faith which makes us certain that God's grace will lead us through
suffering and injustice to the road of blessing. Do not forget that
all human terror has an end and that those who love peace are the
children of God." On August 16 President Scharf, Bishop Krummacher, Superintendent General Fuehr and the President of the
Synod of Berlin-Brandenburg, Fritz Figur, all of whom were living
in the DDR, sent a telegram to Walter Ulbricht and East Berlin's
Mayor Friedrich Ebert, in which they protested against the building
of the wall. The authors of the telegram annoyed the government
very much. They were told that in the future the church would
have to accept orders from the state. On August 18 President Scharf
was called to the city hall by Mayor Ebert and told that the publication of their telegram over the radio of the American sector clearly
indicated the political intentions of the writers. Bishop Krummacher
was called before the president of the district of Rostock. He said
later that he was treated as he had been treated in Russian captivity
by Soviet commissars.

In spite of these attacks, the church continued to work patiently
for the alleviation of the needs which the division of Berlin had
caused. Before Christmas 1961 the two superintendents general of
East and West Berlin conferred with government officials in order to
obtain passenger permits to go from East to West Berlin and vice
versa. It was in vain, as were similar attempts in 1962. The church
asked to leave no stone unturned to obtain visitors' permits for
close relatives. The wall remained impenetrable until Christmas
1963.

After August 13, 1961, Bishop Dibelius was not permitted to return to East Berlin. President Scharf, who on August 24 had been appointed to become "deputy bishop" for East Berlin and for that part of the church of Berlin-Brandenburg which was located in the DDR, was not permitted to return to East Berlin after he crossed into West Berlin on August 31 with a valid permit to participate in a meeting of the council of the EKD. Reasons for the refusal to permit his return were that on August 16 he had signed the telegram to Ulbricht and that as a president of the council of the EKD he was in charge of a warlike and illegal organization.

The council of the EKD protested angrily that such a cynical and dishonest exclusion was a gross interference in the organization of the church. Bishop Mitzenheim intervened with Seigewasser on behalf of Scharf. But it was in vain.

The Synod of Berlin-Brandenburg unanimously declared its confidence in President Scharf and asked the church leadership to work untiringly for his return to East Berlin; but the consultations with Seigewasser, which took place on January 30, 1963, were completely without success. As a reason Seigewasser cited numerous press reports about speeches which Scharf had given in West Berlin and in the Federal Republic and which he termed a defamation of the German Democratic Republic.

Dean Grueber, who had been excluded from East Berlin since the end of September, 1961, could no longer carry on his work in St. Mary's Church and was forced to resign from all his offices in East Berlin. On September 29, 1961, he wrote a letter of farewell to his congregation. He had worked for 15 years for understanding and reconciliation with the socialist government of the DDR.

Church leaders from the DDR now no longer received permission to go to West Berlin, and citizens from West Berlin were excluded from entering the Communist Sector. Thus of the representatives elected to go to the World Council of Churches Assembly in New Delhi in 1961 only eight men from the DDR received permission to travel. The Catholic Bishop of Berlin, Cardinal Doepfner, was not allowed to enter East Berlin because he was not a "lover of peace." The Catholic bishops of the DDR were not permitted to participate in the annual Fulda Bishops' Conference in 1961 and thereafter. When the successor of Cardinal Doepfner, Bishop Alfred Bengsch, a citizen of the DDR, took over his office shortly after the building of the wall, his consecration had to take place on two occasions. On August 19 he became bishop in East Berlin and in his place Cardinal Doepfner appeared at the Cathedral of West Berlin. His enthronement took place a few weeks later, first in the East and then in the West. But the bishop was treated somewhat more kindly than Dr. Scharf. At regular intervals he received permission to visit his congregations in East Berlin. Twelve representatives of the DDR were permitted to attend the Second Vatican Council, but they were not allowed to travel through the Federal Republic. They were obliged to go to Rome by way of Prague and Vienna. When the ambassador of the Federal Republic in Rome asked the German council fathers to come to a reception, the bishops from the DDR politely declined.

Ecumenical cooperation of the Evangelical churches of the DDR was hindered even after New Delhi. While representatives of the churches of the other East bloc states were permitted to travel, Bishop Krummacher could not participate in the work of the commission of the WCC for international relations, which were meeting in Geneva and Paris in the summer of 1962. Bishop Dr. Noth and Director Brenecke were not allowed to attend the meeting of the central committee of the WCC of which they were members. When the conference of European churches at Nieburg was opened in September 1962, five of the 10 representatives of the DDR were missing. For the meeting of LWF in Helsinki, July 30 to August 11, 1963, only 34 of the 62 delegates and official visitors received permission to go.

The building of the wall had been an act of despair. From January to August 1961 a total of 195,828 refugees had fled to the West, and the socialist economy of the DDR had been jeopardized. Later Walter Ulbricht mentioned another reason: "The immediate preparation of an attack upon the DDR by the imperialists and militarists of West Germany made it necessary to build the wall as a safety measure."

The list of intercessions for those arrested increased from two before the building of the wall to 19 on February 27, and to 32 on May 29, 1962.

The church was forced to become more autonomous. The East Conference had established an office in East Berlin. But in spite of the fact that the East Conference had established its headquarters in East Berlin the "progressive pastors" were not satisfied. On October 17, 1961, they issued a call to the synods and governments of the churches in the DDR which urged the separation of the church from the EKD. They said that the confession of guilt which the EKD had made in 1945 had been annulled through the chaplaincy agreement with the military of the West German republic. A continued coexistence of the church in the DDR and the EKD in the West seemed impossible to them under these circumstances.

This request was rejected by the church leadership, including Bishop Mitzenheim. During the meeting of the WCC in New Delhi he announced: "The churches of the DDR will remain member churches of the EKD."

But the Christian Democrats and "progressive pastors" continued to agitate for the severance of the ties between the churches. The DDR was called the home for Christian life. The *Evangelische Pfarrerblatt* reported: "Bishops Dibelius and Lilje, Military Bishop Kuntz, and, in a somewhat different way, President Scharf, through their line of thinking have succeeded in discrediting the church to such a degree that there is no one who can say a single word in their favor. . . . " The report called the wall of Berlin a protective fence which would keep the work of the DDR from being contaminated by disturbing influences.

Prof. Dr. Emil Fuchs spoke in Goerlitz and declared that he was proud and happy to live in the DDR. A few weeks before this meeting Pastor Martin Hertel of Bautzen, only 40 miles from Goerlitz, had written an entirely different letter to the president of the district of Dresden. In it he stated: "Until now we have borne the citizenship of the DDR patiently. But now the burden has become unbearable. As Christians we can never have a positive attitude to a state that recognizes only those citizens who are socialists. . . . It is bad for us to send our children into the DDR schools, which are training them in Communist ideology." He asked that he and his family be released from their citizenship obligations to the DDR. This was a desperate step. The *Saechsische Zeitung* called it a "dirty trick." There were demonstrations. The way in which Hertel was now treated showed what the Communists meant when they spoke about socialist ethics. He was called before a forum of citizens who accused him of being a "provocateur in a black gown." From the whole district of Dresden about a thousand SED functionaries were brought to Bautzen, who forced Hertel to come to their meeting and to accept their judgment. The president of the district, Witek, threatened: "As we have created new conditions in Berlin, we shall also create them throughout the DDR." The pastor was given the choice to retract his letter or to suffer the consequences: expulsion from Bautzen. The city council demanded that Bishop Noth recall Hertel from Bautzen. The bishop rejected this demand. The SED secretary of Bautzen told Hertel that the SED would give him just a little time to make his decision. He said, "Take back what you have written and swear an oath of loyalty to the state." Hertel finally bowed to the pressures and published a declaration in the *Saechsische Zeitung* in which he stated: "I am ready to recognize the government of the DDR as the higher powers which are given us by God. The DDR is the state in which I want to live as a citizen by the will of God and want to work for the welfare of all. I will be obedient to the laws of the DDR and my Christian responsibility and will carry out all the duties of citizenship and enjoy its rights."

After the meeting of the progressive pastors in Goerlitz there was also a Catholic meeting in the same city. It, too, directed an appeal for peace to the West German Catholics and asked the bishops of the DDR to support the just demand for a German peace treaty and a peaceful solution of the West Berlin question. The episcopate rejected this demand.

When Bishop Krummacher was elected on July 6, 1962, by the East Conference of the Evangelical Church to become its president and Bishop Noth took the place of Bishop Mitzenheim as vice president, the "progressive pastors" stated that there was no doubt that the church leadership had lost the trust for which Mitzenheim had so untiringly worked. Secretary Seigewasser also ignored Krummacher and turned to Bishop Mitzenheim for the discussion of problems. In spite of these developments the "progressive pastors" remained a small splinter group which never had more than 200 members including pastors emeriti and preachers from free churches. The building of the wall had led to a complete separation of the two parts of the church of Berlin-Brandenburg. Despite this fact, the church decided to retain their unity, but established a separate consistory for West Berlin. Thus the church met in two regional synods from March 12 to 16, 1962, one in West Berlin, the other in Berlin-Weissensee. Both groups declared their unity with each other. They reported: "Independent action cannot be avoided, but our separation is only relative, for we belong together."

Originally the aged Bishop Dibelius had intended to declare his resignation. Since this would have led to a very difficult situation, he was prevailed upon to continue in his office. Several minority groups stated that the church of Berlin-Brandenburg no longer existed, but the church continued to disregard these attempts to split her.

On December 7 to 9, 1962, the two parts of the synod met again and tried to elect a bishop. This was the last opportunity to decide on a successor to Dr. Dibelius since the term of the synod ended at the end of 1962. Dr. Scharf was the candidate, but there was no possibility that the government of the DDR would recognize him or permit him to return to the DDR. Seigewasser declared to the East Berlin church leaders that the election of Dr. Scharf would definitely cut the ties with the government and would lead to a new trial for him. Nevertheless, the East Berlin synod voted 94 to 48 for him, with six abstentions, and the West Berlin synod 52 to 28, with two abstentions. This was a powerful proof of the confidence which Scharf enjoyed, but the necessary two-thirds majority had not been attained. Thus the question of the succession of Dibelius remained open.

At the beginning of 1963 the two regional synods, which in the meantime had been reelected, met for a third time. But how difficult it was to carry on these separate meetings is shown by the *Law Concerning the Election of a Bishop*. The law that had been passed by the West Berlin regional synod declared that the bishop must be elected by a two-thirds majority from each regional synod. The law that had been passed by the Eastern regional synod, however, stated that while a two-thirds majority of all members of the two regional synods was necessary, one of the synods could elect him with a simple majority. These two versions of the law were brought into harmony, and the Eastern synod elected the Superintendent General of Cottbus, Dr. Guenter Jacob, to serve as deputy bishop in the eastern part of the diocese, while the West Berlin part remained under the direct leadership of Dr. Dibelius.

The EKD faced the same difficulties as the church of Brandenburg. The synod of the EKD met March 10 to 14, 1963, at Bethel, and the members of the Federal Republic, including those from West Berlin, were there alone. The president of the synod, Dr. Puttfagen, had officially told Secretary of State Seigewasser about the planned meeting and had asked for travel permits for all members from the DDR. But Seigewasser declared that no travel permits would be issued. Thus of 100 members of the synod the 35 representatives of the DDR churches were absent.

The rump synod was barely able to muster a quorum. In order to preserve the unity of the EKD, two church laws were passed. These laws did not, as was done in the case of Berlin-Brandenburg, decree two separate synods which could operate independently from each other, but they retained the unity of the one synod, which alone had a right to pass laws, and at the same time provided for mobility and elasticity. The first law determined that the synod could pass laws if there was a majority of its members present. It also made it possible that the eastern part of the synod could meet in the East simultaneously with the meeting of the western part in the West. The synod gave full power to the council of the EKD to determine the time when the laws which had been passed by both sides would become effective.

Also the United Evangelical Lutheran Church in Germany and the Evangelical Church of the Union were split. When the Lutheran General Synod met at Nuremberg on April 21, 1963, the members from the churches of Thuringia, Saxony, and Mecklenburg were missing. Of the 54 members of the synod only 37 were present, a very close two-thirds majority. In order not to endanger her work the church changed her order of business. From now on not two-thirds, but one-half of the members were needed to pass resolutions. The Council of the Evangelical Church of the Union was able to meet regularly even after the building of the wall. On June 24 to 27, 1962, the synod was called to meet in East Berlin. In contrast to the Evangelical Church in Germany and the United Evangelical Lutheran Church, it was unable to muster a two-thirds majority either in the Federal Republic or in the DDR. The president of the synod, Dr. Lothar Kreyssig of Magdeburg, announced the planned meeting to secretary Seigewasser. Seigewasser indicated that a meeting of the entire synod was not desirable but that simultaneous meetings could take place in the East and West according to the example of the synod of Berlin-Brandenburg. He permitted West German guests to participate in the meeting of the eastern regional synod but gave them no vote. The church was not ready to accept this separation. When the synod met, the West German members were kept from entering East Berlin with the explanation that the church of the Union had split herself when she accepted the chaplaincy agreement. A protest to Ulbricht proved unsuccessful. Therefore separate meetings were held in East and West Berlin. Here the same topics were discussed and the same decisions were made.

All these were emergency measures. But carrying out these measures involved technical difficulties. On July 3, 1963, the West Berlin Superintendent General, Hans Martin Helbig, was able to talk with Soviet Prime Minister Khrushchev through the mediation of the Soviet Embassy in East Berlin. The talk lasted two hours and took place at Castle Niederschoenhausen. Helbig asked the Premier to make it possible for separated members of families to meet and to permit sick people to receive medicine from the West and to bring together people who were engaged and married. He also asked that the churches that had been split be given an opportunity to hold synodical meetings. Khrushchev was open to these requests and declared that he was willing to pass on these wishes to the German state officials. But he said that he expected that the methods of the Western partners would be more flexible.

After the building of the wall there was accelerated rearmament in the DDR. On August 18, 1961, all members of the Free German Youth were told: "The Fatherland calls! Protect the Republic!"

The universities too were forced to support this recruitment for the National People's Army. On September 12, 1961, the Martin Luther University of Halle-Wittenberg published a long-winded pronouncement, which contained the whole vocabulary of the SED and called upon students to declare their readiness for the honorable service for peace in the armed forces of the DDR. The theological faculty, however, did not sign this appeal but issued a separate declaration in which they called upon faculty members to respect the measures of the government of the DDR in accordance with the injunctions of Romans 13.

An appeal by the theological faculty of the East Berlin Humboldt University had quite a different slant. Here at first Prof. Dr. Heinrich Vogel had written a declaration which went beyond the opinion of the theological faculty of Halle. He declared: "The theological faculty recognizes the right of defense by the state. The state is appointed to see to it that justice and peace are preserved. On the basis of our interpretation of Scripture, which is in line with the interpretation of the Lutheran Reformation, the theological faculty cannot consent to the idea that a Christian cannot be a soldier. The theological faculty, however, will help those who for reasons of conscience believe that they are not able to take up weapons. But it demands a proof of everyone that he is ready to fight for his people and for his state." This draft of Dr. Vogel was accepted by the council of the faculty on October 14. Although most of the professors could not vote because they were living in West Berlin, a majority was obtained by including progressive assistants and instructors who had been appointed by the state. One of them was a member of the central committee of the Socialist Unity Party.

As early as October 9 the church leadership of Brandenburg had sent to the pastors a letter signed by President Figur, which letter was also accepted by other regional churches. It told them that the council of the EKD had asked the government of the DDR on May 24, 1956, to include the following stipulation in Article 5 of the constitution: "A citizen will not be forced to do military service if he has reasons which, according to his religious faith or moral conviction, prevent him from doing so." This request had not been accepted.

On January 24, 1962, general military conscription was introduced in the DDR. Besides difficulties of conscientious objections an oath which made matters worse was added. The oath read: "I solemnly swear to defend my fatherland, the DDR, and to defend it as the land of the workers and peasants against any enemies. I swear to be ready to fight side by side with the Soviet army and the armies of socialist countries which are allied with us, and to defend socialism against all enemies and to dedicate my life until victory is won. I swear to be an honest, courageous, disciplined, and obedient soldier, to carry out all commands and to keep all military facts secret. . . . If I should ever violate this solemn oath I shall be ready to receive the harsh punishment of our republic and the contempt of our working people." The eastern regional synod of Brandenburg presented the issue involved in this oath, which was not merely an oath to a political doctrine but to an ideology. The final forum to which the person taking this oath was responsible was the working people and the question arose whether this oath should be understood as a call to fight for the ideology of class struggle.

The synod agreed that the state had the right to defend itself and declared its readiness to help all those who, for reasons of conscience, could not serve with weapons in their hands. The church government of the Province of Saxony voiced similar reservations.

It was significant for the situation of the church in the DDR that the leaders and the synods of the Protestant churches were protecting pacifists while professed Quakers and pacifists like Dr. Emil Fuchs in an open letter called to pastors to do their duty in the National People's Army. Before the CDU central committee Dr. Fuchs declared on February 9, 1962, "The 13th of August and the law for compulsory service are necessary because the present situation is dangerous for the forces of freedom." Dr. Fuchs, however, also intervened on behalf of conscientious objectors in many instances.

On March 12, 1962, the discussions of Bishops Krummacher and Mitzenheim with the Deputy President of the Council of Ministers, Willie Stoph, and the other representatives of the state took place.

The subject of the discussions was the freedom of faith for the soldiers in the People's Army, the oath, and conscientious objectors. Stoph declared that freedom of faith was guaranteed also to soldiers but that no outside person could interfere with military life during the period of training. What a soldier did in his off-duty hours was his own affair. As far as the oath was concerned he declared that it was a secular oath and did not require of the soldier any religious confession. Concerning the question of conscientious objectors, Stoph said: "I know quite well how to differentiate between conscientious objections for religious reasons—such an attitude I can honor—and a pacifism which is based on political antagonism and has been abused to make defense arrangements of the DDR impossible."

The experiences of the following years showed that Stoph kept his promises. The intervention of the church on behalf of conscientious objectors had been useful. The soldiers of the people's army were intensively influenced in the direction of materialism. This was unavoidable in a totalitarian state. But there were indications that also pastors who were not among the so-called progressives were invited by officers and soldiers of the people's army. The conditions in the DDR were not uniform. The reality was very complex and varied from place to place. As an example: On September 23, 1962, there was the dedication of a new deacons' home in Pomerania and 1,500 people were present. Although the government had called upon the people to help with the potato harvest, it did not interfere with the festival but placed at the disposal of the church busses and extra food for the participants.

Also in many other instances the SED stayed away from gross interference in the life of the church. It was eager to gain the consent of the church leaders for the political aims of the government. However, serious conflicts between state and church were unavoidable.

An increased propaganda for the approval of the church started when on March 21, 1962, the National Council of the National Front produced a "national document" under the title: *The Historical Task of the DDR and the Future of Germany.* This document proposed a German confederation which would exist within the framework of peaceful coexistence and of peaceful competition until the forces of socialism and of the peace-loving powers in the Federal Republic were ready for reunion.

There was no repercussion to this national document in the Federal Republic. But the churches in the German Democratic Republic were put under great pressure. Seigewasser demanded open support of the students and professors of the East Berlin theological faculty and argued that in the Federal Republic all reactionary and inhuman phenomena of German history had been preserved. He invited President Figur, and after reprimanding him because the church government had rejected the acclamation of the church to political programs, showed him the door. From time to time members of church councils and pastors were invited to participate in discussions of the national document, and the press in the DDR reported great successes. But in fact there was much opposition. The president of the Church of Anhalt, Dr. Martin Mueller, agreed to some of the points, but also offered various criticisms. The council of the theological faculty in Leipzig avoided a clear decision. None of the synods was ready to discuss the national document, let alone to give its consent to it. When the synod of the church province of Saxony was requested to take action by three memoranda, the memoranda were turned over to a committee without debate.

The government did not respond to the refusal of the churches with public attacks. It made great efforts to win large circles of the Christian population for a participation in the dialogue. Pastors and theologians were asked to submit creative proposals. A new statute was prepared by the SED. The central committee defined the policy of the party in its relationship to the religious organizations: "Our party does its effective work by including Christian citizens of the DDR in the program of socialist reconstruction and by winning over theologians and church officers for the peace policy of the DDR."

Of great importance was the statement that citizens of the DDR were united and that explanation of the program by the president of the Council of State of the DDR had emphasized that Christianity and the humanistic aims of socialism did not clash.

During the sixth Party Convention of the SED Walter Ulbricht

had proposed an agreement based on reason and good will for
the regulation of the relationship between the two Germanies. But
the Federal Government did not accept this proposal. It would have
meant the recognition of the German Democratic Republic as a
legitimate German state.

The position of the church was not uniform. The Saxon Synod
meeting from March 18 to 22, in Dresden, admonished pastors and
church councils to show restraint concerning political pronouncements. The "progressive pastors" were enthusiastically for the seven-
point program. Great surprise arose when Bishop Dr. Krummacher
gave an interview to the Evangelical News Service on January 13,
1963. Since he was a member of the commission of the WCC for
international relationship, he was asked whether it was not time
for the commission to help remove the tensions of the German
problem. Dr. Krummacher stated that the commission had been
active in this direction for a long time. He said that he believed
that now after the Cuba crisis it was time to take concrete steps
in international ecumenical endeavors and to try to find a solution
to the burning question of German division. The West German press
in part attacked Dr. Krummacher violently. It called him "a spokesman for Ulbricht." But there were other bishops, like Dr. Jaenicke
of the Province of Saxony and Dr. Mitzenheim of Thuringia, who
voiced similar opinions. They were interested in the restoration of
the unity of Germany.

The documents that showed best that the church was leaving
everything to the wisdom of God were the *Ten Articles on the Freedom of the Ministry and the Church.* They were published on May
27, 1963. They have been compared to the *Barmen Declaration of
1934.* Article I stated that it was the task of the church to preach
the Word clearly and reliably. It warned against disobedience to
the Word of God and demanded that the Word of God should rule
all areas of human life. Article II stated that since God had reconciled man with himself in Christ he had given to man a new meaning and dignity in life. It stated: "We are disobedient if we recognize God as Lord of our life in our church services but in our daily
lives submit to the absolute claims of ideologies and thus try to

escape from the validity of the First Commandment." Article III denied the claim that science could answer all questions. Article IV demanded justice in government. It stated: "We are disobedient if we silently accept the fact that the law has been abused for political and economic interests . . . and if we do not stand up for our neighbor who has been disenfranchised and is threatened in his human rights and if we refuse to suffer with him." Article V was concerned with the command to Christians to be peacemakers. Here, too, there was a clear indication of what the church meant by peace. The authors stated: "We are disobedient if we confuse the secular peace and the peace of God and if we measure peace on earth with the measuring stick of human ideology . . . and with thoughts of revenge." Article VI turned against the idolizing of work. Christ did not want man to become a slave of work. Article VII stated that all those who were entrusted with the higher authority possessed it at the instigation of God, even "if they make themselves lords of conscience and interfere with the ministry of the church." Article VIII spoke of the life and the ministry of the church: "The church is disobedient when she becomes negligent, when she retires behind the walls of the church and leaves the responsibility which is entrusted to all members of the congregations to individual church members and groups. The church is disobedient when she wants to secure the freedom to be active by not remaining faithful to her task." Article IX stated that the form of the church could undergo changes, but that any order of the church must be true to her essence. It cannot be against Scripture and against her commission. Therefore, it stated, "The church is disobedient when she dissolves her order and her laws by human whim and does not keep her order or surrenders it to forces outside the church." Finally, Article X spoke about the hope of the church: "The Christian congregation confesses her faith in the Lord as the decisive confession, even though it is hidden before the world and history. She waits for the day when all the world will know what the church believes now. Rev. 11:15: The kingdom of the world has become the kingdom of our Lord and of his Christ, and he shall reign for ever and ever."

In order to avoid a political interpretation, the Conference of the Church in the DDR declared that the *Ten Articles* were primarily addressed to the church herself. The conference rejected any political abuse of the ten articles. The council of the EKD forwarded the document to the West German church with the request to make it available to all pastors and congregations. It stated: "The *Ten Articles* represent the teaching of Holy Scriptures and of the confessions of the Reformation and are directions for the service of the church in the public and for the obedience of the Christians in the life of society."

The government of the DDR, of course, was not enthusiastic about these articles.

At this point it might be well to draw some comparisons with the churches in other Communist states. While the churches in those states, with the exception of the Roman Catholic Church in Poland, had submitted to the dictatorship of the total state and had become mouthpieces for Communism, the churches in the DDR were able to retain their external and internal independence. They did not repeat Communist doctrines as did the other churches. When they made their declarations, the world knew that they were genuine and truthful and that they were witnesses of consciences that were bound to God's Word.

The reasons why it was possible for the church in the DDR to preserve her freedom were various. Of very great importance was, of course, the fact that the churches in the DDR were member churches of the EKD. Until the building of the wall they were not isolated. The influence of spiritual and intellectual help was of tremendous value. This help was not available to the churches in other countries. Furthermore, the churches had gained a great deal of experience in their struggle against the Third Reich and were able to evaluate more critically a totalitarian ideology. They had learned how to show great courage and to preserve an unbending conscience in their decisions, their pulpit announcements, and pastoral letters. Nevertheless, the church had suffered great losses. But the way in which she had met the challenge of Communism gave reason to hope that she would be able to stand up to all future challenges.

G. LOSSES AND GAINS OF THE CHURCH STRUGGLE

1. Atheistic Propaganda and the Cult of Dialectic Materialism

Atheistic propaganda which was carried on by the SED no longer had the intensity and the enthusiasm of the 19th century and of the first decades of the 20th. There were several reasons for this. The opponent of atheism, the church, had lost her privileged position in church and society, and thus a very important part of the atheistic thunder had been stolen. In a great number of countries the church had been exposed to great persecutions, and the image which she had presented through her courage and her martyrs did not fit into the cliché which freethinkers had traditionally associated with her. The church had acquired a social conscience. She had been reorientated? On the other hand, atheism had lost the pathos of a revolutionary movement in a world which recognized the freedom of belief as a basic freedom of man. It could no longer claim that it had freed the spirit from medieval dogmas. It very often offended with its revolutionary demands. Its concepts of the world and man and the goal of life which it presented as a substitute of faith seemed to be empty and unattractive. Thus atheism had lost the power to be an independent movement. It had become a mere adjunct to a political ideology.

If the state had not helped it to gain recruits, it soon would have dwindled away.

This was one of the reasons why in the Communist countries there was no spontaneity and passion in atheistic propaganda. It had become a calculated program. Specialists were assigned certain tasks to work according to plan, and they fed the apparatus with their mental ideas. They were functionaries who worked in organizations through mass media. The apparatus was rattling.

In the DDR atheism became the willing helper of a state ideology. Its propaganda was at times very primitive. It concentrated on the opposition of superstition *(Aberglaube)* to faith *(Glaube)*.

In the DDR the state, according to its own interpretation, was anti-religious and anti-church. It tried to influence even the smallest details of human life. But the pressures put on people to leave the church were no longer as brazenly carried on as in former years.

The state began to work through various educational institutions, through the people's army, through mass organizations and through factories. Even kindergarten teachers were told to leave the church. The Communists might have wondered whether the people whom they had thus forced to leave the church were really convinced followers of atheistic dialectic materialism.

The great breakthrough for Youth Dedications occurred during the anti-church offensive of 1957-58. In 1958 for the first time the majority of the graduates of the elementary schools participated in Youth Dedications. There were 70% in 1958 and 80% in 1959. In 1960 the number increased to 88%, in 1961 to 97% and in 1962 it leveled off to 95%. The confirmation participation decreased correspondingly. Since 1959 there have been quite a number of congregations where there were no confirmations.

One of the reasons for the victory of Youth Dedications was that since 1958 the youth lessons which served as preparation for Youth Dedications were no longer centered around attacks against the church but had become more neutral in their approach. Furthermore, the tremendous pressure put on parents and children continued. Thus, for example, the parents of the seventh-grade children in the Pestalozzi School in Borna had to sign a promise in December 1961: "We will no longer listen to broadcasts from West Berlin. We will give our vote to the candidate of the National Front. We will see to it that our child becomes a faithful member of the Young Pioneers and wears his kerchief daily. We will establish close contact between home and school and we will send our children to Youth Dedications."

Also the number of kindergartens run by the state increased. The central committee of the SED stated: "The influence of the state on society must be increased so that the three- to six-year-old children can be educated by the state." In 1962, 62 percent of all children in that age group attended state kindergartens.

The rites of baptism, marriage, and burial were also taken over by the state. In the city of Stalinstadt, which was the first socialist city in Germany, an office for the planning of atheistic substitute rites was established. It published a pamphlet entitled *Basic Ideas and Experiences in the Celebration of Socialist Remembrances in*

Connection with Birth, Marriage, and Death in Stalinstadt. This pamphlet was sent to all districts and cities in the DDR. It gained official status. It required that as many people as possible should take part in these ceremonies and that they should be held at the right time. Name-giving dedications should be held on Sundays. It was also stated that celebrations should be accompanied by music wherever possible and that the organizers should try to make a deep impression on those present. The honorarium for the musicians should be paid by private persons so that these celebrations would not be considered handouts by the state, but would become a socialistic enterprise of state and individuals.

Other inducements were also used. Children who were brought to the Socialist Name-Giving Dedications received a savings account of 50 to 100 marks. The party newspapers, which did not accept any other family announcements, were permitted to publish notes of thanksgiving and congratulatory messages for name-giving and marriage dedications. For example, the following congratulatory message to a young couple was published in Bautzen: "Do not trust in miracle-performing idols. If there is a faith that can move mountains, then this faith is your own strength." The Central Committee made certain recommendations about songs, poems, and the like that could be used on these occasions. Certificates were published by the central office of the state and were embossed with the coat of arms of the state. Speakers' bureaus were established in the various districts. The speakers were given the names of all young couples and of all newly born children so that they could visit the couples or parents and convince them of the importance of socialist celebrations.

The most difficult substitute rite, of course, was the socialist funeral. What can dialectic materialism say to the theme of suffering, death, and sorrow? Wolfgang Weinert depicted one of those funerals in his book *Life According to the Red Pattern.* He described how the coffin was put into a small chapel of the cemetery. The walls of the chapel had been covered with blood-red colors and the crucified Lord at the altar had been hidden by these flags. The flag that covered the coffin was also red. On an old reed organ a song was played which glorified the revolution. The widow did not even try to keep back her tears. Also the youngest boy with the blue kerchief of the Young Pioneers around his neck cried without comfort. Representatives of the party, of the labor union, of the cell block, of the factory, sat on narrow benches. The speaker spoke at the grave of the deceased and praised him as the best comrade who had worked in the socialist way. The speaker asked: "Who will continue your work, dear comrade? Who will take your place?" Then the coffin was lowered. Weinert stated that the Communist Party was quite aware of the fact that the socialist way of death did not satisfy the longing of the people. It instructed the speakers: "Our speakers have the duty to comfort the bereaved without giving them religious fare and to acquaint them with the help that the state makes available to them so that they may be able to stand upright in a life that in the days of sorrow may seem hopeless to them."

Since the state forced people more and more to participate in the socialist celebrations, the church conference of the East at the end of 1959 sent instructions to their member churches. In a message to the congregation the church leaders declared that socialist celebrations were atheistic. If someone participated in these celebrations, he would be responsible to God himself. They stated: "We know how difficult it is in each individual case. Therefore we must help each other and carry each other's burden so that our fellow-Christians arrive at the right decision. The Christian must show his faith to a world which does not want to know about our Lord."

In a letter to the congregations the church clearly drew the line between Christian and socialist celebrations. She realized that some Christians who did not want to be godless were wavering since they had been exposed to a great deal of pressure. Concerning baptism she stated: "We cannot deprive our children of this means of grace because they are God's children. We cannot bring them to the name-giving dedications, which have as their basis the opposite idea, namely atheism. When our children have been baptized we have the duty to bring them up in the Christian way. We cannot take them to the Youth Dedications, which have the opposite attitude toward faith. The same restriction applies to marriage and funeral customs."

The most difficult problem was the tremendous pressure to have the children attend Youth Dedications. The churches in the DDR did not have much time to regulate the whole question of confirmation anew. The problem was that if they wanted to continue confirmation as it had been carried on in the "people's church," they would have to disregard the alternative of confirmation versus youth dedication. That meant that all children who so desired would have to be admitted to confirmation regardless of whether they had attended youth dedications or not. There were some voices within the church which denied that there was a basic conflict between confirmation and youth dedications.

There were people who maintained that confirmation should not be denied to anyone who had been baptized and who asked to be confirmed in the faith in Jesus Christ. On the basis of this proposition the four Schwerin congregations decided in 1959 to admit to confirmation all children who had attended confirmation instruction for two years. They considered confirmation a rite of intercession for their faith. At the end of 1959 the Central Committee for Youth Dedications declared: "Every person, regardless of his ideology, can give his consent to our promise because peace, friendship among nations, and socialism are in his interests and correspond to the concept of a happy life and common welfare." Although Ulbricht had said something entirely different when, in the Sonneberg speech of 1958, he stressed that the confession to socialism was also a confession to atheism, the state did not stress this point.

Beginning in 1958 the synods struggled with the question of confirmation. In June 1958 the church province of Saxony ordered a committee to prepare proposals which would make it possible for children who had participated in youth dedications to continue as members of the church. A transition regulation was established in 1959 according to which children who participated in youth dedications could also participate in confirmation instruction and the final examination, but the rite of confirmation was administered only to those who had not participated in youth dedications. In September 1958, the Saxon Synod decided that concurrent attendance at church instruction and preparation for youth dedication was possible. It declared that the instruction in the church should be closed with a divine service at the end of January. Then the confirmands should be confirmed and should receive the Lord's Supper. Young people who had participated in the youth dedications were not to be confirmed at once. But after proving themselves to be Christians through regular participation in church life they were permitted to be confirmed after one year of probation and were admitted to the sacraments. Similar rules were passed in the other churches.

On the whole, these changes meant that the church had given up her frontal attack against youth dedications and was now occupying a position behind the battle lines of youth dedications. She had begun to face the reality that youth dedications were actions which had been dictated by the state and therefore she gave her members an opportunity to decide later whether they were for Christ or for atheistic materialism. The most radical position was taken in Thuringia and Anhalt, while other churches demanded that children who were confirmed later should clearly declare that they did not want to carry out the promise which they had given in the youth dedications. The churches of Berlin-Brandenburg and of the province of Saxony decreed that children who wanted to be confirmed had to surrender their youth dedication certificate to the pastor.

2. Shrinkage of the Church

In the icy climate of the atheistic state and of the storms of anti-religious propaganda, interferences, terror, defamation, prohibitions, and limitations, the whole structure of the church changed both outwardly and inwardly. Most evident at first was the shrinkage of the church, a shrinkage in the number of her members, pastors, and church workers. What was dead in the "people's church" disappeared now, at least in part. Superintendent General Guenter Jacob indicated this fact when he stated: "We cannot speak of apostasy in the strict sense of the word but only of the radical unmasking of factors that have existed for a long time."

Jacob reported that there were totally socialized villages where pastors did not have much work to do. It became necessary to adjust to the conditions by changing the church organization. The lack of pastors made such a change necessary. It had grown worse since 1945. Only Thuringia was an exception. Here in the years 1945-49 11 candidates of theology were ordained; in 1950-54 there were 27; in 1955-59 there were 35; and, in 1961 alone, 45 young men were ordained. In spite of this growth in the supply, 51 of the 772 parishes were vacant, and 100 had to be entrusted to vicars. Also the synod of Silesia, in the German part of Silesia, was in a comparatively favorable position. In 1962 only nine of her 82 parishes were vacant. But in Brandenburg of the 1,000 parishes only about 800 had pastors, including 127 seminarians. The rest were served by lay readers from various occupations. For 416 positions in Mecklenburg only 361 pastors were available. The province of Saxony suffered the greatest shortage. In 1959 only 1,093 of its 1,740 parishes had pastors.

As a result of the growing shortage, preachers with no academic preparation and lectors became more and more important in the church. In the church province of Saxony the right to proclaim the Word in sermons was given to a large number of men and women, including some deacons and deaconesses. About 450 lectors were licensed to conduct reading services. In the Saxon Church 54 lay people were drafted for pastoral services. In Berlin-Brandenburg a great number of lectors were active.

The shortage of men for the ministry was very acute everywhere. The number of students of theology, which had been 930 in 1956, declined to 657 in 1960 and 585 in 1961. That meant that the eight churches in the DDR annually received 120 vicars, while they needed at least 300.

Also the image of the pastor and of his office had changed drastically. In an atheistic state the office of the ministry was thought of negatively. Pastors were considered secret enemies of the state who had to be watched. They were portrayed as comical figures who existed for the comfort of old people. They were publicly ridiculed and scoffed at because they believed in superstitions. They were insulted by mayors, by other officials of the state, by individuals, by party functionaries, by teachers, by salesmen in stores, and by everyone else. Their means of subsistence were more and more limited and their children were treated with contempt in the schools.

And yet the pastor, because he was not a Marxist or a functionary of the state, enjoyed the special trust of a great number of people. There were many "Nicodemus Christians" who came to the pastor by night, including some of those who were members of the People's Police and the Socialist Unity Party. And yet the pastor was very often ostracized. When he tried to visit people, they did not even open the door because they were afraid of repercussions.

The number of baptisms had decreased considerably. In 1950, 96 percent of the children of Protestant parents were baptized in the church of Thuringia, in 1958 only 75 percent. In 1960 it was reported that in big cities of the DDR the number of baptisms had decreased to 10 percent of the normal number. In 1962 only 10 percent of all children of Rostock were baptized. Mothers declared that they could find no one among their relatives and acquaintances to serve as sponsors.

Many parents felt that it was wrong to baptize children when they were later exposed to atheist propaganda and tempted to forsake their baptismal covenant. But after 1961 the number of baptisms was on the increase once more. In some congregations it even doubled. In many cases parents came to the pastor after their child had received the name-giving of the state. Many had recognized that they had been too fearful and had been intimidated by threats. It also happened that people who were active in various occupations and were married but had not been baptized or confirmed wanted to be received into the church. In some cases large groups of baptismal candidates participated in the baptismal instruction. But confirmation instruction continued to decline.

The young congregations had survived. In 1960 there were 650 circles with 7,500 members in Thuringia alone. There are no statistics from the other regional churches. In Saxony about 20,000 young people participated in retreats in 1960, but in 1962 Bishop Noth reported prohibitions and dissolution of the retreats and other forced measures. Church weddings passed through a similar crisis. One church rite that withstood all inroads by the state seemed to

be the church funeral. At last reports 80 to 90 percent of all Protestants were buried by the church.

In the midst of this dismal picture there were some areas of
growth. One of these areas was attendance at the Lord's Supper.
It increased in Mecklenburg between 1960 and 1961. In 1962 about
120,000, i.e. 8 percent of the nominal church members, took part.
In Thuringia it increased from 17 percent in 1950 to 26 percent in
1960. In Pomerania in 1959 over 12 percent of the Christians went
to Holy Communion; in Silesia 26 percent, in Anhalt 27 percent, in
Saxony 24 percent. Also the church province of Saxony reported
a constant increase. Another bright spot was the area of steward-
ship. In 1959 the four collections permitted in the province of Saxony netted 330,000 marks. In the following year, when only two
collections were permitted, giving increased to 358,000 marks and
in 1961 to 394,000 marks. The same trend was apparent in Mecklenburg and the Lutheran Church of Saxony. Many people gave
20, 50, and even 100 marks voluntarily in addition to their regular
church taxes. Thus the collection "Bread for the World" in 1959
collected over 1,400,000 marks in Saxony; in 1960, over 1,150,000
marks. In the three years from 1959 to 1961 the congregations in
the DDR collected almost 11,800,000 marks for "Bread for the
World," which was their relief program for others. Compared to
this, the state subsidies to the churches amounted to only 10,800,000
marks, which was about 114 marks, or about $30.00 per month, for
each congregation.

The charitable work of the church also continued to a considerable extent. In 1949 there were 700 charitable institutions with 34,923
beds. In 1962 there were 753 with 32,400 beds. The number of hospitals increased considerably. The decline in other types of institutions, especially educational institutions, which decreased from
168 in number to 148 and from 7,100 places to 4,300 places, was
due to direct interference by the state. Also the kindergartens and
the nurseries declined from 451 with 21,273 children in 1950 to 330
with 20,740 children 10 years later. They had very strong competition from the kindergartens of the factories and the communities.

The auxiliary organizations of the church continued to exist in
the DDR in the same way as in the Western Federal Republic.

There were women's organizations and men's organizations. There was the Gustavus Adolphus work and the Evangelical League. On Rogation Sunday 1962 over 25,000 women met for the Saxon women's convention. In Thuringia there were 700 women's auxiliaries and 200 circles of mothers. Even the brotherhoods were increasing. In Thuringia they increased from 200 in 1952 to 300 in 1959. Church music had experienced a healthy growth. The number of choirs in Thuringia also increased. There were now 14,500 choir members in Thuringia. Similar encouraging reports arrived from Saxony. There were a great number of Christian organizations for specific occupations, and some of the leading men in the professions were the most active members of the congregations. A constant dialogue was going on concerning faith and science and other themes.

The Evangelical Academies were able to make a definite contribution to the dialogue in the changed environment. The church publications, however, were very much limited. Their number was prescribed by the state and their contents were censored. They were not able to take any independent position concerning any social questions like the collectivization of agriculture, the socialization of the trades, the building of the wall, and so forth. Also the production of books was very much hamstrung by censorship and by lack of materials. The total number of copies printed in 1962 was 4,280,000, the average number was 11,889. But this included all the small publications which had only a few pages. The calendar *Sonne und Schild,* which had been published in an edition of several hundred thousand copies, was limited in 1958 to 100,000. The Bible society of the church had been able to publish one and one-half million Bibles from 1953 to 1958.

Concerning the resignations from the church there have been no statistics since 1961. According to scattered reports, the number of people leaving the church was lower in 1961 than in 1960. The record number of 1958 was not reached again. Besides the resignations from the church, there were a number who rejoined the church. Although their number was small, they were an indication of a trend. Thus, in Thuringia, between 1948 and 1960, 142,000 left and 22,600 rejoined the church. This indicated that even in an atheistic state there were thousands who decided to rejoin the church. Among those who left the church there were a great number of Nicodemus Christians who continued to support the church secretly and who sent their children to instruction in church kindergartens and confirmation classes.

Nevertheless, the majority of the church members had no close relationship with the church. And the church, on her part, for lack of personnel, was not in a position to approach the passive members.

The Catholic Church, on the whole, weathered the storms of time better than the Protestant Church since 1945. As a small church in the Diaspora she was not in the limelight of the attack. Her leadership cleverly avoided a head-on clash and showed great elasticity in facing the problem of youth dedications. There were practically no "progressive pastors" in the Catholic Church. There was no denying that in many places there had been a weakening of the consciences and that there was a kind of spiritual schizophrenia, but it was impressive to see how faithful the people were to the Catholic Church. The number of priests and members of the orders was sufficient and the diocese which had the strongest position in the number of priests in all of Germany was Meissen in the DDR.

3. A New Beginning

Seen from the outside, the road of the church since 1945 was a road of breakdowns, defeats, and losses.

There were many people in the SED who hoped that the church would die. They were not different from those in other Communist countries. The secretary of the central committee of the SED, Albert Norden, declared before the elections on November 16, 1958, that at least 98 percent of the members of the congregations were merely nominal members of the church. He said: "They really belong to us. All that is necessary is to give them a push in order to entice them to separate themselves externally from the church. As far as the other two percent are concerned we have to deal with them more harshly." He said that there was a last remnant of the church members who were very hard to win. Said he: "I am speaking of the 0.019 percent of our population, the pastors. As you know, they are beyond help. But why should we worry about these museum figures? We don't care at all whether they go to the elections or not. They are played out completely." This speech by Norden was received with tumultuous applause, but his diagnosis was completely wrong. The church had been taken out of mothballs. She was getting new and firm contours. In spite of everything, the truth of Christ had not been perverted and the church had not been intimidated.

One of the serious dangers for the Christians in the DDR was resignation to fate. Every disappointed hope for reunion with the brethren in the West led to resignation. The building of the wall on August 13, 1961, increased despair among many people inside and outside the church.

"The church formerly was used to living in the drawing room of society. Now she suddenly finds herself outside the door. There is still the door into the ghetto, where she can exist isolated . . . . But a church that enters through this door commits suicide."

The Bischofswerder Circle, a group of dedicated Christians, in June 1959, published theses on the theme "The Christian in our State" in which it attacked the withdrawal into false inwardness and churchly separation. It demanded that a pastor should not preach generalities, but that he is in duty bound to give help and guidance to his congregation. The director of the Seminary in Naumburg, Johannes Hamel, one of the most dedicated theologians in the DDR, did not tire of calling Christians out of their timidity and their resignation.

There is a certain conservative Christianity. Its representatives are in many cases the trunk of the Christian tree. They are among the regular members who attend services. They observe Christian customs and Christian family life. They work in Christian societies, and they are extremely important for the Christian congregation. But they have often lost a living contact with the spirit of their environment. They do not have the ability to think the problems through. They are not tempted by doubts. They are opposed to all criticism of the Bible and call it the fruit of apostasy. From the first to the last word they consider the Bible God's revelation. When they hear about contradictions between the Bible and science, they always state that not science but the Bible is correct. Their point of view must be respected. Their firm faith can even be envied. They are powerful pillars of the church. But the disciples of dialectic materialism enjoy very much to debunk some of the views of the conservatives. They brag about the results of scientific investigation and they try to glory in the armaments which they have received through scientific enlightenment. They laugh and smile because of the cheap victory of Sputnik which had found an empty sky and no angels and no throne of God and no three-story structure of the world.

In order to counteract the accusation of superstition, it is necessary for the church to think critically. It is necessary for her to ask what the essential message of the Bible is and to understand the dimension of depth and the transcendental truths of the accounts that are found in the Bible, to bring out the great facts of the history of salvation, and to make them available to the 20th century.

This critical work sometimes divides the church. It comes into conflict with the conservative Christians. These conflicts have to be borne. Superintendent General Guenter Jacob, at a time when the controversy between Communism and Christianity was especially heated, gave three reports on the origin of life, in which he treated the problem arising from the biblical story of creation and the theories arising from the interpretation of science concerning the origin of the cosmos and of life. The speeches were published in *Potsdamer Kirche* and caused a lively discussion in the DDR. The state forbade the publication of the brochure. It was published in the West, but read in the DDR by numerous people, especially young people. It was considered a great help for their own clarification and for discussions with representatives of dialectic materialism. But conservative Christians took exception because Jacob had not defended the biblical story of creation in its literalness, and they felt that their faith was threatened if they sacrificed the literal interpretation of Scripture. The leader of the conservatives was the Brandenburg pastor, Dr. Theophil Pfluecke, who in a pamphlet, *The Church and the Monkeys,* wrote a passionate but fruitless defense of the fundamentalist position against Dr. Guenter Jacob. The road which the church has to travel in this matter is clear. She must not merely proclaim an inherited doctrine but must also discover new ways of interpreting it. She must not merely collect the remnant in the house of God—or as Bishop Jaenicke stated, "she must not be a small garden lying idly between chimneys"—but she must go to man outside in the world and must work among those who seek and those who doubt and prepare for them the road for the truth of Christ. Dr. Jacob declared that cells of such Christians were forming everywhere. He stated: "We do not think of the circle of those who are still faithful to the church, nor of the small band of sincere people with churchly loyalty. Neither do we mean conventicles of introverts who turn away in pietistic inwardness from the evil, godless world. We mean cells of Christians who are wide open, who are freed from romantic reminiscences and do not want to restore former models, who realize on the basis of biblical truth that the church exists in the Diaspora. The church is sent among the atheists and the non-Christians. She must meet them and engage them in dialogue."

A further danger would arise for the church if she surrendered to anti-Communism. The temptation is very great since the Communistic ideology is basically anti-religious. It is irreconcilable in its class struggle; it proclaims a one-sided justice, an ethics of class; it is a merciless enemy and killer of whole social groups. It has caused such mass sufferings and killings as never have been seen in history before.

These problems all exist. But they are not solved by calling Communism the incarnation of the devil. At least the church cannot do it and the Christian cannot do it. One cannot drive out the devil with Beelzebub. If she did, the Christian church would fight an ideology by surrendering to an anti-ideology. He who joins an anti-ideology is engaging in black-and-white painting. He is countering the Communist dualism, capitalist exploitation versus the exploited proletariat, with an anti-Communist dualism, middle-class liberal democracy versus Red dictatorship. He is putting Communism into the defendant's dock of history, calling it the enemy of the people and proclaiming the policy of permanent distrust of the armed fist and of a strategy of total destruction.

The church in the East and in the West can never follow such a course. She can neither be completely anti-Communist nor completely pro-Communist. If she could, she would pervert the church into a propaganda instrument for some ideology or order of society and would place the proclamation of the Gospel in the service of secular interests. The church in the West has the freedom to say that there are many weaknesses in either system. She can recognize that in the West, state and society are constructed on the basis of the greatest possible freedom; and she must also admit that in the East socialism has created some good things. But she should never use the Word of God in order to call one system demonic and the other sacred. She would thus disregard the critical function of the Word of God. The Word of God is a two-edged sword and cannot be identified with any human order. The Word of God calls all human beings from their lost estate. If this Word experiences rejection—either by atheism, indifference, or hypocrisy —Christ must not be betrayed. But it is also wrong to use words from God's messengers for the propagation of an anti-Communist crusade. The church must not engage in ideologies and anti-ideologies. If she followed this human inclination, she would give up her real commission. She would no longer be the church of Christ.

The synod of Pomerania, meeting in November 1961, discussed the theme of brotherliness and called upon the congregations to consider that Christ did not refuse to be man's brother. Therefore the Christians should be brothers even to those who are outside the church. They should reject hatred and refuse to act as spies. They should treat their brother-atheists in a Christian way. The guidelines in *The Christian in the DDR,* prepared by the Lutheran Bishops' Conference on November 3, 1960, contained the same basic ideas. The Bischofswerder Circle said similar things: "The Christian congregation is a wanderer in the world, but it does not surrender to the world. It must neither withdraw from nor identify itself with society. It must neither undermine nor canonize society."

The Christian must be free from anti-Communist resentment, but he must also be free from trying to ingratiate himself with the representatives of the Communist state. When the Communist state suppresses the church and outlaws her, the Christian must not see merely human malice in this action, but also a permissiveness on the part of God. God is visiting his church and is using Communism as his instrument in order to tear down hollow Christian façades. If the church accepts this visitation as a sign of the love of God, then she can continue her way in confidence and without bitterness. This freedom should become apparent in the dialogue with the Communists.

The Bischofswerder Circle stated: "When we meet the representatives of the state we must not forget that they are our higher powers to whom we owe respect in our actions and in our speech. We are among the few who as citizens do not simply say the expected *Yes* to all political questions. We should make use of the opportunity to express our opinions sincerely and publicly, but we should never look upon our officials as our enemies. We should always remember that Jesus Christ has also come to them."

In 1960 Johannes Hamel said that Christians must get used to the idea that their number is shrinking and that they are becoming a congregation of volunteers. Seen externally, the church is weak. The congregations are very often small groups in a sea of unbelief. The SED propagandist Norden considered it only a matter of time before the church would be finished. But the believing Christian looks upon these matters differently. Superintendent Albrecht Schoenherr said: "He who can think only in terms of sociology will be afraid that the church will starve and die. But he who believes . . . that the church is the actual reality will recognize in this change that the church has a great chance to come closer to her Lord. The gentle, powerless Lord is the one who is with his congregation. He is the one who bears his own, because he is borne by the Father in whom he trusts. . . ."

This is the mission of the congregation. It must not only be interested in preserving the *status quo* or to collect the nucleus of believers, but it has to fulfill its mission. The congregations must be the salt of the earth, the light of the world, the city on the mountain. Matt. 5:16 says: "Let your light so shine before men, that they may see your good works and give glory to your Father who is in heaven."

Which roads are being traveled to carry out this mission? There is first of all the attempt to reform the divine service. The concern of these attempts is that the service should not be merely a performance by the pastor, but the affair of the whole congregation. The discovery was made that there are many talents in the congregation, especially since the great lack of pastors has made it necessary to rely more and more on the help of lay people.

When a congregation which has become spiritually mature in such a way is confronted by the problem of a vacancy because there are not enough pastors it will always be able to find members who will conduct reading services, who can teach religion classes and who can do administrative work. Under such circumstances one pastor in a district can possibly train more and more helpers in the congregation.

To proceed a step farther: The traditional center and focus of the congregation is the church. But a small congregation that is spiritually tempted and has become a Diaspora congregation needs a different center. Superintendent General Dr. Guenter Jacob suggested at a meeting of Protestant architects in Hamburg in 1961 that a building for the ecclesia should be developed, a building in the center of which there is room for the divine services, but the size of which is determined by those who regularly attend services. There should also be rooms for common meals, for work, for dialogue, for study, and for social activities of the *familia Dei*.

The instruction of Christians is one of the most important tasks of the congregation. At the East Berlin regional synod in February 1963, the church leadership reported that while the older youth were rarely ready to come to youth meetings, there were many more participants than available room. There were all kinds of evangelism activities where the same scarcity of space prevailed. There were many young people who were willing to practice the community of life and to exchange experiences. Bishop Noth stated before the Saxon synod that there were more people than they supposed who were willing to receive help for Christian living. They needed instruction. There had to be evenings of preparation, Bible classes in the homes, weekend retreats, and other activities. There were many reports from cities where this work was done by the men and women of the church.

The smaller circle of conscious Christians in the active congregations has the duty constantly to keep in mind the large number of members who belong to the church but are indifferent. Visitations have gained greater and greater importance in the DDR. In the province of Saxony women go from house to house by twos to visit old and young people. This type of visitation is concerned with the individual. It is not work among the masses. In a church in the Diaspora where Christians are a minority the Christians must not be concerned about merely reaching large numbers of people.

The accommodation to the changes is also seen in the charitable work of the church, e.g. in the Trailer Mission of the Gossner Mission Society. In places where there is no church the trailer is parked and the two missionaries who usually occupy the trailer invite the people to Bible classes and to services. They advise people and even help with the harvest. Worker pastors have been sent to the collective farms and have continued to work there in spite of the threats by the state security service. They have been seen instructing children and driving tractors. This team work has become a very prominent feature of the work of the church in the DDR.

The work of evangelism is flourishing in all the churches. This is also connected with intensive visitation activities. Evangelism among children is increasing. In 1962 there were seven missionary weeks in Thuringia alone, and in many congregations there were Bible weeks. There were even play productions by the Leipzig Play Circle of the Christian Church. In 1960 these plays were performed in 340 presentations to 100,000 people. This large attendance shows that even today it is possible to reach large numbers of people.

This account has demonstrated that many things are happening in the churches of the DDR. The church has had difficult years. There have been fights and defeats, hopes have been squashed. The church has been cut off by the wall of 1961, and some congregations were threatened with spiritual death. Others were cruelly persecuted. But the church has been assigned her field of work by God and has taken her mission seriously. Many of the things which are new are merely in the beginning stage. But there are already fruits. The church is poor and her work is often being done under disheartening conditions. But she also experiences joy in these tribulations. A pastor in the DDR wrote to a pastor in the Federal Republic: "Sometimes I think how much easier it is for you, and yet I wouldn't want to exchange with you. Pastors in the DDR are not allowed to flee, and that is very hard, but it is also good and salutary. What would the people think of us? We have joys here of which you have no idea. . . . In spite of all limitations, we are still able to live and to work, and this alone appears to me a miracle. Again and again there are examples of a rare spirit of sacrifice, and thus in spite of everything we have our great and small joys."

CHAPTER SIX

YUGOSLAVIA

A. RELIGIOUS POLICY OF THE STATE

Yugoslavia is a young state and a state of many nationalities. Its center is the former Kingdom of Serbia. In the peace treaty of St. Germain of 1919 and of Trianon of 1920 the following territories of the former Hapsburg Empire were united with it: parts of Carinthia, southern Styria, Croatia, Slovenia, Bosnia with Herzegovina and two Hungarian countries. The Kingdom of the Serbs, Croats, and Slovenes was renamed Yugoslavia in 1929. According to the census of March 31, 1953, the 16,927,000 inhabitants included 7 million Serbs, almost 4 million Croats, 1.5 million Slovenes, 2.8 million Bosnians, and in addition Macedonians, Scipetarians, Hungarians, Montenegrians, Germans, and Romanians. According to their religious affiliation, 7 million (41.5%) were Orthodox, 5.4 million (31.8%) were Catholics, 2.1 million (12.3%) were Moslems, 150,000 (0.1%) were Protestants, 200,000 (0.2%) belonged to different sects, and 2.1 million (2.3%) were listed as being without religious affiliation. The Serbs are Orthodox, the Croats and the Slovenes are Catholics. Since 1920 the Orthodox Church has been united under the Metropolitan of Belgrade with the title of Patriarch. The Catholic Church is divided into four archdioceses and 15 dioceses.

The union of these numerous territories and nationalities with Serbia after the First World War was a reward to the victorious Serbs. Since they were the rulers of their enlarged state, they caused a constant friction among the nationalities, especially a contest between Serbs and Croats, which was deepened by the difference in religious loyalty between the various nationalities. While the Serbian part of the population is oriented toward the Slavonic East, the Croats and the Slovenes are looking to the Western tradition. Since the attack by the Turks in the Middle Ages they feel that they are the outpost of the Catholic Church in the East and must preserve Christendom before the walls. After 1918 they fought for their full autonomy. Their goal was attained after the occupation of Yugoslavia by the Axis powers in 1941 when an Independent State of Croatia was formed under the leadership of the *Ustasha* movement of Ante Pavelic, which cooperated closely with the Axis powers. The hatred which had accumulated against the Serbs led to many acts of terror. It even influenced the church. There were forced rebaptisms and a mass slaughter of the population. The Yugoslav Foreign Minister, Kardelj, on December 18, 1952, reported to the Foreign Policies Committee of the People's Parliament that the *Ustasha* bands had destroyed 229 Orthodox churches in Croatia, had killed 128 Orthodox priests, and had murdered hundreds of thousands of Orthodox faithful. He told of 900 Orthodox believers who had been ordered to come to a church at Glina for the purpose of rebaptism and had been killed and burned with the church. Furthermore, he stated that 20,000 Jews had been killed by the Croats.

In such actions even Catholic Croat clergymen were involved. Did they act on orders from above? The Communist government claimed that they did and the Archbishop of Agram, Aloysius Stepinac (b. 1898), was made responsible for the forced conversions and the acts of terror. In his speech Kardelj called him "a sinister and inhuman personality who is responsible morally and actually for the killing and the extermination of the Pravo-Slavic and the Jewish population in the Quisling state of Pavelic." But this accusation was wrong. Certainly Stepinac, like all Croats, was for the independence of his country. When Pavelic took over the power, Stepinac wrote in a letter to his clergy: "Be ready for my appeal for increased activity for the preservation and development of the independent state of Croatia. Show it today, dear fellow citizens, fulfill your duty toward the young Croat state." In a letter which he sent on May 18, 1943, to Pope Pius XII he placed the church and the state of Croatia on the same level: "The young Croatian state shows by its actions at every opportunity that it wants to remain true to its glorious Catholic traditions and wants to bring to the Catholic Church in this corner of the world a better and greater respect. In case of its breakdown or unhappy end not only the 240,000 rebaptized Serbian Pravo-Slavs but also the whole Catholic population with all their churches and monasteries would be destroyed."

But such statements do not prove that Stepinac was responsible for the terror against the Orthodox Serbs and had even condoned it. On the contrary, the church demanded again and again that the Croat regime should stop the persecution of the Serbian people and rejected especially the forced conversion of the Orthodox to the Catholic Church. In view of the accusations that had been leveled against Stepinac, Pius XII on October 16, 1946, quoted a note written by the Vatican Secretary of State to the Yugoslav embassy at the Holy See on January 5, 1942, in which the Secretary stated that the Catholic Church would receive adults only through voluntary conversion. "Therefore," he said, "the fact that a great number of dissidents are being received into the Catholic Church causes a great deal of unrest in the Croat episcopate." Pius thought that it was his duty to remind the ecclesiastical officers that the return of the dissidents should take place in full freedom. An episcopal committee was founded which had to see to it that the conversion was the fruit of a genuine conviction and not of force. But these statements of the Pope could not quiet the storm of the passions which arose after the revolution of November 29, 1945, when the Federal People's Republic of Yugoslavia was established under Communist leadership. The hatred that had been generated by the *Ustasha* now backfired and hurt the Catholic Church. This was the primary reason for the severe persecution of the Catholics.

Another element which determined the religious policy of the state was the Communist ideology. The Yugoslav Communist Party is based on dialectic materialism, and in the statutes which were discussed at the Communist Party convention of the fall 1952 it was stated: "Membership in the Party is irreconcilable with a confession of faith or the exercise of religion." The battle against religion was carried on especially in the fields of propaganda and of youth education. Also the churches had to suffer all kinds of administrative interferences and hindrances. After a period of legal and economic disturbances a *modus vivendi* was arrived at in 1950 and 1951. On the occasion of the announcement of the New Economic Plan in September 1951 Marshal Tito declared that he wished for the best possible relationship with the churches of the country. Yugoslavia, he said, was not among the nations that believed that they could get rid of religion by way of decrees. He had learned a great deal from the mistakes of the Russian revolution and did not want to repeat them. At the Party meeting of the Slovenian Communist Party in June 1954 Edward Kardelj objected to the banishment of Christians from public life. He said that the Communists must find a way "to use honest people, even if they are religious, in the system of social reconstruction and must permit them to work on an equal basis in the civil administration for the social reconstruction of the country." He stated that religion should be taken out of politics and should be removed from the influence of the clergy so that it would become the private affair of the individual outside of his socialist activity. A member of the Communist Party should not be a Christian, but religion should not be eradicated over night.

The Constitution of December 1945, stipulated: "All citizens have the same rights without regard to nationality, race, and religious confession. Every action by which citizens receive special privileges or are limited in their rights on the basis of their national and racial differences and on the basis of religious hatred and differences of faith is in contradiction to the constitution and will be punished. . . . Citizens are guaranteed freedom of conscience and freedom of religion. . . . The church is separated from the state. Religious associations have the freedom to administer their own denominational affairs and to hold religious celebrations. Church and school are separated."

According to the *Law on Soil Reform and Colonization* of the year 1945 the authorities of religious communions were given 10 hectares of cultivated soil and 10 hectares of uncultivated soil, and to churches with cultural significance 30 hectares of cultivated soil and 30 hectares of forest were assigned. According to the law of 1951, clergymen of religious associations could be insured by social security if the leadership of the religious association or the association of the clergymen entered into an agreement with the federal administration of social security. Clergymen had the right to organize their own clergy associations in order to foster their professional interests.

A basic regulation of the relationship between church and state was given in the *Law Concerning the Legal Position of Religious Associations* of May 27, 1953. In its general part it stated that citizens are guaranteed freedom of conscience and of religion. In paragraph 1 it stated: "They may belong to any religious faith, to any religious association, or to none. Religious confession is a private concern for the citizens of the state." Paragraph 2 stated: "They may organize religious associations unhampered. All religious associations are enjoying the same rights and all religious associations have the same legal position. The activities of the religious associations must be in accordance with the constitution and the law." According to Paragraph 3 the churches are "free to exercise their pastoral activity and to hold religious services. They are also permitted to publish and disseminate religious printed materials according to the general laws concerning the press." Paragraph 4 repeated the statement in the constitution that school and church were separate. Religious instruction in church buildings was permitted and religious organizations could organize and conduct intermediate and high schools, for the purpose of preparing future clergymen. Important was Paragraph 5 which stated: "The abuse of religious exercises, of religious instruction, and of the religious press, of divine services and other forms of the expression of religious feelings, for political purposes is forbidden. It is also forbidden to create religious intolerance, hatred, and discord. . . . It is forbidden to interfere in religious meetings, in religious instruction, services, and other forms of religious expression." Paragraph 6 promised freedom of faith. It stated: "Nobody can be forced in any form to become a member of a religious community and to abstain from religious expressions. . . . Nobody can be forced in any form to participate in religious services, processions, and other expressions of religious faith. . . . No one can forbid citizens the participation in divine services and other expressions of religious faith. . . . No one can keep a member of a religious organization from exercising the rights that have been guaranteed to him by the constitution and the laws." Equality before the law was guaranteed in Paragraph 7: "In his legal rights no citizen can be discriminated against on the basis of his religious convictions. Religious organizations, their clergy and their members, shall enjoy no privileges, other advantages, or special protection. Membership in a religious association frees no one from the general duties of citizenship." According to Paragraph 8 religious organizations were considered legal persons with civil rights. According to Paragraph 9 clergymen had the right to organize their own professional associations. According to Paragraph 10 the decisions of the religious regulations in matters of dispute in marriage and other disciplinary matters had no legal force outside of the churches. Paragraph 11 stated: "The Executive Committee of the Federation and the executive committees of the various republics may give material aid to religious organizations. They may also determine the purposes for which this help or part of this help must be used. . . . Religious organizations have the right to use this material aid. If the aid is given for a definite purpose, then the religious organization can be required to give an account of the use of this aid." According to Paragraph 12 no one could be forced to give or hindered from giving contributions for religious purposes. The collection of such contributions was free within the church, but outside the church it needed state permission. Clergymen could be reimbursed for the exercise of functions and for other purposes.

A further group of legal stipulations dealt with the exercise of religious rites. According to Paragraph 13 divine services could be held in churches and also in court yards, halls, cemeteries, and other public places which were connected with churches and mosques. However, the organization of processions and other religious rites outside of these areas needed a permit from the officials, if these rites were not religious rites conducted with family celebrations, marriages, and funerals. If there were reasons to protect the health of the people and public order, then religious meetings could be forbidden. Baptisms, according to Paragraph 14, could be administered at the request of one parent or of the guardian. If the baptismal candidate was above 10 years of age, he was to give his own consent. According to Paragraph 15 marriage could be solemnized only after the state had registered the marriage, and baptism could take place only after the birth had been registered by the state. Inmates of hospitals, old folks homes, and dormitories, according to Paragraph 16, could engage in religious exercises within the legal framework of the home where they were living; and clergymen were permitted to visit them if they so desired. Concerning religious instruction, the law stated in Paragraph 18: "Religious associations may conduct schools for the training of their clergy. They are responsible for the program and the curriculum and are free in the selection of the teachers. The state merely exercises the general supervision over the work of the religious schools." In Paragraph 19 attendance at religious instruction was forbidden during school hours. As far as participation in religious instruction was concerned, both parents or the guardian and also the student himself were to give consent. According to Paragraph 20, those who were students at schools for the training of clergymen had the same rights which other people attending schools enjoyed. In the final paragraph, Paragraph 22, it stated that abuse of religious instruction was a criminal act in which case the court could declare the closing of the religious school for a period of from one to 10 years.

It is significant in this law that it expressly forbade any interference with religious life and that it contained no indication concerning the political, ideological basis of the state. The first draft had stated: "That, for the guarantee of freedom of conscience, the instruction in the schools shall be secular and shall be based exclusively on the freedom of the spirit and the attainments of science." The final text merely stated that "the school is separated from the church." In spite of this, the law gave to the state a far-reaching control of church activities and possibly also the means of hampering them. Such a provision was made in Paragraphs 2 and 5. On the other hand, the state did not demand that church offices should be occupied only after previous consent by the state. Also there was no oath of loyalty demanded of church officers. Compared with the religious laws of other Communist states, the Yugoslav law showed liberal tendencies. A state office for the relationship of the state to the religious associations was established. It was called the Federal Commission for Religious Questions, and its chief officer had the rank of minister. Its tasks were as follows: to examine the affairs that touch upon the relationship between the state and the religious organizations, to give opinions in concrete questions, to carry on supervision and to see to it that the stipulations of the laws were observed and to evaluate proposals for the subsidies to religious organizations

B. THE ORTHODOX CHURCH

The position of the Orthodox Church to the state was influenced in two ways. On the one hand, Orthodoxy was opposed to Communist ideology and could not deny its former close relationship with the Yugoslav royal house since Orthodoxy had been the state religion of Serbia until 1918. On the other hand, the church had been closely allied with the people through ancient and most recent history. She had done a great deal in the battle of liberation from the Turks and for the preservation of the language and the national civilization of the Serbs. But last of all, the *Ustasha* mass murders of the Orthodox had created new bridges to the new regime. Many Orthodox clergymen had been active as partisans, and the Orthodox Church had never collaborated with the Axis powers. Among the martyrs of the *Ustasha* were three bishops and 200 clergymen. The Germans too had taken a great number of Orthodox clergymen as hostages and some of them had died in concentration camps.

During the war 665 churches, 72 chapels, and 37 monasteries had been either partially or completely destroyed. Patriarch Gabriel had left the country during the occupation. In the fall of 1946 he returned to his homeland. But as early as Easter of 1946 five members of the Holy Synod had protested in a pastoral letter against the ecclesiastical policies of the state. They had complained that a complete separation of church and state had been carried out and that religious instruction had been removed from the schools, that the state was recognizing only civil marriages, that anti-religious propaganda was being carried on, and that the movement of the godless was supported by the state. In October 1946 there were sharp attacks against the church in the press. The paper *Politika* declared: "The episcopal synod of the Serbian Church is to be numbered among the enemies of the people and of the new Yugoslav state." On March 1, 1948, Bishop Varnava Jastik of Serajewo was condemned to 11 years in prison because he had carried on treasonable activities against the laws of the state and the military security with the intention of breaking up the unity of the Yugoslav people and of creating a favorable climate for the intervention of the imperialists. In order to strengthen the influence of the state in the church and at the same time to create a counterweight against the hierarchy and the clergy, an orthodox peace association was founded in 1949, which published its own magazine, *Vesnik* ("Messenger"), and was financially subsidized by the state. The patriarch did not recognize this association. An improvement in church-state relations, however, took place when the patriarch died in May 1950. His successor would have been Metropolitan Joseph of Skopje, who had administered the church during the war years while the patriarch was abroad. But since the state was afraid that he would take the same position as Gabriel, he was eliminated. On June 10, 1950, the 73 electors were scheduled to meet at the Cathedral of Belgrade to elect the new patriarch. However, the lay people were not permitted to participate so that only 27 electors were present, and the election was made impossible. Joseph was arrested; and under the accusation that he had participated in a monarchical resistance movement, he was sent to an isolated monastery. Thus the way was cleared for the candidate of the association of progressive priests, Vikentij Prodanovic, Bishop of Strumica. On July 1 he was elected patriarch with a majority of 33 votes against 28. Immediately after his election he declared to the president of parliament his readiness in the future to coordinate the interests of the church with the interests of the state.

In this endeavor he succeeded, and the relationship between state and church became free from tension. The patriarch declared to the German journalist, H. A. Fischer: "We had to get used to each other slowly." He still complained about the insufficient opportunities for religious instruction. The fact that the Communist program was atheistic he did not consider too much of a hindrance, for the masses of the people were with the church now as before. He stated that many members of the Party remained members of the congregations. In the fall of 1950 the oldest theological seminary of Serbia and the palace in Srenski Karlovci, which was the see of the patriarch, were returned to him. The bishop of Serajewo was released from prison in August 1951. In 1952 the Orthodox theological faculty in Belgrade was separated from the university and reorganized into a theological academy. In addition to this the church established two seminaries for priests.

In July 1954 Metropolitan Arsenije of Montenegro was accused of crimes against the people and the state with the aim of a *coup d'état*, of dissemination of religious hatred and intolerance as well as of insulting the members of the highest offices of the state. He was condemned to 11 years in prison. As one of the reasons for his sentence his protest in the Western newspapers against the progressive priests' association was given. The help which members of this association received from the state was extended to all church officers on the basis of an agreement which the patriarch concluded with the government in June 1958. Priests, monks, and employees of the church received free medical care and were accepted in the pension plan. Family members of deceased clergymen were also given financial support.

In the year 1958 Patriarch Vikentij Prodanovic died. His successor was German Djoric, born 1899. When he was enthroned at Pec, numerous high representatives of the state participated in the solemnities; and in recognition of his work "for the deepening of peaceful cooperation and friendly relationship between Yugoslavia and other countries," the government bestowed upon him the order of the Yugoslav Banner, First Class. The Minister of Religious Affairs, Dobriovoje Rodosavljevic, said in his speech that a number of important questions between church and state had been solved and that in the future the church could count on the help and cooperation of the state.

Financially the church was quite limited. As a result of the confiscation of her assets and her properties, especially her real estate, she had become quite poor. Her income was derived from perquisites for official acts and from her own candle factory. In the beginning of 1959 Patriarch German Djoric asked the faithful to buy their candles only in the churches. He hoped that by building up this business he would slowly be able to get along without state subsidies. Larger incomes from the sale of candles would make it possible for the patriarch to pay priests those salaries which had been paid by the state until now. According to the census of 1961 the patriarchate of the Serbian Orthodox Church comprised 19 bishops (in 1939 there had been 30 metropolitans and bishops), 1,400 priests (2,734), 310 monks (540), and 385 nuns (416). In addition, there were 300 clergymen active in the central and diocesan administration of the church.

C. THE ROMAN CATHOLIC CHURCH

Its involvement in the battle of the nationalities caused a great blood-letting for the Roman Catholic Church. A pastoral letter of the Yugoslav bishops of September 20, 1945, listed 243 priests killed, while 169 were in concentration camps and 89 were missing. According to a survey made by the Roman Magazine *La Civilita Cattolica* at the end of 1946, of the 1,916 parishes which existed in Yugoslavia in 1939 only 400 were left. Hundreds of priests had fled to foreign countries, but the Archbishop of Agram, Dr. Stepinac, refused to flee. He remained and surrendered to his enemies. After a search of his home at the beginning of 1946, he was arrested on September 19, 1946. The Supreme Croat People's Court accused him of having helped the remnants of fascism and of the war criminals after the liberation of the country and of having abused religious ceremonies for political demonstrations for Pavelic and the *Ustasha* organization. It stated that the archdiocesan see of Agram was a center of the conspiracy against the new Yugoslavia and had been in contact with terroristic organizations in foreign countries. Finally Stepinac was accused of forced conversions among Serbs living in Croatia, Bosnia, and Herzegovina. Stepinac exhibited a dignified behavior against these accusations. On October 11, 1946, when the public trial took place, he declared in his speech of defense: "Before God, before the nation, before the members of the diplomatic corps who are present here, before the representatives of the foreign press, and before the public, I declare that I am completely innocent and that history will judge my actions justly. I was neither a favorite of the Germans nor of the *Ustasha*. I was not a member of the *Ustasha*, and I have never sworn an oath to them as your functionaries have done who are sitting here in front of me as my judges. Many of you may think that we are afraid of them. They should know that whatever may happen we shall remain at our place with a clear mind and a clear conscience. . . . If we have to die, then we shall die in the fulfillment of our duty. Concerning all the acts of terror which are imputed to me, you have no proof, and nobody will believe you. I would like to state once more that 270 Catholic priests were murdered by the partisans, and that the people will never forget it."

The court condemned him to 16 years in prison, stating that he had encouraged the organization of terror groups and had glorified the *Ustasha* in the Catholic press and in pastoral letters. Stepinac refused to ask for a retrial. He said: "I do not ask for mercy." He was taken to the prison at Lepoglava. But the archbishop in prison was a greater embarrassment to the government than the free archbishop had ever been. He was considered a martyr by the Catholics. Rome excommunicated everyone who had been involved in the trial against him. In the Western world there was as much protest against this verdict as there had been in the case of the trial of Mindszenty. The government was unconcerned as long as it remained a member of the Communist bloc. But in 1948 when it withdrew from *Cominform* after violent disagreement and became dependent on the political and material help of the Western powers, the imprisonment of the archbishop was an increasing embarrassment. As early as June 1947 the government offered him freedom if he would ask for a pardon and would promise to go to a foreign country after his release. He refused. In the summer of 1949 Tito discussed these matters with eight Catholic dignitaries and also mentioned his desire to regulate his differences with the Vatican.

In November 1949 Tito declared to five Americans that he did not intend to release Stepinac, for he had done great harm to the state; but he would be willing to expel him. He would not agree to a restoration of Stepinac as had been demanded by the Vatican. In

October 1950 there were new indications that Yugoslavia was ready to release the archbishop if the Vatican would recall him from Yugoslavia. But the Vatican answered that it was refusing the recall of Stepinac if it meant the purchase of his freedom. On June 2, 1951, the government officially communicated to the Vatican that it was ready to reduce the prison term for Stepinac if he would leave the country immediately. On July 2 the Vatican embassy answered that the Holy See had rejected this offer. The *Osservatore Romano* remarked that the Holy See had been informed that the archbishop wanted to remain near his spiritual children because he knew that he was innocent. It stated: "The Holy See can only respect his feelings and does not intend to force him to go into exile which would be contrary to the position which Archbishop Stepinac considers a matter of conscience." In spite of it Tito was forced to prepare an emergency solution. He did this primarily for reasons of foreign policy. The Catholics in the USA had carried on a propaganda campaign without equal for Archbishop Stepinac and had done everything to keep his name in the news. The American government had given Tito large subsidies. It had done so without attaching specific conditions to them concerning the release of Stepinac. However, the Yugoslav embassy in Washington must have informed Tito that it would not be possible in the long run to get along without a concession on his part. On December 5, 1951, Tito announced: "The former Archbishop of the Catholic Church in Yugoslavia, Aloysius Stepinac, is conditionally released." Stepinac was taken to the parsonage of his native village, Krasic, near Agram on the condition that he would carry out the duties of a village priest and would not continue his official functions. But on the day of his release he declared to journalists that he was the Archbishop of Agram as before, that he would at any time accept the orders of the Holy See, but that he would not resign at the command of the government. The essential questions to be settled between church and state had not been solved at all with this minor improvement in the situation. He said: "I shall never leave Yugoslavia unless I am forced to do so. I shall remain here until the Holy Father decides differently." The village and the parsonage were placed under strictest surveillance. In April 1952 the archbishop said to a Belgian journalist: "My freedom is only a farce. I cannot even leave this house to celebrate Holy Mass." Every contact with foreign countries was forbidden. His letters were censored. Since he received numerous visitors, the government commanded that he should not discuss political questions with journalists and should stop preaching in the village church. He declared his readiness to follow the first order, but he refused to stop preaching.

In all these years since 1945 the Catholic Church has been exposed to many harsh suppressions. The clergy was deprived of its means of sustenance, and the charitable activities of the church were forbidden. The Catholic press, with the exception of a few publications, was destroyed. Catholic organizations were prohibited, and numerous Catholic schools were closed and were taken over by the state. The monasteries, which were formerly rich in property and influence, were hit hard by the soil reform. According to Catholic reports, in Croatia, alone, 111 Catholic kindergartens, 73 elementary, 31 vocational, and 21 intermediate schools and two pedagogical institutes were confiscated. These were valued at 3,000,000,000 dinars. Besides 15 of the 27 seminaries were closed, and 11 Catholic printeries were confiscated; 40 book depositories and 80 Catholic newspapers and magazines were put out of action. In Croatia sermons were subjected to preliminary censorship. From now on trips by bishops were made subject to government permission. Processions and pilgrimages were forbidden. Many members of the orders were driven from their houses and places of work, and their contributions were heavily taxed. The clergy were ordered to charge high fees for the administration of the sacraments; 3,000 dinars for baptism; 4,000 for confirmation; 6,000 for church weddings. The amounts had to be surrendered to the civil authorities. Sacramental actions were supposed to be made impossible through these high fees levied on the faithful. Numerous priests were arrested. In the concentration camp Stara Gradiska there were 80 priests in 1948. They were forced to do the most humiliating labors. They had to clean toilets with their bare hands. Every morning they had to stand in front of the camp commander to hear a speech about godlessness. Acts of terror were not rare. The journalist Alfred Joachim Fischer in *Neue Zeitung,* Nov. 15, 1951, told about the faithfulness of the people to their church. The majority of parents insisted on religious instruction for their children. Churches were overcrowded. Abbots assured Fischer that their greatest problem was to make a selection among the great numbers of applicants for the priesthood. Fischer believed that he noticed some letting up in the battle against religion. The number of imprisoned clergymen had decreased to about 100. Anti-church demonstrations had stopped. Processions were permitted again to a limited degree. Some of the clergy had been organized in associations which tried to achieve a better understanding with the state.

Fischer spoke about associations which had been formed by progressive priests and which were to serve the state as vehicles for the establishment of a national church. As early as 1945 the St. Cyril and Methodius Association had been founded in Croatia. From 1950 on further associations were founded, including the League of Slovenian Priests, the Association of the Good Shepherd in Bosnia and Herzegovina. The members were assured their salaries and pensions and freedom from taxation to a certain limit of income and strongly reduced railroad travel for vacation trips. This meant a strong impetus for the lower clergy who were living under extremely straitened circumstances. In return, the state demanded political loyalty. But according to Catholic descriptions, the associations of priests had even more sinister goals. They wanted to create a class struggle between the priests and the bishops. Members of the associations of priests were supposed to act as spies among the clergy. Within the church there was to be a progressive church, which, as a member of the central committee of the Communist Party said, should be "free from the interference of the bishops and the Vatican." The association of priests, according to Communist reports, included about 60% in Slovenia, almost 100% in Istria. In Bosnia and Herzegovina over 80% of all priests belonged to it. This was most certainly an exaggeration. In the Catholic country of Croatia only 5 to 10% were reached. Despite these limitations these associations created confusion in the church and threatened the relationship between the episcopate and the clergy.

In September 1952 the Apostolic Nunciature gave the Archbishop of Belgrade, Dr. Ujcic, a message from the Holy See in which the hope was expressed that the clergy would fight against the great threatening dangers of the priestly associations. The bishops published a declaration concerning the association of priests in which they declared: "It is not permitted to found such associations or to belong to them." But they were unable to do anything against them because the state reacted with counter-measures. When the bishop of Split excommunicated several priests, the government closed his theological seminary. Furthermore, among the high church officials opinion was not united. Bishop Aksamovic of Diakovo was considered a "Red Bishop." The professor of theology, Stanko Cajnkar, in Ljubljana, the head of the cathedral chapter, Svetozar Rittig, of Zagreb, and the provincial of the Franciscan Order in Herzegovina, Jozo Markusic, all insisted on peaceful coexistence between Communists and Catholics. Rittig, once the secretary of Stepinac, during the war had gone into the forests with the Tito partisans and later, until 1952, had belonged to the regional government of Croatia.

Nevertheless, the forces that had been united in the priests' associations were not strong enough to establish a national church. Therefore the state did not undertake such an attempt when it severed its relations with Rome in 1952. The cause for the severance was the decree which the Vatican had issued against the association of priests. In a note of November 1 the government accused the Vatican of interfering in the inner affairs of the state. The press demanded the recall of the Vatican chargé d'affaires in Belgrade. Burnings of several Catholic parsonages increased the tension. It culminated on November 29, 1952, when Archbishop Stepinac was created a cardinal. Violent propaganda against the Vatican was the result. Marshal Tito called the nomination a hostile gesture of the Vatican and accused the Vatican of supporting the imperialistic policy of Italy and of trying, with the help of the Italian government, to hamper the foreign aid program for the development of the Yugoslav economy and defense. In a note of November 15 the Holy See rejected the complaints of the government and underscored the constant attempts of the Vatican to create better relations with the Yugoslav state. It had the duty, it said, to protect the rights of religion. Over 200 priests were in Yugoslav prisons, and further arrests were taking place constantly under false pretenses. In the last few years 30 priests had been killed, almost all seminaries had been closed, religious instruction had been abolished, and students had been sent home on account of their religious attitude. The Vatican was ready to improve the relationship if the government would carry out a number of definite conditions: for example, the restoration of complete freedom for church attendance and for Catholic schools, for baptisms and for church weddings; the readmission of the Catholic press and of Catholic organizations; the reintroduction of law and of the right to support the church through monetary gifts; unhampered religious activities of the priests and of members of the religious orders.

On December 18 the chargé d'affaires of the Apostolic Nunciature in Belgrade, Silvio Oddi, was handed a note in which the Vatican was asked to withdraw its representative from Belgrade. Foreign Minister Kardelj stated that the Catholic hierarchy had never been ready to order its relationship with the state on account of the pressure exerted by Rome. He accused the Vatican of artificially increasing the tensions between church and state. Instruction in the catechism had often been used to educate the children to hate Yugoslavia and the socialist system. In the same sense the church press, the religious organizations, and the pulpits were being abused. Even simple churchly ceremonies were sometimes changed into political demonstrations. This conflict between the church and the state had been responsible for some of the excesses that had taken place. He said: "I am convinced that such conflicts and excesses cannot be avoided as long as the church does not try to eliminate the causes." He stated further that the government had been forced to take a few preventive measures against the church, but talk about persecution was a free invention. The faithful were not hindered from attending church services and the priests were not hindered from carrying out their official duties. Kardelj stated: "The state subsidizes religious schools; gives material help to churches; assumes the expenses for the social insurance of the priests, for the upkeep of historically valuable churches, for the salary of the church's faculties; and supports the priests through local government authorities. The clergy are in no wise discriminated against in the life of society. Of the total of 82,000,000 dinars which the state gives to the church annually, 30,000,000 is given to the Pravo-Slavian Church, 32 million to the Catholic Church, and 19 million to the Mohammedan believers."

The government tried to regulate its relationship with the church by direct negotiations with the episcopate. On January 5, 1953, Marshal Tito called together seven bishops for a two-hour long discussion in which the relationship between church and state was to be regulated "within the framework of the constitution and in connection with the breaking off of diplomatic relations with the Vatican." The results of his conversation were disappointing. The bishops gave Tito a list of grievances. They complained that churches and chapels had been destroyed, that they had received no permission for buildings and repairs, that processions had been forbidden in most provinces and that religious festivals had been hampered. The freedom of preaching was threatened; the positive exposition of the faith was being considered an action against the state and the existing order of society. Priests were forbidden to fight against atheistic propaganda among the children. The police demanded of one priest that he should give to the faithful the advice to stay away from church. Religious instruction was not only forbidden in schools, parsonages, and other church buildings, but also in the sanctuaries themselves. The church was burdened with unjustifiably high taxes, and if she was unable to pay, the church property was confiscated. In numerous churches the collection of alms was forbidden. A shipment of used clothing, shoes, and powdered eggs, which was given to priests and monks by American Catholics had to be returned at the port of Fiume at the beginning of 1952, because the government demanded a tax and duty of 6,000,000 dinars. The arrest of priests was continuing and the punishment which was meted out to them surpassed in strictness anything that had been done in ordinary courts. Thus the 75-year-old pastor and Dean of Zuzemberk, Karlo Gnidovec, was condemned to death by the firing squad for certain crimes that he was said to have committed during the war. There were still over 200 priests in prison. It could be said that in the last eight years the majority of priests had for shorter or longer periods suffered the shame or harshness of prison terms. Assaults on priests were not a rare occurrence. In the last seven years 30 priests had been killed from ambush. The bishop of Ljubjana, Anton Vovk, was soaked with gasoline on January 20, 1952, was set on fire, and only because of his quick thinking, was saved from a fiery death. The perpetrators were punished with nine days' arrest. In many places bishops were hindered by terrorists from visiting their congregations. Atheism was being taught in schools as the religion of the regime. It was being preached in meetings, was propagated in the press and forced upon the officials of the state and the members of the army. Professors and teachers were formally forbidden to attend church, and he who did not follow this command was dismissed from the service of the state. Also school children were held responsible when they attended the church and showed their religious feelings.

In the conversations with Tito on January 5, 1953, the bishops declared that they could not discuss an agreement with the state without the consent of the Vatican and could not sign such an agreement. But they were willing to form a joint committee which was to prepare a memorandum concerning the wishes of the Catholic Church and the government. This was a very small accomplishment. Pressure continued to mount. In the summer of 1953 all secretaries of the party in Croatia received secret orders to support intensively the spontaneous expressions of displeasure on the part of the population against the bishops. The police were ordered not to interfere in such cases. But serious bodily attacks were to be avoided since they might hurt the reputation of Yugoslavia abroad. In every case the demonstration was to give the impression of a completely spontaneous expression of the feelings of the population which had been provoked by the bishops. Such a spontaneous expression of opinion led to the attack on Bishop Ludwig Budanovic on his way to the church of Sugotika. He was beaten, his gown was torn from him, his bishop's mitre and watch were stolen, and his eyeglasses were broken. The apostolic administrator of Banjaluka, Bishop Carolus Celiky, was attacked and mistreated, also the private secretary of the Bishop of Split. The Dean of the Cathedral of Split, Dr. Paval Pasan, was pelted with rotten eggs when he went to Dubrovnik (Ragusa) and was pushed into the sea. An 80-year-old bishop had a vase broken over his head, and his clothing was torn from his body. Priests were chased through the gardens and the streets like rabbits. After a speech by Tito in Sibenik, the population stormed the seminary of the town, plundered it and threw the books of the library into the street. At an election meeting on September 29, 1953, at Ruma, Tito finally stopped this wild orgy. He said that such a way of fighting was not worthy of educated people, but it was understandable because the priests had incited the people to an extreme degree. He stated: "I have a very simple system. Have nothing to do with them. Don't pay any attention to their words and don't listen to them. Isolate them, for when they are isolated they can no longer exist."

The anti-church measures had not reached the hoped-for goal. In a confidential letter the commander of the secret police, General Stefanovic, wrote to the secret police of Croatia and Slovenia in the fall of 1955: "In Croatia and Slovenia there are state officials who get up at 5 o'clock in the morning in order to go to church before they go to their offices." In many places the clergymen had a greater reputation and a stronger influence on the people than party functionaries. The attendance at church had increased in Croatia by 60%, in Slovenia by 40%, in Bosnia and Herzegovina by 30% over against the prewar time. Almost everywhere in Croatia Cardinal Stepinac was more popular than any Communist leader, including Marshal Tito. As long as the Croats and the Slovenes were bound so firmly to the "foreign Catholic Church" Yugoslavia could not be consolidated and Communism would not become an integral part of the people. The president of the Croatian Parliament, Dr. Bakaric, confirmed this estimate in a confidential memorandum to the local Communist Party committees. Socialist thinking had not penetrated the majority of the Catholic families, and the Communists were still a very small minority in the Catholic part of Yugoslavia. As an example of the influence of the church he quoted that funerals in all of Croatia, except for a very few, were conducted according to the rites of the church, and even party members and former partisans had indicated in their last will that they expected to be buried by the church. Therefore he had ordered the presidents of the local Communist Party organizations not to wait for a church funeral to get underway when a party member died. Furthermore, Dr. Bakaric complained that reactionary priests in villages and small cities were still very highly regarded. When two neighbors were fighting in the outlying villages, they asked a clergyman for his advice and called him in as an arbiter. The church was the greatest hindrance on the way to Communism, and her influence prevented every influence of the Communist Party. Therefore the eradication of religious thinking in the hearts of the younger generation during the next decade was important. The time was short, and with increased effort the battle had to be fought, he said, "against the shadow of Stepinac, against his spiritual and secular disciples."

In the spring of 1955 the seminary of Rijeka (Fiume) was closed for five years and its director, Joseph Kapch, was condemned to six years' imprisonment and four of his co-workers to up to three years' imprisonment, because they had defamed the regime and had been active fascists. Concerning this occurrence the NCWC news service reported: Dr. Bakaric requested of Kapch that he should give a speech that had been prepared for him at the celebration of the tenth anniversary of the liberation of Yugoslavia. Since the text contained false accusations against the Holy See and Cardinal Stepinac, Kapch refused to do so. On the next day he and his co-workers were arrested. At the trial they were led into the court room in chains and were received with the shout: "Kill the fascist dogs." In July 1955 the father superior of the Salesian monastery in Zagreb (Agram), Anton Bajak, was accused of shady financial deals and illegal activities and of violation of the law concerning foreign currency, because he had accepted packages sent from abroad for his monastery. Shortly before, the well-known preacher of Zagreb (Agram), Michael Schkworz, S.J., was condemned to two years in the penitentiary because he had encouraged discord and hatred between Croats and Serbs and had opposed the theory that men are merely groomed monkeys and thereby had proved that he was a propagandist of reaction and anti-scientific theories.

In the following months open terror declined. There were reasons for this. In Western foreign countries the impression that the Catholic Church was persecuted had to be avoided because the government feared that this would adversely influence the tourist trade that was bringing in foreign currency. Also the occurrences in the USA, where Tito's planned state visit in 1957 was canceled because American Catholics had protested violently to the government, had given cause for reflection. But anti-church propaganda continued, including trials of priests and the closing of churches and religious institutions. The religious freedom which had been promised in the constitution was limited through regional and local police measures, through intimidation, boycott, and terror. In a report of the Herder Correspondence of April, 1957, one could read: "Churches are filled with people who, because they are old or are workers and small farmers, have fewer reprisals to fear. To others the clergymen often say that they had better not attend services because they would thus endanger themselves and their families." Stepinac's shadow continued to exert its influence. In October 1954 the Pope appointed an archbishop coadjutor in the person of Bishop Franz Joseph Seper. At that time he declared expressly that Croatia's spiritual head now as before was Cardinal Stepinac. In 1957 Belgrade tried to establish contact with papal diplomats by way of Switzerland and France in order to find out the condition for a resumption of diplomatic relations. Numerous priests were released from their prisons. In the spring of 1958 the government in a surprise move gave permission to pay the *ad limina* visit to the Vatican to three members of the episcopate, among them Archbishop Ujcic and Bishop Seper. At that time they were supposed to find out about the *modus vivendi* between church and state. In the meantime there were no official discussions.

On February 10, 1960, Cardinal Stepinac died. He had always insisted on his innocence, and the government had tried with great care of documentation to prove his guilt. But the Croatian sculptor Professor Mestrovic, who had emigrated to the USA and later had visited his homeland and had been a guest of the government, reported a conversation with Communist Party leader Djilas, who was later deposed by Tito, in which Djilas declared to him: "If I may honestly say the truth I think—and I am not the only one—that Stepinac is a man without blemish and of a firm character which cannot be broken. He has been condemned innocently. But it happens very often in history that the just are condemned in order to serve political ends. We would have had nothing to say against his Croat nationalism, but we could not endure his loyalty to the Pope."

Stepinac, who since 1953 had been suffering from an abnormal increase of red blood corpuscles, and in addition since 1955 from prostate troubles, had been an invalid during the last few years of lis life—as he expressed it, he "was dragging his bones around the house with the help of a crutch." When the district court of Osijek subpoenaed him to be a witness at a trial, he answered: "If I fight against the ideology of the party in the conviction that it is absolutely wrong, is that a fight against the state? If it is permitted to the Communist Party in Yugoslavia for 15 years to fight against the church with fire and sword, to separate her members from her, to hinder the baptism of children, and to make impossible Christian instruction of the youth in the churches; if it is permitted to the Communist Party to destroy the Catholic establishment in schools, to suppress Catholic newspapers and their property, and to commit numerous acts of repression—how can one dare to accuse me of a crime if I raise my voice in the defense of the sacred cause of the Catholic Church? Have I violated the charter of human rights of the United Nations? Or has this charter not been violated by others when after these bloody injustices and so many suppressions, certain people would like to torture me by long inquisitions about accusations to which I will never confess myself guilty? . . . I tell you that I am a man who is standing with both feet in the grave. As a very sick person, I cannot accept your summons. You may try to torture me with questions either on my sick-bed or during the painful walks in the courtyard. But I shall from now on refuse to give any answers. Furthermore, I reject any responsibility for the public scandal which will arise if the international press will make known your stubborn attacks against a man who is already half-dead. If the government is of the opinion that I am dying too slowly, then it should order my physical liquidation as it commanded my legal liquidation 14 years ago. St. Cyprian gave 25 pieces of gold to the executioner who was to behead him. I have no gold. I can only pray for the person who will perhaps execute me. I can ask the Lord to pardon him in all eternity and to let me die in peace.

If I, goaded on by you, have talked about this inhuman treatment during these long years, please do not take it amiss. The Roman proverb says: 'Everything has its limits.' My keepers can continue to keep their guard following your instructions and can make life miserable for me. But I know where my duty lies. By the grace of the Lord, I shall fulfill this duty to the end without the least hatred, without the least feeling of revenge against anyone, but also without fear of anyone."

After the death of Stepinac, the government permitted a splendid funeral for him in the Cathedral of Zagreb (Agram). Besides 22 bishops from Yugoslavia and foreign countries, members of the consular corps, officials of the Yugoslavian Federal Office and the Croatian Regional Office for Ecclesiastical Affairs attended the obsequies. More than 100,000 faithful took leave of the dead prince of the church. A few weeks later Tito bestowed upon Archbishop Ujcic on his 80th birthday the highest order, the People's Order of Merit, First Class. The president of the commission for ecclesiastical affairs, Radosavlievic, at the presentation of the order declared that in the relationship between the Catholic Church and the state the wish for cooperation had come into its own more and more. This wish would certainly lead to a normalizing of relationships. Archbishop Ujcic replied that he "in the future will work in the direction of normalizing the relationship between church and state. I am a convinced theologian and an obedient Catholic. I am devoted to my highest authority, the Holy Father, and as a citizen of this country, I am devoted to the country and to its highest authority, the President of the Republic. I ask all priests to work for the welfare and the increase of the reputation of our country as well as for peace within and without." He stated that it was the wish of many faithful Catholics that negotiations should be resumed between the Holy See and Yugoslavia and that the relationship should be normalized.

During the following months, Pope John XXIII nominated eight bishops, who, without exception, were accepted by the government. The question about the boundary of dioceses which had their episcopal see on Italian territory was finally regulated. Five bishops were given permission to travel to Munich to take part in a Eucharistic

Congress. Visits of bishops to the Vatican were in no way hindered. The polemics of the press against Rome lost their sharp edge. The Vatican on its part saw to it that the attacks which were leveled against Yugoslavia by Croatian emigré priests in *Radio Vaticano* were stopped.

The Bishops' Conference which met from September 20 to 23, 1960, at Zagreb (Agram) worked out a memorandum which was handed to the government commission on ecclesiastical affairs on October 8. It has not been published. According to press reports the episcopate recognized the full validity of the constitution and of the laws which were regulating the relationship between church and state. The church also approved of the principle that citizens should be loyal to the present regime and should do their duty. She promised that the episcopate would abstain from propaganda and any action which might disturb the development of the Yugoslav community of nationalities. The memorandum also contained a number of wishes and demands: (1) It demanded the full application of the laws which had been passed concerning religious organizations and which up to the present time had been interpreted in a very narrow sense by the local authorities. (2) It demanded the return of chapels located on cemeteries and of parsonages which had been confiscated by the state. (3) It demanded greater freedom for religious instruction as well as stipends for students of theology and, in general, all the help which the state was giving to other students. (4) It demanded greater freedom for the religious press and permission to publish additional Catholic newspapers and magazines. (5) It demanded direct discussions between the government and the episcopate for the purpose of regulating the various church-state problems and a discontinuance of all discussions with the Association of Priests which up to now had been subsidized by the government.

In the middle of November 1960 the government informed the bishops that on the whole it was in favor of the memorandum and its demands, but that individual points had to be discussed. The government was ready to recognize the authority of the Pope in all religious questions. But the government also insisted that the relationship between state and church was an internal affair of Yugoslavia. This provision, however, did not mean that the clergy would be forbidden to obey the Vatican in religious questions. The government stated that it was firmly convinced that within the framework of the society of Yugoslavia the Catholic Church also could take her rightful place. At the time of the publication of this declaration by the government, Archbishop Ujcic went to Rome to discuss directives for further discussions with Belgrade. But the Vatican rejected all offers of Tito. It stated that they were of such little consequence that the condition of the church was hardly changed. This was the state of affairs at the end of 1960.

But the Catholics admitted that the condition of the church in Yugoslavia was much more favorable than in other Communist states. The bishops were permitted to travel to Rome unhampered. Priests could be transferred without difficulties from one parish to another. The seminaries for priests were not closed. In Zagreb (Agram) alone there were in 1961 about 250 students of theology and 320 pretheological students. But the confiscated property of the church has not been returned to her. Collections and gifts for the church are subjected to high taxation. The Archbishop of Belgrade, Dr. Gabriel Bukatko, in the fall of 1961 reported to Vienna that divine services were very well attended. The number of priests and members of religious orders who were called to serve parishes was satisfactory. In the Byzantine eparchy, which he also directed as co-adjutor to the Latin Archbishop of Belgrade, he reported that there were one priest and two members of the religious orders for each 1,000 members. The church was in touch with the Holy See at all times and especially for the purpose of preparing for the Vatican Council, bishops had at various times traveled to Rome. In every case the permission to leave had been given. He stated that the church was publishing two monthly magazines and besides that the individual dioceses had hectographed bulletins. From time to time also religious and theological books were allowed to be printed, which were quickly sold out after their appearance. Thus some time ago an edition of 50,000 Bibles had been sold out within a week after publication.

D. PROTESTANTISM

The Reformation had originally been introduced among the Slovenes and the Croats, but during the Counter-Reformation the Protestant congregations were destroyed. It was not until the 18th century that Maria Theresa and Joseph II called in farmers and craftsmen to populate the country that had been evacuated by the Turks and as a result Slovaks, Hungarians, and Germans immigrated to Yugoslavia. Among them were also Lutherans and Reformed. After World War I there were three Protestant churches: The German Evangelical Christian Church of the Augsburg Confession (Lutheran), founded in 1923, numbered 130,000 members of whom 100,000 were Germans and the rest were Slovenes and Hungarians. The Slovakian Evangelical Christian Church of the Augsburg Confession (Lutheran) had 62,000 members. The Reformed Christian Church (Calvinist) had 65,000 members of which 50,000 were Hungarians. The three churches were independent of each other, but cooperated in running a Deaconess Motherhouse.

World War II was a catastrophe for the ethnic Germans. They had numbered 600,000 souls and had lived in the Bashka, the Banat, Syrmia, Croatia, and Bosnia. When the German armies retreated, part of these people were evacuated. About one-half remained in their old homes. On the basis of a law which was issued by the Anti-Fascist Council for National Liberation of Yugoslavia on November 21, 1944, the entire ethnic German group was expropriated without payment. The Germans who had remained in the country became victims of mass liquidations, of forced deportations, of mass starvation, and forced labor in concentration camps and work camps. About 200,000 ethnic Germans were killed in this way. The property of the ethnic Germans—including the areas of best acreage, about 70% of the total industrial output, and over 80,000 houses and 90% of the stores—was expropriated. There was no longer a German Evangelical Christian Church. Her bishop, Philip Popp, was taken to Moscow where he died in 1953. The possessions of the church were expropriated. The churches were often demolished and the rubble was used elsewhere.

In the meantime, at first only in Zagreb (Agram), the work of the church could be carried on by Pastor Edgar Popp, the son of the bishop. Later regional Lutheran churches were organized. Protestantism reorganized into five denominations: The Free Lutheran Church of Slovenia with 24,000 souls; the Lutheran Church in Croatia, Bosnia, and Herzegovina with 10,000 souls; the Evangelical Lutheran Church in Serbia and Vojvodina with 17,000 souls; the Reformed Christian Church in Yugoslavia with 36,000 souls; and the Slovakian Evangelical Christian Church of the Augsburg Confession (Lutheran) with 55,000 souls. The Reformed Church, which also belonged to the World Council of Churches, after 1945 became the chief supporter of the Deaconess Motherhouse in Neu Verbas. In 1952 the Protestant Churches united in the Association of Evangelical Churches in Yugoslavia.

The statistics indicated that these churches in the Diaspora were very small minorities. The churches and their property were restored by the state after evangelical groups had reorganized into congregations and had submitted a request to the government for the return of their churches. The congregations were poor, but spiritually they were alive. The Reformed Church, for example, needed annually 18,000,000 dinars, but was able to raise only 6,000,000. The case of the other churches was not very different. They needed and were given the helping hand of their sister churches in foreign countries. The government did not hamper this work at all. The living standard of pastors was extremely modest. The work of the church had to be carried on with very primitive means. In the Reformed Church, for example, because there was no Sunday paper, Swiss devotional calendars were used, translated, mimeographed, and disseminated in the congregations. In the Slovakian Church, where for 27 congregations and 12 filial congregations only 18 pastors and one deacon were available in 1962, reading services were given by lay people in the congregation which did not have a pastor. Very difficult was the education of theological students. The Lutheran World Federation provided stipends for foreign study. In 1961 the Slovakian Church established a seminary for the education of lay preachers and choir directors and organists. The secularization of the Deaconess Motherhouse in Neu Verbas was a heavy blow. The leadership of the Reformed Church was ordered to surrender the home so that a part of the district hospital could be lodged in it. All attempts of the synod to keep it were in vain. At the end of March 1957 the Deaconess Motherhouse had to be evacuated. The church was permitted to continue the work of the Deaconess House in the former orphanage of Feketitsch, and a theological school was planned to be erected there. The treatment of the church by the state authorities was different in the various parts, but on the whole it was very unfriendly. Thus, for example, in 1962 it was reported that several Lutheran pastors had been condemned to long prison terms—one of them because he had accepted a car which had been legally shipped from the West as a gift.

CHAPTER SEVEN

ROMANIA

A. STATE AND THE CHURCH

After the occupation of the country by Soviet troops, a Communist government under Groza was formed on February 27, 1945. Then the coordination of all political organizations took place; and after the abdication of King Michael, at the end of 1947, a People's Republic was proclaimed, which gave itself a first constitution on May 1, 1948, and a second constitution on September 21, 1952.

Besides the Romanian people, who make up 85.7% of a total population of 18,300,000, according to the census of 1959, there were several minorities: the Hungarians numbered 1,500,000; the ethnic Germans (Transylvanian Saxons and the Swabians in the Banat and around Sathmar) with 350,000; and the Jews, with 138,000. To the Orthodox Church almost 14,000,000 souls belonged. Since 1928 Catholicism was divided into two branches: the Roman Catholic Church with 1,174,000 and the Uniate Church with 1,500,000 souls. Smaller church bodies were formed by 830,000 Reformed, 204,000 Lutherans, 66,000 Baptists, and 30,000 Adventists.

According to Article 84 of the Constitution "freedom of conscience is guaranteed to all citizens of the Romanian People's Republic. Religious cults can be organized freely. The freedom of the exercise of religious cults is guaranteed to all citizens of the Romanian People's Republic. The school is separated from the church. No denomination, no religious order or congregation may open institutions of general instruction and maintain them, but may open only special schools for the training of personnel needed for its specific cult. The nature of such organizations and the functioning of religious cults are regulated by law."

On August 4, 1948, a Law Concerning the Cults was promulgated to maintain the constitutional basis of complete religious freedom. It stated that "no religious cults are permitted which have not been legally recognized." All religious cults were required within three months to obtain permission to function and to submit their constitutions, outlining their organization and activities. Furthermore, it was stipulated that no religious organization was permitted to maintain contact with co-religionists in foreign countries, except through the Ministry of Foreign Affairs. The clergy had to take an oath. The text of the oath for the higher clergy was as follows: "As a servant of God, as man and citizen, I swear to remain faithful to the people and to the nation and to defend the Romanian People's Republic against all internal and external enemies. I swear that I will respect the laws of the Romanian People's Republic and will see to it that they are respected by my subordinates. I swear that I will keep my subordinates from doing anything that will violate public order and the authority of the Romanian People's Republic and that I myself will do nothing against the state. So help me God." The oath for the lower clergy was briefer, but it stated basically the same thing. All religious communions were placed under the immediate control of the Minister of Cults. The law stated: "The Romanian Ministry of Cults is the authority by which the state exercises its right to supervise and control religious communions, the freedom of conscience, and the freedom of exercise of religion. Therefore the Minister of Cults will supervise all religious communions and their organizations, their parishes, orders, clubs, and foundations. The Minister of Cults also will supervise the religious instruction and give his consent to the organization of new parishes. Furthermore, he will supervise the property of religious communions of any type and origin."

Atheistic propaganda was less strongly developed in Romania than it was in Hungary and Czechoslovakia. There were, to be sure, certain circles in which free-thinkers were prevalent, but there was no large scale organization of the godless. Also the Communist Party did not seem very much interested in atheistic propaganda. At the beginning of 1960 the president of the University of Bucharest, Alece Oprescu, wrote in the official student paper, *Viata Stu-*

denteasca: "The total liquidation of religion is a process which will take a long time, since the roots of religion are deeply anchored in the consciousness of people." This liquidation could only be the result of untiring reeducation of the people under the supervision of the party.

A year later the same paper worried about the tendencies toward ideological deviations among the students. Thus the president of the Union of Student Associations, Cornel Burtica, stated that there was a "remarkable lack of political and cultural work of education in the associations." He criticized the fact that many students were under the influence of primitive mystical concepts. The secretary of the Student Associations was angry with Bucharest co-eds who had stated at a meeting that they attended church because they were interested in good organ music. He demanded that these influences of a foreign ideology should be combatted with harshness. Students who refused to withdraw from church should be excluded, for they had no business to be enrolled "in the citadels of our culture which are our universities."

At the beginning of 1960 the Bucharest youth paper *Scinteia Tineretului* complained that there was very little success in the atheistic propaganda among the youth. Clubs for naturalists among the youth which had been organized by the Communist youth organizations in order to "convince the youth of correctness of scientific understanding in the fields of nature and society" were accused of "superficiality, formalism, and laxity." It was stated that in the club of Toporo, for example, the responsible leader in a monotonous voice read an essay concerning the origin of life on earth. After he had finished his reading, the other boys took their caps and went home. When they passed a church on their way home, they made the sign of the cross and continued to believe that God had created the world. The writer said that it was necessary to have some spirit in these clubs and to fight against outdated religious concepts.

A Danish church delegation, which visited the Orthodox Church of Romania in 1956, reported after its return: "The government clearly confesses the materialistic ideology of Communism, but since it knows how much religion means to the people it has given to the 18,000,000 inhabitants of the country the right to follow the faith of their choice, if doing it does not militate against the interests of the state. The minister of cults sees to it that the state keeps contact with recognized churches. Bishops and clergymen are elected by the church, but they must be confirmed by the state in order to be able to function. All clergymen receive state subsidies to supplement their own modest salaries which are raised by church contributions. The state, as a matter of principle, does not interfere with the doctrines of the church and with the church services and is satisfied that the theology of the church is different from the ideology of the state. Discussions concerning materialism and Christianity are carried on in a scientific manner and not as propaganda. The churches are not allowed to engage in propaganda against each other. The minister of cults has about 100 inspectors throughout the country who represent the state to the local ecclesiastical offices. The clergy are not permitted to touch upon political questions in divine services. There is no religious instruction in the schools, but the churches are permitted to conduct religious instruction in church buildings."

B. THE ROMANIAN ORTHODOX CHURCH

The Orthodox Church was divided into five metropolitan dioceses with 8,568 congregations and over 9,400 pastors (1963). There were 199 monasteries and convents with over 8,500 monks and nuns. But their number has declined and during the last few years an undisclosed number of them have been disbanded. The Orthodox Church is historically the Romanian people's church and as such is closely allied with the life of the nation. Its compliance with the new political conditions has taken place without much tension, especially after the death of Patriarch Nicodemus toward the end of 1947, when the former country priest Justinian Marina (b. 1901) became Patriarch. He was in agreement with the social aims of the Communist Party and saw to it that all opposition in the church was removed. Priests who objected were imprisoned or taken to remote monasteries. Justinian was anxious to reestablish communications with the Moscow patriarchate which his predecessor had rejected. He insisted on a reform of the monasteries which had great importance in the life of the church. The state paid considerable subsidies toward the salaries of the priests, supported the monasteries and the theological seminaries, and helped with the reconstruction of the churches that had been destroyed during the war. In 1950 the theological faculties were separated from the universities and were transformed into academies which were relocated in Bucharest and Hermannstadt. There were also six seminaries at the disposal of the church which were connected with some of the larger monasteries and served for the education of the priests. The church press was relatively large. Besides the official organ of the synod and two theological magazines, there were five papers published by the metropolitan sees. Besides the two theological magazines a large number of theological works were published. Through these publications and through regular theological training courses for priests the theological work of the Romanian orthodoxy is carried on. Orthodox clergymen formerly enjoyed a high degree of education. Under Justinian's influence Orthodoxy returned to a new appreciation of the fathers of Orthodoxy and to a better education of its priests.

Indicative of the relationship between the state and the Orthodox Church were the reports about the celebration, in October, 1955, of the 17th anniversary of the autocephalous Romanian Church and the seventh anniversary of the return of the Uniate Church. The Minister of Cults, Petru Constantinescu, declared to a German reporter: "As Communists we are free-thinkers, but we recognize the realities. . . . We live in coexistence with the church and we have established coexistence in practice." The reporter said: "Indeed the Orthodox Church helps to keep the faithful loyal to the party line. The priests admonish the people to do the seeding and harvesting at the right times and to follow the planned economy. In return the clergy are paid like officers of the state, and the state takes care of the buildings of the church and of the monasteries." During a banquet which was held in the course of the celebrations on October 9, the President of the State, Petru Groza, said that no nation which has been organized into a state could visualize this state without the church. He emphasized his own personal relationship to the church and her leading men and characterized the relationship between the state and the Orthodox Church as one of close cooperation for the welfare of the people. The development of this relationship in the spirit of esteem and cooperation had been indicated by the great historical and spiritual significance of the Orthodox Church for the self-understanding and the autonomy of the Romanian nation.

Until now there has never been a conflict between church and state in Romania. This does not exclude occasional difficulties. Thus in September 1958 in the course of actions taken against the intelligentsia 235 Orthodox priests and monks in Bucharest and surrounding districts were arrested. They were accused of having engaged in activities against the state and of having sponsored secret religious meetings. This action of the state was based on the fear of the government that Romania would develop into another Hungary. A large number of the arrested priests were punished with severe prison terms in a secret trial.

Concerning the inner life of the church there were only a very few reports. The above-mentioned delegation of Danish churchmen who were in Romania in 1956 had noticed that services were well attended and that the relationship between clergy and people was one of natural cordiality. The fact that 90% of the infants were baptized and 85% of the marriages were solemnized in church might indicate that the tradition of the people's church has been preserved without interruption. Remarkable is also the inner strength of the monasteries. More and more they have become centers of religious renewal and exercise a strong attraction upon the students.

C. THE ROMAN CATHOLIC CHURCH

The Catholic Church has been treated much more harshly by the Communist regime. We must differentiate between the Roman Catholic Church and the Greek Catholic Uniate Church. The latter began in the year 1607, when, through the efforts of the Hapsburgs, all arch-priests of Transylvania with 1,600 priests and 200,000 Transylvanian Romanians under the leadership of Metropolitan Sereni forsook the Orthodox Church and submitted to the Pope while retaining the Byzantine rite. Since then this church has been a cancer in the Romanian body politic. To lead her back into the Orthodox Church has been the goal of the leading men of Romania. After the Second World War the reunion of the church was accomplished. The Uniate Church was reunited with the Orthodox Church in the same way in which she had been reunited in Ruthenia. In September 1948 her priests were put under pressure by the police and party functionaries. They were told to sign a declaration that they desired reunion with the Orthodox Church. Only 423 of the 2,340 priests signed this declaration. On October 1, 1948, 38 of these signers met at a conference in Cluj. Then they declared: "In our own name and in the name of those who have delegated us, we are deciding to break off our relationship with the Vatican. From now on we shall obey only the superior who has been placed above us by the authorities of the Orthodox Church." These 38 delegates were taken to Bucharest, where, on October 3, their reception into the Orthodox Church took place before the Holy Synod. On October 21 the restoration of the religious unification of Romania was celebrated in Alba Julia with a national festival. The government decisively rejected a protest by the apostolic nuncio and called it "an impudence against the Romanian state and the population of Romania." On December 1 the government decreed that the Uniate Church had been dissolved, and expropriated all her institutions and property. The six uniate bishops were arrested. One of them, Bishop Aftenie, apostolic vicar in Bucharest, died in the insane asylum. Bishop Frentiu of Grosswardein died in prison. Bishop Suciu, apostolic administrator of the archdiocese of Alba Julia, died in the hospital. Bishops Rusu, Hossu, and Balan, who were all over 70 years old, were interned in a monastery. After the compilation of the International Christian Study Seminar in Assisi about 450 Uniate clergymen who opposed the forced reunion were interned in a work-camp near the Danube Black Sea Canal. Later 210 of them were deported to the Soviet Union and only a few old priests were permitted to return to their homeland. The Uniate Church, as far as she resisted the reunion with the Orthodox Church, continued to exist underground. Services were held secretly in homes. At the end of October 1957 a trial was held in Bucharest for several leading clergymen and a number of sisters. The accusation read: "Relationship to a hostile foreign power." The Vicar General of the Diocese Lugosch, Joannes Ploscariu, was condemned to 15 years in the penitentiary.

Also the priests who made the switch to the Orthodox Church did not do it completely voluntarily. How much their conscience was bothered by this forced reunion was made clear by a declaration which a uniate priest gave after signing his consent to return to the Orthodox Church: "I too have signed this terrible document through which I now become a schismatic. I too did the thing which I thought would be impossible. I have become a traitor to my faith." He reported that after his arrest he was placed in a narrow cell in which he could not move at all. After four days and three nights in this cell he had lost his will to resist and subscribed. He said: "In this moment I would have signed anything, even my death warrant if they had told me that they would release me from this terrible cell. At first I was happy to have escaped from this frightful condition. But soon my conscience started to hurt on account of the action which I had taken, and the pangs of conscience in the long run were much worse than the things I suffered in the cell." The Uniate churches were closed or were transferred to the Orthodox. But many Orthodox priests—76 have been mentioned—refused to take over these former Uniate churches and preferred to be arrested themselves. Also elsewhere in Orthodox circles there was a strong sentiment against the methods that had been used to bring about this forced reunion.

At the same time at which the Uniate Church was destroyed the battle against the Roman Catholic Church began. The Concordat that had been signed in 1929 was declared invalid on July 17, 1948. Seminaries for priests and all Catholic schools were closed. Any contact with the Vatican was made dependent upon the permission of the foreign ministry. According to the law on cults, the bishops of both rites—the Uniate church was still in existence at that time—on August 26 to 27, 1948, worked out a statute consisting of 46 articles. The minister of cults rejected 42 of these 46 articles. He insisted that all points which indicated a stubborn dogmatic attitude of the Catholic Church, which declared the infallibility of the Pope and his canonical rights, and which proclaimed the right to give religious instruction in the schools should be eliminated. The bishops, however, agreed to no compromises. Thereupon all subsidies of the Latin Church were stopped on account of the "anti-democratic position of her bishops."

The measures of the state against the Catholic Church now became even more rigorous. The speakers for the episcopate, the Bishops Aaron Marton of Alba Julia, and Anton Durcovici of Iasi, were arrested. By a decree of the Ministry of Cults of August 31, 1949, all religious orders were dissolved and their property was confiscated. In Article 2 the members of these religious orders were permitted "to continue their monastic life. Within 15 days after the publication of this decree they may become members of two monasteries for men and three convents for women." Article 3 stated: "Those who do not want to continue their monastic life may work unless they are too old. Those who are too old and are not physically able to work will be admitted to public asylums. If they want to follow a trade or want to be trained for any occupation, they shall go to the labor offices which will assign them to their proper places."

The progressive pastors assembled, and a Catholic Peace Congress was held at Targul Mures on April 27, 1950. Forty of the 120 participants were priests. The peace movement soon was transformed into a Catholic Action Committee under the leadership of the excommunicated priest Andreas Agotha. But there was not much response to this movement. In retaliation the remaining three bishops of the church were arrested: the Archbishop of Bucharest, Alexander Cisar, Bishop Johann Scheffler of Oradea (Grosswardein), and finally, on July 18, 1950, the aged Bishop of Timisoara (Temesvar), Augustin Pacha. In September 1951 the last mentioned was condemned in a trial in Bucharest to 18 years' imprisonment. An additional four clergymen and four lay people, among them the secretly ordained Bishop Joseph Schubert, were condemned to terms of 10 years to life imprisonment for alleged espionage for the Vatican and the USA, for monetary manipulation, and for conspiracy against the regime. On July 7, 1950, the leader of the Bucharest nunciature, Archbishop O'Hara, was expelled because he had interfered with the inner affairs of the Romanian People's Republic.

A congress of about 130 clergymen and 270 lay people was called on September 5, 1950, to Gheorgheni, with the aim of separating the church from Rome. It decided, "To separate from the reactionary bishops and priests, to support the People's Republic, to ignore the political directives of the Vatican, and to work together with the state on the basis of mutual trust." In order to put this movement on a wider and firmer foundation, the *Status Catholicus Transylvaniae* was changed into a *Status Romano-Catholicus Romaniae*. This status was a corporation which had been established in the 17th century to represent the interests of Catholics in the regional diet of Transylvania, to administer the schools of the church and her charitable institutions, and to exercise a certain right of nomination for the appointments to ecclesiastical offices. In the year 1932 its name was changed by agreement between the Vatican and the Romanian government into "The Council of the Latin Diocese of Alba Julia." In 1948 the Bishop of Alba Julia suspended the activities of this council because the government had confiscated its property and because there was danger that it would be used as a tool against Rome. The Communists restored the status to new life in 1950. A regional commission was formed which was given jurisdiction over the Catholics of all of Romania and which claimed far-reaching independence from the Pope. At the end of 1950 a preparatory commission organized meetings in several cities at which about 200 representatives of Catholic parishes of all of Romania were elected to discuss the future meetings of the status. Of the 601 parishes only 410 were represented. The general convention met at Cluj (Klausenburg) on March 15, 1951, with about 240 clergy and lay people present. It certified that the status had been expanded to all of Romania and that its executive organ was a permanent council which had the task to see to it that the church would operate within the framework of the laws of the state without getting preferential treatment. The government reduced the number of dioceses from five to two, Iasi and Alba Julia. On November 25, 1951, the council of ministers made the nomination of bishops dependent upon the consent of the government. The resistance of the clergy against the aims of the status to establish a national church was counteracted by numerous arrests. About 500 priests were imprisoned. A Romanian, Asra Berkovitz, who was imprisoned from 1949 to 1955 in various prisons of the country, reported concerning the prisons of the ministry of the interior where prisoners were herded together in painful confinement. He stated that they had to do heavy work in spite of undernourishment and constant maltreatment. He wrote: "The most difficult and at the same time the most humiliating tasks, as for example the cleaning of the latrines and the disposing of trash, were reserved for members of the Catholic clergy. The willingness of these young priests for sacrifice knew no bounds. They not only tried to make the lot of the imprisoned ecclesiastical dignitaries easier, but they also gave comfort and courage to the other prisoners."

The church had been deprived of her leadership. Her organizational life had been reduced to the congregational level. On March 27, 1952, Pius XII sent an apostolic letter to the faithful. In it he painted a picture of the destruction of the church and admonished the Catholics to suffer banishment, imprisonment, and loss of all goods rather than to deny their faith and to lose the strong bonds which connected them with the Holy See. The congregations remained steadfast, and the great majority of the priests refused to cooperate with the government. After the death of Stalin there was a lessening of tension. A number of reliable reports mentioned celebrations in the churches, consecrations of priests, confirmations, and first communions. But the episcopate had died out almost completely by this time. Bucharest's Archbishop Alexander Cisar, who had been condemned to enforced retirement in a monastery, was allowed to return later but did not receive complete freedom of movement and died in 1954. Bishop Pacha died during forced labor at the Danube-Black Sea Canal. The Bishops Durkovici and Scheffler had died in prison. The Bishop of Alba Julia, Aaron Marton, who had been condemned to life imprisonment, was released in 1955 and was allowed to return to his diocese. Two seminaries for priests were allowed to operate for the two dioceses. In the diocese Alba Julia the Franciscan nuns of Mallersdorf received a certain measure of freedom of action. They were permitted to work in large groups in hospitals. The former teachers among the sisters received a state pension. The services in the churches were well attended.

D. PROTESTANTISM

Protestantism had not become part of the Romanian national scene. It was represented to a large extent among the national minorities of Germans and Hungarians. Among them it had found an early entrance during the Reformation. In the 16th century Transylvania had been the center of the new faith and had advanced so much in its historical development that as early as 1541 toleration of all religious confessions was granted by law. Thus, for example, among the Hungarians a few decades later a strong Unitarian group came into being which continues to exist today. The Hungarian Reformed Church in Romania had diocesan sees in Cluj (Klausenburg) and Oradea (Grosswardein). The news from these two sees had been very sparse. The secretary general of the Reformed World Federation, Pastor Marcel Pradervand, of Geneva, in a report of his travels in the year 1956 praised the openness of the younger generation to the Christian faith. He stated that despite the general poverty, the willingness to sacrifice was increasing in the congregations which were building new churches in numerous cities and villages in order to be able to take care of the great numbers of people involved in the church life. In some areas 80% of the inhabitants were attending church services; in Cluj the Reformed congregations built not fewer than four chapels and one large church in eight years. In the spring of 1963 in the area of the District Synod of Oradea alone, which comprises one-third of the territory of the church, 22 new pastors were ordained. In connection with the persecution of Hungarian intellectuals in Transylvania after the Hungarian people's revolt of 1956 also Reformed clergymen were arrested. The pastor of Cluj (Klausenburg), Dr. Laszlo Dezsö, was condemned to eight years in prison. Among other things he was accused of having sympathized with the Hungarian revolt.

The ethnic German Lutherans, like the entire German group, suffered more serious losses as a result of the catastrophes of the last decades. Thus in September 1940, 80,000 Germans of Bukovina were transferred to Germany. But their resettlement in the Warthegau, that had been intended by Hitler, did not take place. Today most of them are living as refugees and uprooted people in several countries. A small part of them have returned to their old home. Also the 93,000 Germans in Bessarabia and 15,000 Germans in the Dobrutcha were resettled in 1940 and suffered a similar fate. Among the total of about 190,000 resettled Germans 120,000 were Lutherans. The ethnic Germans of Transylvania and the Banat suffered greatly from the ravages of the war. When the German troops entered, the young men were conscripted to the *Waffen SS*. They fled into the Reich before the advancing Red Army. With the retreating German army a large part of the German population left their homes. On January 11, 1945, about 70,000 of those who had stayed behind were deported to Russia. Many of them died of exhaustion. Others returned after having served as forced laborers. Their farms were expropriated by the government, and they lost their houses and property. They continued to live as hired hands and laborers with their families in the stables of their former farms while former workers and imported people from the South Roma-nian area were living in the farm houses. Dirt, decay, and poverty took over the villages. In order to end this condition the govern-ment a few years later decided to return the houses, if not the land, to their former German owners. They were organized into collective farms to which the Germans were admitted. One collective farm had 300 or more members. Sometimes these farm collectives were formed by only Transylvanian Germans and their economic condi-tion was comparatively good. But other collectives were forced to accept a large number of gypsies and also to pay for the debts from former mismanagement and their condition was oppressive.

In 1961 the German Protestant Evangelical Church of the Augs-burg Confession in Romania had 303 congregations with 191 pas-tors, compared to 513 congregations with 292 pastors in the year 1940. The Hungarian Lutheran Church in Romania had 34,000 members. The German Lutheran Church at one time was the center of the ethnic Germans in Transylvania and the source of a rich cul-tural life. She maintained more than 600 schools in addition to kin-dergartens, orphan homes, hospitals, libraries, and museums. Her

Bishop, Dr. Glondys, in 1940 was forced by the Nazis to abdicate, but wanted to resume his office after the war, after his successor, Schaedel, who had been appointed by the ethnic group leader, had fled. But King Michael I refused to accept Glondys' reinstatement. In his place the pastor of Hermannstadt, Dr. Friedrich Mueller, was elected bishop. In 1948 the church accepted a new constitution. This constitution was subject to the new conditions but essentially followed the outline of the old constitution. During that year the church was deprived of its school system, which in 1944 had consisted of 263 elementary and 12 secondary schools. The continuation of the schools had been a heavy drain on the church since the impoverished parents could no longer pay the high tuition. The German church schools now became German-speaking sectors of the Romanian school system.

On February 22, 1949, a Theological Institute with the rank of a university of the Protestant Churches was opened at Cluj (Klausenburg) with the permission of the state. The Reformed Church placed her dormitory at its disposal. The state agreed to pay the salaries of the professors and of the administration and to subsidize the cost of running the institute, which had the right to bestow doctorates and was divided into three sections: Lutheran, Reformed, and Unitarian. The Lutheran section in turn was divided into two linguistic groups: German and Hungarian. All courses, except dogmatics, were taught to all three sections. The German-speaking branch of the Lutheran section in 1956 was moved to Sibiu (Hermannstadt) where the home of the bishop had been returned to the church by the state.

The church life of the congregations was unbroken. There were hardly any dissidents. Baptism and confirmation, weddings and funerals were generally observed. In many congregations the old brotherhoods and sisterhoods which had first been dissolved by the nationalists and Communists had been reorganized. The financial needs of the church were met largely by voluntary contributions. Because of the general poverty the church was able to get only very little support from her congregations. The church had lost all her real estate. Religious instruction and confirmation instruction had been eliminated from the schools. According to an agreement with the ministry of education Saturday afternoons and Sunday mornings were reserved for religious instruction. But in order to block the weekends these days were often assigned for duty with the Young Pioneers and for obligatory attendance at movies and concerts. By such means and by the use of threatening letters, written by the leaders of the schools to parents, the state in 1959 tried to interfere with the confirmation in Brasov (Kronstadt). A year before, Pastor Konrad Moeckel and a church elder, Roth, had been arrested because a group of students had formed an Edwin Erich Dwinger Club, which was to serve the purpose of preserving German customs. The club was suppressed. The young people were given prison terms of 10, 15 and 20 years. Pastor Moeckel had admonished them not to try such foolish schemes, but he had failed to denounce them to the police. Therefore he and Roth were condemned to death. The verdict was changed to life imprisonment. A few years later Moeckel was released and Roth was put under surveillance.

These occurrences and the changes in the environment, the harsh attacks of the last decades, were responsible for the fact that the ethnic Germans did not feel at home in their old homeland. The majority of them wanted to emigrate. But it often took years before passports were issued to them. Their emigration resulted in the fact that the congregations lost ground. At times there were congregations which still had a church, perhaps even a sexton, but only two or three members. Most difficult were the problems which husbands and wives and families had to face who had been torn apart by resettlement and flight, beginning in 1943.

CHAPTER EIGHT

BULGARIA

A. THE BULGARIAN ORTHODOX CHURCH

There are no statistics about religious affiliations in Bulgaria. The Bulgarian Orthodox Church estimated that about 6,000,000 of the 7,000,000 inhabitants of the country belonged to her. According to a census of 1961 she numbered 3,500 churches, 2,363 priests, 232 monks, and 289 nuns in 117 monasteries and convents. For the education of the priests the church had three seminaries. Besides the Orthodox, the other confessions represented small minorities. There were about 550,000 Moslems under the leadership of a Grand Mufti, 50,000 Catholics, 20,000 Protestants, and about as many Jews.

Orthodoxy in Bulgaria occupied a position similar to that of the Catholic Church in Poland. For over a thousand years it had been the faith of the nation and had grown together with her in her long history. For centuries it had been the chief bulwark of resistance against the Turks. The monasteries had been the centers of Bulgarian nationalism and of its resistance against Greek influences. This fact led to a cooperation between the church and the Communists from the very beginning. The clash between the two forces was not influenced by negative premises as in Russia. The Orthodox Church had been a center of resistance against the Nazis; and in the People's Front, which was formed in 1942 to combat the Nazis, the Orthodox Church and the Communists had been united. In the revolt which broke out in 1944 the Orthodox and the Communists worked together.

The coalition government, which was formed soon afterwards, under the pressure of the invading Soviet armies, was cleansed of its democratic members so that it consisted only of Communists. On the occasion of the one thousandth anniversary of the famous Rila monastery in 1946 the Communist leader, Georgi Dimitroff—famous in the Reichstag fire trial of 1933—praised the historical accomplishments of the church. "Our Bulgarian Orthodox Church is the church which has historical merits for the preservation of the Bulgarian people. In the struggle for the liberation of our people from the foreign yoke the Bulgarian Church was the preserver and the protector of the national spirit during the days of the most difficult testing of our nation." He stated that at the time when the nobility and other important people became traitors to the people "our Bulgarian national church in her monasteries supported the national self-consciousness and the national feeling of the Bulgarian people. We can say without fear of contradiction that we would not have the new democratic Bulgaria today if in the past, in the times of darkest servitude, our monasteries, like this monastery of Rila, had not existed. They preserved the national consciousness, the national aspirations, and the national pride of Bulgarians, and preserved the people from losing their identity as a nation. We, our Fatherland Front, and also we as individuals, as Communists, express our gratitude to the clergymen of the Bulgarian National Church, to those patriots and friends of the fatherland. I can sincerely state that as a Bulgar I am proud of the Bulgarian Church."

Thus the relationship between the state and the Orthodox Church was under this sign of cooperation which at times may have shown some tensions, but has never been seriously challenged. These tensions were apparent especially during the first few years. In September 1944, shortly after the Communist takeover, Archbishop Stephan of Sofia became head of the church. After two years the parliament decided to prohibit religious instruction in the schools and to confiscate the property of the church. The press engaged in sharp anti-religious propaganda and numerous clergymen were arrested and condemned to prison terms.

The constitution of December 4, 1947, stated in Article 78: "All citizens have the freedom to follow their religion, conscience, and cult. The church is separated from the state. A special law will regulate the legal position and the type of material support for the various religious confessions and their right to self-administration."

It also stated: "It is forbidden to abuse the church and religious faith for political ends and to form political organizations which are based on religion." In Article 79 it declared that the education of children is an affair of the state. A decree by the minister of cults of 1948 demanded that pictures of political leaders should be hung in the rooms used for the cult. The Holy Synod did not accept this decree. It declared that the decree had not been accepted and was considered invalid. This led to the application of pressure by the state. Metropolitan Stephan was forced to resign from his office and was banished to a remote monastery, but in the face of the increasing resistance by the believers, the government was forced to state in a law in February 24, 1949, for the protection of the canonical purity of the Bulgarian church: "The Bulgarian Orthodox Church is the traditional church of the Bulgarian people and inseparably united with it in her history. She is a democratic church in her structure and her spirit." In this special law the church was recognized as a legal person. Interference with her divine services was made punishable and the publication of church literature was permitted. Also the state declared its readiness to continue the payment of subsidies toward the salaries of clergymen in the amount of 7,000,000 to 10,000,000 leva, the amount which had been paid since 1944.

As a successor of Metropolitan Stephan, the Archbishop of Plovgiv, Cyrillus, was appointed as commissar, and the government accepted him. He was an important church historian and a member of the Academy of Sciences. He carried out the separation of the Bulgarian Church from the Ecumenical Patriarch of Constantinople. After the Turks had captured the then Bulgarian Patriarch in 1393 the church had remained until 1870 under the spiritual leadership of the Patriarch of Constantinople. Then an independent Bulgarian exarchate was established. In 1951 the Holy Synod promulgated a canon law which provided for the reestablishment of the Bulgarian patriarchate, and in 1953 Cyrillus was elected patriarch.

The state left it to the patriarch to take measures against anti-Communist clergymen. In order to support him, an amnesty was declared on the occasion of his enthronement. A number of priests were released from prison. The Communist Party stopped its attacks against the clergy. In February 1954 the government returned certain expropriated buildings of the monasteries to the church. In order to encourage closer cooperation between the church and the government, a state office for religious affairs was established in 1954. The Orthodox Church was able to weather a critical phase in 1955 without difficulty. The Association of Spiritual Brotherhoods, which had been founded in 1903, was dissolved by the Holy Synod because it was militating against the authority of the church. This organization of priests originally had the purpose of supporting its members and their families in case of necessity and of publishing popular religious tracts. Since the early 1920's a group of leftist clergymen also belonged to the association. After the Communist takeover in 1944, this minority of fellow-travelers gained the leadership. When their progressive tendencies became too strong and when there was danger that the church would be forced to make compromises with the state and the party, the Holy Synod decided the dissolution of the association; and the state did not interfere. The social and economic assets of the association were taken over by the church.

Attempts to reintroduce religious instruction in the schools were, however, without success. When the Holy Synod made this demand, it was sharply rebuked. But this did not change the cooperation between church and state. In a message of the Holy Synod to the parish priests, published on March 15, 1958, the Synod stated that there were some priests who did not accept the instructions of the Holy Synod concerning their duties as pastors as well as their duties over against the state. This message reminded the priests of their basic Christian duty to give unto Caesar the things that are Caesar's and unto God the things that are God's and admonished them: "We will always remember the spirit of understanding which is evidenced in the Constitution of the Bulgarian People's Republic and in our laws concerning this question. If we abuse these laws for political purposes and for propaganda against the People's Democracy and its institutions through speeches, publications, and other actions, we have to bear the responsibility." According to this message, a sermon which did not reflect this spirit was not in accordance with the spirit of the Gospel and should be avoided. The message urged the support of collectivization. It stated: "We should encourage it because it is in accordance with the teaching of the Gospel and the spirit of Christianity that brothers should live together in unity and work with each other."

The financial needs of the church were met by state subsidies, to which were added high grants for the restoration of the many historical churches and monasteries that had artistic value, and by the sale of candles. The church had a monopoly for the manufacture of wax candles, which were sold in the monasteries and churches to the faithful. Since the cost of making these candles was only 2% of the price for which they were being sold, the church made a tremendous profit. That the state was protecting this candle-making monopoly of the church was made clear in the trial of 1959, at which the prosecutor demanded long prison terms, and even the death penalty, for employees of the church who had obtained candles illegally and had sold them privately. Only through the intervention of the Prime Minister and the Patriarch were the criminals able to escape the death penalty.

The church life had developed in a favorable way since 1953. On May 9, 1959, the official organ of the Holy Synod issued a survey of the religious developments since the restoration of the patriarchate. It mentioned the restoration of church buildings, especially of the Rila monastery, and the erection of new churches. Through the founding of agricultural collectives and through industrial plants owned by the church, the income of the church had been increased. The number of the faithful had also increased. The publication stated that "there is a real religious reawakening. The attendance at church is large. The press is growing. There is an active brotherly life in the Christian Orthodox brotherhood."

According to press reports in the West about 30,000 to 40,000 people of Sofia participated in the Easter services in 1957 in the overcrowded Alexander Nevski Cathedral, and the majority of them were young people under 30 years. The church attendance on Easter was greater than at any other time during the preceding five years. One could also consider the fact that the black market in Bibles had increased considerably as an indication of the spiritual hunger. The books had been smuggled into the country from

Poland by the tens of thousands and were sold at exorbitant black-market prices. The Bulgarian Minister of the Interior in 1959 was forced to admit that these Bibles had now become best-sellers on the black market.

B. THE ROMAN CATHOLIC CHURCH

The churches of foreign origin, i.e. the Catholic and Protestant churches, were treated more harshly. The law of February 24, 1949, which has been mentioned, also contained stipulations which were used especially against these churches. In order to secure full independence the churches of Bulgaria were forbidden to continue their contacts with foreign organizations. The church law of the spring of 1952 guaranteed the free exercise of religion in the framework of the constitution and of the laws, but all clergymen who had to deal with foreign countries had to have the consent of the Foreign Ministry before they could enter into their offices. In the same way every material help from a foreign country had to be cleared through the Foreign Ministry.

It was the intention of these laws to force the Catholic congregations to form a national church which would be independent from Rome. At the beginning of 1949 when the Holy See appointed Monsignor Francesco Galloni to be apostolic legate for Bulgaria without diplomatic status he was refused permission to reside in Bulgaria because he was considered "an agent of a power which is pushing the world into a new World War." In spite of the imprisonment of numerous priests, the resistance against the separation from Rome could not be broken. In August 1952 two of the three bishops of Bulgaria were arrested: Bishop Cyrillus Kourteff, Latin exarch for the Byzantine rite, and the apostolic vicar of Sofia, Johann Romanoff. The third bishop, Dr. Eugeni Liwidiovo, was brought to trial before the supreme court with many other defendants in the fall of 1952. The accusation claimed that he had been schooled in the Vatican for counter-revolutionary work and espionage and that he was the leader of a Catholic secret society. He was alleged to have had transmitted to the Vatican confidential information and also to have supplied the diplomatic representatives of the imperialistic countries with this information. A diocesan conference which had been called by him had decided "to fight against Communism by conducting religious meetings throughout Bulgaria and by carrying on an activity which he called mission." The bishop and three priests were condemned to death, 36 others, among them 26 priests, were condemned to prison terms up to 26 years. It is not known whether this verdict was carried out. Bishop Kourteff, who was released after his arrest in 1952, was again arrested in 1956. With his imprisonment every possibility to consecrate new priests in Bulgaria was stopped. According to the latest reports there were only a few Catholic churches in the country. The faithful were subjected to strong pressures, but they were continuing an intensive religious life.

C. THE PROTESTANT CHURCHES

There are about 20,000 Protestants divided among the Methodists, Baptists, Congregationalists, and Pentecostals. As early as 1948 they had been deprived of their spiritual leaders. Accused of high treason, espionage, foreign money manipulations, and relations to military and economic espionage groups in foreign countries and to representatives of international reaction, 15 clergymen were arrested—among them the leader of the Congregational churches, Vassil Ziapkoff; the superintendent of the Methodist Church, Janko Ivanoff; the leader of the Baptists, Nikola Mihailoff; the leader of the Pentecostals, Georgi Tscherneff; and the leader of the Supreme Council of Evangelicals in Bulgaria, Nicolai Naumoff. The deputy foreign minister declared that they had confessed during their pre-trial imprisonment and had admitted that they had tried through contacts with diplomatic representatives of foreign powers to get the foreign governments to intervene in the inner political affairs of Bulgaria. An inquiry made by England in January 1949 as to the reasons why these leaders had been imprisoned was not answered. At the end of February 1949 the trial began at Sofia. It was a show trial, well prepared; and everything went according to the plans of the stage managers. The accused were anxious to outdo each other with confessions, self-accusations, praise of the Communists and of the trial judges, and with promises that they would reform. Naumoff said with a broken voice that he now believed that under Communism a new world of justice had begun. After the solution of the social questions there would be more room for Christianity. He stated: "The security police of the state has made a new man of me." Ziapkoff hinted: "Behind the American Protestants stands capitalism, which is the greatest enemy of humanity. The leaders of the World Council of Churches are the agents of that capitalism. . . . I know that I am a great criminal, but I ask you not to make of me a useless martyr but to help me to become a hero of the fatherland front and of the people." Ivanoff said: "I have to confess, to my regret, that I can find no extenuating circumstances except my complete confession. Nothing excuses me, not even my age." Finally, Tscherneff stated: "You have helped me to repent and to place my strength at the service of the Bulgarian people."

The verdict was life imprisonment, loss of property, and 1,000,000 leva fine each for Ziapkoff, Ivanoff, Naumoff, and Tscherneff. Four other accused were condemned to 15 years in prison and 200,000 leva in fines; three accused got 10 years in prison; one got six; and two got one year in prison. After the verdicts had been passed, all the accused thanked for the mild punishment. There was no attempt made to review the sentences since the prosecutor and the defendants had agreed beforehand concerning them. The trial found a strong international echo. The confessions were rejected as incredible, probably induced through torture. The USA, England, Canada, Australia, New Zealand sent protest notes to Bulgaria. The World Council of Churches declared that its relation with the Bulgarian pastors had been one of a purely ecclesiastical nature and could not be considered a betrayal of a government which was interested in arriving at an understanding with the church. The Reconstruction Committee of the World Council of Churches, with whom the defendants had been in contact, had only one task: to help all Christians of the world with the equalization of financial burdens by assisting churches in need to carry on spiritual and charitable work. Concerning the fate of the condemned men very little is known. When the Danish Lutherans visited Bulgaria in 1956, they were told that at least 10 pastors were still in prison, but that their release from prison was to be expected shortly. Two years later it was

reported that Ziapkoff and the leader of the Baptists, Mihailoff, had
been released from prison, while no news was released concerning
Ivanoff and Tscherneff.

Concerning the life of the congregations hardly anything can be
said because all their activities are covered by a thick veil of censorship. A reporter found out from the Pentecostal congregation in
Sofia that it had about 300 members and conducted four services
per week which were very well attended. Only sickness kept members away from these services. It was stated, "We are quite free to
exercise our faith as we see it. Our difficulties are economic. It is
difficult for us to pay our pastor."

D. ANTI-RELIGIOUS PROPAGANDA

The anti-religious propaganda of the Communist Party was still
in its infancy as far as its inner strength and productivity were concerned. Not until 1959 was a club of intellectuals formed with the
help of the Communist Party, which established a house of atheists.
But the speeches and discussions which had been arranged and an
atheistic exhibition did not find much response among the people.
The activities were directed exclusively against the Catholic Church.
At the beginning of 1961 an anti-religious conference in Sliven decided to introduce atheistic Sunday morning programs in theaters
and cinemas and to sponsor the broadcasting of a variety of satiri-
cal radio shows which were to ridicule religious prejudices. In order
to keep young people from attending church services the atheists
worked with more drastic means. In a number of cases youthful
church members were excluded from the Communist youth organization. Besides, young people who were considered religious suffered discrimination in their education, in the selection of their
vocation, and in advancement. The army newspaper *Narodna
Armija* deemed it necessary in the spring of 1962 to create a well-
thought-out system of scientific atheistic education which would
include all classes and groups of the population and hinder the dissemination of religious ideas. It stated that this program should be
carried out especially among children and among young people. It
also claimed that there were several reasons for the toughness of

religious remnants: tradition, which was a mark of the old society; propaganda of the bourgeoisie; and the fact that religion no longer came to the people in its old biblical hide but in modern imported dress and was using science as a pretext. Besides, there were people who were tired of certain difficulties in the socialist reconstruction and had become weak and had succumbed to anti-socialist propaganda.

In the spring of 1962 the central committee of the Communist Party decided to introduce a systematic intensive program of anti-religious activities. In its resolution it stated: "Under present conditions the fight against religious prejudices is of the utmost importance. . . . In committees of the party and its organizations, commissions, councils, and other organs for anti-religious propaganda should be established. Special attention should be given to atheistic propaganda among the Turkish population, among Bulgarians of the Moslem faith, and among gypsies."

The numerous orthodox holidays were a stumbling-block. The Communist Party paper, *Wetscherni Novini,* in December 1948 considered religion a hindrance in carrying out the economic planning, for it was keeping the population from working for the welfare of the fatherland. The faithful were losing too much time through participation in religious festivals. The church calendar was crowded "with hundreds and thousands of saints and apostles." In spite of the healthy atheistic traditions of the people more and more were leaving their places of work, even during the agricultural season, in order to participate in church festivals and to attend observances in the monasteries. Therefore it was advisable "to break with this harmful tradition so that our development is not stunted." The Bulgarian Communist Party was different from other Communist parties in that it considered religion primarily from the point of view of economic progress. Before Christmas 1961 Radio Sofia stated: "It is a crime to waste costly time just to keep religious holidays and holy days." And the newspaper *Tschernomorski Front* declared threateningly in June 1960 that any attempt to influence workers religiously would be considered sabotage, for it was a fact that churches and sects were leading people away from active participation in the socialist construction and the people's economy was suffering material disadvantages. In the press and at Communist Party meetings the complaint was heard again and again that during the holidays the workers were leaving their factories, and the farmers were leaving the collectives. At the end of 1961 the Communist Party organ *Septemwrijska Pobeda* stated: "The end of the month of December and all of January are crowded with religious holidays which are still celebrated by a large part of the population. First there is Christmas, then there is St. Stephen's Day, then St. Wasilli's Day, then the Day of the Baptism of the Lord, then Ivan's Day, and so on until Atanas' Day at the end of January. . . . Even under the present conditions of socialism these holidays are observed with great zeal and fervor." Through the church festivals the discipline of the workers had been adversely influenced and the fulfillment of the socialist production plans in January had been made difficult. The newspaper *Otetschestwen Glas* remarked that there were also some health reasons for opposing religious holidays: "The strict and uncontrolled carrying out of religious rites and demands of church dogma leads to a physical weakening of the faithful." The paper indicated that Islam, for instance, demanded five prayers per day during which 40 light and 80 deep bows had to be made. People should fight actively against these and other religious exercises, the paper said, "since they hinder the acceleration of economic development, the construction of the socialist society, and the transition to Communism."

Also in other respects Islam was the aim of many attacks. Thus the South Bulgarian Communist Party organ, *Now Schiwot*, complained about numerous party members who carried the red party books in their chest pockets while Allah was spooking in their heads. The paper was especially incensed about members of the Communist youth organization. It stated: "It is almost impossible to get them to attend meetings of *Komsomol*, but they are seen quite regularly in the mosques."

CHAPTER NINE

ALBANIA

"RELIGIOUS FREEDOM" AND BARBARIAN SUPPRESSION

According to the census of 1945 there were about 827,000 Moslems, 230,000 Orthodox, and 142,000 Catholics among the 1,200,000 inhabitants of Albania. With some limitations, the constitution guaranteed to all citizens full freedom of religion. The spiritual head of the Mohammedans and also the archbishop of the Orthodox and the bishops of the Catholic Church had to have the approval of the chief of state before they could function. But this religious freedom was mere paper freedom. Especially the Catholic Church was persecuted in a most barbarous way. As early as 1945 the Apostolic Nuncio, Leon Nigris, was arrested and expelled. In the following years deadly blows were carried out against clergy and hierarchy. Of the five bishops only the Archbishop of Skutari, Kaspar Thaci, died of natural causes. A successor to him could not be elected. In 1948 the Archbishop of Durazzo, Nicholas Prennushi, was condemned to 30 years of forced labor, and in 1952 he died in prison. Bishops Volai of Sappa and Gijni of Alessio were condemned to death and shot in 1948, and also the Apostolic Administrator of the Free Abbey of St. Alexander of Ovosci, Monsignor Gigni. After the arrest and the death of their bishops, the clergy elected administrators for the chapters. But the vicars of the chapters of Skutari and Sappa were also arrested and interned. Since 1948 only the Bishop of Pulthi, Bernardin Shlaku, remained of the whole episcopate. He was later banished to a mountain village in the extreme north of Albania and kept under house arrest. His deputy, the Auxiliary Bishop of Skutari, Monsignor Goba, was the only active bishop of the Catholic Church.

Of the 100 secular priests of the country 17 had been liquidated and 39 had been cast into prison, 10 had died and 3 had fled by 1956. Of the 94 priests of the Jesuit and Franciscan orders 31 were expelled, 35 were condemned to prison and forced labor, and at least 16 were shot while another 6 died of natural causes. The seminary for priests at Skutari was closed, also all Catholic printeries, schools, children's homes, and old folks' homes. The entire property of the church was expropriated. The orders were dissolved, nuns were forced to take off their habits, were declared released by the government from their vows of celibacy, and were sent home. But of the 62 former nuns only 3 married.

In order to create a new way to function for the remnants of the church the remainder of the clergy decided on June 26, 1951, to separate from Rome and to change the church of Albania to a national church. On August 3, 1951, the Praesidium of the People's Chamber agreed to the *Statutes of the Albanian Catholic Church,* which had been accepted by the national church convention and had been signed by Bishop Shlaku, 42 secular priests, and 21 members of the orders. The document had the following text: "(1) The Albanian Catholic Church is a national church. It is a legal corporation and has no organizational, economic, or political ties to the Pope. (2) Besides strengthening the religious convictions, the Catholic clergy must also encourage the faithful to be loyal to the Albanian People's Democracy and to their fatherland. (3) The Catholic Church must be subject to the laws of God, the laws of the Republic and to canon laws as far as the latter do not conflict with the laws of the republic and militate against public order and morality. (4) The education of the clergy takes place in the seminaries which are conducted according to the directions given by the Albanian Catholic Church at the request of the Catholic episcopate and in keeping with the educational standards of the state. (5) Contact with foreign churches can be carried on only through the official agencies of the Albanian Republic and only for the purpose of coordinating religious affairs."

With this development the Catholic Church was completely isolated from the outside world and was made subject to the state in her administration. The state had declared that it would give to the church regular annual subsidies, but these subsidies were reduced from year to year. In 1955 they were 4 million leka; in 1956 1.4 million leka; in 1957 1.1 million leka; in 1958 one million leka, or the equivalent of $20,000.

The faithful were poor and could do little for the support of the church. In 1957 the government gave permission for the reopening of the seminary in Skutari but declared that it would give no financial aid for the maintenance of this institution. The result was that the seminary had to remain closed. The few future priests were prepared by a private system of studies. In the year 1956 only four priests were consecrated, in 1957 only three.

The Orthodox Church, too, suffered great persecution. Her property was confiscated. Two bishops were imprisoned, and the Primate of the Church, Christopher Kissi of Tirana, was removed from office in the fall of 1949. In his place a party-line priest, Paisi Vodiza, who was married and therefore according to the laws of the Orthodox Church could not become a bishop, was given the dignity of Archbishop of Tirana. Under his leadership the small autocephalous church submitted to the Moscow Patriarchate.

In order to remove the influence of Islam, those of its leading personalities who were suspected of resistance against the Communist government were liquidated. In a very clever way the government encouraged enmity between the various Islamic factions. Like the political pressures, also the atheistic propaganda was directed against both Christians and Moslems. The primitive caricatures which were exhibited in the windows of the party offices attacked the "superstitions" of religion. Sputniks and rockets were depicted shooting holes into the vestments of both Peter and Mohammed.

An insight into the present conditions in Albania was given in a report to correspondent C. E. Buchalla, who visited Albania in 1961. On a Sunday morning at seven o'clock he went into the Catholic Cathedral of Skutari. In spite of the policemen who were standing at the portal and scrutinizing all church-goers very carefully, the church was filled to about three-fourths of capacity, mostly with simple, impoverished people—workers, peasants from the mountains, who knelt with their wives and children, and old people. One felt clearly that those who had come here to church were not just nominal Christians. They were the suffering, suppressed, and tortured congregation of God. Buchalla reported: "More than half of the Catholic churches of the country have been closed or are decaying or are being used for storage. On both sides of the highway from Durazzo to Skutari we see these churches and chapels with windowless holes, their doors nailed shut, their crosses torn away." At Tirana a Greek Orthodox church was being used as a combination dance hall and garden restaurant. During weekends a band was playing dance music under its portico and in the church liquor was being served. The counter was at the front side of the church where the altar used to stand. Also one of the formerly most beautiful mosques of Albania, the lead-roofed mosque of Skutari, was no longer being used as a house of worship. The lead covering of the four minarets had been removed and the indescribably dirty interior of the mosque served as a cow barn. In Tirana, West German visitors wanted to inquire at the Office for Ecclesiastical Affairs concerning the situation of the churches and the interpretation of the constitution which guaranteed religious freedom to everyone. But they reported: "In the Office for Ecclesiastical Affairs they did not think it necessary to give us information. They stated that the wording of the constitution was quite clear."

CHAPTER TEN

CHINA

A. STATE, RELIGION, AND CHRISTIANITY

At Peking on October 10, 1949, after a long and confusing battle, the People's Republic of China was proclaimed under the leadership of Mao Tse Tung. With this proclamation Marxism-Leninism in its most radical form became the master of a people which today numbers over 650,000,000. Thus began the most powerful and most terrible experiment ever witnessed in the history of the world: the re-education of a giant nation in the ways of total conversion of the souls of its people; the coordination of man, the change of an entire empire into one giant factory which is run by the people's communes with their millions of buzzing worker bees. A tradition of thousands of years was wiped out over night. A rich and honorable civilization was cut down. From one day to the next it was replaced by the idols and mottoes of dialectic materialism. This had a tremendous effect also in the realm of the religious life.

Christianity had been just a small minority in China. Islam was much stronger. Estimates of Moslems regarding their number varied from 20 to 40 million believers, while the official state figures acknowledged only ten million. The mass of the Chinese people nourished themselves from other sources. In his book *Religious Life in Present-Day China*, Prof. Wing-tsit Chan differentiated between the religious life of the "people" and the religious life of the enlightened. According to him 85 percent of the Chinese belong to the "people" and 15 percent to the enlightened. He stated: "Masses of people venerate thousands of idols and natural objects of ancient Buddhist, Taoist and other provenience, and sacrifice to the gods from whom they expect to receive power and influence in their lives.

The enlightened people, however, venerate only the heavens, their ancestors, and sometimes also Confucius, Buddha, Laotse, and some great historical personalities, but not any spirits."

The "people's religion" with which Communism clashed was primarily pagan superstition. The temples of the Chinese were on the whole not much more than places for consulting with evil and with good spirits. They were information bureaus where one could find out about good and evil days. Mao Tse Tung recommended that the Communists should be slow in destroying these religious connections of the people. Thus, at first there was no fight against the magical concepts and practices of the people's superstitions. The Communists were satisfied to substitute in the public places the picture of Mao Tse Tung for the picture of the God of Welfare and to change the text "The source of welfare is in heaven; the spirit of happiness is among the people" to read "Savings and more production. To save more is more glorious." In the first few years of Communism the professional soothsayers, geomancers, oracles, and the Taoistic secret society, Tao Hui Men, continued to flourish.

But their activities in this business of superstition had become very loathsome to the Communists. They needed a strict discipline of work for their economic reconstruction. What could the Communists do if superstitious people did not come to work or tried to hinder the construction of new buildings and waited for weeks for a favorable time to travel, or opposed the new hygienic measures and artificial fertilizer or prohibited sensible marriages? The Communists were anxious to build water reservoirs and did not want to wait until the gods of weather would be favorable or could be persuaded. They wanted to build factories at the right time and could not permit consulting a horoscope which predicted misfortune if anything was done under the wrong constellation of the moon. The god of the kitchen had to make room for the agricultural expert; the god of rain had to make room for irrigation canals. Therefore in 1953 the professional soothsayers and sorcerers were forced to enter the work cadres, and the Communist Party presented itself as the giver of all happiness and the source of all salvation in place of the gods. Every time an economic accomplishment had been achieved, the Communist Party functionaries tried to explain that not the imaginary gods but the party had helped. For the same purpose courses were held to combat illiteracy. There were monthly film presentations, radio broadcasts, and other measures which were conducted under the motto: "Communism Is Heaven and the People's Commune Is the Way to It." But when the cult of the ancestors was suppressed, and family graves were desecrated in connection with the introduction of the people's communes in the summer of 1958, there were revolts and a great deal of opposition. On August 16, 1958, the *Red Flag* of Peking declared, "The basis for the superstition has not disappeared and the masses are still superstitious. There are still magicians, sorcerers, Ying Yang experts, and soothsayers who make a living of this superstition."

More is known about the work against the other religions, Buddhism, Islam, and Christianity. Here the state was confronted by more or less well-organized forms of religion and by certain doctrines. They, too, had to disappear. But the methodical elimination of religious faith demanded time. For the present, religion still had some utilitarian values in the eyes of the faithful. As long as this was the case they had to be handled with kid gloves. This was stated in official decrees. Article 87 of the constitution of the People's Republic of China declared: "The citizens of the People's Republic of China enjoy freedom of speech, freedom of the press, and freedom of assembly." Article 88 declared: "The citizens of the People's Republic of China enjoy freedom of faith." The government, according to Shu Ping (*New Times,* Oct. 1, 1957), had taken the following measures for the preservation of the faith: (1) It had decided to protect the places of religious cults, to rebuild important temples that had been neglected and destroyed, and to exempt temples, churches, and administration buildings of religious bodies from the payment of taxes. (2) It had established pensions for old and invalid workers of the religions. (3) It had decided to support religious corporations in their endeavor to establish their own schools. (4) It had decided to help religious corporations to found their own patriotic and other organizations.

All of this sounded very helpful, but much of it was only on paper. The crucial point was Point 4. What was meant by these "patriotic organizations" was made clear by Chang Chihyi, a member of the

permanent party committee and director of the ministry of nationalities, when he stated in the Chinese magazine *Union of Nationalities*, April 1962: "The policy of the party demands that freedom
of religions must be understood correctly and carried out correctly."
He further stated that it was in the interest of the party that the
millions of believers who represented an important social force
should ally themselves with the party and government so that they
could serve the cause of the revolution. In this way it would be
possible to educate the great majority of the faithful and to re-
educate them, to isolate reactionaries, and to eliminate counter-
revolutionaries. Therefore patriotic societies should be created for
the religious. Thanks to these organizations, the party could place
religion under the control of the fatherland, and religion would
completely disappear when the rule of man over nature had been
established and when the exploiting classes had been liquidated.

The government program of the Communist Party of China could
be formulated as follows: Religion was permitted as long as it had
utilitarian value for the faithful. It would automatically lose this
value in the course of socialist reconstruction. As long as it was
still existing, it would be used for the socialist construction of the
nation. Religion therefore had to commit suicide voluntarily and
under the supervision of the state. For this reason patriotic societies
had been established to fight against religion. The Communist Party
did not plan to carry out an all-out attack against religion, but as
was stated in a newspaper editorial, "it plans with great care to
kill religion in the long run."

In accordance with this program of the government, as it was
interpreted by Shu Ping, patriotic organizations were founded at
the initiative of the state in all religious groups. Thus there was
a Chinese Buddhist Association, a Chinese Taoist Association, a
Chinese Islamic Association, and others. Their functions were to
express the will of the government to the religious groups and to
incorporate the faithful into the work of socialist construction. Only
when this condition had been fulfilled was there any freedom of
belief, which was defined in an article in the magazine *Philosophical
Research* as follows: "Only when followers of a religion obey the
social and political system and incorporate themselves into it, can

their faith be tolerated." Since this social political system was dialectical materialism it meant that religions had to sacrifice essential parts of their faith.

The official magazine *Modern Buddhism* condemned the fact that Buddhist monks and nuns renounced earthly things and gave themselves to study and prayer. It demanded that they should surrender and dedicate themselves to productive work and should become exemplary workers. Shirob Jaltso, the president of the Buddhist Association, declared that the killing of creatures "is not against our religion. For we are killing only imperialists and counter-revolutionaries." Numerous pagodas were destroyed and their monks were driven out. Only such temples as were visited often by foreigners were kept intact by the government. Lily Abegg, who was in China in 1956, reported: "The number of totally decaying temples which I saw in China is legion." On October 4, 1956, Radio Peking declared with satisfaction that the Buddhist faith was slowly being extinguished. Terror and the force of arms were used against the Lama-Buddhism of Tibet. A *White Book* of the International Lawyers Commission stated in 1959: "The collected material shows clearly a planned attempt to exterminate religion in Tibet."

Islam presented greater difficulties, since its followers were also members of national minorities, as for example the Huis and the Uiguris of Sinkiang. The government at first tried to be obliging. The Moslems had their own schools, but Arabic instruction was forbidden and religious instruction was limited to a minimum. In the course of time Moslems were forced to subject their religious ideas to the political demands. In 1955 an Institute for Islamic Theology was organized in Peking which had the monopoly for the education of Islamic teachers and was under the supervision of the state. Islamic national minorities repeatedly, seven times since 1949, fought against their absorption into the Chinese Han population.

The Christian churches were treated in a special way. There were reasons for that. Christianity had come to China as a Western religion, as a foreign import. It was always considered as something foreign to the Chinese spirit. The attempt to find an amalgamation between Christianity and Chinese life ended in a fiasco in the 18th century when the Pope forbade the Jesuits to permit the converted

Chinese to follow ancestor worship and Confucianism as "civil rites." When missionary work was resumed with renewed vigor in the 19th century, it remained a tremendous problem to translate the Christian message in such a way that it became accessible to the Chinese spirit without estranging it. The number of Christians increased, but in spite of the devoted work of thousands of missionaries, there was never a mass movement toward Christianity.

It was the misfortune of missions that they appeared in connection with the spread of Western imperialism. These were the imperialistic invasions of China; the Opium War of 1839-1842, which ended in the Treaty of Nanking and opened five harbors to Europeans; opium trading; the English-French war against China, 1857-1860; and the treaties of Tientsin and Peking, 1858 and 1860, which opened the doors of China to European trade and to Christian missions. These were concessions for the economic exploitations of the people, for which missions were also made responsible. The hatred against foreigners was directed equally against Christians. This became apparent during the Boxer Rebellion of 1900. Furthermore, it was a misfortune that quite a number of the missionary institutions acted at the same time as promoters of Western civilization. The General Conference of Protestant Missionaries in 1877 declared that Christian education should not only serve the education of pastors and strengthen the self-confidence of the native church, but should also introduce the superior culture of the West and its science and arts. The result was that conversion often became a Westernization of the Christian Chinese.

But not only Christian missions, but also secularism came from the West. China opened up to this secularism especially after the Russo-Japanese War of 1904-1905. As early as 1922 there was an anti-Christian league nourished by the hatred of foreigners, secularism, and Communist ideas. It was successful in forcing the government to forbid Christian instruction in the missionary schools. Chinese Communism took over this hatred of foreigners and increased nationalism. Thus an enmity which was motivated both by nationalist ideology and Communism clashed with the mission churches. They were considered enterprises that had worked in the service of the rapacious capitalism and imperialism of the West, especially of the USA and the Vatican and now intended to obstruct the work of Communist construction, to spy against the state and to fight against the people of China. The whole complex of hatred which had accumulated against foreigners during the past generations unloaded itself now against the Christian missions. Thus it became the hour of spiritual temptation for the Christian missions at a time when they were small minorities with very little firmness, separated from their missionaries, isolated from their mother churches and completely left to themselves.

B. THE ROMAN CATHOLIC CHURCH

1. The Attempt to Coordinate the Church with the Help of the Three Autonomies

After the abortive attempts of the Nestorians to Christianize China in 635 and of the Franciscans to do the same in 1294, the missions of the Jesuits in 1583 had greater success. When large numbers of missionaries came into the country after the treaty of Nanking in 1842, they found a remnant of 300,000 Catholics. Under the protection of Western powers, the various protectorates for missions of 1858 and 1888, missions were able to carry on extensive activities. In 1909 the first Catholic University, the Aurora University of Shanghai, was founded. In 1926 Pius XI consecrated the first six Chinese bishops. In the following years the number of Chinese in the episcopacy increased constantly, and in 1946 a Chinese Bishop, Tien, became a cardinal. Thus in 1949 there were about 4,000,000 Catholics in 20 archdioceses, 85 dioceses, and 39 apostolic prefectures. Besides 116 foreign bishops there were 27 Chinese bishops among them. Side by side with 3,080 foreign priests and 2,351 foreign sisters, there were 2,557 Chinese priests and 5,112 Chinese sisters. The church owned three universities at Peking, Tientsin, and Shanghai; over 156 intermediate schools; 1,546 elementary schools; 2,742 catechetical schools; 216 hospitals; 781 ambulances; five leper colonies; 254 orphanages; and 29 printeries. The Catholic Central Office in Shanghai, which was under the episcopate and the nuncio, coordinated the entire work.

In the "old liberated areas" of northern and northeastern China the church had been exposed to severe persecutions for many years. In 1946-1947 over 100 priests had been killed. The most horrible occurrence was the murder of the Trappist nuns of Yan Kia Ping. Also 183 churches had been converted into state offices and 123 into theaters and cinemas; 166 were completely robbed, 25 devastated, 101 were closed, and 12 were burned. Of the mission stations 549 had been destroyed or occupied. In the territories which were liberated later there was at first a relatively lenient treatment, especially in the larger cities. But the Catholics were confused. In order to counteract this confusion the Catholic Central Office appealed to them that the missionary work and the pastoral care should be supplemented by the printed word and the lay apostolate wherever priests were hampered in their work. At that time the *Legio Mariae* gained great importance. Founded in 1921 in Dublin by Frank Duff as a lay organization for the purpose of self-sanctification and the apostolate through personal contact and visits in the homes, it had been working in China since 1935 and by 1948 was spreading rapidly. It was hated by the Communists especially on account of its courageous decisions and of the success of its activities. On October 4, 1951, a Peking newspaper wrote that it was "nothing but a gang of secret helpers of imperialism." Since religion had been used for the deception of the people and as a mask for the criminal movement of the imperialists, it was especially dangerous. The newspaper claimed that the legion was planning the establishment of counter-revolutionary forces and the ruin of the entire people's economy. It stated: "The Marists are sworn enemies of the entire Chinese people and therefore also sworn enemies of all patriotic Chinese Communists."

Soon after the establishment of the People's Republic there were strong interferences in the affairs of the church. Until 1951 all universities, the larger part of the intermediate and elementary schools and all catechetical schools had been confiscated. The priests were treated badly and were hampered in their pastoral work. Until December 31, 1950, 3,280 foreign priests, brothers, and sisters had left China. At the same time an attempt was being made to coordinate the church with the Communist nationalist way. As early as March 1949, shortly after the Communist takeover of Peking, two pamph-

lets were published, *An Open Letter to the Clergy of Peking*, written by the so-called Chinese League of Progressive Catholics, and
an *Appeal of the Society of Progressive Chinese Catholics.* The *Open
Letter* accused the church of having used the methods of feudalist
fascism. The clergy were asked to limit themselves to the administration of the sacraments. Only on this condition would the government be ready to protect the clergy. In the appeal it was claimed
that the church and Communism were following the same goals and
that there would be a complete accord if the church would give
up her feudalistic despotism. Beginning in 1950, the government
tried to introduce into the church the "Three Autonomies." This
program demanded that there should be no financial assistance from
foreign countries, no foreign priests in China, and no contact with
the Holy See. A proclamation of the gospel with a socialist interpretation was demanded. This movement began with a manifesto
issued by 40 Catholics of Kwangyuan in northern Szechwan. In order
to win the faithful for this program the name of a very popular
priest, Father Wang Ling-Tso, was placed under the manifesto.
He protested against this abuse of his name and was arrested and
shot. The manifesto was published on December 16, 1950. According to Chinese custom Chou En-Lai gave a tea for two bishops and
several other Catholic leaders. The bishops suggested the following form for the three autonomies: "Churches, Catholic foundations,
and institutions must be maintained exclusively by Chinese subsidies. The spreading of the faith must be solely and exclusively
by Chinese priests, but without bias against foreigners. The authority of the church must be centered progressively in the hands of
the Chinese clergy, but the church shall remain in communion with
the Holy Father." Chou En-Lai was not satisfied with this statement. On March 18 the news bureau Hsinhua demanded the separation from Rome. From then on manifestos were published by
allegedly authorized Catholics which followed this line. Thus, for
example, 793 Catholics in a *Declaration of Nanking* demanded that
all political and economic relations with the Vatican should be
broken off and only purely religious relationships be retained. But
all these declarations which demanded the separation from Rome
were not signed by priests. In order to make them pliable com-

mittees of so-called Parish Soviets were organized. They were instructed to lead the parishes democratically and to become cells for the reform of the church. Since not only the priests but also most of the lay people refused to cooperate with these committees, the Communists themselves appointed their members.

In March 1951 the Catholic orphans' homes were attacked. The nursing staff was accused of having murdered children, and indignation was aroused in mass protest meetings. A wild propaganda against the church was started. Imaginary figures were given of children who had been beaten to death in Catholic orphanages. In Canton in the presence of 6,000 people a travesty of a trial was held against two Catholic nuns. They were condemned to five years' imprisonment because they allegedly had mistreated, neglected, and murdered orphans. Five Franciscan nuns were accused of having killed 120,000 children. They were tried before a gigantic People's Court in the public gardens of Chengtu in the presence of 40,000 people. In the mission's home in Wuchang only 126 of 57,317 children were said to be still alive. The missionaries were often treated with unspeakable cruelty. After their return to Switzerland several sisters reported that three Chinese clergymen had died at the stake. In this bloody persecution there were many examples of heroic faith. The Chinese priest who was the leader of the Marists had twice refused to give declarations which had been demanded by the priests. He went home to set his house in order, celebrated communion in his church, and went to the police. He did not return from there. The Italian priest Alfeo Emaldi, who had been arrested at the beginning of 1951 at Honan, was tortured for many weeks and finally cut off his own tongue in order not to be forced to make statements during these tortures.

The press carried on a continuous campaign against the Pope. Caricatures showed him as the slave of American imperialism. For example, there was a picture of an opened curtain in front of the Pope's room. He was seen kneeling on the floor with his tiara on his head, looking up with a terrified look. In front of him was the Bible, behind him were the money sacks of the imperialists. On the wall were the pictures of Hitler and Mussolini. In his hand the Pope had a bloody hatchet, and behind him there were the cannons and bombs of the imperialists. Or the Pope was shown putting a mask in front of his face and acting as the angel of peace. His wide gown covered a big revolver which he was carrying in his belt. In his right hand he was holding the Peace Encyclical, in his left hand a sword. Or, a group of upright progressive priests was in the process of sawing off the branch on which the Pope was hanging so that he would fall into the abyss.

The anti-church measures reached their high point with the expulsion of the papal nuncio, Archbishop Anton Riberi. The government succeeded in winning the support of a few progressive Catholics to sign the petition for his expulsion. Riberi was arrested on June 28, 1951, and after long questioning about espionage and the undermining of public security he was expelled from the country in a degrading way on September 4. On June 8, 1951, the Catholic Central Office in Shanghai was closed by the police. A *Committee of the Reform Church* was organized with the help of a small number of progressive Catholics and was recognized by the government as the only church leadership. The government even toyed with the idea of appointing a Chinese pope. It approached the Archbishop of Nanchang and the Apostolic Administrator of Tientsin. But both refused to be candidates.

The wave of arrests continued. The Communists imprisoned numerous priests and lay people in order to force them to subscribe to the Three Autonomies Movement. But the episcopate opposed it unanimously. At its head was the Bishop of Shanghai, Kung Pingmei, administrator of the archdiocese of Nanking, who after the expulsion of Riberi became the leader of the Chinese church. The Jesuit Tsiang Beda, director of the Catholic gymnasium at Zikawei near Shanghai, was asked to become the head of the Reform Church. When he refused he was arrested on August 9, 1951, and died in prison on November 11. At the end of 1951 the *Legio Mariae* was forbidden. The government announced that all Marists had to follow the order to leave the organization. They had to have a certificate that they had left the order and had to present themselves at the local government office to register their resignation from the order.

Episcopate and clergy were further weakened through expulsions.

Thus the 74-year-old bishop Jean de Vienne of Tientsin was expelled because he had opposed the reform of the church. Archbishop G. X. Jantzen of Chungking because he refused to sign the petition for the expulsion of the nuncio. Archbishop Pollio of Kaifeng was interrogated 22 times before his expulsion, mostly at night. He was led from prison through the streets ten times and attacked by the people. The Belgian bishop, Leo J. de Smedt, died 48 hours after being released from prison as a result of maltreatment. Bishop Cypriano Cassini of Pengpu, an Italian Jesuit, died of a heart attack. The German Archbishop, Theodor Buddenbrock of Lanchow, had to appear at the open door of his house again and again, so that thousands of people who were assembled in the courtyard could revile him and attack him. He became so sick that he had to be released from arrest. Bishop Alexander Carlo died three weeks after his release as a result of maltreatment during public hearings. As a precaution before his expulsion the nuncio had asked all bishops to nominate a number of priests who could take over the leadership of the diocese if the bishops should be impeded in the exercise of their functions. In 1951, 1,371 missionaries were forced to leave the country, in 1952, 1,093 had to emigrate, and in 1953, 488. At the end of 1954 only 61 were still in the country of whom 21 were in prison. In 1955 there were still two foreign bishops and 20 priests in China. Of these one bishop and 17 priests were imprisoned. Of the Chinese priests about 500 had been imprisoned.

The number of the vacillating among the native clergy was small. In 1952 the Vicar General of Nanking, Li Wei Kuang, was excommunicated because he had called Riberi a criminal and had thanked the government publicly for the expulsion of the nuncio. More difficult was the case of the Vicar General of Tsinanfu, Tung Wen-lung. The Communists had succeeded in converting him by threatening him with most severe punishment for his former anti-Communist activities. Now he was accusing his own bishop, the German Cyrill Jarre, of imperialism and caused him to be imprisoned. When he died and was buried by the faithful in his red episcopal garb, Tung informed the police about the significance of red as the color of the martyrs. Thereupon the body was exhumed. Tung himself disrobed his dead bishop of the red garb and was hindered only by the protest of the Catholic people from putting on him the clothing of a common criminal. Later he was named bishop because he was "a pillar of the patriots."

On January 18, 1952, Pius XII sent an apostolic letter to the Chinese Catholics. He rejected the allegation that the missionaries had tried to gain worldly profit and earthly rule. He stated that the attack against the missionaries was in truth an attack against the faith. The church was not interested in worldly power, but was looking for brotherly unity among fellow citizens and trying to support the poor and to strengthen the basis of human society through Christian virtues. The Pope stated that Catholics loved their fatherland and tried to obey the higher authorities according to the laws of God and the dictates of conscience. The church was not interested in one people alone, but loved all people. Therefore no one could demand of the church that churches in individual nations should be separated from the Holy See where Peter, the vicar of Christ, would continue to live in his successors until the end of time. The Pope stated that the church had taken great care to educate a native clergy in China and 25 years ago had begun to entrust Chinese dioceses to the care of Chinese bishops. The foreign missionaries had tried to lead the church of China to that degree of maturity which would no longer make it necessary for them to continue work among them. The Pope continued: "In the course of centuries, the church has suffered so many persecutions. The soil of your country is red with the blood of the martyrs. But you too can claim for yourselves the well-known word: When they kill us they increase us. The blood of the Christians is the seed of the church."

In the encyclical *Ad Sinarum Gentem* of October 7, 1954, Pius XII took issue with the three autonomies. As far as the national autonomy of the Chinese Church was concerned he declared: "If your Christian communion wants to belong to our Redeemer and to the society which has been divinely established by him, it is absolutely necessary that it should be completely subject to the Supreme Shepherd, the Vicar of Jesus Christ on earth, and should be in closest communion with him in its religious faith and morality. With these words we want to emphasize that the whole life and activity of the church is meant, including her constitutions, her leadership, and her discipline, for everything depends upon the will of Jesus Christ, the Founder of the Church." He stated that the power of jurisdiction was given to the bishops only through the mediation of the successors of Saint Peter. The Pope said: "To him not only the simple believers, but all bishops are subject in perpetuity, and they are united with him in the reverence of obedience and through the bonds of unity. According to the same divine right also the people and the civil authorities are not allowed to trespass into the areas of the rights and administration of the ecclesiastical hierarchy." Concerning the economic autonomy, the Pope said that he would welcome the day when the Chinese faithful would be able to take care of their church by their own means. The gifts which had been collected in other nations had not been used for political and other secular reasons, but had been given from Christian love which felt itself driven to spread the kingdom of Christ everywhere. Concerning the autonomy of proclamation the Pope asked: "By what right can people interpret the Gospel of Jesus Christ in different ways to different nations according to their own ideas? The bishops have the task to proclaim the Gospel and to teach first what Christ himself has proclaimed and has taught and what this apostolic see with all bishops subject to it has preserved for centuries and has passed on unchanged and unadulterated."

The encyclical was partly responsible for the fact that the attempt to establish a Reform Church met with failure. Until the end of 1954 only fifty to sixty priests had been won for the new church. In the book *Chinese Martyrs Speak*, Monsterleet wrote concerning the results: "In spite of all the attempts by the government the Reform Church continues to consist only of a few parishes which are administered by a minority of the progressive Catholics. Its symbols are similar to a propaganda symbol. In any case the movement for the establishment of the three autonomies has been a decided defeat for the Party, perhaps the only defeat until now. Through this movement all of China has become acquainted with the church. The Catholic Church has proved herself to be the only power which is in a position to resist the dehumanized omnipotence of the Party and its demands, which are fundamentally opposed to all human rights."

2. The Patriotic Association Takes Over

That was a premature assessment. The Chinese Communist Party, of course, did not relent. It now started to attack the problem from another angle. Under the motto: "Love the Fatherland and destroy Capitalism!" a new movement was started. The excommunicated Vicar General, Li Wei Kuang, and a group of people's priests placed themselves at the disposal of this movement as traveling missionaries. In December 1954 this action resulted in a new wave of arrests. Three Chinese bishops, 175 priests, 13 monks, several sisters, and about 2,000 lay people were thrown into prison. Now the Communists destroyed the strongest Catholic bulwark, the congregation in Shanghai, with its bishop, Kung. In Shanghai there had been numerous institutes and intermediate schools, the most important center of the press and above all the Great Seminary at Zikawei near Shanghai with seven Chinese professors and 350 seminarians and preseminarians from 24 dioceses. Bishop Kung, an outstanding personality of tremendous ability, had united the 50,000 Catholics of the city in a firm communion. None of his priests had joined the Reform Church. In view of the threat to the church an intensive liturgical life had developed. It was reported: "Every day in Shanghai is like Easter Sunday morning. The people not only fill the churches, but there are more people than the churches can hold. The Reds are very much alarmed." This was reported at the end of 1954 by the Jesuit Gerald McKernan. In the nights of September 8 and 9, 1955, the bishop and 40 priests and about 300 lay people were arrested. The seminary was deprived of its professors. Several dozens of the seminarians were put into prison. The larger part were sent back to their home congregations. The students who remained in the seminary, about one-third of the students, were instructed in Marxism, and the seminary was placed under the supervision of a patriotic priest. On September 25 about 15,000 Catholics were assembled on a dog race track and were forced to approve the arrest of their bishop. Between 300 and 400 lay people refused to consent and were arrested. Toward the end of 1955 another 600 Catholics were put into prison. Of the "criminals" who had been arrested during the nights of September 8 and 9, 17 were shot. Later the seminarians who had been arrested and Catholic young men of Shanghai were transferred to a concentration camp in the extreme north of Manchuria where they remained in a forced labor camp until they had changed their opinions.

Also in other dioceses there was a wave of persecutions. In five provinces two bishops and 28 priests and 12 monks and at least 4,000 lay people were arrested. In the diocese of Yan only one of the 50 priests who had served the 53,000 Catholics remained free. In Han Yang in the province of Hupeh two Chinese priests and one nun were executed. Among the lay people who had been arrested there were especially young men and women. They were reeducated in training courses. A participant reported: "The discipline was very strict and the atmosphere was cold. The harshness was indescribable. Sometimes the training sessions continued until the early hours of the next morning. During the whole period of retraining no recreation was permitted, not even on Sundays." At the end of the stay they had to write a confession. Then they were forced to continue their training individually and to report two or three times weekly to the police. One of them stated: "We are convinced that they will never leave us in peace again." The police subjected the priests to a system of imprisonment by rotation. In order to demoralize them they arrested them periodically and then released them. With the financial help of the state, Catholic magazines were printed in Tientsin, Shanghai, and Hankow, which made propaganda for the Communist church policies.

After the terror there was in 1956 a time of relaxation. After the demoralization the next step followed. Now there was no longer any talk about the autonomies. The emphasis switched to the patriotic associations. These patriotic associations recognized the authority of the Pope but with certain reservations. The new motto read: "Love the Fatherland, fight against Imperialism, and love both Fatherland and Church at the same time!" This was a cleverly devised motto, for it appealed to the patriotism of the Chinese and did not at the same time demand the complete separation from

Rome. Thus it was a trap in which many Chinese priests and even bishops were caught. A conference which met at Peking from February 12 to 16, 1957, under the chairmanship of the leader of the state office for church affairs, Ho Cheng-hsiang, decided to make possible through a recruitment campaign the founding of the Patriotic Association of Chinese Catholics. At a congress which met in Peking from July 15 to August 5, 1957, the Association of Patriotic Priests was founded. At this meeting the following theses were proclaimed: "Catholics are citizens of China and not of the Vatican. The Vatican is a capitalist state which is doing the work of the imperialists. Chinese Catholics who are loyal to Rome are spies and traitors. Members of the patriotic association are favoring the expulsion of foreign missionaries and bishops."

In a final declaration the delegates promised "to propagate among the believers the policies of the government and to help the government to carry out its religious policy." The congress decided to do away with all political and economic ties to the Vatican. It stated that Chinese Catholics would obey the Vatican in dogmatic and ethical questions, but would "reject energetically any plans promoted by the Vatican—even those clothed in religious garb—which would try to interfere in the inner affairs of our country and its sovereignty and might impede our patriotic movement against the imperialists." Such interferences which were clothed in religious garb were always present, the association stated, for "the Vatican has a large number of decrees to convince the Chinese Catholics that they should fight against their own government and thus become tools of imperialism against the socialist construction of China."

In this position toward the Vatican the negative points were emphasized more than the positive ones. To a representative of the Reuter Agency the general secretary of the Patriotic Association, Ly, declared that Chinese Catholics did not see why they should try to explain to the Vatican the purpose of their new patriotic association or why they should send a mission to Rome to discuss the relationship of the Chinese Church with the Vatican. He stated: "The Vatican is stubbornly opposed to all socialist countries. The Catholic Church of China is determined to follow the path of Socialism so that religious affairs can be taken care of by Chinese Catholics." He stated that it was not their intention to sever their ties to Rome. As before they would consider the Pope the leader in spiritual questions and would submit all appointments to the Vatican for its approval. But, he stated: "We do not confess that Communism is evil. In case there should be decisions by the Vatican which are anti-Soviet or anti-Communist, we shall not approve them." In these remarks there was a definite indication of defiance. The promise of limited obedience toward the Holy See was merely window dressing. It was clear that in the final analysis there was a complete separation from Rome. This movement of patriotic priests had established itself under the leadership of the Communist regime and was supported by the Communist regime as a counterchurch that would undermine and take the place of the church that was bound to Rome.

The members who had participated in this congress did not all agree with the basic assumptions of the patriotic associations. There was a great deal of opposition. A motion by the state that the excommunication of Vicar General Li Wei Kuang should be rescinded was defeated. The final declaration of the congress stated that a "rightist minority" had been present. Among the 240 participants there were 11 bishops and 72 priests. The bishops were part of the small remnant of the hierarchy, for, according to the statistics of Cardinal Tien, at the end of 1956 17 archbishops, 70 bishops, and 29 other superiors were no longer able to exercise their office—19 had been expelled, five had died in prison, seven were in prison, four were in exile, and 11 were hindered in some other way from carrying out their office. Bishop Chao Cheng-sheng of Tientsin, who opposed the plan of the congress because the founding of a Catholic organization without the approval of the Vatican would "kill the soul of the church," was sent to prison for eight months. But other bishops more or less voluntarily placed themselves at the disposal of the patriotic associations. The Archbishop of Mukden, Ignatius Pi Chou Shi, became its president. Among the eight deputy chairmen there were also several bishops. There was an additional leadership committee of 150 members.

Many of the bishops who acted as leaders of the patriotic association had been won over through reeducation. Thus Archbishop Pi Chou Shi gave the impression of being a person hypnotized by the Communists for their propaganda purposes, as was reported by the Herder Correspondence in 1959. On account of his loyalty to Rome he had spent five years in prison and under house arrest. Now he boasted in an article: "Freed from the colonizing guardians who insisted that only foreign missionaries should receive the dignity of being bishops, we are now carrying on our life of faith in freedom. Nobody interferes with our faith, nobody hinders us from reading the Bible." After the congress Bishop Chao Cheng-sheng was brainwashed in prison until he confessed all his crimes. From this reeducation the 60-year-old man returned looking like a man of ninety. In a similar way Administrator Alfons Chao of Tientsin was "turned inside out." In front of a people's court he confessed that he had done everything against the Communists because he had been loyal to Rome and that he had influenced his priests. But he had been wrong in all these attempts and he proclaimed that the separation from Rome was justified.

How many priests became members of the patriotic association was not known. Whether they did so voluntarily or under duress was a difficult question to decide. People who resisted were worked on with all means at the disposal of the police, with accusations, with third-degree methods day and night, with public condemnations. The young people were made ready for a break with Rome during frequent reeducation courses. Whoever resisted was considered an enemy of the people and of the state, was sent to prison, or removed to outlying districts, or sent to the mines until his power of resistance was broken. Bishops of the opposition were called before the courts. Thus the apostolic administrator of Nangcheng, Jacob Yang, was condemned to ten years' imprisonment, the vicar-general of Hankow, Odoncus Liu, to 20 years, and the Franciscans Wu and Cheng of Hankow to ten and four years respectively. Bishop Tang of Canton, under whose leadership not a single priest of the diocese had joined the patriotic associations, was arrested on February 5, 1958, together with five priests and 20 lay people. All Catholics, even school children, were forced to participate in the meeting at which the bishop was accused of being a people's enemy. Tang had endured 20 public pre-trial interrogations. Bishop Fan Hsueh-Yen of Paoting was condemned to 15 years in prison because he had sabotaged the patriotic associations, had stated that participation in the associations was a betrayal of the church, and had declared that the religious freedom which had been guaranteed by the constitution was only a paper guarantee. Bishop Simon Chu of Haimen, who had been under house arrest since September 8, 1955, wrote in his last letter before his death, which occurred on February 22, 1960: "I was condemned as a revolutionary because I did not support the attacks against the Vicar of Christ and because I did not join the National Church. I am quarantined like an infectious leper."

The Patriotic Association showed its true character as a Communist nationalist counter-church to Rome when, on February 27, 1958, it announced a step which was of greatest consequence: "In order to sabotage the Chinese church, the Vatican has attacked the patriotic priests and is continuing to control the appointment of church dignitaries in China. We have no illusions about the position of the Vatican. Therefore we must take into our own hands the responsibility for the problems facing our bishops. . . . Many bishops have been expelled from China because they were the agents of the imperialists. Others are in prison because they have betrayed the fatherland. Therefore it is urgently necessary to appoint new bishops who have been elected from the ranks of the patriotic priests. They alone can lead the believers to love of religion and of the fatherland." Tsian Kia-Shiu, who was later elected Bishop of Shanghai, declared to a correspondent of the *Corriere delle Sera*: "The Vatican has placed us before a dilemma. Either we have bishops who are opposed to Communist ideology or we have no bishops. Since bishops are necessary for the welfare of the church, we have the right to appoint them ourselves. The Vatican demands that we should have political bishops. Therefore the Vatican has taken a position against justice and against Christ."

As early as December 16, 1957, the consecration of Father Li Hsi-ting as bishop took place after he had a training course in Szechwan. Two other clergymen were consecrated as auxiliary bishops. On February 8, 1958, the patriotic association of Suchow "with the help of the Holy Spirit" elected the patriotic priest Shen Chou-Ming as bishop, and he solemnly took possession of the cathedral. On March 18 and 19 the patriotic associations of the province of Hupeh elected the priests Tung Kwang-ching and Yuan Wen-hua as bishops of Hankow and Wuchang. The election was communicated to the Holy See, but the Congregation for the Propagation of Faith sent a wire that it would not accept the election and referred to the decree of April 9, 1951, according to which those who consecrate a bishop who is not nominated or accepted by the Holy See and those who have been consecrated in this way are excommunicated *specialissimo modo* by the Holy See even if they assume their office under the influence of extreme fear. Immediately the Bishop of Puchi, Li Tao-nan, refused to consecrate the two elected bishops. He declared: "If I had two souls, I could consecrate the bishops with one soul and save my other soul for eternal life. But since I have only one soul which I must save for eternal life, I cannot consecrate these bishops without the permission of the Holy Father." The consecration was scheduled to take place on Easter Day 1958 but had to be postponed on account of the refusal of the bishop. In the meantime he was isolated and reeducated. On April 10 the patriots had a meeting and rejected the Roman order as a "shameless intimidation." Bishop Li was reeducated to such a degree that on April 13 he was willing to administer the consecration. But this act did not take place in the cathedral. It was transferred to a small chapel, probably because Bishop Li had been so changed physically by the treatment he had received that he could not be presented to the public. In the following months there were further elections of bishops. The vows that were uttered at the consecrations of these bishops made it clear in which sense the bishops wanted to carry out their office. When Li Hsi-ting took the oath as bishop of the Chengtu, he promised: "I fear personally that I am not able to assume such a heavy responsibility. . . . From now on I will lead the clergy of the whole diocese and the 40,000 believers on the road of socialism under the leadership of the Communist Party. I shall actively participate in the construction of the socialist society in this country. I will work for the anti-imperialist patriotic movement in this diocese and in the province of Chengtu.

I will resist any interference of the Vatican in any form and will guarantee the complete independence in church affairs. I am willing to remain in communion with the Vatican only under the condition that the prestige of the fatherland and the welfare of the people do not suffer thereby and that this communion concerns only questions of dogma." At the consecration of four bishops, which took place under the leadership of Archbishop Pi with the assistance of Bishop Francis Xavier Chao, the following dialogue took place. Chao turned to Pi with the request to consecrate the four priests to the office of bishop. Pi asked: "Have they been elected by the people?"

Chao: "Yes."

Pi: "Thanks be to God."

Pi now turned to the four priests and asked them 16 questions. Some of them were like this.

Pi: "Will you love your fatherland in imitation of the example of Christ? And under the leadership of the Communist Party and the People's Government will you direct all priests and believers to be participants in the socialist construction of our country?"

Candidates: "Yes, we promise."

Pi: "In accordance with the principle of the unity of love to fatherland and to religion, and to the greater honor of God and to the salvation of your souls, will you lead the church of China on the road of autonomy and independence?"

Candidates: "Yes, we promise."

Pi: "Will you use your natural talents and your education to do what the Holy Scriptures tell you?"

Candidates: "Yes, we promise."

The scope of these patriotic consecrations of bishops is not quite clear. The *Osservatore Romano* of January 16, 1959, spoke of more than 30 forced consecrations of bishops. Twenty of them had been clearly sacrilegious. In the meantime the number of patriotic bishops increased further. What Li Pai-shan wrote in *Stimmen der Zeit* in November 1958 was important: "Both the consecrating bishops and the consecrated priests are victims of inhuman pressures and of delusions after long periods of political brainwashing. As regrettable as such consecrations are, they are not a clear indication of schism. For these bishops are not acting of their own volition. To be sure, there is a greater danger of schism than ever before. For the most part it is a forced schism." This also agreed with the remark made by Father Johannes Fleckner, who stated that many bishops who had been consecrated sacrilegiously had previously enjoyed a good reputation. Liturgy, church order, celibacy, monasticism—nothing had been destroyed by these consecrations (*Rhein. Merkur,* March 25, 1960).

In view of these threatening developments, Pope Pius XII, on June 29, 1958, addressed the encyclical *Ad Apostolorum Principis* to the episcopate and clergy of China. He reminded them of his former letters and complained that through the clever action of the Communists' founding patriotic associations of priests, the church had fallen into very bad ways. With all the means at their disposal these associations were forcing their members to consent; and under the very superficial pretext of working for the fatherland, they were trying, step by step, to inculcate in Catholics the tenets of atheistic materialism. The encyclical discussed the abuse of love of fatherland and of peace and then turned against the progressive priests. It stated: "They are not ashamed to limit the authority of the supreme *magisterium* of the church according to their own ideas with the claim that there are questions of a social and economic nature where Catholics may legally circumvent the doctrines and rules given by the Holy See. It is completely superfluous to emphasize that this opinion is false and in error." Pius XII also quoted a few sentences from his address of November 2, 1954, to the episcopate: "The power of the church is not bound to the area of what people may call purely religious affairs. Rather, the whole compass of natural law, its definition, its interpretation, and its application as far as ethics are concerned, is subject to the church. The observance of the natural law according to the will of God is part of the way in which man can attain his supernatural goal. Therefore the church is the leader and the guide of man on the road to this supernatural goal." He declared that the patriotic priests not only limited the supreme *magisterium* of the church, but they also went so far in their boldness as to pay lip service to the idea of obeying the Pope in matters of faith and in what they called the norms of the church, but in reality they refused to accept the firm and clearly defined concepts and orders of the Holy See by claiming that these orders were the result of a secret conspiracy against their people. A further sign of their defection from the church consisted in the fact that they tried to proclaim a new law according to which Catholics could elect bishops on their own initiative so that pastoral care would be assured and that the dioceses could be directed by men who were accepted by the state. Pius XII stated: "The law of the church declares clearly and expressly that only the Holy See has the power to decide whether someone is worthy of the office of bishop and thus it gives to the Pope the right of free appointment of all bishops. Even though in certain cases it is permitted that other persons or corporations take part in the election of a candidate for an episcopal office, this is done regularly only on the basis of a permission expressly given by the Apostolic See to certain persons and corporations under certain definite conditions and presuppositions. From this it is clear that bishops who have been neither nominated nor approved by the Holy See or who have been elected and consecrated against its expressed orders, have neither the right nor the jurisdiction to teach, since this jurisdiction can be given to the bishops only by the Pope." The argument that the consecration of the bishops was necessary in order to assure the pastoral interests was disavowed in the encyclical by stating that such consecration often took place in dioceses where the bishops were in prison and were hindered in the free exercise of their jurisdiction. The Pope continued: "Therefore we are saddened that the priests who had such great zeal for the souls in the midst of all this persecution have been replaced by false shepherds, and the hierarchical order of the church has thus been destroyed and the authority of the Pope has been resisted in a rebellious manner."

A change in the conditions did not take place as a result of this encyclical. The patriotic elections of bishops did not stop. On March 17, 1960, the Bishop of Shanghai, Kung Ping-mei, was punished with life imprisonment after four and a half years of pre-trial imprisonment. In addition 13 priests of his diocese were condemned to from five to 20 years imprisonment. In the verdict it was stated that the "entire revolutionary clique of Kung Ping-mei has been an important instrument in the hands of the imperialists in order to undermine the regime of the People's Democracy. Its cooperation with the imperialists and its betrayal of the fatherland under cover of religion must be considered a crime of high treason. The imperialist agent Kung Ping-mei was always opposed to Communism and to the people. In the year 1950 he took over the position of Bishop of Shanghai with the intention of carrying out a plan that had been devised by the American spies Edward Walsh and Antonio Riberi." It stated that this clique had sabotaged the laws of the government and the patriotic movement of the Chinese Catholics. It had started rumors and spread them. It had worked for the invasion of the country by American imperialists. It had sabotaged the peace movement and had made contact with spies, had collected the secrets of the state, had given asylum to spies, had forced young people to leave the country, had hidden weapons and ammunition, had retained secret connections by radio, had delivered information concerning the number and the strength of the air protection of the volunteer army in Korea and the national defense establishment, had identified itself with the aims of the American imperialists and Chiang Kai-shek for the reconquest of mainland China, had supported anti-Communist organizations, had organized groups of resistance in the environment of Shanghai, complete with ammunition dumps, radios, and flags in churches and schools, and had established secret prisons where it persecuted Catholics. The court had taken care to draw up long lists of all possible crimes. On March 18, 1960, it was announced that the American Bishop James Walsh, who had directed the Catholic central bureau in Shanghai from 1948 until its abolition in 1951, had been condemned to 20 years in prison for the same crimes as Bishop Kung. A protest by the American government was rejected. Bishop Walsh had remained in China when most foreign missionaries left China in order to share the fate of the native clergy. At that time the Communists had recognized his courage. In 1958 he was, however, arrested.

The picture of the church that was portrayed in the few news items that came out of China was indeed a saddening picture. In the country most of the churches had been converted into schools, movies, sheds, exposition buildings, or meeting places, or had been destroyed. The former Bishop Vitus Chang reported: "My cathedral in Sinkiang has become a market hall. The monks and sisters work in it as sales people." Only in the big cities in districts where the priests had joined the patriotic associations were churches still open. But even here church life was suffering since priests were very often drafted for reeducation courses and for work duty and since also many of the faithful had been taken from their home congregations in order to fulfill the production quota of the state. Two Catholic Canadians, Jacques Hebert and Peter Trudeau, who from September 18 to October 22, 1960, made a trip through China at the invitation of the Chinese government, in 1961 published a very positive book about their impressions. In Chang Chung they wanted to visit a church on Sunday. It was empty. They knocked at the door of the parsonage, but the priests were in the fields as farm workers. On another Sunday they wanted to attend Mass in Shanghai. They reported: "The large cathedral in which formerly the entire congregation of Shanghai was assembled for services was almost empty. Only about 100 believers, mostly women and old men, were there. There were no young men, with the exception of five altar boys, who were in the sacristy." On the third Sunday they attended Mass in Canton. Again they reported that only about 40 believers were present, among them also a few young people and a few families.

On the whole, only those bishops and priests were able to function who either voluntarily or under duress had become members of the patriotic association. They were followers of the Communist ideology and accepted Communist orders. The clergy who had been loyal to Rome were either in prison or in forced labor camps and would be released only when they renounced their allegiance to Rome. Others were engaged as craftsmen. Old and sick priests were sent to church institutions which they were not allowed to leave. The seminaries were closed, since the seminarians had left them after they had joined the patriotic movement. Many seminarians had been sent into work camps, and no new seminarians had been admitted. The patriotic priests were enjoying the favor of the regime. Their economic condition was secure since the state gave them 40 percent of the income of the confiscated church property. The Party considered them representatives of the official Catholic Church and used them as proof to tourists from foreign countries that China still enjoyed religious freedom.

The German journalist Dr. Peter Schmidt reported that in the Catholic Church of St. Joseph in Shanghai, where he attended mass, nothing had been changed externally and there was no visible evidence that the priests had broken with the church of Rome. A loyal Catholic layman complained to him: "We do not know whether they have signed the declaration of loyalty. Brainwashing is done very discreetly, and nobody notices anything of it. We have only one criterion by which we can recognize the truth. The true church today is very poor. On the altar there are a few miserable flowers. The lights are extinguished as soon as daylight makes it possible to see what is going on. Electricity is saved. We find out about the betrayal of our priests only through devious ways. When they have lots of flowers on the altar and when the lights are burning in the church in the daytime we know they have been unfaithful. For the devil is very much interested in giving to his own all these gifts with which the churches can be renovated externally and can be shown to the world as beautiful empty shells, as proof of how pious the Communists are" (*Stuttgarter Nachrichten*, May 5, 1956). At the beginning of 1957 Chinese Christians requested the world not to visit Red China. They stated that the government frequently invited Christians in order to show them that religious freedom still existed in China. But they said that the priests and the faithful whom these visitors saw in China were all progressives who had been placed into their position of authority by the government. Places which were shown to foreign visitors had been prepared in advance for these visitors, and no foreigner was allowed to move around freely. Also the people who received the visitors —the chauffeurs, the servants—were all trained to carry on conversations with foreigners. There was no free conversation. There were no free, unsupervised visits.

A large part of the faithful did not want to have any traffic with the patriotic priests. They preferred to get along without the sacraments rather than to receive them from the hands of such priests. Added to this were the difficulties brought about by the establishment of collectives. The form of existence which was forced upon man in the collectives left no room for a Christian life. Since life in the people's communes did not allow for privacy, it was not even possible to pray in the family circles. Many Christians had to be satisfied with a silent prayer in their hearts. It was often the case that Christian families did not take their children to the "patriotic baptismal font" and they did not even baptize them themselves. They said: "Why should we do it? Our children will be taken away from us anyway. They will be taken into a Communist nursery, into a Communist kindergarten, and into a Communist school. They will wear the red kerchief of the pioneers, and later they will become fullfledged members of the Communist youth organization. We cannot give them any Christian education, and they will hear all day long that God is merely a myth. What sense would it make to baptize them in such an atmosphere?" At this point the whole program of the Communist Party in China becomes reality. "We shall not destroy the church; the church will disappear by herself."

C. PROTESTANTISM

1. The End of Missionary Work

Protestant missionary work in China began in 1807 when Charles Robert Morrison, missionary of the London Mission Society, arrived in Canton and laid the foundation for the missionary activity with his Bible translation into Chinese. The German Karl Guetzlaff showed to the Western Christian world the importance of missionary work in China. The actual missionary work began after 1842. American, English, German, and Scandinavian missionaries arrived in China in growing numbers. Older and new mission societies, especially the China Inland Mission, founded in 1865 by James Hudson Taylor, took up the work. The various denominations transplanted their peculiar beliefs to China. Among the thousands of missionaries there were teachers, doctors, deaconesses, who were supported by large amounts of money. Schools, colleges, medical institutes, universities, and hospitals were founded, and the YMCA began a flourishing activity. During the whole period the Anglo-Saxons were the leaders in Chinese mission work. In the year 1948 they did 80% of the missionary work in China. Also a number of German-speaking mission societies cooperated in China—since 1847 the Basel and the Rhenish Societies, since 1882 the Berlin Society; since 1897 the Hildesheim Mission to the Blind; since 1899 the East Asian Mission Society and the Liebenzell Society; and since 1921 the Breklum Mission Society. According to the World Christian Handbook of 1949 Protestant mission churches immediately before the Communist take-over numbered 623,526 communicants, 1,401,-777 baptized members, and 2,024 Chinese pastors.

Since no less than 132 mission societies of the various denominations and theological persuasions had worked in China, Chinese Protestantism consisted of a great variety of denominations. Although many of these missionary congregations united with each other, the atomization of mission work was very discouraging. Of 1,400,000 Protestant Christians 86% belonged to 12 large denominations while the other 14% were split among 40 denominations. A thorough cleanup work was necessary. Larger church bodies were the Presbyterian United Church of China, which included almost 30% of all Protestants; the Anglican Chinese Holy Universal Church; the Chinese Evangelical Protestant Church; the Lutheran Church of Justification by Faith; and the Methodist Church. Since 1922 the National Christian Council united the larger part of the non-Roman churches. At the same time it followed the goal of making them independent under Chinese leadership.

Chiang Kai-shek, who took over the leadership of the National People's Party, Kuomintang, after the death of Sun Yat Sen in 1925, also took over the alliance which Sun had formed with the Soviet Union in 1923. From the Soviet Union the propaganda against the imperialistic powers, especially England, was carried on; and the aim of the attack was primarily directed against the mission schools whose students were called the "hounds of foreigners." Most missionaries left the interior of the country. When Chiang Kai-shek broke with the Russians, the mission work continued undisturbed. Chiang Kai-shek himself became a Christian in 1930. When Japan attacked China in 1937 and occupied half of the country, the missionary work suffered great damage. When Japan capitulated in 1945, missions started up again. But the time of peace was soon interrupted by the civil war between Chiang Kai-shek and Mao Tse-tung, which lasted from 1947 to 1949.

The Protestants were more friendly to the Communists than the Catholics, since they had no connection with a foreign Pope. On the other hand, their predominantly American background became a heavy burden. But since the connection with a foreign mission society was not a matter of faith for them, it was clear that they could free themselves from the suspicion of imperialistic influence by separating from the foreign mission societies. There were in the Protestant congregations definite followers of Mao Tse-tung. That was understandable. Chinese Christians were and always had been—as Wilhelm Fahlbusch wrote in the *Evangelische Missionszeitschrift* of April 2, 1959—a minority in an unchristian state and had basically only the choice between the Kuomintang and the Communists. Both movements were revolutionary and totalitarian and had tried to gain absolute power. Fahlbusch wrote: "Historically we could say it this way. The Chinese civil war was a confessional war between two branches of one and the same movement. The schism of these branches had come through the power struggle of their leaders. The branch which was victorious was the one which originally had fought for the common interests of the Chinese people in the most radical and the most promising way. There was no choice or decision in this ideological confrontation. The criterion was only the carrying out of the goal of the revolution, the salvation of the people, and the liberation from civil war. Therefore it was an option neither for the West nor for the East. The ideological horizons were not even clear. To say the least, they were very hazy. The decision for Mao was an option for China, a position which was represented in the most powerful way in the Communist Party."

After this victory the Chinese had the alternative either to cooperate positively with the reconstruction of the new society or to retire into the ghetto of the persecuted congregation by confessing their allegiance to the Western mission countries. But why should they not cooperate? The government had accomplished a new organization of the people and the state. This was an undeniable accomplishment. Corruption, highway robbery, opium trade, prostitution, and many other evils had disappeared. A people that had been the political playball of foreign powers had developed into a proud nation which was respected and feared in the world. Should this not find enthusiastic consent among Chinese Christians? To be sure, it was a dictatorship with its lack of freedom for the individual and also the lack of freedom of confession of faith. But this fact, too, at least at the beginning, did not bring into focus the conflict for Chinese Christians. The leader of the missionary institute in Tsingtau, Dr. Wilhelm Seufert, gave the following reason: The Chinese were determined by their past. The battle for the freedom of personality, which was important in the spiritual history of the Western powers and had been influenced by Greece, was completely unknown to the Chinese spirit. The Chinese word *tse-yu,* which was used in the Bible as a translation for "free," had a social background. It originally designated the person who had freed himself from his social background and was serving his own self, who was asocial; and thus it designated a very questionable condition. The jump from "natural thinking" to the freedom of the children of God was much greater for the Chinese Christian than for a person who had been grounded in the Western tradition. The Chinese Christian accepted the obligation to the new state, especially since the state made great social progress; and they tried to work for that free development of life within this framework. In this sense he had not finished the war of liberation, but was beginning to fight it for himself.

From all this it became clear that when the Chinese churches were ready to cooperate with the state, they were not betraying or even forsaking Christianity. In the spring of 1950 a group of Christians in Peking discussed these matters with Chou En-lai. Their leader was the executive secretary of the Chinese YMCA, Wu Yao-tsung. He had formerly studied at Union Theological Seminary in New York and had earned the M.A. degree at Columbia University. He had access to Chou En-lai by the fact that Chou himself had been a member of the YMCA in Tientsin. The result of this discussion was the founding of a committee for the reform of Christianity in China under the presidency of Wu. The motto of the reform movement was: "Back to the pure faith! Away from foreign lying priests! Away from foreign imperialists!" In May of 1950 members of the National Christian Council also had a meeting with Chou En-lai. On June 24 the Korean War broke out. The wave of hatred against the imperialists which went with it, especially against the USA, strongly influenced the work of the mission societies and the inner position of the Chinese Christians. After further discussions of the National Christian Council with members of the government, a manifesto signed by 40 church leaders and theologians was published in August 1950. It treated the way of the Christian church in the present epoch of reconstruction and laid the foundation for a National Organization of Evangelical Christians that had been demanded by the government. It gave itself the name *Three Self Reform Movement.* This word "Three Self" came from a motto which had been coined about the year 1850 by the American Rufus Anderson for the independence of the younger churches: "Self-extension, self-preservation, self-administration." In the Chinese manifesto the work of the missionaries was recognized, but it was added that they had been influenced by the fact that they came from imperialistic countries that had penetrated China at the same time as the missions. It stated that it was now their task to create a church that would be free from foreign influences. The manifesto demanded of the churches and their congregations that they "should fight under the leadership of the government, without wavering, against imperialism, feudalism, or bureaucratic capitalism and should try to build an independent democratic, peaceful, united, flourishing, and strong China." The National Christian Council at its meeting in October 1950, supported these aims and put pressure on the churches affiliated with the council to take over the task of self-administration and self-financing. Besides, the denominations were called upon to cooperate with each other and to come closer to each other with the goal that one day a common Chinese church could be created. The congregations and churches raised offerings for Korea, and on banners exhibited on the streets one could read: "He who was nothing let him sell his clothing and buy a sword." Under these banners was written: "Every congregation buys one cannon." One of the Chinese airforce planes in Korea received the name

"Pursuit Plane of the Threefold Self-Reform of the Church in China." The Church of Christ in China had collected a large amount for this airplane.

In April 1951, 151 representatives from all denominations were brought by the government to Peking, where they were told to subscribe to a strongly worded political manifesto. In this manifesto, Russia and China were praised as powers of peace, Americans were condemned as imperialists, and the Christian world organizations were called masks of American imperialism, every connection with which should be broken off. It stated: "We believe that the Church of China trusts in God and can be built up under the splendid leadership of President Mao Tse-tung through its own strength as a more complete and purer church which will serve the people in a better way." Furthermore, the manifesto contained a consent to the confiscation of all missionary property by the government, to the policy of the government, to the battle in Korea, to the peace movement, to soil reform, and to political education. The churches were asked to purify themselves by "establishing meetings of self-implications through which all imperialistic connections would be uncovered and the souls of all Christians would be cleansed for the new ideas." Furthermore, the cutting off of all connections with the foreign mission societies and the establishment of complete self-administration and the enthusiastic participation in the movement against America and for Korea were entrusted to them. The missionary societies were accused of many crimes. It was said that the first English missionary to China, Robert Morrison, had been the author of the degrading peace treaty after the opium war; that Livingstone had been a cultural aggressor in Africa and had prepared the enslavement of the Africans; and that missionaries were murderers of orphans, of the sick, and of the refugees; that they were deceivers and spies.

The year 1951 was the year of large-scale expulsions of missionaries. Already during the civil war their number had decreased from 4,000 to 2,000. After the victory of Communism their work had been limited or had been made completely impossible. Their free movement was limited to their places of residence. They were allowed to preach in their own churches, but they had to expect that certain members of their congregations one day would declare to them that they should leave the difficult task of preaching to a Chinese brother. With a few exceptions they were forbidden to give instruction. Since many of them had become completely inactivated, they were recalled by their mission societies. The 1,200 missionaries who, during the summer of 1950, were still in the country after the outbreak of the Korean war were accused of being representatives of Western imperialism and of espionage; and they were suspected in every way so that any contact with them became very dangerous for Chinese Christians. Therefore, further missionaries were recalled by their mission societies. Others were expelled, among them about 500 American missionaries. Others again were arrested. In the late summer of 1950 the European bishops of the Anglican Church resigned. In their places Chinese bishops were appointed who then separated the church from the mother church in England. The London Mission Society was forced to relinquish all of its Chinese mission fields and to stop its 145-year-old missionary activity in China. About 50 German missionaries left the country in 1951. The last German missionary who returned home in the fall of 1952 was Felix Paulsen of the Breklum mission, who had been arrested on November 9, 1950.

Expulsion of the missionaries was in part accompanied by the enthusiastic consent of the Chinese Christians. The work of the foreign missionaries was condemned in summary fashion. The rector of the seminary in Chungking, Marcus Chen, published a prayer in which he wrote: "Father, Lord of the Heavens and of the Earth, the thing that is most difficult for me to bear and that worries me most is the fact that the honorable name of Jesus Christ and the holy name of God are mixed up with imperialism. Unfortunately imperialism has used the Christian church. Thus, for example, the way for the proclamation of the Gospel in the interior of China was opened through the Opium War and the Treaty of Nanking. For many years Western missionaries enjoyed privileges of unjust treaties and special rights to bring the glad tidings. Now the revolution in China has destroyed imperialism. But many missionaries are still fighting against giving up their special rights. Many are still sympathetic to imperialism and are impatient to see their privileges restored. Therefore I ask you, God, to open the eyes of the missionaries through the Holy Spirit, to lead them to a new awakening and to a right understanding so that they may lift themselves up with us Chinese Christians and may rise with us to resist imperialism and especially to consider America the instigator of war through her aggressive words and actions."

But there were also other voices. Thus the Hakka Church addressed the following farewell to the Basel mission society: "Dear Brothers and Sisters, in this great and difficult hour when our missionaries are taking leave of us, we would like to send to you a greeting of cordial remembrance. We thank you that you have sent to us the messengers of the Gospel from a far land across continents and oceans. We thank you that you have worked first for us and then with us for more than a hundred years in the work of our Lord Jesus Christ. Also in the future we shall continue to live under the Gospel of Jesus Christ alone. We recognize Jesus Christ as our sole Savior and Redeemer. We shall remain part of the church which is ecumenical and world-wide and exists in all countries. Therefore we shall struggle to remain the light and the salt in our country and to witness to our Chinese brothers of the Gospel in word and deed. We know that the kingdoms of this world will all pass away and that the kingdom of God will come to us, and we are willing to prepare ourselves also in China through our suffering. We stay behind in great need. We ask you to think of us in the future and to pray to God constantly. Pray that the kingdom may come also to China. Pray for the leaders of the Chinese church that they may be strong in the hour of temptation. Pray for the congregations which are often sheepfolds without shepherds that they may remain faithful to the great Shepherd. Pray that we may find the right way to serve our people and to remain faithful to our Lord and Savior. Pray for us as we shall pray for you."

In the course of the soil reform the possessions of the church were expropriated. After the cultural institutions, all schools, welfare and other institutions which had been directed by foreigners were registered with the state on December 29, 1950, the expropriation of all missionary property was decreed in September 1951. Schools, hospitals, and other institutions were taken over by the

state. Included among these were also the high school for missions
of the East Asia Mission at Tsingtao, which had been founded by
Richard Wilhelm and which was directed by Dr. Seufert. It was
transformed into a Communist propaganda school, and the hospital
connected with it became a hospital for workers while the former
employees were subjected to reeducation. Before that time the German church in Tsingtao had been surrendered to the government
because the taxes had become unbearable for the small German
congregation. It was used now for meetings and dances. Also other
foreign churches were dissolved because most of their members
had emigrated.

2. The Patriotic Three-Self Movement

Chinese congregations and churches had in part become leaderless through the expulsions. Separation from the mission societies
and the expropriations of the possessions of the church deprived
the church of her financial basis. Her charitable work was made
impossible and her proclamation was strictly limited. In addition,
there were the arrests of leading Christians. The secretary of the
National Christian Church, the Methodist Bishop W. Y. Chen, was
arrested in Shanghai because as an emissary of imperialism he had
"Americanized" the Protestant Church of China. The same accusation was leveled against the secretary general of the YMCA, the
Anglican Bishop Y. Tsu, who had fled abroad. On March 11, 1952,
three professors of the Christian university Yenching near Peking
were arrested. Among them was the professor of theology, Dr. Tsu-
Chen Chao. He was one of the six presidents of the World Council
of Churches and had welcomed the victory of Communism as a
fulfillment of his national aspirations. He renounced his former connections with capitalist and imperialistic circles and on April 8,
1951, declared his resignation from the praesidium of the WCC in
protest against the Korean resolution of its Central Committee. But
he was not able to escape arrest. The National Christian Council
accused him of having served aggressive policies of American imperialism under the mask of religion and of having remained passive
toward the Reform Movement. As one additional crime was men-

tioned his personal relationship to the men of the World Council of Churches. For this there was no excuse. The Communists released him that he might have an opportunity to think about his crimes. The magazine of the University, *New Yen-ching*, accused him of having placed faithfulness to Christ above love to fatherland and of having written: "Religious faith goes beyond national and racial boundaries." Furthermore, he was accused of having insisted on love of all human beings, on the ecumenical dimensions of the church, and on the independence of Christians from the "people's ideology."

The churches were not spared self-incriminations in public meetings that became a typical phenomenon of Chinese Communism. Church buildings were often abused by the holding of incrimination meetings against clergymen, who were then forced to confess their sins before the people. The bishop who had years ago baptized Marshal Chiang Kai-shek and his wife and had received them into the Methodist Church was now forced to condemn himself publicly on account of this action. In a great self-incrimination meeting in Shanghai, 10,000 Christians were forced to curse themselves and the mission society which they had served. Above the meeting place the following motto was printed: "He who does not hate his father and mother is not worthy of me." The only daughter of the president of Yenching University, Lu Chih Wei, brought the following accusation against her father during the meeting: "I accuse my father of having blinded me and of not having placed me at the side of the people." This self-criticism which the father was expressing did not please the masses or the daughter. She accused him that he was a Christian who had no feeling for the Communist Party and had criticized the party instead of being thankful to it. When the father broke into tears at this accusation of his daughter, she said: "Lu Chih Wei, why should I not fight against you? Why should I protect you and ask for your life and give credence to your devilish lies? Do you believe that your tears can bribe my conscience?"

There was much apostasy in the young congregations. The number of Chinese Protestants today is estimated at 700,000. Pastors left their office and denied their faith. Students at missionary schools swore off their faith. After he had attended a Communist university for half a year, a former student directed the following letter to his former missionary: "I am no longer the person whom you used to know. Apart from my body, which is the same as formerly, my whole feeling and thinking has changed. I have become a new man within the classless body of revolutionary pioneers, one who believes loyally in Marxist-Leninism. I shall never again live for myself, but only for the masses. The things that occupy me completely are the advancement from socialism to perfect Communism. In this new thinking I have been incomparably blessed and have found happiness. I hope very much that you will very carefully examine the differences between religion and materialism and that you will recognize what religion really is. I am sorry that I have to tell you that I no longer believe in God or pray to him. I can no longer consider you my spiritual father, but I send you my greetings in revolutionary love."

As sad as they were, these occurrences should, however, not be generalized. Intoxication for revolutionary changes carried away those people who were not firm in their faith and blinded them. Such aberrations had also happened in the old established churches of the Christian West. But there were also signs of unshakable loyalty to the faith. Three representatives of the World Council of the YMCA, who visited China in 1957, wrote about these years: "From 1949 to 1952 the Christians of China passed through a period of great uncertainty and anxiety. At that time many members left the churches and the Christian movement. Without a doubt, many church leaders have been arrested and some of them are still in prison." But even where there were no longer divine services, the Christian life did not become extinct. In many congregations the secret work for Christ continued on a person-to-person basis. A pastor who could no longer take care of his work officially and who was employed in a small milk distributing plant during the day, in the evening visited homes in order to strengthen the faithful. Bible women did their work and doctors proclaimed the Word of God in the hospitals. Family devotions were conducted. Of the Hakka congregations it was reported that with few exceptions public services had stopped completely four to five years ago, but that secretly the services had continued. In a certain district a leading personality assembled members of the congregation in his own house for family devotions. The number of participants continued to grow; and when there were over a hundred, the government in September 1956 was asked to restore normal divine services. The request was granted. Thus a total of 41 congregations were reestablished in the Hakka church.

The Three-Self Movement became the official leading organization of Chinese Protestantism. It established its own organ in the weekly *Tien Feng* ("Heavenly Wind"). Besides Wu, the leader of the theological seminary in Chungking, Marcus Chen, became one of its leading men. At first the movement did not try to interfere with the spiritual substance of the individual churches but wanted merely to free them from foreign influence. It had no intention of establishing a uniform confession of faith or liturgical order in the churches or changing their constitutions and organizations. But it insisted that the existing differences should no longer be sources of dissension, and that all Christians should live peacefully side by side. This principle of mutual esteem culminated in amalgamating a number of theological seminaries so that Nanking Union Theological Seminary, which was founded in 1952, served members of 11 different communions and the Yenching Union Theological Seminary in Peking served seven groups.

The combination of modes of theological education which was carried on in five theological seminaries in Nanking, Peking, Shanghai, Canton, and Chunking had after a time a definite effect. A further motive for the overcoming of the traditional divisions was found in the experience of the revolution. In the task given to all churches to prove their faith in this new situation and in the desire for unity, Wu Yao-tsung declared at the end of 1954 that "it is natural that the Chinese Christians should try to find inspiration for the new viewpoints in the meaning of the Gospel and that they should consider the situation in which they are placed. There are many indications that Chinese Christians grasp for the treasure of the Gospel from new perspectives. This is a healthy development; and if it matures, it will constitute an enrichment of the life of the Chinese church."

Under the leadership of the Three-Self Movement, churches have subjected themselves to the Communist state. To be sure, the Anglican Bishop Kwong Hsun Ting stated in an address to the general committee of the Christian World Student Council in Tutzing in 1956 that there was a deep contrast between the Christian faith in God and Communist atheism, and he declared: "We do not automatically support everything that the Communists are doing." But the official pronouncements of the Three-Self Movement were completely identical with the propaganda of the state. Thus the Pan-Chinese Congress, meeting at Peking in 1954, called the World Council of Churches Assembly at Evanston "a tool of Anglo-American imperialism." The churches were forced to accept expressly all actions of the state. They were forced to remove from their hymnals certain hymns which were considered imperialistic remnants, including those that were considered to be critical of the happy socialist society and those which indicated that the world was a vale of tears. All forms of healing by prayer and exorcism were forbidden. The biblical hope that Christ will return at the end of the world, which was being attacked furiously by the Communists, was retained but was made harmless. The magazine of the Three-Self Movement stated that although Christians could not give up this hope since it was taught in the New Testament, this did not mean that they had to deny the world. Belief in the approaching end of the world was declared to be compatible with the Communist idea of progress; for the biblical writers had exaggerated somewhat in order to lead people away from sin and had painted the world in dark colors. It was stated that in the New Testament there were also statements that the world was getting better.

That the Three-Self Movement had no chance to say anything critical about the state was shown by the following occurrence. In 1957 Wu Yao-tsung, in the Consultative People's Conference of which he was a member, had thanked the government and the party for its religious policy, but he had also criticized that there had been interference by government and party organizations in the life of the congregations. This accusation was taken up by his fellow delegate, Marcus Chen, who declared that discrimination against Christians on account of their faith in God must be rejected in the same manner as the desecration of the graves of the ancestors. But, he said, the mistakes made in carrying out the policy against religion did not prove that there was no religious freedom. In other areas of public life the government had made even greater mistakes. All one had to do was to see these deficiencies and to do away with them. Christians also were not without mistakes. But, thanks to the help of the Three-Self Movement, the church had cleansed her proclamation from the poison of imperialistic, feudalistic, and capitalistic thinking. Soon after this speech, Chen was denounced by his fellow Christians under the leadership of Wu and was subjected to brainwashing. Since he had considered the mistakes of the government in religious matters less serious than its shortcomings in other fields and at the same time had compared the former to the desecration of graves, he had defamed the government, the party, the constitution, and socialism in the worst possible way. And since he had spoken in the name of the church, he had brought the Christians into conflict with the government and the party.

The desire for the removal of the traditional denominational boundaries was fulfilled in 1958 through the initiative of the Three-Self Movement. In August 1958, 65 congregations in Peking decided to unite into four congregations, one each in the north, the east, the south, and the west part of the city. The magazine of the Three-Self Movement justified this move by means of the declaration that of the 65 congregations more than 10 had no single member left, 5 had not more than a dozen, and another 20 had been under the leadership of rightist deviationists and other evil influences. The Sunday services in all these congregations had been attended by less than 500 people. The amalgamation of the 65 congregations into 4 led to the freeing of large numbers of pastors, Bible women, and students of theology. Of these 150 were employed as laborers in the agricultural communes. In September 1958, 200 congregations in Shanghai united into 12 or 15 congregations. Similar changes took place in other large cities. The process of unification was in all cases very simple. Representatives of various congregations met and decided that their leadership and organs of control no longer existed and that the local Three-Self Committee had taken over the supervision of all possessions and of all employees. Existing differences in doctrine were eliminated. Thus, e.g. in Chinchow, Province of Liaoning, the amalgamation of the Church of Christ and the Seventh Day Adventists took place under the following ground rules: (1) The designations of both churches were abolished and the church was to be known in the future as the Christian City Church of Chinchow. (2) The organizations, buildings, properties, and persons serving the church were combined. Superfluous property was given to the socialist movement. (3) The Adventist practice of giving a tithe was abolished. Each member could give as much as he wanted to give. (4) After the union, former patriotic resolutions were adjusted to the new conditions. Preparations were made for the brainwashing of the individual church members. (5) As an answer to the appeal of the government to produce steel, the church was to erect its own people-owned factory and was to be responsible for it. The dean of studies of the theological seminary in Peking, Chao Fu San, assured the world that the combination of congregations had not been forced upon the church by the government. He admitted that there had been a certain movement from above in the direction of unity, but the strongest impetus had come from the congregations themselves. He stated: "I believe that it had become clear to many people that the differences had to be eliminated after the liberation. These differences were historical accidents. They sapped our strength and hindered us in carrying out the task of spreading the kingdom of Jesus Christ. We had to overcome them in some way."

There was no lack of opposition to the Three-Self Movement. Again and again accusations were published against pastors who did not follow the party line, or news was published about the expulsion of those who did not want to go along with progress. There were also arrests of parish pastors and church leaders, among them Kimber Den, the Anglican Bishop of Chekiang, who was released in 1956 after four years in prison. According to the report of missionary Helmholtz, who was expelled in 1959, Christian students were degraded to become janitors, or they were sent to workcamps. In prison a pastor was promised that he would be released if he would stop praying, for his praying showed spiritual instability.

But he did not stop praying and thus remained in prison. Another pastor was harshly criticized because he had admonished people in an appeal to pray for China's liberation from spiritual darkness. Local interference led to the arrest of whole groups of pastors and their co-workers, the closing of churches, and the confiscation of Bibles and hymnals as reactionary materials.

An important means to free pastors and congregations from oppositional ideas was the continuous and intensive retraining for the purpose of "thought reform" which was a refined form of brainwashing. The English missionary Geoffrey Bull, in his book *At the Door of the Yellow Gods,* wrote about how he himself became an object of brainwashing. He had come to Tibet in 1947 and was captured by the Chinese when they invaded that country and was kept in prison for three years. Since he showed himself to be a stubborn opponent of Communism, they looked upon him as a lost soul which had to be saved. Therefore he was transferred to a prison which was not an institution for punishment but an eerie caricature of a theological seminary. He wrote: "Communists look upon these institutions as a kind of hospital whose inmates are infected by the bacillus of reactionary ideology and false social concepts. These institutions are supervised by functionaries who are considered physicians. Symptoms of the sickness of the patients are collected and analyzed by the hospital attendants, the leaders of the cells, and other functionaries. On the basis of the diagnosis, the 'doctors' recommend a fitting therapy: useful books, colloquia, and 'battle discussions,' also solitary imprisonment, handcuffs, and chains, and finally work education in concentration camps." In Bull's case the treatment began with solitary confinement and Communist propaganda materials. From time to time he was brought into a dark court of justice and was asked about his attitude. Behind a large table hung with black drapes sat three or four functionaries, as immovable as idols. Bull was forced to sit on a low chair opposite them. The hearing was carried on in an icy atmosphere. The inscriptions on the wall told him: "Confess Your Crimes and Live. Hide Your Crimes and Die. Harshness and Mildness Are Combined Here." At the hearings the prisoner was left in the dark about what was desired of him and of what he had been accused. He could save himself only through a complete self-analysis. After some time Bull was placed in a cell with other prisoners. They were called fellow students. From now on the main emphasis was on group discussions. These were led by a fellow prisoner who was advanced on the road of progress. With great zeal many of the fellow prisoners tried to propagate Communist doctrine. With even greater passion than the Communist functionaries they wrestled with the souls of their resisting comrades. They often showed vehement hatred which they tried to cover up with the motto: "Our Fellow Student Needs Our Help." These newly-converted outdid each other in sycophancy in the hope that they would be sent to a work education camp and would finally be released. He who was slow to understand was chained with handcuffs and was instructed for about a week without interruption so that he could scarcely go to sleep for more than one or two hours. Another method was "battle discussion," a debate of a whole group of converts. At this "squeezing session" prisoners who made difficulties were given to understand that they would be completely destroyed by the advance of the masses. Indeed their fellow prisoners often attacked them physically with hysterical shouts and asked the functionaries to use force. If several battle discussions were carried on at the same time, the whole prison resounded like a madhouse. All prisoners were expected to apply regular self-criticism. As a typical example Bull quoted the self-criticism of a prisoner who had understood what was wrong. He stated: "As far as my daily life is concerned I must confess that when I washed the hallway this week I did not show the necessary zeal and thoroughness. I could have done more, but I didn't do it because my thoughts were not concentrating sufficiently on my daily work. I think daily about my case. I must change. Beginning with today I will fight constantly against egocentricity, this hereditary sin of the bourgeoisie. I will try to arrive at truly proletarian thinking and will consider the welfare of the masses in the first place. Many signs indicate that I have not yet overcome my class-consciousness. I am thankful to my fellow students for every bit of advice which makes it easier for me to remove my faults." From time to time all prisoners were assembled, and each one had to make a general confession and had to mention all the laws against which he had transgressed during the first half year. After this, changes in personnel often took place. The old leaders of the cells were frequently deposed and other prisoners took their places. Bull, who did not give in, was finally dismissed and expelled. When he was dismissed, one of his oppressors, probably with sincere conviction, told him: "We hope that you are leaving Communist China with good memories."

One of the victims of this brainwashing was Pastor Wang Mingtao of Peking. Without any connection with a mission society he had independently built up his congregation and had done great work through evangelization and through writing. During the Japanese occupation he had resisted the demand to show reverence to the Emperor. With the same determination he refused to bow to Communism and called the work of the Three-Self Movement a service of Baal and a discipleship of Judas. As late as 1954 he wrote in his *Spiritual Food Quarterly:* "Christians will obey all higher authorities and governments, but Christians who obey God's will to keep the church pure and to spread the Gospel of salvation will not permit anyone to interfere. . . . But what a misfortune! Now there are a great number of preachers who seemingly have the understanding that the church should in all things obey the higher authorities and the government. These people are deceiving many Christians who cannot fully understand the words of the Bible. The faith and life of the church become subject to human systems, human powers, and human control. The result is that the church is covered up, the Holy Scriptures are perverted, and the essence of the church is falsified." In September 1955 he and his wife were arrested. The first trial led to no result, because his followers took his side. In the second trial, when patriotic Christians accused him of having stated that dogma was more important than patriotism, he was condemned to 15 years in prison because he had conducted illegal Bible classes and had served as a spy. But a year later he was released. Shortly after September 30, 1956, he made the following confession of guilt at a meeting of the Three-Self Movement: "I owe it to the patient attitude of the government and to the reeducation which I have experienced that I have recognized my mistakes. . . . As a citizen of my country I should have followed its laws and should have supported its program and the policy of the government, but I have always made reactionary statements and have tried to sabotage various plans of the government and the social program of reconstruction. I sincerely confess this in the presence of the people and the government and I hope that those who have been led astray by me will return to the right road." Pastor Wang Ming-tao was, as Dr. Seufert wrote, one of those rare men who, from the recognition of Christ alone, tried to influence people's life and to build a congregation. As long as he was bound to Christ he was free. Therefore his brainwashing was a catastrophe which could not be underestimated.

Also two denominations which were closely allied with Pentecostalism lost their independence. The *Jesus Family* had been founded in 1921 by Ching Tien Ying from Shantung. Educated in the religion of Confucianism, he had joined the Christian church; and after intensive Bible study he had come to the conviction that the church was the communion of those who had been called out of this world and that the Christian had to live a life of poverty and self-sacrifice. In the village of Ma Chung he collected a large number of followers as the Family of Jesus. In other parts of China a hundred or more such families came into being. Membership was offered to those who would renounce the world. Members had to give up parents, children, home, and property. Children no longer belonged to the parents, but to the whole "Family." As the center of the religious experience it was felt that the consciousness of a living relationship with Jesus Christ must be established through definite religious experiences. The first of these experiences was called the receiving of faith, a kind of ecstatic prayer with the characteristic physical phenomena which accompanied it. Training in Holy Scriptures was considered as an indispensable part of this education. These Families of Jesus were respected by the Communists because they were of purely Chinese origin. Also during the period of Japanese occupation they had refused to venerate the Emperor and had gone underground. They had welcomed the Communist victory and had anticipated the new order in their own way on the basis of original Christian Communism. But a tragic occurrence brought about the end of their independence. Their founder, Ching

Tien Ying, was accused of moral aberrations. The interference by the state, which had started in this way, soon spread to the whole group. All of Ching's followers were subjected to brainwashing. They were organized as a church and incorporated into the Three-Self Movement. Similar to Ching's group were the origin and the work of the "Small Sheepfold," an evangelistic movement which originated outside of the official churches and gained considerable strength. In the Province of Chekiang alone it had 362 places of worship and numbered 39,000 members. After the arrest of its leader it was cleansed of counter-revolutionary elements. During a conference in the summer of 1957 it decided to participate in the Three-Self Movement.

Dr. Seufert stated with resignation: "After all these catastrophes, we are confronted in China by Christians who have completely accepted Communist coordination and who believe that the message of salvation in this world can be reconciled with the Gospel of the kingdom of God. All other voices have been silenced, at least for the present." But it must also be stated that Chinese Christians who have been shut off from the outside world and for many years have been exposed to a continuous attack of one-sided propaganda are not in a position to have a valid picture of reality. Thus they do not have the ability to look at themselves critically, and this lack again has had its consequences for their decisions concerning their faith.

Significant was what the reporter Dr. Peter Schmidt wrote in the *Stuttgarter Nachrichten* of May 5, 1956, about a conversation which he had had with the director of the Yenching Seminary, Dr. F. F. Li, and with its Dean of Studies, Chao Fu San. He said that the latter was the most brilliant person he had met on his trip. Both assured him that today the churches were in a better position than ever before, for they had been cleansed of the so-called "rice Christians." They told him that the economic improvements in China had given new impetus to religion. Christians were completely free to live according to their faith, and the applications to enter the theological seminary had never been so high before. Dr. Schmidt asked: "Why are there so many arrests of pastors and priests?" Chao answered without hesitation: "Because they have broken the laws as enemies of the state or through immoral conduct. Do you know that the papal nuncio has for two years associated with reactionary circles which had intended to blow up our President Mao Tse Tung at a festival?" Schmidt looked at the highly intelligent face of his partner and asked him with amazed incredulity: "Do you really believe that? This is truly an absurd invention." Chao was shaking with laughter: "It is absurd, it is unbelievable, I know. But I have seen proofs at an exposition. The confession, the bomb, everything." Schmidt said: "Don't you know that all of this is pure invention and falsification like the whole Korean bacterial warfare?" Again he was interrupted by the laughter of the two clergymen. Dr. Li said: "I have seen those airplanes myself when they were spreading the bacteria. I had been invited to visit the border region. The airplane was flying high above us, hardly to be seen. Soon the searchers went out and came back with infected ants and with pieces of paper covered with infected bacteria. No, you can believe that everything our government says is true." With brains stuffed with such fairy tales and the continuous self-praise of the Communists it was not surprising that instances like the following occurred. A certain pastor, Sha Yi, explaining Genesis 2:15 that "he built and preserved" in a sermon praised the Communists in the following words: "They, the Communists, build and preserve us. They who kill the aggressors in Korea and liquidate our inner enemies are the preservers in the sense of this word. In this way they are leading our country on the road to fame, strength, peace, and blessings."

Dr. Schmidt reported: "He who has been coordinated can live in peace in China." And Chao stated, "The status of the Christians in China has been raised in the measure in which Western influence has decreased. We have become indigenous churches; we are standing on our own feet; we are recognized the same as the Moslems and other theists." The church buildings which had been taken over during the expropriation of the land have been returned to the churches in various places. The state has even contributed to the restoration of the churches. The self-support of the congregations has been facilitated by the fact that since 1952 no taxes had to be paid for church property. Evangelization was permitted but was strictly limited to church buildings. A new Bible translation was being prepared.

Concerning the inner life of the churches very little was known. The knowledge was naturally limited to a few highlights. In 1955 a Quaker delegation spent three and a half weeks in China. Duncan Wood reported later that the churches modestly but steadily were increasing in numbers. Basic theological instruction was given to the future clergy in common seminaries. The delegation found no planned Marxist indoctrination in these seminaries. The demand to be admitted to these seminaries was greater than their ability to receive these candidates. The Christians had identified themselves to a large degree with the national concerns of China. He stated: "They say that Christianity and Marxism are incompatible. But, like the other citizens, they are not free to show any opposition to the policies of the government. They are placed on the same level with other citizens in that political information from the outside is available to them only to a limited degree." Representatives of the YMCA who visited the Chinese YMCA in 1956 told that the YMCA movement was very active. There were YMCA's in 26 big cities with 140 full-time employees. The number of visitors at the meetings of the YMCA could be estimated in the hundreds of thousands, and the cooperation between the YMCA and the churches was excellent.

From March 16 to April 3, 1956, Professor Hromadka spent a few weeks in China at the invitation of the theological seminaries of Peking and Nanking. He spoke at a Pan-Chinese Conference of the Three-Self Movement and returned with tremendous impressions. In his reports he agreed completely with the ideas of the Three-Self Movement. Entirely different was the tone of a letter which was written by a Chinese Christian in Shanghai a few months later, on October 10, 1956: "The Gospel is still being preached, but it is confused with other ideas. The churches, as far as their membership is concerned, are only half as strong as they were formerly. As far as their material resources are concerned, they have less than half the strength they possessed formerly. Some people are afraid to go to church. Others do not want to hear any politics in church because they can hear these things elsewhere. They are looking for food like hungry sheep and are finding no nourishment."

A group from the Anglican Church of Australia under the leadership of Archbishop Howard W. K. Mowll was in China at the end of 1956 and visited 10 of the 15 Anglican dioceses and met all Anglican bishops. The Archbishop reported: "Several bishops emphasized to us that Christianity and Communism are fundamentally divided because one has faith in redemption through Christ and the other is a man-made ideology. But the bishops are of the opinion that the accomplishments of the present-day government are remarkable and that they are good for the people." Many Christians were elected to local, provincial, and national committees. A three-man committee of the church to which Wu Yao-tsung belonged had the task to examine immediately every violation of religious freedom and to report it to the government. Concerning the prohibition of church mass meetings outside of the churches, the Chinese church leaders were not very much worried because the attendance of non-Christians at church services had increased. However, the Christian education of the youth was very difficult because the state had taken over all Christian schools and other agencies. Discrimination against Christians did not exist. Many former students and pupils of Christian universities and missionary schools today had leading positions in hospitals, schools, and universities. The period of the drastic liquidations was past and forgotten and only indoctrination continued.

An idea of the financial needs existing in the church was shown in a letter which the church in South China (that had had its beginnings in the work of the Basel Mission) wrote to the Chinese sister churches in Northern Borneo on July 6, 1957. From that letter it became clear that pastors and preachers received about 12 People's Dollars per month and that many of the poorer congregations could not even pay 10 People's Dollars to their pastors. Therefore it was decided to send subscription lists to the Chinese congregations in Hong Kong and Northern Borneo in order to help the poorer congregations on the Chinese mainland in their emergency.

More detailed was the report by Dr. Walter Freytag after his trip to China in the year 1957. He admitted that he did not have a complete view concerning the position of the Christian church there. But he said: "As imposing as the new buildings of the new churches are; as much as we notice that the services in the cities are attended by 50% to 100% of the members of the congregations; as much as we are impressed that in one big city where there are 50,000 Christians there are not less than 15 full-time and 130 part-time co-workers in the youth work; as much as we must notice that the publication of Christian literature in comparison to the number of Christians is much greater than it is in our country, we must not gain the impression that this is all that can be said. It may look entirely different in the villages, and the health of the church cannot be defined by statistical figures." In conversations with Chinese Christians Freytag everywhere met the apparent desire to say only good things about Communist China, to emphasize the freedom of faith, to point out that discrimination against Christians had ended, and to tell about friendly acts of the government and of the party. He had the impression that these Christians were concerned with the defense of their country and of themselves. They wanted to show the foreign visitor that the outside world had a false picture of the Chinese Christians. They wanted to be recognized as Christians.

Freytag said: "People freely admit that the party and the state have made mistakes. But there is no fundamental criticism of the new system. It is difficult to get into a conversation about the events of 1949-1953, about the arrests, the accusations, and the executions of leading Christians which have been reported in our press." He had the impression "that they do not merely want to be silent about these things but have probably forgotten them or do not want to see them any more." But on the other hand, there was a clear borderline between Christians and their Communist environment. Christians proclaimed publicly: "We are not atheists. We believe in God, in the resurrection, and in eternal life. We are praying." Nowhere was there any talk about a theological undergirding of the present ideological system. The Christians declared: "We are convinced that the Gospel is entirely different from anything that has existed or exists now in this world and that we must proclaim this Gospel. But we are also convinced that we can do this only if we are loyal to our people." Strikingly rare was a tendency to retreat into other-worldliness. One could see again and again that Christians said their table prayers openly in public. It happened that young people answered correctly the ideological questions put to them in state examinations, and added: "This I have learned, but my Christian faith tells me differently." Professor Freytag was very much impressed by the fact that 70 Christians participated in a lay course in a theological seminary which met five evenings per week for a period of three years and prepared them for voluntary service as witnesses. Chinese Christian congregations were growing. More adults were being baptized in China than in some churches of India and Indonesia. In one big city the Christian church had increased during the previous year by about 10%. In conclusion Freytag admonished the churches of the West not to forsake the Christians in China. He stated: "Nothing could be worse in this situation than a policy of spiritual blockade and aloofness. We should keep our political interests out of our relationship with the Chinese Christians."

In 1960 the former German Chinese missionary Gerda Buege was allowed to travel to China. While in almost all other cities Christians had to be looked for with a magnifying glass, Mrs. Buege found that in Shanghai church life seemed to be quite active. The Methodist pastor of that city told her that all pastors met at stated times and that the differences between the denominations did not play an important part. He told her that in his church there were three services every Sunday with an attendance of about 300 at each. In the churches of other cities, however, there was often only one service and the number of people who attended was rarely more than 60. Mrs. Buege stated that pastors in general worked in a factory on certain days or even during the entire week. She also met Christians in leading positions. But, she said: "They have no illusions. They recognize the increasing helplessness of the church and the decreasing possibilities for her work. They are suffering from the fact that there are things which cannot be said and which cannot be done. They are burdened by the past, tempted by the present, and worried about the future. They are looking for fellow-members in the faith whom they have known and they do not find them. They know what the words of the Bible mean: 'And Jesus did not trust in them for he knew. . . . They are afraid of him who will appear as the angel of light.' "

Thus it was quite clear that reports from China were contradictory. No one could see what the future held in store for the Christian congregations, for Catholics and the Protestants. It depended more than in any other Communist country on political and ideological developments. Every liberalizing tendency would make the possibility for the life of the Christian congregations to continue easier. But if ideological education and reeducation were to be continued with their present intensity, the danger would be very great that the congregations would die out because they would have no future generation. The Italian journalist Virgilio Lilli, who visited China repeatedly before and during the revolution and for the last time in 1960, in his book *Red China: Danger for East and West?* compared the Catholic Church of China with a wrecked boat which was somewhere in the corner of a harbor and was being taken apart. The retired captain who had to supervise this taking apart was the Archbishop of Peking and the president of the Patriotic Association. The leading technicians for the wrecking operations were the bishops who had been elected without the consent of the Vatican. The workers who crushed the boat into a heap of scrap iron were the patriotic priests. Lilli stated: "For the Vatican, when it looks at these conditions with the look of faith and of supernatural hope, the Catholic Church in China may still be alive and may merely be under the cross of martyrdom. But to the secular, purely natural view she is as dead, finished, and bereft of life as a corpse. She is like a ship of which one knows that its fate has been sealed although it is still floating." The prognosis for Protestantism was no different. The Christian civilization which had been nurtured by the two mainstreams of Christianity in China had been uprooted. This uprooting was quite different from what had happened in the Communist states of Europe, where the leaves had been blown off the trees of Christianity, but where the roots had remained unharmed.

CHAPTER ELEVEN

LOOKING INTO THE PAST AND THE FUTURE

I.

Communism proclaims a message of salvation. This salvation is to take place in collective society in a highly technological world. It presupposes that all people, all human associations and activities, and the whole area of values, of ethical demands, and ideological premises have to be reformed on the basis of Communist ideology. Communist ideology makes a total demand which includes all areas of life.

The Communist message of salvation is radically this-worldly. "Radical" means that this ideology demands the complete, undivided devotion and loyalty of man. Communist salvation cannot tolerate that anyone should know about, or look for, another salvation outside of this secular salvation. Such actions would weaken him in his struggle for this-worldly salvation or turn him into a doubtful supporter.

The foundation of Communist ideology is dialectic materialism. It is the source of all its values, motivations, and aims. It contains all the principles for its interpretation of the world, the directions for its political strategy, and the order for its collective society. Atheism is one of its essential component parts. It is not only a theoretical or philosophical atheism, but a militant antitheism. Philosophical atheism may declare that there is no God, but militant antitheism declares there *must* be no God. Philosophical atheism uses reason. Militant antitheism uses suppression. It wants to make secure the this-worldly message of salvation through which Communism offers its exclusive right to exist, and to make impossible the escape into the realm of a different other-worldly salvation.

Communist ideology is thus opposed to every type of religious faith. Since the Christian message also has a claim to totality, namely the demand to be obedient to God, the conflict between the Christian message and the Communist message of salvation cannot be bridged. It can be eliminated neither through synthesis nor through compromise. Coexistence may be a temporary expedient, but it is not a permanent condition because it leads to schizophrenia in man and society. Collaboration is possible only in the limited field of political activity which is ideologically neutral, and even here it is burdened by differences of motives and by suspicions which arise from ideological enmity.

In the fight between Christianity and Communism both are convinced of the final victory of their cause. For the Communists the Christians are merely religious remnants which will disappear as Communist society is constructed more perfectly. For the Christian the Communists are a grievous visitation by permission of God. Communism has a limited commission in the framework of the aims of history. It is used by God and will then disappear.

II.

When Communism came to power it had to come into conflict with the churches of all countries. But the conflict developed in varying degrees and led to various results. There are many reasons for this.

There is no one way of Communism. Communist countries are influenced in their actions not only by their common Communist ideology but also by their historical, social, and religious backgrounds. Communism in the Soviet Union is different from Communism in China or in Yugoslavia. This difference is also noticeable in the relationship of Communism to the churches.

There was also no unified church or unified Christianity which faced Communism. The type and form of the church was important for the kind and development of this confrontation.

One must differentiate between churches that were closely identified with the governments and the social orders that had been overthrown by Communism and churches which had their firm roots among the people and were even considered centers of resistance against former oppressors. The basic contrast between Communists and the church was brought into sharper focus in case of the former, but was not completely eliminated in case of the latter. However, it was definitely lessened.

One must also make a distinction between denominations. They all have in common the proclamation of an other-worldly salvation. For this reason they are all opposed to the this-worldly Communist message of salvation. But the Christian proclamation of salvation in the various denominations is different in its relationship to the world.

In the Orthodox Church this proclamation is vertical. The supernatural world of salvation and the power of salvation come down upon the secular world and offer themselves to the faithful as a confrontation and a participation.

In Protestantism the proclamation of salvation is dynamic. Protestants offer salvation in the person of a God who confronts the believer with his demand to be obedient. This forces the believer to live according to the laws and the expectations of God in all his relationships, including the social and political relationships.

In Roman Catholicism this dynamic is intensified into an ideology. The demands have become a system of definite order and of rules for the political and social attitudes of the faithful.

From this it is clear that the reactions of the various denominations are different in their attitude toward Communism.

Orthodoxy is basically opposed to the atheistic thesis of dialectic materialism but leaves the ordering of political and social relationships to Communism and is satisfied to be present in the secular world as the embodiment and the offer of the gifts of the supernatural world.

Protestantism, on the other hand, demands to be heard in public. It rejects dialectic materialism and atheism but is not in a position to declare that the Communist order of society is of the devil. Neither can it declare that the Western order of society is sacred.

It accepts the order of society in both cases as reality and sees its own task in carrying out its critical function on the basis of the Word of God. The church is the watchman and must see to it that the actions of the state do not violate the laws of God, that justice and right are preserved, and that freedom of faith and obedience to God are respected.

The Roman Catholic Church gives a content to her claim to act in public, which is firmly expressed and binding in its norms and whose aim is the guidance of the Christians in state and society. These norms are in opposition to the norms of Communist ideology. Thus the clash between Communism and Catholicism is not merely an ideological conflict, but at the same time a clash between opposite concepts of state and society.

We can see that coexistence between Communism and orthodoxy is probably possible because their opposition is limited to ideology.

The relationship between Communism and Protestantism can be changed to some extent. The church can recognize the Communist state as the higher powers in the sense of Romans 13 and can work for a positive cooperation of all Christians in all affairs which are politically and ideologically neutral. There will be occasions for conflict when the total state claims the total man and forces the Christian to violate the laws of God and tries to force dialectic materialism upon the faithful by destroying the freedom of faith and of proclamation.

For coexistence between Roman Catholicism and Communism all presuppositions are lacking. Here the contrasts are clear, and both are facing the other with total claims. Therefore wherever Communists and Catholics meet the battle is hardest. It is increased even more because the Roman Catholic churches are dependent upon a foreign power, the papal see, and must obey the Pope's orders. This situation cannot be tolerated in a total atheistic state.

The final aim of Communism in all these encounters with the Christian denominations is the same. They are considered remnants of an outmoded spiritual attitude, and their destruction must be accelerated as much as possible. But the immediate aims are different.

Communism demands of Orthodoxy that it should remain non-political. The church must not try to influence the public mind. The church must place herself at the disposal of the state with her whole power.

The Protestant churches must be hindered from carrying out their public critical functions, and they must be limited in their proclamation to the cultivation of pious inwardness.

The Roman Catholic churches must be separated from Rome, be changed into national churches, and be forced to give up the norms which they have for the ordering of state and society.

A survey of the conditions in Communist countries indicates that as far as Orthodoxy is concerned the immediate aims have been reached.

After more or less drastic destruction the Catholic churches have been coordinated in the Soviet Union, Czechoslovakia, Hungary, Romania, Bulgaria, Albania, and China, but this coordination for the present is limited to the leadership and a part of the clergy; and it is an open question whether this is a genuine, or merely an external, tactical acceptance of the Communist order. In Poland the church has preserved her independence. In Yugoslavia the decision has not yet been made.

Wherever the Protestant churches were German ethnic minorities, as e.g. in the Soviet Union, Poland, Hungary, Yugoslavia, and Romania, they have been hurt by expulsions and resettlement of the Germans and have been partly destroyed. In the Protestant heartland, the so-called German Democratic Republic, the church has been able to preserve her independence and her right to be heard in public. In all other countries the churches accepted the coordination demanded by the state, partly voluntarily and with theological reasoning, as in the case of Hromadka, and partly under duress.

The long-range goal of Communism, namely the destruction of the Christian faith, has been attained in no country. The churches have suffered heavy losses. Their opportunities for work have been limited; their congregations have decreased in numbers. But faith has not been extinguished. On the contrary, often it has started again with new power and has been refined in the fire of atheist propaganda. Loss of membership is often compensated for by an intensified life of the communions. The hardest battle is being fought over the youth. If the churches want to win this battle and want to spread the work of missions, they must restate and thoroughly live their message. This message based on a bourgeois tradition must be restated to such an extent that it will be accepted as a pertinent answer to the questions confronting man and his existential needs in a Communist society. Here we have the most difficult problem posed to the churches. But here the church also has her greatest opportunity. For dialectic materialism is unable to give an answer to the decisive questions of life, to the question concerning the meaning of existence, to the riddle of fate, to the interpretation of contradictory occurrences, of suffering, sickness, and death.

III.

The battle between Communism and Christian faith will continue. How will it end? We shall not try to prophesy, but we shall merely continue along the lines which have been drawn in the history of Communism and its clash with the churches.

The development of Communism is influenced by the question: Can an ideology succeed in changing man, or will man succeed in changing ideologies? Communism is not a petrified force, but like all historical phenomena it is subject to the law of change. A basic trait of this change is that in most Communist nations of the Western world—in China Communism is based on entirely different philosophical presuppositions—a process of humanizing has started since the death of Stalin. This process is slow and sometimes excruciating. But it is based on the eternal human desire which fights against all aspects of an ideology that is foreign to life. It demands room for its own needs. At the center of these demands is the right of man to have his own individuality.

In every revolutionary movement, after a period of "first love"— the phase of the beginning, of battle and victory—there follows a phase of growing cold and getting tired of it all. The Communist movement, too, is not immune to this development. In the second and third generations there is a decrease of the ideological interest, a lessening of the enthusiastic expectation of salvation, a reaction against ideological overfeeding. In place of the dogmatic thinking which is dictated by ideology there now arises a pragmatic thinking which is interested in reality. This too is a very slow process. But one can call it a process of sobering up or a process of accommodation to the realities of life.

After the first period of more or less heavy attacks with terror and legal administrative and propagandistic measures, the battle of Communism against the churches has now entered a period of pacification. The hope of Communism is now focused on the growing generation and on the fact that the older generation will die out and with it the religious remnants. Nowhere is there a resumption of a general attack against religion. The more the Communists stop being ideologists and become pragmatists, the less reason is there for an anti-religious battle and the greater is their willingness to tolerate religion.

The result will be a secularized society in which the churches and communions may lead a limited existence in relative peace. The revival which they have experienced in times of battle will make room for weariness after the attacks have been forgotten, because human impulses and movements cannot be continued and preserved at all times; and with the lessening of resistance to Communism, the church will get used to the changed environment.

IV.

The Christians of the non-Communist West must clearly see the opposition between Communism and the churches. They must recognize that the problems about which these two powers are clashing are basically the same problems which all the churches in the West are facing. The Communist ideology is merely a radical chiliastic message of salvation based on secularism. But the Western world, too, is to a large extent under the dominion of secularism. This secularism has not been crystallized into ideological formulations at all or only to a very limited extent. Western secularism does not lead to an open battle against the churches and their proclamation, but it is a slow-moving apostasy from the churches; it leads to religious indifference under the sign of a thought process which is determined by this-worldliness. It has become a mass phenomenon. If this process continues, there is a possibility that the position of the churches in the West will also change in state and society. The privileges which they possess as inheritors of their past existence in a pluralistic society will disappear as an anachronism. The Constantinian era is past both in the East and the West. The churches must not cling to things that are past, but must prepare themselves for new situations. They can learn a great deal from the experiences that have been presented to the churches in the East.

The Christians of the Western world must remain aloof from fanatical anti-Communism. They look upon Communism falsely if they consider it only as a plague for the world and as a danger for humanity and judge everything that is done in the name of Communism negatively. They must at least recognize that Communism did not originate out of the blue and that it has grown into a powerful movement. It has developed from nothing to its present state. They must recognize that in its battle against capitalism it is the answer to the social sins of the old society and that in its battle against Christianity it is exacting payment for a debt which the churches of the Constantinian era have contracted. In its stirring up of the colored nations it is a form of revenge against colonialism and against the racial supremacy of the whites. It is—and that a Christian must see—a judgment of God against the whole Western world, and it is a call to repentance, which God directs through Communism to all states, societies, and churches of the West.

Is it true that the churches are free in the West and enslaved in the Communist countries? Certainly, to all churches in the West constitutions and laws grant freedom in the proclamation of the Word. It is true that in the Communist countries these freedoms have to a very large extent been taken away. But there is also a sublimated form of the Babylonian Captivity of the church. It is the captivity of a Christian church that has become conformed to the world and that harmonizes her proclamation with the values established by this society. Who will deny that the churches in the West are living in this type of captivity or at least are threatened by it? The churches in the Communist countries, on the other hand, are forced to oppose their environment. They are like the congregations of the New Testament, the "ekklesia," the people who are called out of this world. In them the word of Jesus which has lost its meaning so completely in our traditional churches and in our national churches becomes actuality: "Behold I send you as sheep among wolves." It is the freedom of the sheep that they can at no time be tempted to make an agreement with the wolves or to accommodate themselves to them. The churches in the West in time must see the road of this opposition and seek their freedom. Only in taking a stand against secularism will they be the light and the salt in a secularized society.

INDEX